CRASH

CRASH
Cinema and the Politics of Speed and Stasis

Duke University Press
Durham and London **Karen Beckman**
2010

© 2010 Duke University Press

All rights reserved

Designed by Heather Hensley

Typeset in Warnock Pro by Tseng Information Systems, Inc.

Library of Congress Cataloging-in-Publication Data appear on the last printed page of this book.

Sections of chapter 3 were originally published in *Discourse* 30, no. 3 (fall 2008). An earlier version of chapter 5 appeared as "Crash, Semen and Pop," *Grey Room* 12 (summer 2003), 94–115. An earlier version of chapter 6 appeared in Karen Beckman's and Jean Ma's edited volume *Still Moving: Between Cinema and Photography* (Duke University Press, 2008).

For Diana Fuss

CONTENTS

ix ACKNOWLEDGMENTS

1 INTRODUCTION

25 CHAPTER ONE
"Jerky Nearness": Spectatorship, Mobility, and Collision in Early Cinema

55 CHAPTER TWO
Car Wreckers and Home Lovers: The Automobile in Silent Slapstick

105 CHAPTER THREE
Doing Death Over: Industrial-Safety Films, Accidental-Motion Studies, and the Involuntary Crash Test Dummy

137 CHAPTER FOUR
Disaster Time, the Kennedy Assassination, and Andy Warhol's *Since* (1966/2002)

161 CHAPTER FIVE
Film Falls Apart: *Crash*, Semen, and Pop

179 CHAPTER SIX
Crash Aesthetics: *Amores perros* and the Dream of Cinematic Mobility

205 CHAPTER SEVEN
The Afterlife of *Weekend*: Or, The University Found on a Scrapheap

235 NOTES

275 BIBLIOGRAPHY

289 INDEX

ACKNOWLEDGMENTS

I would like to thank warmly all those people who have responded to sections of this book at various stages, and who have supported me during the time of its writing. I first began this project while at the University of Rochester, where I found a generous and stimulating intellectual community at the Susan B. Anthony faculty workshops and the Visual Studies rehearsals. Sharon Willis was a generous and inspiring mentor during my time there, as was Bette London, and I am very grateful for all their help. Douglas Crimp has been a wonderful interlocutor and friend since I first walked into his office. Jeannine Korman helped me through the day-to-day challenges of my first film-teaching job, and the multimedia librarians at the University of Rochester were absolutely indispensable. Rachel Ablow, Janet Berlo, Elizabeth Cohen, Ken Gross, Tom Hahn, Rachel Haidu, Rosemary Kegl, John Michael, Russell Peck, and Jeff Tucker all helped to make Rochester a supportive and exciting place to work.

My collaboration with Jean Ma on *Still Moving* was a terrific experience, and I learned a great deal from her during that process that has helped me think about this book. Jonathan Kahana and Jenny Horne not only came up with more car crash cartoons and references than I ever imagined existed, but they have also been incredibly generous to me over the last few years, and I thank them for that. Callie Angell, Eduardo Cadava, Oliver Gaycken, Rita Gonzalez, Tom Gunning, John McCoubrey, Caitlin McGrath, John Mowitt, Melissa Rangona, David Rodewick, Marc Siegel, and Liliane Weissberg have all made great suggestions along the way, and I am very grateful to them, and to those people, whose names I don't know, in conference audiences who asked useful and challenging questions. Elizabeth Shepard at the Cornell Medical School Archive was extremely helpful, and I am indebted to her for making images and documents available to me. I am grateful to my fellow editors at *Grey Room*—Branden Joseph, Reinhold Martin, Tom McDonough, and Felicity Scott—for their collegiality and for the inspiring way in which they all work. Juan Suarez and James Meyer carefully read the Warhol chapter in its later stages, Paula Marantz Cohen and Dana Polan offered wonderful last minute feedback on chapter 2, and Leo Charney gave careful attention to an early version of chapter 6. Thank you all.

At the University of Pennsylvania, Heather Love and David Kazanjian provided highly illuminating responses to my early work on Andy Warhol. Heather Love and Mara Mills have also been terrific friends during my time at Penn—and in London most of all. The Penn Humanities Forum offered a lively and stimulating context in which to present my early work on the film *Weekend*, and the history of art department's weekly colloquia have served as a very generative space in which to present work. All my colleagues in this department are terrific, and I am grateful for the support and friendship offered to me by everyone in the Jaffe building. The Cinema Studies Program at Penn has offered me a warm and stimulating environment in which to work, and I deeply appreciate the collegiality and friendship of Timothy Corrigan, Peter Decherney, Meta Mazaj, and Ellen Scott. Nicola Gentili works miracles and saves my life on a daily basis. Thank you, Nicola. Stephen Lehman, Paul Farber, and Bijan Oliai set the bar very high for all other librarians, and I count myself lucky to have had the chance to work with them. I would also like to thank Deans Rebecca Bushnell, Dennis DeTurck, and Ann Matter for their support of me and of this project. Lacey Baradel has been a phenomenal research assistant.

Ken Wissoker, of Duke University Press, has been a helpful and thoughtful adviser not just about book publishing, but about academic life in general. Thank you for your support, Ken. Special thanks also go to the three anonymous readers at Duke, who so carefully helped me to shape this book with their enlightening comments, and to the Duke editorial staff—especially Mandy Early, Tim Elfenbein, and Patricia Mickelberry. I am also grateful to Nancy Davenport and Chip Lord for making images available for publication.

Family members on both sides of the Atlantic have enriched my own life by allowing me to share theirs. I want to thank, in England, Barbara Redrobe, Ruth Wright, Jane Robin, Lucy and Suzanne Johnson, Claire Redrobe, Torben Steeg, and Janek, Freya, and Mikkel Redrobe-Steeg; and in the United States, Robert and Merrilee Beckman, Mari Beckman-Lau, and Eric Lau. You are all so different from each other, and I love each of you differently.

There is no one in the world more fun to watch movies with than Siduri, Lua, and Bruno, but watching them is best of all. Michael Beckman—you know what I think of you—thank you so much for everything, and bring it on.

This book is dedicated to Diana Fuss, who has been a kind and thoughtful adviser and friend for what now seems like a long time. I continue to aspire to the standard she sets, and offer this strange book as a token of my thanks for the ways in which she has enriched my life and work.

INTRODUCTION

"Little Bastard"

On 30 September 1955, James Dean died in a car crash on the road to Salinas. He was driving his silver Porsche Spyder, "Little Bastard," which is perhaps the best known of the many celebrity-crashed cars that have been absorbed into the landscape of postwar art, writing, and film (in fact, it became a celebrity in its own right, touring the United States as part of a safe-driving campaign for teens). While I will focus neither on Dean in particular nor on the celebrity crash in general, I want to invoke momentarily the name of Dean's car because it encapsulates the dialectical tensions embedded within the cinematic car crash, one of film's earliest and most persistent self-reflexive tropes. Through the lens of the crash, I will explore tensions that exist at the heart of the film experience: between stasis and motion, body and image, proximity and distance, self and other, and inside and outside. In invoking the figure of a "little bastard," I hope to emphasize, rather than explain away, cinema's inherent impurity at a time when some critics, especially within the field of art history, are calling for a renewed focus on the medium, a parallel reinvigoration of traditional epistemological structures, and a disciplining of the messy field of cinema studies. Yet if film is, as Hollis Frampton suggests, "a deeply hybridized, bastard technology . . . , as rickety a collection of electromechanical devices as a Model T Ford," then perhaps it makes sense to embrace the discourse of cinema studies less as a discipline than as a thoroughly bastardized field, one unable to contemplate its impure object of study, as Frampton's gesture toward the Model T Ford suggests, without some acknowledgment of the way cinema's high and hybrid technology binds it inextricably, if complexly, to capitalism's industrial systems and to a wide variety of other media, technologies, and disciplines.[1]

The renewed interest in aesthetic autonomy and the medium within the field of art history has emerged at least partly in response to the growing presence of projected moving images both in the contemporary art museum and in urban public spaces. This presence (along with other factors) raises concerns about the transformation of the museum into a space of entertainment, the expansion of art in other media (such as painting) to a cinematic scale, the disappearance of monitors and feedback mechanisms in video-art practice, and the increasing prevalence of narrative as a defining feature of contemporary art in a variety of media closely related to film. Furthermore, mainstream industrial films now also commonly appear as crowd-pleasing, thematically related program supplements to museum shows, an approach to film programming that not only reductively posits cinema as "easy" and accessible, and art, in contrast, as difficult and elitist, but also displaces those more experimental films that are excluded from mainstream cinemas and have historically found a place only within museums' film programming. Unless museums more effectively foreground the tension between multiple modes of moving-image production, art institutions will miss the opportunity of exploring the complex and increasingly intertwined relationships among commercial narrative cinema, art cinema, experimental film and video, and art across the course of the twentieth century and the twenty-first. At a moment of increasing anxiety about the prevalence of projected moving images in the museum, scholars addressing the relationship between the museum's moving images and cinema may be better off confronting and engaging cinema with all its bastard traits than trying to purify it in order to make it good or pure enough—politically and aesthetically—for the discourse of art history. For this reason, *Crash* consciously strives to consider the trope of the car crash across genres, historical periods, exhibition spaces, and geographical locations, not in order to disregard, but to draw attention toward and to reflect on these categories and their limits, a reflection integral to the practice of film theory.

Commenting on the state of film theory in the digital age, David Rodowick suggests, *pace* those who claim that we are "post-theory," that this discourse is uniquely equipped to engage what Rosalind Krauss has called the "post-medium" condition, not because it has successfully defined the nature of the medium, but because it starts from the difficulty of grounding "filmic ontology in a single medium-specific concept or technique."[2] Like Rodowick, I think both that "film studies . . . has never congealed into a discipline in the same way as English literature or art history," and that this is "a positive thing."[3] Yet in recent years, in a version of the art historian's anxiety about the arenas of entertainment, spectacle, and popular culture into which this hybrid or "mongrel medium" leads, film-studies conferences have become increasingly focused around caucuses and interest groups within the field.[4] While, on the one hand, these increasingly specialized forums—early cinema, documentary, ephemeral film, art cinema, experimental cinema, the Hollywood film industry, and so on—reflect the growth and success of the field, they may also run the risk of factionalizing the scholarly film community and hindering the kind of critical exchange about the contradictory impulses to be found within film practice, history, and theory that could usefully inform contemporary critical engagement with artists' moving images. This is not to say that one would be better off erasing all distinctions between different modes of filmmaking and areas of specialization within the study of film. But there is perhaps a way of at once recognizing that there exist stronger affinities between some kinds of filmmaking and artists' practice than between others, while keeping open the possibility that some of the critical questions that emerge in areas of film studies less closely or obviously tied to the field of art than, say, avant-garde film might still usefully be introduced to contemporary discussions of the medium within art history.

In recent years, "the medium" has sometimes been proffered as an antidote to the confusion that has followed in the wake of what one might think of as a critical *and* aesthetic "crash," a widespread loss of faith in "high" or "grand" theory, but also in the political movements out of which many aesthetic and theoretical practices and discourses grew. Yet while the language of aesthetic autonomy, the medium, and critical distance offers a seductive fantasy of resistance to the encroachment of advanced capitalism on every area of human existence, this discourse is also rife with a vocabulary that borders on a kind of moralism in its disdainful condemnation of a range of qualities, concepts, and spectators that have come to be associated with capitalism's images and their consumption, including promiscuity, scale, speed, desire, thrills, pleasure, sensation, immersion, emotion, and spectacle. It is almost superfluous to point out that many of the terms that have been negatively associated with capitalist image production and consumption have often found a positive resonance in the historically intertwined discourses of film studies, feminist theory, and queer theory, all of which have been more willing than art history to engage the full range of modern visual technology's "excrements."[5] I highlight the tension between these two strands of contemporary visual criticism, not to take up one pole or the other, but rather to ask how one can avoid caricaturing critical positions—with regressive, medium-specific disciplinarians on the one hand and pleasure-seeking, interdisciplinary populists on the other—and to instead consider how one might think more productively about the relation between aesthetic resistance to advanced capitalism and the operations of desire at this moment of transition.

The "crash" of theory, political movements, and utopian visions of interdisciplinarity's possibilities has produced an intellectual environment that can seem at once confused, defensively dogmatic, and stifling, as scholars and critics, blinded by their proximity to the present, attempt to adopt and articulate a clear critical stance for their times. While this moment of critical disappointment and loss of clarity or direction urges some to move on, to identify the next new thing, I locate this book firmly in the center of the crash, the traumatic and uncertain moment of inertia that comes in the wake of speed and confidence. The crash, with its suggestion of high speed and collision, pleasure and recklessness, violent encounter, uninvited entry, contingency, and failure or depression, provides an apt and urgently needed metaphor through which to consider a series of closely interrelated concerns that persist throughout contemporary art and film criticism. The crash—as critical metaphor, narrative device, and visual image—is something to think through, not to just gawk at or avoid. It functions as an enabling critical and visual trope that insists on the continued usefulness of the hybrid, messy, and contaminated discourse of film theory.

Automobile accidents occupy as significant a place in film history as the staged train collision, the importance of which has been carefully demonstrated by Wolfgang Schivelbusch and Lynne Kirby. Though the car crash mutates as it migrates from the "cinema of attractions" to slapstick comedy, industrially sponsored films, experimental film and artists' videos, and global art cinema, these varied forms of halted auto-mobility form a generative counterpoint to the more familiar critical paradigm that repeatedly aligns the automobile with the moving camera, the moving filmstrip, and the illusion of movement created in the act of projection. Jean Baudrillard writes, "The vehicle now becomes a kind of capsule, its dashboard the brain, the surrounding landscape unfolding like a televised screen," just as

Virilio suggests that "what goes on in the windshield is cinema in the strict sense."[6] Similarly, Edward Dimendberg notes that "the highway provides a controlled visual experience analogous to the montage and multiplicity of perspectives afforded by cinema," while other film scholars view the "road movie," with its penchant for filming the world through the windshield of a car, as one of cinema's most self-reflexive spaces, presenting a genre in which, as Timothy Corrigan claims, "the perspective of the camera comes the closest of any genre to the mechanical unrolling of images that define the movie camera. As with the movie experience, time on the road becomes figurative space."[7] In *Crash* I both extend the tradition of thinking about cinema through the frame of the automobile and challenge the tendency of this discourse to privilege movement above film's other qualities.

Tracing lines of flight from the cinema of attractions to pop art, from slapstick comedy to industrial-safety films, I explore how the crash gives visual form to overlapping fantasies and anxieties regarding speed and stasis, risk and safety, immunity and contamination, impermeability and penetration. Rather than viewing this movement of a visual trope across aesthetic and ideological categories either as something that has to be cleanly categorized into positive and negative uses of the figure in question, or as evidence that each and every generative or disruptive figure produced by artists and filmmakers has been fully appropriated by the ideological visual spectacles of capitalism, the imbrications and collisions I track not only expand and refine our understanding of the medium of film and related moving image technologies, but also illuminate something of the affective, social, and political resonance of these media, and the way in which both our possibilities and vulnerabilities are dramatized, challenged, and shaped by the images that pass before our eyes.

The Body and the Spectator

Within film studies, the disembodied spectator of psychoanalytic film theory has largely given way to an embodied spectator who is engaged through sociological and phenomenological approaches that focus on haptic vision, body genres, and audience responses.[8] Yet while these critiques of film theory's repression of the spectator's body have been crucial in moving scholars away from an overly dogmatic and homogenous conceptualization of the absent cinematic spectator, one must nevertheless be wary of fully dismissing the complex relationship that psychoanalytic film theory posited between the spectator's psyche and the apparatus.⁹ It is particularly important, in the context of this project, to consider the embodied, physical responses of a spectator alongside other possible modes of viewing film because of the intensely corporeal, and at times overly literal, tendencies that mark existing critical engagements of the cinematic car crash.

One can clearly see the ethical questions surrounding the representational crash, as well as the tensions that emerge at the intersection of aesthetic experimentation and traumatic bodily experience, in Vivian Sobchack's angry response to Jean Baudrillard's essay on J. G. Ballard's novel *Crash*, an exchange that was published in *Science Fiction Studies* in 1991. Sobchack describes Ballard's use of the crash as "cautionary," moral, and ironic, drawing evidence from Ballard's introduction to the French edition of the novel, in which he specifically asserts the cautionary nature of the crash. By contrast, Sobchack condemns Baudrillard's essay on the novel as "celebratory" and indulging in a "postmodern romanticism" that is indifferent to the suffering of the lived body. Writing in the wake of major cancer surgery on her left thigh, Sobchack declares, "The man [Baudrillard] is really dangerous. Indeed, as I sit here with a throbbing, vivid 'inscription' on my left distal thigh, I might wish Baudrillard a car crash or two. He needs a little pain (maybe a lot) to bring him to his senses, to remind him that he has a body, *his* body, and that the 'moral gaze' begins there."¹⁰ This exchange, in which crashes are almost cast like spells and the suffering body of the critic becomes inextricably bound to an argument about embodiment, comes close to a crisis of criticism. The possibility that the infliction of physical pain could be used as an instructive tool marks the borders of Sobchack's essay and is symptomatic of the fraught and murky territory that texts like Ballard's *Crash* enter when they take the site of trauma as the starting point for aesthetic and relational possibilities.

Though Sobchack firmly aligned her embodied "moral gaze" with Ballard's own position, this alliance became more complicated when, three years after Sobchack's response, Ballard retracted his defensive moral claims about *Crash*, on which Sobchack's critique of Baudrillard at least in part depends. Ballard states, "I went wrong in . . . that introduction . . . [when] in the final paragraph, which I have always regretted, I claimed that in *Crash* there is a moral indictment of the sinister marriage between sex and technology. Of course it isn't anything of the sort. *Crash* is not a cautionary tale. *Crash* is what it appears to be. It is a psychopathic hymn. But it is a psychopathic hymn which has a point."[11] To note this shift in Ballard's position is not to dismiss Sobchack's claim that the novel's morality is grounded in the body, but it is perhaps to suggest that the complexity of the body's "moral gaze" may in part be responsible for Baudrillard's disembodied style. As an organ that is both of the body and the bridge beyond it, the eye in cinema exceeds the limits of the physical body and "throws" us into the space of other "bodies" that are themselves cinematic projections and images that combine with spectators' imaginations in idiosyncratic ways. Though fantasies of a complete transcendence of the body certainly have a terrifying dimension, one might also argue that without this ability to dream ourselves out of our bodies—through cinema or speed, for example—we would never feel anything for or with another. *Crash* explores the modern technological landscape and its impact on those who inhabit it. If it has a moral dimension, it lies in the novel's persistent exploration of the line between inside and outside, self and other, private and public. In this way it is typical of many of the texts I will explore here. Crash films are cinematic quests, undertaken in the spaces whose outer limits are marked by terrestrial speed taking flight on the one hand, and by the mutilated body on the other; by the immobilized corpse, which throws film into crisis, and the speeding imagination taking a camera for a ride. Neither denying nor submitting to the logic of materiality, the crash film invokes a complex network of dialectical tensions that pry open spaces in which to reflect on the place of the body in the film experience, and begs the question of how one might think through, against, and about cinema, and its relation to oneself and others.

In *Crash* I ask why artists, writers, and filmmakers—including Cecil Hepworth, Andy Warhol, Jean-Luc Godard, Ousmane Sembène, J. G. Ballard, Alejandro González Iñárritu, and Nancy Davenport—have repeatedly turned to immobilized and crashed cars as they wrestle with the political, ethical, sexual, and aesthetic conundrums of the modern world. This book is fundamentally concerned with work that engages the continued potential of film's hybridity and illegitimacy, qualities that frequently lead us into spaces of hybrid identity and non-normative sexuality, and that demand exchange across disciplines and media. Many of the works I consider emerge at the border of at least two media, media that, in colliding with each other, seem formally to mimic the subject of technological collision they depict. As these media encounter each other at their own limits, each one seems to yearn across the boundaries of what appears possible within itself, as though seeking to extend its capacity by creating an imaginary life for itself in the space of another. Film and photography, literature and film, film and television encounter, threaten, and enrich each other through the figure of the crash. The aesthetic encounters of this highly commercialized medium with other media highlight the way film places us within a conceptual paradigm of relationality, rather than of purity and autonomy, and the collisions I analyze provoke us repeatedly to consider the ethics of the border, the line dividing self from other, the world of the spectator from the world of the image. Existing in close proximity to the concepts of the accident and the disaster, the crash often constitutes a rupture in the membranes that seem to divide us, leading to an association of this term with penetration, contagion, disease, and corruption. Consequently, the cinematic crash brings concepts like responsibility, autonomy, movement, vulnerability, victimhood, and citizenship into focus, and asks how our understanding of them has been shaped by technological innovation and its accidents. It challenges us to consider the value of different types of risk-taking—physical, political, and critical—at a time when the discourse of citizen safety is wielded in ever more oppressive ways. This volume is not a sociological study of how car accidents affect people, but rather an attempt to explore why the fantasies, anxieties, and traumas associated with the automobile and its collisions have been so closely aligned with cinema.

Crash Methodology

My methodological strategy takes its cue from the hybrid nature of film itself, and draws on four related but distinct approaches to the question of the technological, mobile, and accident-prone subject: (1) the discourse surrounding the modern mobile spectator that has emerged in conversation with the writing of the Frankfurt School, particularly the media theory of Walter Benjamin (leading figures in this discourse include Wolfgang Schivelbusch, Tom Gunning, Miriam Hansen, Jonathan Crary, Ann Friedberg, and Lynne Kirby); (2) the discourse of speed and disaster, most closely associated with Paul Virilio, in which cinema, transportation, and war emerge as intimately related capitalist technologies; (3) the discourse of the avant-garde, and most notably futurism, which embraces technologies of speed and their accidents as vehicles for creative transformation and radical possibility; and (4) the psychoanalytic discourse of "the drive" as it appears in the work of both Sigmund Freud and Jean Laplanche. Of course, at times these discourses become incompatible with each other, and in juxtaposing them, I intend not to obscure these points of difference, but rather to bring them to the fore in order to create a productive critical matrix through which to engage the specific complexities and possibilities of the trope of collision and disaster.

PANORAMIC VISION AND THE MODERN MOBILE SUBJECT

Over the last twenty years, scholarship in the related fields of visual studies, art history, and film studies could be characterized by an ongoing interest in historicizing how modernity has transformed the human subject's experience of and formation by perception, movement, and time, perhaps sometimes at the expense of an interest in modern media's equally complex engagement with stasis. The works of authors such as Wolfgang Schivelbusch, Lynne Kirby, Jonathan Crary, Tom Gunning, Anne Friedberg, and Giuliana Bruno share a common interest in what Gunning has described as "the archeology of the film spectator, modes of viewing that seem to have first been rehearsed within the urban environment."[12] Repeatedly, these authors establish strong links between the emergence of cinema as a technology, the visual and psychological experience of modernity, and the development of a wide range of high-speed transportation systems, including the railway, the streetcar, and, later, the automobile (among these, the railway is privileged). Kirby, drawing on the work of Schivelbusch, has explored in detail the role that shock plays in the "perceptual overlap between the railroad and the cinema," noting that in addition to the stimulation offered by rapid shot changes, cuts to close-ups, and "attacks on vision" (like a "train charging headlong into the camera"), staged railway collisions repeatedly emerged as a thematic preoccupation in early films.[13] But as Gunning points out, the early "aesthetic of attractions" offers the modern spectator not just a potentially dangerous experience of shock, but also the kind of thrill previously found at amusement parks, resulting in a mixture of "pleasure and anxiety."[14] Unlike later narrative cinema, Gunning argues, this early cinema of attractions acknowledges, even directly addresses, the spectator, and is marked by a "reach outwards," rather than by the absorption of the spectator into the film world, absorption that has come to be associated (perhaps reductively so) with classical narrative cinema. This outward reach to an embodied spectator parallels one of the central conundrums explored through the cinematic crash: how to make conscious the effect of modernity on the relation between subject and object, body and mind, inside and outside.

Addressing this question of the modern subject's limits, Wolfgang Schivelbusch, in his seminal discussion of the shocks and assaults of urban life, draws on Freud, Georg Simmel, and Walter Benjamin to describe the modern subject's "stimulus shield," a semi-permeable, inorganic membrane that would, according to Freud, filter out some of the intensity of the stimuli.[15] Yet for Benjamin, as Miriam Bratu Hansen brilliantly demonstrates, the radical possibility of cinema depends in part on one understanding this stimulus shield as "a bit less of a carapace or armor and a bit more of a matrix or medium—a porous interface between the organism and the world that would allow for a greater mobility and circulation of psychic energies."[16] Focusing on the term *innervation*, Hansen contrasts the two-way process Benjamin articulates, which allows for the recovery of "split-off psychic energy through motor stimulation," with the unidirectional models of innervation Freud develops in his writing on hysteria and dream analysis, where mental and affective energy simply take somatic form.[17] Furthermore, Hansen foregrounds Benjamin's statement that "people whom nothing moves or touches any longer are taught to cry again in the cinema," in order to recognize the importance of "a regeneration of affect" to Benjamin's vision of cinema and technology as a counterpoint to technology's negative impact on modern subjects.[18] Within this paradigm, the spaces newly configured by transportation, advertising, and cinema enable a movement of "energy" across and between layers, which in turn constitutes both our (potentially traumatic) reception of the world and our response to it. At this time of heightened anxiety about the demise of criticism, the impossibility of critical distance, and the spectacularization of the world, including the art museum, Hansen usefully draws attention to Benjamin's exploration of the critical possibilities of *nearness*, speed, and American cinema, a nearness forced on us by advertising, which "'all but hits us between the eyes with things,' in the same way that 'a car, growing to gigantic proportions, careens at us out of a film screen.'"[19]

While Gunning, like Benjamin, does see in the cinematic thrills exemplified by a cinematic train rushing outwards toward the spectator a radically disruptive and critical potential, this is *only*, Gunning insists, because these early projections run "counter to the illusionistic absorption," their two-dimensionality exposed, for example, by the sudden animation of a projected still image or by the live performances that accompanied projection.[20] For Gunning—and this point is essential—the real shock of cinema lies precisely *not* in a naïve spectator's faith in the realism of a train rushing at the screen, but rather in the exposure of the "loss of experience" reflected in cinema's phantom image; and he insists that the screams of delight and terror recounted from those early screenings were not those of naïve spectators beholden to a new realism, but those of a modern audience aware of cinema's reflection of a modern world "freighted with emptiness."[21]

PAUL VIRILIO: TAKING THE ACCIDENT SERIOUSLY

For Hansen, Benjamin's speculations on technology "cannot be easily assimilated to contemporary media theory, certainly not the teleological variant (for example, in Paul Virilio, Friedrich Kittler, or Norbert Bolz) that marshals a vast number of sources to demonstrate—celebrate or decry—the subject's inevitable abdication to the *a priori* regime of the apparatus."[22] Like Hansen, I resist the teleological approach Virilio takes in relation to technology, as well as his separation of human subjectivity and experience from technology, yet Virilio's work poses important questions.[23] The problem of how to discipline the crash, how to make its mediation serve an ethical purpose, haunts Paul Virilio's exhibition catalog *Unknown Quantity*, published by the Fondation Cartier pour l'art contemporain in 2003. The catalog, Virilio explains, offers a premonition of a future "Museum of the Accident" that would expose, with critical distance, the accident "as the major enigma of modern Progress," containing the possibility of both our survival and our collective finitude.[24] If "the *visible velocity* of substance—the velocity of a means of transport or the speed of calculation or information—is only ever the emergent part of the iceberg of the—*invisible—velocity* of the accident," and if "accident production" is indeed the "unconscious industry" of Progress, then, Virilio claims, one needs to find ways of making "perceptible—if not visible—the speed of the emergence of the accident, of those accidents that plunge history into mourning."[25] While Virilio denies advocating a "millenarian catastrophism" or taking "*a tragic view* of the accident for the purpose of frightening the masses, as the mass media so often do," and claims instead only to be "taking the accident seriously," one cannot help but find a resonance between his use of large, bold, and italicized fonts for key words—**finitude, media tragedy, live coverage, what is happening**—with the moralistic and apocalyptic discourses of homeland security and terrorism that mark the post-9/11 era.[26]

While I share Virilio's desire to take the accident seriously, I argue, perhaps paradoxically, that this requires one also to engage its comic and thrilling dimensions. Virilio positions his museum of accidents as a necessary step toward combating the present's "troubled times," times governed by "threats of a love of madness taking as its motto the drunken driver's words to his passenger: '*I'm an accident looking for somewhere to happen.*'"[27] Here, Virilio adopts—without reflection—a foreboding rhetoric that resonates in uncomfortable ways with the moralistic safe-driving discourse of the late 1950s, found both in social-science journals and educational films, such as *None for the Road: Teenage Drinking and Driving* (Centron Corporation, 1957) and the bizarre animation short *Stop Driving Us Crazy* (General Board of Temperance of the Methodist Church, 1959).[28] This discourse of safety conflates the dangers of speed with the threat of the "human" element in technology, which is deemed unpredictable, unconscious, and beyond rational comprehension. James L. Malfetti, for example, in "Human Behavior—Factor X," written for the *Annals of the American Academy of Political and Social Science*'s special issue on highway safety and traffic control in November 1958, opens his essay by stating, "Man's greatest enigma is himself," and then goes on to argue that the increased tempo and mobility of society has led to the destruction of the sacred society, as well as to a condition of anonymity among strangers who consequently feel no responsibility toward each other.[29] Of greatest danger in this society, according to Malfetti, is the part in each of us that takes "calculated risks" in order to inject a little excitement into the day. It is this desire for just a little excitement that reduces the difference between the "normal driver looking for a change of pace" and the "social deviate." And this deviate, Malfetti asserts, like Virilio, "can be described as an accident riding around looking for a place to happen."[30]

While Virilio, like Malfetti, may be right to caution that the excess desire for speed threatens life, any moral discourse that bases the notion of responsibility on the condemnation of the common human element that is blindly driven by desires that work beyond one's capacity for self-knowledge slips easily into moralism. Such moralism rests, as Judith Butler has recently argued, on a negation of our shared vulnerability to our own opacity, which makes us human in the first place, binds us in responsibility to each other, and is the condition for the possibility of ethics.[31] Furthermore, just as the sociological discourse of traffic safety has long associated risky drivers with social deviance and otherness (menstruation, miscegenation, poverty, and homosexuality repeatedly emerge as markers of risk), so Virilio's critique of the human drive for speed rests on a fundamentally problematic association of women with technologies of transportation: "Man is the passenger of woman, not only at the time of his birth, but also during their sexual relations. . . . In this sense, woman is the first means of transportation for the species, its very first vehicle, the second would be the horse."[32] It is the "woman of burden" who provides man with the "potential for movement" that is also the "potential for war": "Her back will be the model for later means of portage, all auto-mobility will stem from this infrastructure."[33] Tracing a direct lineage from woman to the horse or mount, of which the automobile is a later manifestation, Virilio argues that "it is the invention of the mount and the vehicle which will attain its greatest extension, the mount will be the warrior's first 'projector,' his first weapons system."[34] Later, the straight line of the road, the railway, and the roll of film on a spool all emerge as violence in the form of movement without purpose, and this violence is again equated with a sexualized image of women: "As is the case for the courtesan, its success is nothing, all that counts is the pursuit; its seduction at first tempts, its innocence is the snare of the trip, attracting, it leads toward the horizon like the prostitute leading the soldier to her chamber."[35]

Resisting Virilio's misogynist vision of technology, which emerges in opposition to subjectivity, sexual desire, and femininity, while recognizing the imminent threat of the accident to which his work draws attention, I wish to explore how film, through the recurrent trope of the car crash, stages, excites, and disciplines the unconscious *drives* that pull us toward speed, risk, and the vulnerability of the self that is forged by these drives. I am interested in how cinema forces us to grapple with the ethical, political, and aesthetic challenges that emerge at this intersection of transportation and cinematic technologies in the midst of experiencing these challenges. Rather than either condemning or celebrating the destructive, ecstatic impulses of the careening and speeding drivers in the films I examine here—drivers who are often "under the influence" of alcohol, anger, sexual desire, or modernity itself, caught between transcendent fantasies and the material vulnerability of the body—I explore how cinema technologically embodies and visually represents the contradictory impulses of modern human subjectivity, without which there would be neither need for nor the possibility of ethics or politics. In doing so, I attempt to mobilize some of the spatial, physical, and psychic structures made available by the hybrid medium of film, including the juxtaposition of still images to create the illusion of movement, and the technology of projection, with its requisite distance between screen and spectator, understanding these structures, like the stimulus shield, as vehicles for exploring rather than repressing our journeys between an interior subjectivity, always inevitably marked by an external other, and the world we perceive as "outside" ourselves. I thus expand Virilio's thesis to take account of the repressed question of the human *desire* for speed and exhilaration, and to avoid a critical position that, in attempting to resist the destructive effects of advanced capitalism's progress and its concomitant accident industry, inadvertently condones a moralistic opposition to pleasure and desire per se. As Mikita Brottman, in a refreshingly honest moment, admits, "Let's face it: we all feel a slight thrill at the thought of any serious accident."[36]

FUTURISM: "TRAUMA THRILLS"

In his work on futurism, speed, accidents, and the modern sublime, Jeffrey Schnapp makes an important intervention into the critical discussions of speed and crashes by distinguishing the works he discusses, from futurism through Warhol and J. G. Ballard, from what he calls the "traumatocentric accounts of modernity" (by which he means those writing in the tradition of Benjamin, Simmel, and Schivelbusch), claiming simply that in the former tradition "trauma thrills."[37] Taking F. T. Marinetti's "The Founding and Manifesto of Futurism" (1909) and its formative crash as a starting point, Schnapp differentiates his own account of the relation between the accident and modernity from others in the following way: "The accident, in short, will emerge as the locus of a form of trauma that, contrary to prevailing traumatocentric accounts of modernity, engenders neither psychic blockage nor new sure-fire forms of regimentation or alienation."[38] As he historicizes the co-development of individualism and transportation systems, Schnapp identifies two separate cultures of transportation: the first, "thrill-based," he describes as "the province of drivers" and "akin to cruising," while the second, "commodity-based," is centered on the passenger, isolating and enclosing human passengers "as if they were packages."[39] But how, exactly, we understand the relation *between* these two conceptions of the traveler, between the thrill-seeking cruiser and the safe little package—particularly with regard to the impact of this duality on our comparisons of the cinematic spectator with a modern passenger—remains to be explored. Such an opposition raises questions about the relation between desire and safety, between sexual freedom and social communion, between individuality and collective responsibility, and how all these tensions shape the landscapes we inhabit.

While Schnapp's discrimination between traumatic and thrill-based crashes is useful, it may ultimately be a little too rigid or reductive, may too easily erase the messy spaces of overlap in which the politics of modernity's technological aesthetics may emerge a little less cleanly than he suggests. To his credit, he does acknowledge that "the dichotomy is perhaps too sharply drawn," and that he allows the distinction between critical discourses to stand so clearly primarily "as a heuristic device."[40] But while this strategic intervention may be both important and useful, there are two areas in which the distinctions Schnapp asserts erase complexities that may need to be reintroduced as one explores the crash and its political, sexual, and aesthetic possibilities.

Shock, Trauma, Innervation

First, Schnapp critiques the exclusive association of the accident with trauma, psychic blockage, the stimulus shield, paralysis, aloofness, and indifference, a tendency which he finds in the writing of Benjamin and Freud and which dominates the "traumatocentric" studies that follow from this tradition.[41] While Schnapp correctly identifies what one might think of as an overemphasis on the stimulus shield at the expense of the metaphors of communion and fusion that permeate the transportation texts on which Schnapp focuses, Hansen's careful and corrective reading of Benjamin's writing on the "second technology" shows that Benjamin was actually exploring the question of how to *resist* "paralysis" and "psychic blockage" through a new alignment of the body, the psyche, and modern technology, suggesting that his work has much more in common with the radical possibilities for subjectivity that Schnapp sees in a pre-fascist futurism than Schnapp allows. As Hansen argues,

Innervation as a mode of regulating the interplay between humans and (second) technology can only succeed (that is, escape the destructive vortex of defensive, numbing adaptation) if it reconnects with the discarded powers of the first, with mimetic practices that involve the body, as the "preeminent instrument" of sensory perception and (moral and political) differentiation. . . . Benjamin seeks to reactivate the abilities of the body as a medium in the service of imagining new forms of subjectivity. For Benjamin, negotiating the historical confrontation between human sensorium and technology as an alien, and alienating, regime requires learning from forms of bodily innervation that are no less technical but to a greater extent self-regulated (which ties in with Benjamin's autoexperiments with hashish, gambling, running downhill, eroticism).[42]

While Schnapp shifts the historical emphasis of the discourse of speed away from the nineteenth century, the railway, and the motorcar to the pre-motorized era of the eighteenth century and the introduction of the paved road, it is ultimately in early cinema's car crashes that he finds a figure designed to "impress the viability of a volatile new mode of being upon the audience."[43] But how, if at all, does Schnapp differ from the models of spectatorship explored in the so-called traumatocentric accounts of cinema and their relation to transportation? For him, this discourse is marked by "an iconography of tedium, discomfort, and reification that appears unrelentingly critical in its new attitude towards new transportation technologies," an attitude that contrasts strikingly with his own "less intentionality-driven reading," which finds in cartoons ("a medium always already implicated, like its cinematic successor, in a rhetoric of collision") a space of laughter, of surprise, of magical transformation, where the real and the fantastic merge; which finds in early films, such as Cecil Hepworth's *How It Feels to Be Run Over* (1900), a display of "dismemberments, shocks, and explosions whose effects are gleefully displayed and quickly overcome"; and which finds in amusement park rides "the transformation of passengers into modern whirling dervishes."[44] Though Schnapp, in an early footnote, acknowledges an overlap between his framework and that of Gunning, and though Gunning's essay "Cinema of Attractions" clearly prefigures the continuity Schnapp traces from early cinema to futurism, there is an important distinction to be made between the way these two authors understand the relationship among a culture of thrills, early cinema, and modern subjectivity. For Schnapp, early cinema is one of several technologies to offer modern subjects transcendent experiences of speed that "so blur the distinction between the categories of realism and the hallucinatory or the fantastic that they demand a rethinking of the commonplace notion that modernism marks a revolt against naturalism."[45] But for Gunning, again, the "cinema of attractions" less "blur[s] the distinction between . . . realism and the hallucinatory or the fantastic" than exposes, through recourse to antiillusionist strategies, the traumatic emptiness lying at the heart of a daily experience which, having lost its coherence, leaves the spectator "hungry for thrills."[46] Yet to recognize this traumatic aspect of the cinematic disaster does not necessarily negate the comedy, magic, and variety that mark the early years of cinema, as Schnapp seems to imply. Similarly, while the crash, for Schnapp, prevents the routinization of speed, at least until the crash too "become[s] normalized," engendering "not relaxation and tedium, but bigger living," for Gunning, the early cinematic disaster rather *exposes* the ennui of the modern subject, creating a self-reflexive space in which critical consciousness and dialectical thought become possible.[47]

"From Shock to Sexual Shudder"

One can locate a second point of tension between these discourses in the fact that Schnapp finds the traumatocentric accounts unwilling to recognize that "the step from shock to sexual shudder remains small."[48] In contrast to Freud and Benjamin, he argues, Marinetti's manifesto inverts the traumatic meaning of the crash, "recasting trauma as ecstasy, accident as adventure, death drive as joy ride," just as in later futurist writing, "shocks figure as engines of bliss: as orgasm, rapturous play, release from the constraints of analytic reason."[49] On the one hand, Schnapp's efforts to reintroduce the sexual dimension into contemporary discussions of technology, speed, and modernity resonate with my own resistance to Virilio's demonization of desire;[50] and, like Schnapp, I turn to J. G. Ballard's novel *Crash* to illustrate the centrality of the orgasmic aspect of the crash. But on the other hand, Schnapp and I diverge in our approaches to the sexual dimension of the crash in that his analysis sidesteps the gendered question of whether the (often) phallic texts to which he refers leave open any liberatory sexual possibilities for female readers (and drivers). Early in the essay, he does give a brief nod to the question of gender, noting that while some of the "vascular, muscular, perceptual and erotic" childhood intoxications "appear to have greater purchase upon the masculine psyche," most "are common features as well of girlhood development."[51] But this early gender parity of pleasure seems to vanish as one zips from "the son of the Sun god" and the "keys to dad's car" to James Dean, Mr. Toad, and the "miracle of penile tumescence overcoming death."[52] Repressed from this discussion of futurism's founding crash is also the way femininity emerges not through a discussion of renewed sexual possibility for female "individuals," but rather as the sludge-producing site of the modern man's second (technological) birth.

> The words were scarcely out of my mouth when I spun my car around with the frenzy of a dog trying to bite its tail, and there, suddenly, were two cyclists coming towards me, shaking their fists, wobbling like two equally convincing but nevertheless contradictory arguments. Their stupid dilemma was blocking my way—Damn! Ouch!... I stopped short and to my disgust rolled over into a ditch with my wheels in the air....
>
> O maternal ditch, almost full of muddy water! Fair factory drain! I gulped down your nourishing sludge; and I remembered the blessed black breast of my Sudanese nurse.... When I came up—torn, filthy, and stinking—from under the capsized car, I felt the white-hot iron of joy deliciously pass through my heart![53]

Though the driver-based, thrill-seeking cruisers of Schnapp's speedy futurist discourse may well appeal to those in search of less constrained sexual paradigms, one might also usefully remember the manifesto's assertion that the futurists will not only "glorify war ... militarism, patriotism, the destructive gesture of freedom-bringers, beautiful ideas worth dying for, and scorn for women," but also that they will "fight moralism, feminism, every opportunistic or utilitarian cowardice."[54] While I build on Schnapp's emphasis on the sexual possibilities of the crash, I also highlight the way the potentially radical creative energy of the crash so often emerges in opposition to women and feminism, and ask how, within the discourse of mobility, one might avoid aligning feminism with a moralistic rejection of thrills, speed, and humor.

Feminist scholars such as Janet Wolff and Jean Franco have shown that metaphors of movement are gendered, with mobility frequently cast as masculine, and stasis as feminine.[55] Wolff warns that because these metaphors of mobility operate as ideologies or technologies of gender, cultural theory that relies on them should carefully consider how it is that "metaphors of movement and mobility, often invoked in the context of radical projects of destabilizing discourses of power, can have conservative effects."[56] Following Wolff, I draw attention to the sometimes uncritical operations of the ideology of movement in aesthetic and critical practice by offering the crash as a wry counterpoint, a different metaphor through which to consider the media of film, literature, and photography. While narratives of male mobility are often, as Wolff points out, construed as a "flight from women," the images and narratives I consider, each one structured around the figure of the crashed or jammed car, present scenarios and spaces defined by that which male travelers have tended to flee: touch, penetration, vulnerability, emotion, stasis, and radical uncertainty. Just as Kirby has argued that the early "train compartment" films offer a "heterotopia" that seems to exist outside of any particular space and time, resulting in staged transgressions across lines of race, class, and gender, so the crashed car opens up potentially productive temporal and spatial uncertainties, in spite of the motorcar's privileged position in patriarchal sexual structures.[57]

Many of the texts and images I analyze position the crash as a catalyst for potentially radical and transformative encounters that exist in close proximity with avant-garde celebrations of creative destruction. However, as feminist critics have repeatedly demonstrated, such encounters all too frequently enact violence on images of the female body, and images of the maternal body in particular—in this sense, the Futurist Manifesto is exemplary. Yet this book both allows for the possibility that the sexual politics of the collisions it considers will be complex and contradictory, and suggests that rather than turning away from such images altogether, dismissing their aesthetic strategies as deriving from a definitively "male avant-garde," or addressing them solely in relation to their treatment of gender, one might benefit from a renewed attempt to understand, from a contemporary feminist perspective, how, when, and why radical transformational aesthetic practices seem so often to rest on misogynist foundations. I build on the pioneering work of Susan Rubin Suleiman and her articulation of a complex formal allegiance between feminism and the avant-garde, a type of feminist doublespeak: "One may—one must—criticize the misogyny of male avant-garde sexual and cultural politics, and still recognize the energy, the inventiveness, the explosive humor and sheer proliferating brilliance of such male avant-garde 'play.'"[58]

DRIVE THEORY/THEORY DRIVE

Though Hansen offers a nuanced and dialectical paradigm for understanding the interaction between modern subjects and technology, in her reading it is only Benjamin, and not Freud, who understands "innervation" as a "two-way street," as a potentially enabling, rather than paralyzing force. For Freud, she argues, innervation is a process that moves only from the psychic to the somatic.[59] While Freud's later writing on the drives confirms the movement from psychic stimulus to somatic discharge that Hansen argues is present from his early writings on hysteria, one may nevertheless want to be wary of dismissing too quickly Freud's writing on this topic as unidirectional or of constructing a simplistic Freud to set off Benjamin's complexity.

Like many of the car-crash films this book addresses, Freud's writing on the instincts and the drives cannot be understood to refer simply to the penetration of one's "stimulus shield" by external forces, or as a unilinear movement from the psychic to the somatic, for these texts are fundamentally engaged with the difficulty of knowing how to distinguish mental from physical, and inside from outside. "An instinct," for Freud, appears "as a borderland concept between the mental and the physical."[60] Though the stimulus shield can protect the subject from excessive excitation, Freud states, "toward the inside there can be no such shield."[61] In certain instances, however, internal operations are experienced by the subject as coming from the outside, and it is in this phenomenon, Freud suggests, that one finds the "origin of projection."[62]

Building on and expanding Freud's theory of the drive, and the relation it posits between mental and physical, inside and outside, Jean Laplanche sees the drive as "the impact on the individual and on the ego of the constant stimulation exerted from the inside by the repressed thing-presentations, which can be described as the source-objects of the drive."[63] Rejecting any notion of a body initially closed upon itself as a "biological idealism or solipsism," he invokes a model that "implies from the outset an opening to the world and, in terms of both perception and motor development, an opening of the organism onto its own environment."[64] Instead, what the drive reveals is the fact that "the adult world is entirely infiltrated with unconscious and sexual significations to which adults themselves do not have the code."[65] Stemming from these "enigmatic messages" from the Other, "drive" becomes, for Laplanche, not a concept to be put to use within analytic practice, but rather the precondition for theory itself, with the theory of the drive emerging as an exploration of "how, in what conditions, with what results and failures, and at what cost, the subject 'theorises' or metabolises the enigmas that are posed to it from the outset by interhuman communication."[66]

Though Laplanche's understanding of "the drive" in many ways involves a departure from Freud, it shares with Freud's own drive theory the belief in the primacy of the act of theorizing. In *Beyond the Pleasure Principle* Freud repeatedly dismisses the question of the accuracy of his metapsychological claims. Early in the fourth section of the book, he insists on the necessary centrality of the unknown to his theory of the drives: "The indefiniteness of all our discussions on what we describe as metapsychology is of course due to the fact that we know nothing of the nature of the excitatory process that takes place in the elements of the psychical systems, and that we do not feel justified in framing any hypothesis on the subject. We are consequently operating all the time with a large unknown factor, which we are obliged to carry over into every new formula."[67] And toward the end of the text, he again insists on the irrelevance of the truth of his theory, insisting rather on the right to "throw oneself into a line of thought": "It may be asked whether and how far I am myself convinced of the truth of the hypotheses that have been set out in these pages. My answer would be that I am not convinced myself and that I do not seek to persuade other people to believe in them. Or, more precisely, that I do not know how far to believe in them. There is no reason, as it seems to me, why the emotional factor of conviction should enter into this question at all. It is surely possible to throw oneself into a line of thought and to follow it wherever it leads out of simple scientific curiosity.... And in any case it is impossible to pursue an idea of this kind except by repeatedly combining factual material with what is purely speculative."[68] Theory involves speculative thinking not apart from but *as* an experience. Laplanche writes, "Theory too is an experience.... There is a living experience of concepts, their borrowings, their derivations, their straying or wandering."[69] Though the movements of a concept may ultimately end with a crash, a dead end, or a limp, Freud points out in the final line of *Beyond the Pleasure Principle* that limping is not a sin ("es ist keine Sünde zu hinken").[70]

At a time when contemporary film theory is widely perceived to have lost its momentum, this book foregrounds the space of "the crash"—evocative of collision, contestation, trauma, failure, and disappointment, as well as vulnerability, thrills, and the transgression of uninvited participation—in order to consider what might be salvaged from the wreckage. However successfully cognitive theories of vision might be able to prove the errors of psychoanalytic film theory's conceptualization of how we look at moving images, film theory usefully maintains a space for the kind of speculative theory Laplanche describes as "the living experience of concepts," distinct from the question of scientific accuracy. For if the drive to theorize stems from our constitutional opacity, from our inability to fully know ourselves, then perhaps we would do well to put the inaccessibility of the knowledge we strive to access at the center of the projects we undertake. Instead, what we *can* now know—whether through brain imaging, audience questionnaires, or detailed examination of our own bodily responses—threatens to displace, rather than explore, what we *cannot* know. Yet to transform film theory into a discourse of forgetting the unknowable is to be blind to cinema itself, to lose sight of the philosophical gift of the medium of film.

Speed Limits: The Problem of Movement

Limping, unglamorous, lunging forward while glancing backward, accidentally contaminated by the impure spaces one was trying to critique from a distance: such is the clumsy fate of the contemporary critic. Yet the challenge of movement is not limited to the problem of velocity, nor is it a purely aesthetic question; for the contemporary confusion about the direction and speed at which to move as a critic is also part of a more general skepticism about the very idea of collective movement, that is, about the possibility of moving or acting at all *with or in relation to others*. Honing in on this current disenchantment with political movements, which significantly impacts the identity of critical theory, Julia Kristeva writes,

> The entire history of political movements proves that they are permeable to dogmatism. One wonders if the realization of the revolt I am referring to is possible only in the private sphere: for example, in the psychoanalytical self-interrogation that people practice with themselves, or in an esthetic framework (literary and pictoral creation), or maybe in certain contexts that are not directly political, but at the meeting point between different religiosities that question the sacred. I am increasingly skeptical about the capacity of political movements to remain places of freedom.

Liberation movements are often threatened and monitored.... We saw this with the feminist movement which rapidly became a movement of chiefs where women crushed women inside the same group.[71]

Similarly, Virilio cautions one to be wary of valorizing all movement as necessarily progressive, as necessarily a "revolt . . . against the *constraint to immobility* symbolized by the ancient feudal serfdom."[72] He writes, "But no one yet suspected that the 'conquest of the freedom to come and go' so dear to Montaigne could, by a sleight of hand, become an *obligation to mobility*. The 'mass uprising' of 1793 was the institution of the first *dictatorship of movement*, subtly replacing the *freedom of movement* of the early days of the revolution."[73]

"Movement," like revolution, is now burdened with the bad reputation of involving oppressive and dogmatic collectives that require the total submission of the individual to the collective. Though this moment of inertia may seem pessimistic or even destructive, I ask whether and when such resistance to movement might also prove to be an enabling force, one that resists the speed or acceleration that aligns itself with advanced capitalism and clears a space for the slow pace of recursive and critical thinking. As Avital Ronell states, "That's part of our whole Western logos: to finish with something, to get it over with, to have a decisive or clean-cut decision, rather than passing things through the crucible of undecidability. Taking your time and recognizing the impossibility of making a clean-cut decision would render some of our moves more flexible, strange, deviant."[74] I go in search of these flexible, deviant, implicated, cross-generational, and cross-disciplinary exchanges through the suspension and confusion that the crash creates; I seek contested spaces, a community, rather than a communion, of intellectuals, writers, artists, and filmmakers.

In *The Inoperative Community* Jean-Luc Nancy describes "communion" as a type of fusion that produces a singular subject, a singularity that destroys the possibility of both communication and community as he understands these terms. Though the absence of "communal fusion" or shared collective identity may produce disorienting "phantasms of the lost community," Nancy argues, "What this community has 'lost'—the immanence and intimacy of a communion—is lost only in the sense that such a 'loss' is constitutive of 'community' itself."[75] Neither fusion nor atomization, community is, for Nancy, "the *clinamen* of the 'individual,'" the yearning of the individual beyond herself, at and to her limit, toward the other, "the ecstasy of the sharing: 'communicating' by not 'communing.'"[76] One may understand the compulsive "car crashing" of contemporary artists, writers, and filmmakers at least in part as a desire to capture, and perhaps provoke in others, the risk, feeling, and transformational possibilities of this clinematic ecstasy of sharing, of leaning toward the other without fusion. The notion of sharing, of thinking and being "at and to the limit" of oneself may offer not only a model for understanding certain aesthetic practices and concerns, but also for thinking productively about the continuing role of theory in the twenty-first century.

In this book I participate in and take inspiration from the ongoing work of antiracist, radical feminism, always both a political practice and an endlessly mutating, contested critical methodology. Feminism challenges one to explore the relationship between politics and epistemology, to engage the problems and possibilities of coalitions and communities (intellectual and otherwise), and to insist that the ongoing crises of criticism, its utter provisionality, might also be its greatest asset. As Judith Butler argues in "The End of Sexual Difference?," radical politics ultimately depends on the willingness to allow oneself to be open to questions whose answers may force a rethinking of one's political position: "To remain unwilling to rethink one's politics on the basis of questions posed is to opt for a dogmatic stand at the cost of both life and thought."[77] While some readers may view this openness to provisional alliances and positions as a form of weak moral relativism or pluralism, a "paradigm-of-no-paradigm," I share Janet R. Jakobsen's conviction that "articulating morality through complexity opens moral possibilities, in part, because the more connections among specific social units, the more complex the interactions, and the more complex the interactions the more opportunities for freedom."[78] Focusing on collisions that bring difference to the fore within a framework of uncomfortable, sometimes painful, and even fatal, proximity, I examine how we articulate, police, and transgress aesthetic, discursive, disciplinary, and physical boundaries, and consider how we might better understand the relationships among ourselves by examining how filmmakers and artists explore, explode, and transform the borders between different modes of representation.

chapter one

"JERKY NEARNESS"

Spectatorship, Mobility, and Collision in Early Cinema

Today the most real, the mercantile gaze into the heart of things is the advertisement. It abolishes the space where contemplation moved and all but hits us between the eyes with things as a car, growing to gigantic proportions, careens at us out of a film screen. And just as the film does not present furniture and façades in completed forms for critical inspection, their insistent, jerky nearness alone being sensational, the genuine advertisement hurtles things at us with the tempo of a good film. Thereby "matter-of-factness" is finally dispatched, and in face of the huge images across the walls of houses, where toothpaste and cosmetics lie handy for giants, sentimentality is restored to health and liberated in American style, just as people whom nothing moves or touches any longer are taught to cry again by films. —WALTER BENJAMIN, "ONE-WAY STREET" (1928)

For Walter Benjamin, the cinematic car careening toward the audience "out of a film screen" becomes a privileged figure illustrating not only mass culture's destruction of contemplative space, but also its ushering in of an intensified physical experience of "jerky nearness," of virtual collisions with the material world that catalyze affective awakenings.[1] As reflection becomes impossible in the face of these hurtling images, their sensational proximity and speed break through the defenses of those who had forgotten how to cry, allowing them to be moved and touched anew. Though the merits of this sentiment continue to be debated in discussions of the ideology of popular cinema, for Benjamin it is mass culture's ability to arouse this sense of "insistent, jerky nearness" to the material world shown within the film, rather than any fateful absorption into that world, that displaces critical distance and vanishes a "matter-of-fact" approach to the world. And it is in this notion of cinema as a world close-at-hand but stuttering, just beyond our grasp, that Benjamin locates the radical possibilities of film. Though the specter of capitalism's gargantuan face and the destructive threat of the oncoming motorcar caution against a naïve and uncritical embrace of Benjamin's utopian vision of modern media, this passage nevertheless invites us to discover—through the figure of the cinematic car zooming straight at us—a mode of thinking about the world that grows out of, and has an affective openness to, the physical intensities of the virtual world of film. While the futurists celebrate the crash for its ecstatic potential and the regenerative orgasmic energy that arises in the wake of its destruction, Benjamin here suggests that feeling and the capacity to be moved emerge not through an actual collision, but through the sensation of nearness that the *illusion* of a vehicle about to collide with the apparatus of cinema is able to heighten. The paradigm of spectatorship as a virtual collision is not new to cinema; it can be found in descriptions of earlier projection technologies. Dionysius Lardner, for example, writing in 1859 of the common practice of gradually moving the magic lantern away from the screen in order to increase the size of the projected image, describes how "it sometimes appears as if the object would approach so as to come into actual collision with the spectator."[2] Yet perhaps because cinema combined these sensations of sudden changes in distance and proximity, enabled by projection, with repeated images of actual technological collisions, the popular as well as the philosophical conceptualization of cinema is increasingly aligned with the experience of being run over by a car, as in this 1907 advertisement for Liebig's Real Meat Extract, a product which implicitly promised to fortify and restore its consumers after their daily encounters with the physical challenges of the modern world (figure 1).

Benjamin is not alone in linking cinema's utopian potential to its ability to elicit in spectators a kind of affective awakening in response to the speed and thrills represented on and experienced in film. Writing in 1926, only two years prior to Benjamin's publication of "One-Way Street," Virgina Woolf sees as the medium's promise in its ability to bring the true velocity of thought and emotion before our eyes in a way that writing never could. In the face of cinematic images, she suggests, the brain sees that "it is time to wake up."[3] But for Woolf, too, the surprise, the affective and intellectual potential of cinema does not lie in any real threat that the objects on-screen will break through and hit us; and Woolf quite explicitly notes, "The horse will not knock us down. The King will not grasp our hands. The wave will

FIGURE 1 Advertisement for Liebig's Real Meat Extract. Courtesy Werner Nekes, private collection, Mülheim, Germany.

not wet our feet."[4] Rather, she envisions a yet-to-be-realized cinema that maintains a nearness that never resolves itself into the "present" of the audience, one made up of pictures that are "real with a different reality from that which we perceive in daily life."[5] "Then," she claims, "as smoke pours from Vesuvius, we should be able to see thought in its wildness, in its beauty, in its oddity, pouring from men with their elbows on a table; from women with their little handbags slipping to the floor. We should see these emotions mingling together and affecting each other."[6] Though Woolf thought cinema had yet to find its form, she saw intimations of its potential less in cinema itself than "in the chaos of the streets, perhaps, when some momentary assembly of color, sound, movement suggests that here is a scene waiting a new art to be transfixed."[7]

For contemporary film theorists, the questions raised by Benjamin and Woolf regarding the role of critical distance and affective proximity; the relationships among thinking, seeing, and feeling; the intellectual possibilities of sensational and affective experiences provoked by both new media and the street; cinema's destabilization of the relationship between inside and outside, self and other; and the screen's effect on the relationship between spectator and world—all these burn with renewed intensity, not least because of the pressure put on these issues by the transition from analog to digital forms of image making, which leaves us having to deal with new uncertainties before we have had time to resolve the old ones. As David Rodowick argues in his important book *The Virtual Life of Film* (2007), "What characterizes the medium is our awareness that it occupies a continuous state of self-transformation and invention that runs ahead of our perception and ideas."[8] And now, as then, the virtual collision of the automobile—with the audience, camera, screen, pedestrians, lampposts, and other equally reckless objects—provides a compelling and recurrent cinematic figure through which to think our changing phenomenological experience of moving images.

Three early British examples of these "car-crash films" serve as sites for exploring the aesthetic, philosophical, and ideological limits of cinema, for testing, representing, and shaping the emerging space of the frame, the experience of the screen surface, the relationship between moving objects and the camera, and the axis between spectators and the moving image. I begin in the early years of cinema, not in order to provide a comprehensive and chronological account of the cinematic car crash, but to foreground those moments in film history when car crashes become particularly prominent—namely, the 1900s, the 1920s, the 1960s, the 1970s, and the present—and to explore how our experience of these virtual collisions is shaped by the culturally and historically specific roles that technology, cinema, and disaster occupy in the collective imagination. Nevertheless, as I open with a period in which the medium's codes and practices had not yet been standardized, I explore how early experimental uses of film technology emerged in relation to the equally new technology of the automobile. While the relationship between a later, more linear and codified narrative cinema and the automobile's promise of speed and freedom-as-movement has been widely discussed within the generic context of the Road Movie, less attention has been paid to the cinematic fantasies, social visions, and experimental aesthetics that have emerged in conjunction with the early automobile as a malfunctioning technology, one that fails to start, stalls, crashes, explodes, and falls apart. While this aspect of the automobile is most visible in cinema's early period, when *both* technologies, cinema and the automobile, were at early stages of development, this early self-reflexive preoccupation of the camera with the car as accident-prone, as a machine of risk, surprise, and potential disaster, persists throughout the history of the medium, even as both technologies become more stable. The early trope of the crashing car thus persistently functions as a vehicle for testing and at times transcending the perceived limitations of cinema.

The films *How It Feels to Be Run Over* (Cecil Hepworth, 1900, 50 feet), *Explosion of a Motor Car* (Cecil Hepworth, 1900, 97 feet), and *The (?) Motorist* (Walter R. Booth, 1906, 181 feet) yoke the erratic, crashing, mutilated, and immobilized cars to explorations of the formal possibilities of the medium, including the space of the frame, and the use of camera movement, written text, and editing.[9] Simultaneously, these formal experiments become sites for the articulation of social fantasies and anxieties regarding modern public and private space, personal mobility and paralysis, changing gender roles and familial structures, and social circulation and contagion.

How It Feels to Be Run Over (1900)

The title of Cecil Hepworth's film, *How It Feels to Be Run Over*, immediately emphasizes cinema less as a medium of vision than as a feeling machine. The short opens with a view of an empty, receding country road, a strikingly pastoral contrast to the popular short films depicting busy urban street scenes and the infiltration of modernity into public life that began to emerge around 1900, and a scenario chosen deliberately by Hepworth for its "essentially English character and for the peculiar beauty of the countryside of this land."[10] As if to emphasize the incursion of modernity into the English countryside, the film begins with a horse and cart appearing at the most distant visible point of the road, driven by a single male passenger toward the off-screen camera, a forward movement that highlights the image's depth of field and draws attention to the camera's invisible presence.[11] Later, as an automobile approaches the camera, the behavior of its passengers, who wave directly into the camera, underscores this presence, making explicit that we are watching a game of "chicken" between the twin technologies of motion: car and camera, at a moment when the camera's ability to move relied largely on a parasitic relationship with transportation technologies.[12] Unlike the car, the horse veers gently away from the camera; as it exits the lower-right-hand corner of the frame, the motorcar appears in the distance, followed by a young man on a bicycle (a second modern vehicle often excluded from synopses of the film).[13] The car contains a male driver, a female passenger in the front seat, and a male passenger standing behind the other two, and together, they form a pyramidal structure evocative of a circus act, making the status of the drive as performance quite explicit. As the car heads directly for the camera, the bicycle retraces the alternative path taken by the cart and exits (almost unnoticed) off to the right. Meanwhile, the men in the car gesticulate wildly at the camera while the woman wags her finger at it, but we rapidly lose perspective on their actions as the car's body and the woman's skirt gradually fill the frame until the screen is fully overwhelmed by the car, at which point the image of the car becomes a black screen. This black screen–car body is immediately followed by one of the earliest known, and extremely dramatic uses, of intertitles. A series of single, white, hand-drawn words and punctuation marks appear, each starring in its own frame, possibly painted or scratched directly onto the celluloid–car surface: "?? / !! / ! / Oh! / Mother / *will* / be / pleased" (see figures 2–6).[14]

SMASHING THROUGH THE SCREEN

Though Hepworth's film has been compared with contemporaneous railway films, including one reading that has seen it as a possible ironic commentary on the supposed terror felt by the first audiences of Auguste and Louis Lumière's *L'arrivée d'un train en gare de La Ciotat* (1895), the differences between the railway film and the automobile film remain undertheorized.[15] As Jeffrey Ruoff noted, "While much work has been done linking the development of the train to new modes of vision associated with film (Kirby 1997), comparatively little has appeared on the relations between the automobile and the cinema, despite the historical coincidence of their development."[16] Though it is certainly tempting simply to fold the cinematic automobile accident into Wolfgang Schivelbusch's and Lynne Kirby's excellent work on the railway accident, panoramic vision, traumatic neuroses, and early cinema, it is necessary to suspend this ready-made reading in order to explore the extent to which early car accident films may tell a different, if related story. If many of the railway films Kirby discusses showcase the spectacle of train transportation and its accidents, the enigmatic and animated text that closes *How It Feels to Be Run Over* marks a place where the promise of a direct visual experience of the accident ultimately seems to destroy the possibility of cinematic vision, but in doing so gives way to the incorporation into cinema of another medium: writing. Noël Burch counts Hepworth's film as one in a "series of battering rams beating on the 'invisible barrier' that maintains the spectator in a state of externality," all early efforts to interpellate the early film spectator into the space of the diegesis, making *How It*

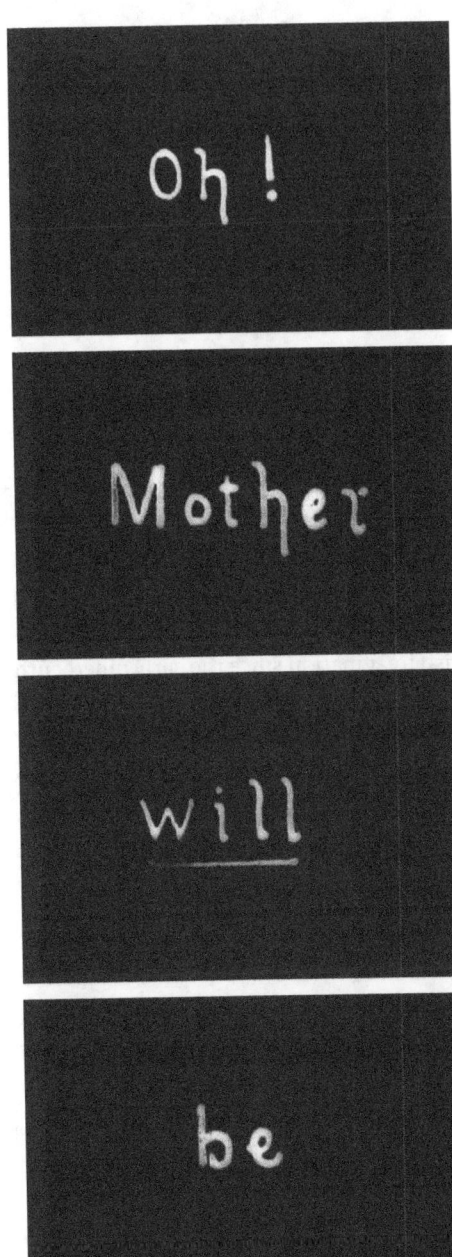

FIGURES 2-6 Intertitle from *How It Feels to Be Run Over*.

Feels to Be Run Over, for Burch, "a remarkable 'epistemological' résumé of the formative phase of the IMR [Institutional Mode of Representation]."[17] Yet this is only one way of reading a film that also draws attention to the fixity of the camera through its comparison with moving vehicles; introduces movement not as a simple opposite of stasis, but as a range of velocities; experiments with the gap between spectator and image; and equates the destruction of the image in the form of the collision and the resulting black screen with the medium's expansion via cryptic on-screen writing.[18]

Though Hepworth's car films obviously share common interests with turn-of-the-century railway films and local films depicting other forms of mechanized transportation in urban life, one need only look at films like M&K 186: *Jamaica Street, Glasgow* (1901) or M&K 183: *Ride on the Tramcar through Belfast* (1901) to note the motorcar's absence from the streets of British cities at this time, and to understand that its presence in British cinema at this moment signifies in quite different ways from that of the railway, which had occupied the British imagination since the early nineteenth century (figures 7–8).[19] Although cinema's visualization of the subjective experience of train travel may have contributed to new modes of representation deriving from a newly available mode of "panoramic perception," as Jonathan Crary, Schivelbusch, Gunning, and Kirby, among others, have argued, it is important to note that, unlike the car and cinema, the railway was *not* new but was, rather, as Burch states, "entering its golden age," about to be displaced.[20] While the train becomes a vehicle to create expansive and often breathtaking illusions of movement through space for early filmmakers, the use of the motorcar is often more fantastical, comic, puzzling, and disaster-ridden, suggesting that the full range of its technological possibilities—like those of cinema—had yet to be discovered. And the accident becomes a prime testing ground.

Spectators may or may not have been overwhelmed by the approaching train featured in the Lumières' 1895 film, *L'arrivée d'un train,* but formally speaking, this train film and Hepworth's *How It Feels to Be Run Over* are very different.[21] In both films the effect of screen depth is created by receding, converging lines. In the former the train itself visually traces the left-hand line, while the waiting passengers on the platform form the right-hand line. The camera is located in the middle of the two lines and is turned leftward to catch the train as it passes. By contrast, in *How It Feels to Be Run Over* the converging lines are traced by the two edges of a country road, and the

FIGURE 7 View of Jamaica Street in Glasgow, Scotland, showing no evidence of motorcars. Still from *Jamaica Street, Glasgow*.

FIGURE 8 Street view in Belfast, Ireland. No motorcars are visible. Still from *Ride on the Tramcar through Belfast*.

camera faces the oncoming car directly. While in Hepworth's film the car approaches the camera, in *L'arrivée d'un train* the train does not move directly toward the camera, but rather passes it at an oblique angle.

Though the myth of the first film spectators exiting the Grand Café in panic still persists, this narrative of naïve spectators has been challenged by Gunning's compelling argument that the terror of the Lumières' oncoming train may have stemmed less from a belief in the material threat of screen rupture than in the way projected moving images—illusions of life with their "vividness and vitality... drained away"—reflected an encounter with modernity that was experienced as a "loss of experience," an uncanny encounter with emptiness and death.[22] In support of Gunning's reading, a close look at *L'arrivée d'un train* reveals that in addition to offering spectators a sensational encounter with an oncoming train, the film also reminds audiences of the impossibility of a physical encounter with the illusory train, through something like a metacinematic commentary on the spectator's experience of cinema. Though the most discussed aspect of this short film is undoubtedly the escalating scale of the approaching train as it fills the screen, the film's frequently neglected second part focuses on the gleaming side of the train as it pulls into the station, a metallic surface that reflects the blurred and slowly creeping reflections of the crowd waiting on the right-hand side of the frame, making this a literal as well as an allegorical "train of shadows."[23] As the train doors swing open, the reflections of the ghostly passengers glimmering in the train's side suddenly disappear; but this transitory glimpse of the passengers' doubles underscores the virtual, rather than material, quality of the cinematic train, and reminds us that it was not only moving glass windows, but also the shiny metal surfaces of modern machines, that made procinematic visions—and the sense of nearness such visions provoke—a ubiquitous part of the modern landscape (see figure 9). Though the train's approach animates and highlights the axis between screen and spectator, implying the possibility of breaching the division between the projected world and our own, this dream of permeability is held in check by the film's simultaneous representation of the space *between* the on-screen bodies of the passengers and their ghostly reflections in the mirror-like second "screen" of the train's surface. Even as this film activates the illusion of screen rupture, it stages a scene that reveals that there *is* nothing behind the screen and that if the distance between screen and spectator is diminished, if the screen, like the train door, were to "open

FIGURE 9 Passenger reflections in the metallic surface of a train. Still from *L'arrivée d'un train*.

up," then cinema—along with all the terrors and pleasures of its "jerky nearness"—would also vanish.

The scene of the cinematic car accident highlights cinema's struggle simultaneously to cross and maintain this distance. Repeatedly, the figure of a mechanical collision is articulated through the use of formal devices that attempt in different ways to exceed the limitations or parameters of the medium, and at times this produces an interesting correlation among scenes of mechanical accident, the expression of liminal or transgressive social desires, and experimental or innovative formal gestures. In early cinema this frequently occurs through the movement of objects toward the camera, creating the fantasy that these objects may somehow be capable of moving "beyond" the screen without disappearing. Yet if, as Benjamin and Woolf suggest, such moments of spectatorial proximity to the cinematic image somehow awaken our affective openness to both the world and to the speed of thought, in spite of, or perhaps because of, the impossibility of the encounter suggested by them, then perhaps a close examination of the cinematic car crash's virtual encounters can heighten our understanding of cinema's capacity to shape the relationships between self and other, and among body, vision, and thought. In many ways, the impending collision with the audience or camera suggested by so many cinematic accidents functions in a similar way to the look at the camera. Miriam Hansen has argued that though this look stages a "failed encounter" between film world and spectator, this failure may also "project a spectator not yet in place."[24] And it is here, in the simultaneous visualization of both the desire for a complete encounter with the other and the realization that the recognition of the other requires some separation and is therefore always, of necessity, incomplete, that cinema's ethical potential can be located.

FLESH, FILM CRITICISM, AND SUBJECTIVE VISION

In recent years, as scholarship transitions away from models of film theory primarily grounded in psychoanalytic theory, phenomenological studies of film have increasingly emphasized the ethical superiority of the embodied spectator who experiences cinema in a fleshy way. And, like the car careening toward the screen, phenomenological film theory challenges us to articulate the physical body's relationship to the cinematic image, and attempts to understand the consequences of this relationship. Few contemporary film scholars have made as sustained an attempt to develop a phenomenological approach to film as Vivian Sobchack, and her recent work provides a useful point of entry into the question of what the future potential of phenomenology for film theory might be. In her first book, *The Address of the Eye: A Phenomenology of Film Experience*, she worked against the vagueness of the cinematic phenomenological tradition, trying, for example, to categorize phenomenological film theorists into three distinct groups: (1) transcendentalists, influenced by Husserl; (2) existentialists, influenced by Merleau-Ponty; and (3) those with an "enthusiastic but methodless 'feel' for existential phenomenology."[25] In contrast to the rigor and philosophical discipline Sobchack asserts in *The Address of the Eye*, however, her more recent work *Carnal Thoughts: Embodiment and Moving Image Culture* (2004), though guided by the existential philosophy of Merleau-Ponty, celebrates a lack of philosophical discipline and introduces autobiography and anecdote as tools for enabling an embodied film theory that pays attention to the subject's corporeal, historically, and culturally located experience of cinema, to ask what cinema feels like, how the feelings film inspires can shape one's thinking about it, as well as how cinematic feelings in turn affect one's relation to and understanding of the world. If Sobchack's turn to phenomenology is motivated by feminist concerns—she states that her interest in embodiment is rooted in her experience as a female of "the inconsistent and often contradictory ways in which [her] material being was regarded and valued (or not)"—her turn away from a more disciplined application of Merleau-Ponty is equally feminist, inspired by Judith Butler's rigorous feminist critique of Merleau-Ponty in "Sexual Ideology and Phenomenological Description."[26] Having identified the fact that for Merleau-Ponty, there is no such thing as gendered subjectivity, but only a universal and implicitly masculine subject, Butler declares, "For a concrete description of lived experience, it seems crucial to ask *whose* sexuality and *whose* bodies are being described, for 'sexuality' and 'bodies' remain abstractions without first being situated in concrete social and cultural contexts.... The terms of this inquiry will not be found in the texts of Merleau-Ponty, but in the works of philosophical feminism to come."[27] Sobchack's work plays a vital role not only in the development of film phenomenology, but also in the sustenance of a dynamic tradition of feminist participation in film theory. (Whatever the faults of psychoanalytic film theory may be, some of its most important texts were written by feminist scholars, such as Laura Mulvey, Kaja Silverman, Mary Ann Doane, and Teresa de Lauretis; and as this earlier model is dismissed by the likes of *October* editor Malcolm Turvey as "fashionable nonsense," his newly rigorous film theory, modeled on analytic philosophy, runs the risk of becoming an exclusively male affair—and one need only look at Turvey's footnotes to see evidence of this emerging pattern.)

As one transitions from a feminist psychoanalytic-semiotic to a feminist phenomenological-film-theory paradigm, what questions arise? Reading Sobchack suggests three questions that may provide useful starting points for further discussion. First, does contemporary phenomenological film theory have a politics and an ethics? Second, as one insists on developing a vocabulary to describe the embodied film experience, is one to assume that the idea of a disembodied, psychological, or virtual film experience has been fully discounted? Third, is it possible to critically engage a discourse that relies so heavily on "thick description" of a subjective film experience, or do such subjective responses "undermine theories," as Turvey fears ethical and epistemological commitments also do?[28]

It should come as no surprise that car-crash texts, including J. G. Ballard's *Crash*, Cronenberg's *Crash*, and Abraham Zapruder's film of the Kennedy assassination, play a prominent role in *Carnal Thoughts*.[29] Without a doubt, the ethical questions surrounding cinema's ability to mediate "how it feels," and the extent to which we can (or should) directly experience the feelings of another, are central to Sobchack's critical endeavor. Historically, when positioned in contrast to the structuralist-semiotic approach, phenomenological film theory has emerged as seemingly apolitical. As Dudley Andrew writes, "Structuralists are typed as cultural radicals while phenomenologists are accused of neutrality, if not rightism. The former . . . can envision a utopia of signs, of knowledge, and of communication, a cinema which will be clear, just, and demystified. The latter are anxious to change nothing but instead to comprehend a process which flows along perfectly well on its own."[30] Yet in what is almost a total reverse of this claim, Sobchack links disembodied screen experiences to an indifference to "AIDS, homelessness, hunger, torture, the bloody consequences of war, and the other ills the flesh is heir to outside the image and the datascape," allowing her critical position to accrue an almost overwhelming moral force.[31] The embodied viewer, described by Sobchack as the "cinesthetic" subject, "both touches and is touched by the screen—able to commute seeing to touching and back again *without a thought*."[32] The rich sensory experience of the cinesthetic subject, who is "ambiguously located both 'here' offscreen and 'there' onscreen," is contrasted to the impoverished (and pathologically feminized) alternative of those viewers "who would reduce sensorial experience at the movies to an impoverished 'cinematic sight' or posit anorexic theories of identification that have no flesh on them, that cannot stomach 'a feast for the eyes.'"[33]

Ethically, the phenomenological approach makes available a space of cinematic intersubjectivity that recognizes the embodied other. Discussing her experience of Jane Campion's *The Piano* (1993), Sobchack writes, "*My fingers knew what I was looking at*—and this *before* the objective reverse shot that followed to put those fingers in their proper place," and she describes how her own fingers "'felt themselves' as a potentiality in the subjective and fleshy situation figured onscreen."[34] According to Sobchack, these fingers' perspicacity derives not from the viewer's familiarity with cinematic codes, but rather from her apparent ability to engage in an intense form of cinematic empathy, to experience physically the subjective experiences of others through the projection of her own body into that of another, a movement beyond the self that that is accompanied by a simultaneous subversion of "the very notion of *onscreen* and *offscreen* as mutually exclusive sites or subject positions."[35]

Sobchack offers neither Benjamin's "jerky nearness" nor Woolf's secure knowledge that "the King will not grasp our hands." On the contrary, for Sobchack, we *will* touch and be touched: "At the moment when Baines touches Ada's skin through her stocking, suddenly my skin is both mine and not my own.... I feel not only my 'own' body but also Baines's body, Ada's body, and what I have elsewhere called the 'film's body.'"[36] But what is the consequence of dissolving the gap between subject and object, viewer and world viewed, of shifting the cinematic paradigm from nearness to presence?

Though cinema enjoys a privileged relation to the world, being, unlike the other arts, for André Bazin, "a discourse of the world, not men," it remains crucial to maintain a tension between our embodied experience of cinema as subjects in the world and an awareness of the virtual dimension of the moving image of the world we view, a fact emphasized by Stanley Cavell and Rodowick—"that film presents to me a world from which I am absent, from which I am necessarily screened by its temporal absence, yet with which I hope to reconnect or join."[37] As Sobchack invokes the discourse of phenomenology to describe her embodied cinematic experiences, our awareness of this virtuality begins to disappear. But what is to be gained (or lost) from maintaining the gap between the viewing subject and the world viewed? For Cavell and Rodowick, our separation from the world, made visible by both photography and cinema, raises the ethical question of how we are positioned subjectively in relation to the world by such images, and provokes what may be regarded as an ethical (if impossible) desire in viewers to be present for the objects viewed. This desire is close, but not identical, to the desire that is experienced *and fulfilled* for Sobchack's off-screen subjects. But how is it possible that Sobchack's on- and off-screen subjects can more easily and more materially commingle than those of Cavell and Rodowick?

It is here that one encounters a certain slipperiness on the part of Sobchack regarding the status of the subject in her version of phenomenological film theory. Clearly, there is something deeply disturbing about idealizing a medium that would allow subjects to enter fully and completely into the subjective world of another. Indeed, as Judith Butler argues in *Giving an Account of Oneself*, ethics itself is grounded on the fact not only that the other is inaccessible to us, but also that we are only partially, and necessarily, accessible to ourselves. Sobchack is aware of the disturbing ethical consequences of the porous quality she attributes to the screen, and perhaps as a result of this awareness, the status of the cinematic subject in *Carnal Thoughts* is very unstable. At times, she prevents her inhabitation of the on-screen subject's body from being a kind of invasion or occupation of the other by making the subject-object paradigm disappear altogether, allowing cinema to transport us into what seems to be the material equivalent of Lacan's Imaginary, in which the sensory experience of the other emerges as "primary, prepersonal and global," relating "not to our secondary engagement with and recognition of either 'subject positions' or characters but rather to our primary engagement (and the film's) with the sense and sensibility of materiality itself."[38] Yet, at other times, the subject seems firmly in place, as when Sobchack sees cinema as the mechanical projection and making visible of "not just the objective world but the very structure and process of subjective, embodied vision—hitherto only directly available to human beings as an invisible and private structure that each of us experiences as 'our own,'" as a vehicle for experiencing *directly* the subjectively structured vision of another.[39]

The problem with describing a sensory cinematic experience as "primary" or "prepersonal" in order to circumnavigate the difficulties of the ethical subject-object relationship from a phenomenological perspective is that phenomenology is rooted in the conscious experiences of the subject. Sobchack seems to want to have her cake and eat it too, allowing her cinematic viewer to be exempt from the ethical obligations of the subject toward the object by describing the encounters between the two as "primary," but then also allowing that "prepersonal/presubjective" experience to be fully transparent to the viewer, suggesting that it is conscious and subjective after all.

The implied persistence of the subject throughout Sobchack's book makes her phenomenological approach to film theory hard to reconcile with the work of Gilles Deleuze. In spite of the fact that Sobchack explicitly aligns her phenomenological interpretation of cinematic spectatorship with Deleuze's celebration of "sensory thought" in Eisenstein's work, these two theoretical discourses ultimately pull in opposite directions.[40] For Sobchack, Deleuze not only misunderstands and misreads Merleau-

Ponty, but, more importantly, "Deleuze neglects the *embodied situation* of the spectator and of the film," even as he, in a project that Sobchack identifies as similar to her own, asserts "the *direct* and *preverbal* significance of cinematic movement of images."[41]

Yet it is a dramatic underestimation of Deleuze to say that he simply neglected the *embodied situation* of the spectator, for his position is far more conscious than the word *neglect* implies. For Deleuze, cinema never gives us "the presence of bodies" as theater can, but, further, he understands "true cinema" as constituting the unknown, unthought, and yet-to-be visible body, as contradicting "all natural perception" and "making [the everyday body] pass through a ceremony" until "at last the disappearance of the visible body is achieved."[42] The absence of the subject for the cinematic spectator rests less on a sense of a "preverbal" or "presubjective" experience than on a belief that cinema comes after the subject. For Deleuze, cinema leaves phenomenology behind: "It will be noted that phenomenology, in certain respects, stops at pre-cinematographic conditions which explains its embarrassed attitude: it gives a privilege to natural perception which means that movement is still related to *poses*. . . . As a result, cinematographic movement is both condemned as unfaithful to the conditions of perception and also exalted as the new story capable of 'drawing close to' the perceived and perceiver, the world and perception."[43] One can see how Sobchack might align her theory of the preverbal and direct subjective experience, as well as Merleau-Ponty's phenomenology, with Deleuze's "grounding of cinematic signification as immanent" at moments such as those when Deleuze writes, "But the cinema perhaps has a great advantage: just because it lacks a center of anchorage and horizon, the sections which it makes would not prevent it from going back up the path that natural perception comes down. Instead of going from the acentred state of things to centered perception, it could go back up towards the acentered state of things, and get closer to it."[44] Yet Deleuze immediately follows this passage by stating, "Broadly speaking, this would be the opposite of what phenomenology would put forward."[45]

Although Sobchack allows some movement away from subjectivity and consciousness in order to create an intellectual space in which to think how a material intersubjectivity might be possible, and ethical, in the cinema, her project ultimately repeatedly returns to the task of trying to narrate, through a subjective consciousness, those intersubjective experiences. By contrast, in Deleuze the subjective consciousness fully disappears. As he declares in *The Movement-Image*, "My body is an image, hence a set of actions and reactions. My eye, my brain, are images, parts of body.... External images act on me, transmit movement to me, and I return movement: how could images be in my consciousness since I am myself image, that is, movement? And can I even, at this level, speak of 'ego,' of eye, of brain and of body? Only for simple convenience; for nothing can yet be identified in this way. It is rather a gaseous state. Me, my body, are rather a set of molecules and atoms not distinct from worlds.... [I]t is a state of matter too hot for me to be able to distinguish solid bodies in it."[46]

THE ABSTRACT ACCIDENT

With these problems regarding cinema's relation to the physical body in mind, I now return to *How It Feels to Be Run Over*, as well as to the other aforementioned "car crash" films from cinema's early years. By 1900, British film audiences would certainly have been familiar with the onstage magic illusions of two-dimensional paintings and playing card figures "coming to life" and appearing on stage as three-dimensional bodies, often by ripping through the flat images that initially represent them. Yet, though *How It Feels to Be Run Over* gestures back toward these earlier theatrical tricks, this brief film is perhaps less interesting for how it resembles the trick film and onstage magic acts than for how it differs from them.[47] Gunning has already highlighted this film's use of nontheatrical framing, yet in addition to this observation, one must note that, unlike *How to Stop a Motor Car* (Percy Stow, U.K., 1902), in which Hepworth acted, or *Extraordinary Cab Accident* (W. R. Booth, 1903), both of which show men miraculously jumping up after being knocked down (by a car in the former and a horse-drawn cab in the latter), *How It Feels to Be Run Over* marks the apparent moment of the car's collision with the camera not with a staged spectacle or substitution trick of any sort, but with a black screen that subsequently gives way to writing.[48] Producing a black base for a text whose meaning we struggle to decipher, the car's implied "crash" with the camera manifests not a physical sensation of what it feels like to be run over by a motorcar, but rather what Deleuze describes as a "pedagogy of the image" through which we learn "that the image is not just given to be seen. It is legible as well as visible." And, for Deleuze, it is particularly in the case of the white or black screen where we learn that "we do not know how to read it properly."[49] Though this film promises to show how something feels to another through the subjective view of the camera, it ultimately reminds us—through the turn to (almost nonsensical) writing—that cinematic images are, just like words, inscriptions of an enigmatic world that are, like the world itself, in need of interpretation.

And so the intertitle erupts into cinema at the scene of the accident, further hybridizing the already bastard medium in the wake of a technological collision, a direct consequence of the camera's apparent inability to move quickly enough in the face of the moving world. Unspeakable punctuation marks followed by shaky, scrawled single words and signs implicitly acknowledge the awkwardness and tentativeness of this birth of words into cinema. Furthermore, this dramatization of the limits of live-action cinema's mobility through a turn to the graphic will persist in other similar films, analysis of which trend requires first that one consider how to read this semantically obscure intertitle.

Though the film's title foregrounds more explicitly than perhaps any other title in film history the idea of cinema as a vehicle for transmitting the feelings of another, it nevertheless adopts a grammatical form that lacks a feeling subject, using a verbal phrase to express an abstract notion of sensation disconnected from any specific embodied subjectivity. Can this abstract structure, doubled in the film form by the representation of an encounter between two technologies, the automobile and the camera, transmit to the embodied spectator a subjective sense of what it feels like for a person to be run over, even in the absence of a subject? This is unlikely, for as the image disappears, the crash refuses rather than invites the fantasy of experiencing directly the subjective visual and physical sensations of another, dissolving the image completely and offering words instead. Though this reading may simply demonstrate a failure to give myself over to embodied cinematic viewing, it is the conceptual third space or gap between the world and me, made visible precisely by the experience we have here of cinema's technological, nonhuman gaze, a gaze from no place, that allows film to open into the realm of ethics. Rather than giving us the opportunity to directly and physically experience the subjective experiences of another, Deleuze suggests, the cinematic image offers a place where the distinction between subjective and objective "tends to lose its importance," not because the two are confused, but because "we do not have to know and there is no longer even a place from which to ask."[50]

Prefiguring Woolf's vision of a cinema made up of "something abstract ... something which calls for the very slightest help from words or music to make itself intelligible, yet justly uses them subserviently," cinema here turns to writing less to communicate a joke than to exceed itself.[51] Though cinema's inherent and ever-expanding hybridity may ultimately prevent it from successfully colliding with or exceeding its constitutive, formal limits (those limits are always too fuzzy), it is in this space of attempted collisions with other media that one becomes aware of film's ability to expand into its own "outside." Here, then, cinema emerges as an analogy to "the Open" (a term Deleuze links to the process of changing and unfolding in the absence of a given, graspable whole).[52] While an alignment of cinema with the Open does not negate the possibility of thinking about cinema in relation to questions of the medium, it does suggest that however consciously film aims to construct its encounters with other media—writing, drawing, painting, music—as collisions or conflicts, these encounters will ultimately only ever be able to emerge as variations. Though this quality of cinema in part explains the medium's affiliation with capitalist culture's gluttonous incorporation and subsequent destruction of difference, cinema's constant and excessive variation, which renders it structurally incapable of formal aesthetic conflict, might also, in the manner of the Open, offer a form of resistance to a capitalist culture in which the representation of conflict repeatedly transforms critique into product. As Deleuze explains in his discussion of the theater of Carmelo Bene, "For the representation of conflicts, CB claims to substitute the presence of variation as a more active, more aggressive element. . . . Now is not continuous variation precisely that which keeps overflowing—by excess or by defect—the representation of the majoritarian standard? Is not continuous variation the becoming-minoritarian of everyone, in opposition to the majoritarian face of Someone?"[53]

Explosion of a Motor Car (1900)

One can further explore the relationship between the automobile accident and the emergence of a cinema of variation by turning to a second Hepworth film made in 1900, *Explosion of a Motor Car*. For Hepworth, this film marked "something of an epoch" in his life, primarily because of the attention it attracted and the sales figures it achieved, which were his highest to date.[54] Hepworth's frame lends support to Burch's critique of the bourgeois nature of British cinema in general (in comparison with the popularism of early French cinema, for example), and of Hepworth's films in particular, where Burch sees the presence of the automobile as primarily an indicator of "the social status of its film-maker owner."[55] Burch's reading is in some ways underscored by the fact that the driver in the film is played by Hepworth himself; and yet a more dialectical approach might see these films as emphasizing not the car's, and by extension, cinema's forward motion and economic success, but rather the unpredictable, unstable, and potentially explosive nature of new technologies.[56] Though the explosions within this film and others like it certainly have the potential to be incorporated into a bourgeois economy of spectacle, they also contain seeds of aesthetic rupture and experimentation.

As an automobile carrying two men and two women appears at the remote end of the street, Hepworth again uses the road to establish an illusion of spatial depth. As the car moves into the foreground, it suddenly explodes in a puff of smoke, leaving only a few spare parts behind (figure 10). A policeman approaches from the left-hand side of the frame and pulls out what we might initially mistake for a truncheon, but which turns out to be a telescope. In a gesture that suggests the automobile's alien and unpredictable nature at this historical moment, the policeman gazes upward with his telescope, only to find himself showered with body parts that fall from the sky (figure 11).

Though the film uses two familiar tropes from early cinema—the substitution trick and the exploding machine—its entertainment value may have resided as much in its representation of the public attitude toward automobiles at that particular moment as in the reiteration of familiar visual spectacles.[57] In contrast to the train, the car was regarded not as a speeding, space-swallowing demon, but rather as a hopelessly unreliable and unstable technology, one often incapable of moving in the way that drivers needed to move. As Hepworth writes of his first car, "The carriage was of dog-cart design, completely without protection, and so balanced that if the occupants of the front seats got out first the whole thing tipped up and pitched out the others. In suitable conditions it would run for five or six miles without requiring filling up with cooling water, but in that time it generally shed a journal-box, which you had to walk back along the road to recover and refit. It had no reverse, but that didn't matter for if you wanted to turn round in a narrow road you just got out and lifted up the front wheels and turned it round."[58]

FIGURE 10 Cloud of smoke indicating a car explosion. Still from *Explosion of a Motor Car*.

FIGURE 11 Policeman looking up through a telescope as body parts rain down. Still from *Explosion of a Motor Car*.

While the automobile's movement and its companion film genre, the Road Movie, would gradually become inextricably intertwined with the vehicle's "swallowing" of space, through mounting the camera on the vehicle, in a manner similar to those early films that mounted the camera on a train, and through the parallel (and related) horizontal expansion of the screen, in the early days of these twin technologies of motion the unpredictable technology of the automobile becomes a vehicle for exploring not only the screen-audience axis through a theatrical and conscious address of the audience, but also the fantastical and soon-to-be-repressed of the screen's vertical dimension, which we see here associated with magic, flight, and extraterrestrial space.[59] Partly because we are not privy to a telescopic view of the space beyond the scene of the road, the off-screen space from which the bodies fall enters our imagination less as a concretely conceived location (sky, planet, etc.) than as a marker of the infinite possibilities of cinematic space, as a space of unfolding and becoming, a space immanent to but not collected within the image.[60] Though the transformations are obviously comic, they gesture toward cinema's unseen and underutilized spaces, to the possible role new and uncertain mobile technologies (like the spontaneously combusting engine) could play in our efforts to employ these not-yet-spaces in the representation and creative imagining of the modern world. In particular we might note the way the halted horizontal motion of the automobile activates the screen's neglected vertical axis. And though the question of the screen's vertical dimension rarely emerges within film scholarship, the car's stunted forward progress often gives way to a simultaneous formal emphasis on a vertical axis aligned with fantasy, flight, and dreaming.[61]

The (?) Motorist (W. R. Booth, 1906)

Like Hepworth's *How It Feels to Be Run Over* and *Explosion of a Motor Car*, W. R. Booth's *The (?) Motorist* shows comedy to be at least as central as the thrills of movement and collision in early cinema's depiction of the automobile. Though cinematic auto-mobility would eventually become increasingly steeped in ideologies of speed, desire, gender, sexuality, responsibility, and risk, these early shorts seem less interested in specific social questions than in the automobile's ability, as a still-unregulated, moving technology, to open up cinematic space, and to engage the camera's (in)ability to capture the movement of the modern world. In these films, men and women seem equally involved in the quest to push the limits of the camera and the law.[62] *The (?) Motorist* opens with a man and woman driving, once again, down the middle of an empty country road toward the camera. A policeman suddenly emerges from the right-hand side of the frame and attempts to interrupt their journey by signaling them to stop. They hit the policeman, whose body lies splayed across the front of the vehicle, and the female passenger energetically beats that law-enforcing body. As the film cuts to a new shot of a curved road, the policeman is thrown from the car onto the road and then run over by the car, only to stand up and begin chasing the vehicle again, running directly toward the camera. Introducing a dramatic contrast with the perspectival depth in the two previous shots of receding country roads, the next shot emphasizes the flat two-dimensionality of the screen rather than its illusory depth by showing a street running not into the distance, but horizontally across the bottom of the frame. A frontally framed house on this street then fills the frame, and the madcap couple, driving across rather than along the horizontally aligned road, seem to head straight for a collision with the building, an Ale House.

While *How It Feels to Be Run Over* suggests that an on-screen car will smash through the screen into the space of the spectator, *The (?) Motorist* offers a counter-illusion in which the car promises to crash into and expose the implied unseen world *behind* the image on the screen—the world behind the wall of the Ale House.[63] But at the anticipated moment of collision, the car ruptures not the wall, but only our "realist" cinematic fantasies, as it suddenly drives up the surface of the wall (figure 12).[64] Through its radical shift from the perspectival depth of the outdoor street to the flat frontality and vertical orientation of the car driving up the front of the Ale House, *The (?) Motorist* seems deliberately to draw attention to the boundary between the diegetic and spectatorial worlds using the figure of the car, which approaches the camera only in order to abandon the axis linking the spectator and the world of the diegesis and thus to emphasize the unexpected vertical movement of the car up the front of the house, offering a prime example of what Burch describes as "the surprises of a booby-trapped surface," the early film screen.[65]

Following this street scene, the film cuts to an animated sequence of a car driving across the sky of a painted landscape, passing through stars and clouds, circling the moon, and racing around Saturn's ring as if on a speedway. When the car eventually drops off the ring, the animated vehicle falls

FIGURE 12 Car driving up the Ale House wall. Still from *The (?) Motorist*.

down the center of the screen (figure 13) — again drawing attention, through its downward motion, to the neglected vertical axis — and crashes through the roof of the "Handover Court." Astonished by the sight of this white, ghostly apparition, which appears in its animated, not live-action form, in the middle of a live-action court scene, the policeman once again gives chase, but as he lays hands on the driver, a substitution trick transform the urban motorists into country folks driving a horse and cart.[66] As the bemused judge and policeman question their vision, removing their glasses and staring up at the sky, a gesture that recalls the vertical gaze of *Explosion of a Motor Car*, the horse and cart transforms back into a car, and the motorists gleefully exit the scene.

As *The (?) Motorist* yokes together the aggressive formal exploration of cinematic movement and the screen's surface with the social and legal reception of the motorcar in the early 1900s, the motorists' transgression of the law and class boundaries, as well as the tension between urban and rural populations, functions as a skeletal narrative that allows the filmmaker to experiment with movement and stasis, the possibilities of cinematic mobility in live-action and animated sequences, and the capacity of fantastical

FIGURE 13 Car falling through space. Still from *The (?) Motorist*.

movement to transport us to previously unimagined places. Although the camera cannot move alongside or in contradistinction to the movements of the car as it will later do—and it is worth noting that Deleuze's somewhat stubborn attachment to camera movement and montage as essential to the movement-image prevent him from exploring early cinema's resonance with his own ideas—this film is striking for the way it activates a tension between the static camera and the car's movement to push against the horizontal linearization of on-screen movement and to explore the cinematic potential of screen direction and location.[67]

In contrast to the horizontal space marked out by the contemporary street films of Mitchell and Kenyon, in which electric trams and horse and carriages pass before the eye of a camera that occasionally pans to unfold the space depicted by the film, but only in the direction of the moving bodies, the short film *The (?) Motorist* offers a series of shots in which the car—in both its live-action and animated forms—systematically traces almost every single movement possible in and around the space of the screen. In the course of this very short film, the car delineates paths running in the following directions on-screen: vertically from top center to bottom; diagonally from top left to bottom right; vertically from bottom center to top; horizontally from left to right in the upper half of the screen; horizontally, with undulating movements, from left to right in the center of the screen; in a circular pattern; and diagonally from top right to bottom left.

Mary Ann Doane has usefully pointed out the extent to which film historiography, in spite of its current "antiteleological thrust," continues to perceive the absence of what André Gaudreault calls "double mobility"—"mobility of objects depicted and motility of time-space segmentation"—as "a limitation, as a primitive moment."[68] Doane rightly sees Deleuze as espousing "a fairly predictable and teleological history in which the early, 'primitive' cinema is really not-yet cinema"; and yet it might be possible to find in these spaces of the "not-yet cinema" a quality that is resonant with Deleuze's idea of a cinema of becoming, in which becoming signals not a movement toward a teleological goal, but rather a desirable process that highlights the immanence, and the constant unfolding, of cinema, and by extension, of the world.[69]

In the serial variations of the movements traced by the car in *The (?) Motorist*, we find a quality that invites us to think not only the time-image but also the movement-image back into early cinema. Although the splicing of several different shots in this film clearly enables some of the film's variations of movement and trajectory, the movement-image, understood as the unleashing of the vehicle's movement into and for the space of cinema itself, cannot be reduced to the use of editing alone, for individual shots also contain within themselves, even in the absence of a mobile camera, unexpected movements that allow the spectator to experience the divergent paths of expected and actual motion of the vehicle depicted. This, in turn, may approximate, or at least have an affinity with both the movement-image of Deleuze, and the "double mobility" celebrated by Gaudreault, the radical potential of which may be more vulnerable to regulation or appropriation (e.g., through the perception of the disarticulation of the moving camera and the moving vehicle as a "misframing") after the fact of the technological realization of camera movement.[70] To invoke the movement-image requires us neither to repress or misread the limitations of Deleuze's own historical paradigm nor to posit film theory as a universal discourse somehow outside of or immune to film history; it is, however, to insist that "theory" is not a static collection of fixed ideas but rather, as Jean Laplanche reminds us, "a living experience of concepts, their borrowings, their derivations, their straying or wandering."[71]

As *The (?) Motorist* works to exhaust the possibilities of a moving object on-screen, it not only offers a multidimensional experience of cinema that shifts us between flat and perspectival space, but also invites us to dream of an imagined, not-yet-established mobility into the film world. Although frustratingly aware of the limitations on the camera's movements, *The (?) Motorist* animates every corner of the screen space, inviting what Burch describes as a "topographical reading" in which the decentered but not absorbed spectator can "gather signs from all corners of the screen in their quasi-simultaneity, often without very clear or distinctive indices immediately appearing to hierarchise them, to bring to the fore 'what counts,' to relegate to the background 'what doesn't count.'"[72]

For Deleuze, film's ability to mediate the state of becoming depends on its capacity to extract movement from the bodies it depicts: "The essence of the cinematographic movement-image lies in extracting from vehicles or moving bodies the movement which is their common substance, or extracting from movements the mobility which is their essence."[73] Deleuze ties this process of extraction to the mobility of the camera on the one hand, and to montage on the other, and argues that when the camera is fixed, "movement is . . . not extracted for itself and remains attached to elements."[74] Yet even in the absence of camera movement, these early cinematic examples show how the figure of the out-of-control car—exploding, colliding, disappearing, cutting across laws of time and space—registers the traces of cinema's yearning toward its own becoming. As the medium develops, these acentric and "topographical" movements within screen space will be largely checked by the implementation of narrative codes governing screen direction, position, and perspective, just as the automobile's movements and drivers, both on- and off-screen, will become increasingly regulated throughout the 1920s by social mores that attach themselves quite firmly to drivers and their vehicles. Yet the desire for a continuation and expansion of the dance between the camera and the motorcar—a dance that might somehow emancipate the car's movements into cinema—will persist. While the urban street films of Mitchell and Kenyon, as yet devoid of cars, are full of people, these early automobile films show streets in which, like

Carmelo Bene's minoritarian theater, "the people are missing."[75] They offer a view of a modern world not as it is, but as one yet-to-come. As we watch these films, the fear is less that we will be run over, for we know, like Woolf, that we will not be, than that we will fail to live up to the variation and infinite becomings that these films suggest.

chapter two

CAR WRECKERS
AND HOME LOVERS

The Automobile in
Silent Slapstick

In spite of the initial prominence of the motorcar in early British films, by the 1920s the British government had become mired in endless disputes among the domestic car industry, motorists, the Board of Trade, the Treasury, and the Ministry of Transport about how to tax motor vehicles in order to pay for the new roads needed to accommodate them. Early taxation of petrol and horsepower led British car manufacturers to produce cheap and lightweight vehicles they saw as a niche market that catered to British regulatory standards, but these cars could not compete with their American rivals. This decision inhibited the exportation of British cars, encouraged the importation of stronger and faster American cars—1925 was the year with the highest level of car imports between the wars, and consolidated the image of the United States as a country of speed.[1] The skyrocketing popularity of the automobile in the United States was also accompanied by a rigorous and contentious process of regulation and standardization, not unlike the parallel process that worked to regulate the social impact of that other modern technology, cinema, and the prominence of the automobile in the comedies of the 1920s in part reflects the central place it occupied during this period in nationwide discussions about public space, urbanization, vision, responsibility, citizenship, and national identity.[2]

The Roaring Twenties: Regulating the Automobile

As American cars grew in popularity at home as well as abroad, and as people started to think of the expanding road system as a national product, as something "of which we in America are beginning to be proud," public attention turned increasingly to the impact of the automobile upon public and private life.[3] If the frequency of crashing, exploding, immobilized, and otherwise malfunctioning automobiles in slapstick comedy can, on the one hand, be traced to the early film tradition of the "mischievous machine" that Gunning highlights, it also participates in a historically specific anxiety about the impact of the automobile on American life, which reached a peak in the 1920s and was commonly referred to as "the Traffic Problem."[4]

In November 1924, for example, the Philadelphia-based American Academy of Political and Social Science devoted a special issue of its annals to "The Automobile: Its Province and Its Problems." Gathering together representatives from car companies, the arts, the government, the police, and educational institutions, this issue offers a glimpse of the promises and problems of the nation's ever-expanding auto-mobility. In an article entitled "Safeguarding Traffic: A Nation's Problem—A Nation's Duty," George M. Graham, chairman of the Traffic Planning and Safety Committee of the National Automobile Chamber of Commerce, and vice-president of the Chandler Motor Company, celebrates the automobile (which he sees as working in conjunction with the mass media) as "a boon of progress" for its capacity to replace the individual with the family as the primary American "unit of pleasure," a unit whose growing resilience proves as problematic for Harold Lloyd in *Hot Water* (Sam Taylor and Fred Newmeyer, 1924) as it does for Laurel and Hardy in *Perfect Day* (James Parrott, 1929).

> Along with the victrola, the radio and the moving picture, the automobile has changed the daily life of our people, made the family rather than the individual the unit of pleasure.
>
> Before the days of the automobile, members of a family often took their diversions apart. Now on Sunday the whole family gets into action together. Everybody goes to the big picnic.
>
> Into the little car are crowded father, mother, five children, grandmother, the dog, rugs, newspapers, fishing poles, bird cage, and even mother-in-law, for it is a day of truce when all natural hatreds cease.[5]

The car-driving family was regarded as an improvement on the individual traveler, who had previously had to resort to the eroticized space of public transport, with its chance encounters and physical proximity to strangers. Yet while traveling alone on public transport was seen as risqué, driving alone was regarded not only as a rejection of the new unit of pleasure, the extended family, but also as a spatial and social irresponsibility that made excessive demands on the space of the city. The Philadelphia architect John Irwin Bright, for example, laments the fact that "at one stroke, the city has burst its bounds," and complains that "from all points of the compass, these intensely modern vehicles converge towards the City Hall, each car occupying at least 150 square feet of the roadway. Often, there is but one occupant. Twenty years ago, this same citizen was content with four or five square feet. The streets are no wider than they formerly were, but there are many more people and they insist upon many times more elbow room."[6] Bright offers here a paradoxical vision of isolated people jammed together, immobilized within a crowd of private cars. Still more problematic than the solo driver, however, was the "dead vehicle," a vehicle whose driver "is absent or unable to move [the] vehicle," and which traffic regulators considered to constitute "not only great inconvenience to the general public and injury to business, but a veritable menace likely to result in uncontrollable conflagrations."[7] As Bright details the horror of a city brought to a standstill by a series of these "obstructing valves," he can only imagine, in an urban vision resonant with Fritz Lang's *Metropolis* or the multilayered infrastructure of J. G. Ballard's 1970s London, the vertical expansion of roadways: "We are pouring more into our streets than they can hold, and if they cannot bulge sideways they must be increased in size vertically.... A two-, three-, or four-tier roadway will relieve some of the immediate pressure."[8]

As town planners worked on solving the impediments posed by the increased ratio of cars to urban space, others struggled to manage the social problems that the car seemed to usher in. While the superintendent of the Detroit police department remarked that "two men in an automobile were more effective than six men on foot," especially when driving one of their specially designed, high-speed "flyers," this benefit was offset by the parallel emergence of new types of crime and criminals—hold-ups and car thefts committed by newly anonymous criminals capable of entering and leaving a state within a matter of hours without being recognized by anyone.[9] A direct counterpoint to the family outing, the lone, anonymous, and criminalized driver tainted the automobile with an aura of strangeness, criminality, and danger, something which rubbed off on even the most middle class of drivers, who were all potentially capable of turning the car into "a deadly weapon."[10]

By 1924, the danger of strangers not only produced a new kind of policeman—the traffic cop—but also led to the gradual implementation across states of legislation that required a new and instantaneous legibility of both people and their automobiles through the introduction of tags, titles, insurance, and permits, and through the regulation of roads, which were also increasingly designed for optimum transparency. Billboards, one author prescribes, should be erected "above the ground to prevent the commission of nuisance or the hiding of criminals in connection with them," and should not hide "something dirty or ugly, for it is obvious in increasingly sanitary America that we do not want to hide anything unsanitary or dangerous, but to bring it to light and remove it."[11] The car, it seems, was creating a fantasy of an utterly transparent American landscape and citizenry.

Kristin Ross has detailed at length the importance of the automobile to the standardization of the film industry and its industrial structure.[12] The perceptual, ideological, and technological affinities she notes between these two industries of modern mobile vision were being explicitly articulated and widely disseminated within the American context both by the educational films of the motion-picture department at Ford, established in 1914, and those of Chevrolet Motors's Jam Handy production company, founded in 1917.[13] These films were designed to instruct spectators not only about good citizenship and driving safety, but also about the scientific basis of cinema, as we see in a film like *How You See It: How Persistence of Vision Makes Motion Pictures Possible* (Jam Handy Organization, 1936).[14] Through a series of shots that foreground Chevrolet cars—including rollovers, crashes, diagrams of an eye looking at a car, and people diving off the top of a car—*How You See It* mobilizes the rhetoric of education to advertise two products—cars and films—simultaneously, and to forge the link between the experiences of driving and cinema for an audience whose attention has been heightened by the promise of scientific learning (figures 14–15).

Yet in spite of all efforts to align cinema and the automobile with education and progress, throughout the 1920s cinema and cars would persistently be regarded as technologies that "[had] not proven [themselves] an unmixed blessing," as potent technologies in need of censorship, standardization, and stringent regulation.[15] Just as the industries mimicked each other at the level of production, so the parallel processes of self-regulation intersected in complex and interesting ways.[16] On the one hand, traffic-safety officials (who were often also prominent employees of car companies, lead-

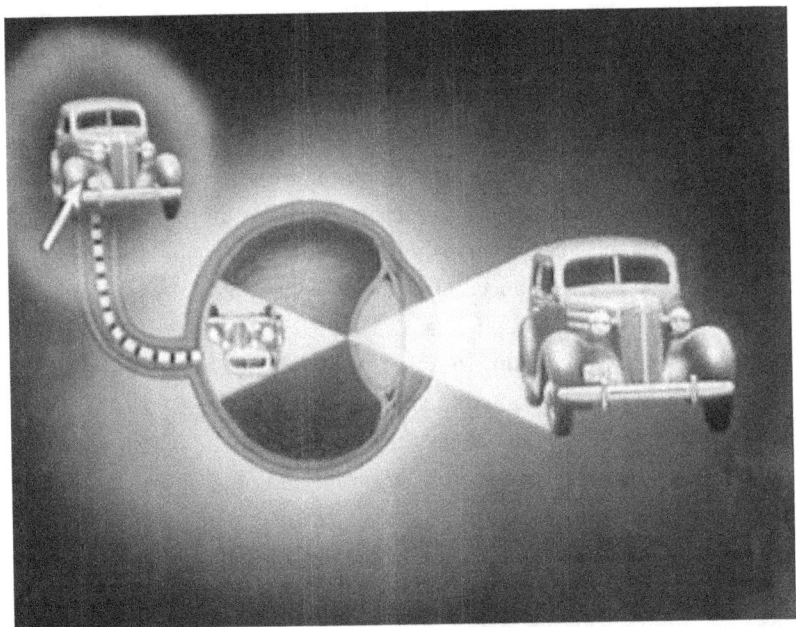

FIGURE 14 Diagram of how the eye envisions an automobile. Still from *How You See It*.

FIGURE 15 A woman dives from the top of an automobile. Still from *How You See It*.

ing to a situation in which "education" and "advertising" became somewhat indistinguishable) encouraged the production of educational safety films and lantern slide shows, which they regarded as central to their mission of drilling the nation in the rules of the road. As George M. Graham of the National Traffic Planning and Safety Committee advocated, "Films and slides are a most effective means of presenting the safety story at any meeting. Such slides may also be shown at motion picture theaters before, during, or after the regular performance. A list of safety films and slides available may be obtained from the National Safety Council."[17] On the other hand, the reckless driver was beginning to emerge in Hollywood's narrative films as a character type perfectly suited to an increasingly self-censoring movie industry's need to justify sensational thrills with a didactic function. Driving becomes a vehicle for expressing other prohibited compulsions, as Cecil B. DeMille, the "first master of the preemptive measure," made clear in *Manslaughter* (1922), the tale of a speed-addicted female driver who learns her lesson well enough, after killing a traffic cop and going to prison, to marry the prosecutor who put her away.[18]

Compared with those films operating within the paradigm of dramatic realism, comedy certainly enjoyed more leniencies from the Motion Picture Producers and Distributors Association (MPPDA), and it is within the realm of comedy that we continue to find bad drivers and ridiculous traffic cops aplenty, in spite of the contemporaneous seriousness about the danger of cars and drivers. As Henry Jenkins has convincingly demonstrated, slapstick or "anarchistic" comedy thrives as an alternative to the increasingly regulated (both morally and formally) narrative films well into the early 1930s, after which "the studios either jettisoned declining comic stars or brought their vehicles into greater conformity with classical storytelling conventions and established social standards."[19] This did not mean that film comedy existed completely outside of the moral and institutional regulation of this period, and Lea Jacobs stresses the need to understand comedy's greater freedom in relation to the fact that industry censors "gave much attention to the ways in which comedy could be used for strategic purposes, as a means of justifying otherwise unacceptable material."[20] Yet it seems that slapstick may have offered at least some degree of shelter from the increasingly regulated studio environment. At the formal level, it was certainly possible, as numerous critics have noted, for these films to continue exploring the creative possibilities of the earlier "cinema of attractions."

Yet as we try to understand the coexistence of two distinct film styles, it is important not only to note the continuities between early cinema and slapstick—such as the repetition of familiar gags, or the use and abuse of mechanical devices—but also to examine how the function of these gags' well-known ingredients—such as the irresponsible driver; the car that moves wrongly, stops, crashes, or fails to move at all; and the traffic cop—mutate as we move from one film period to another.[21] While in early cinema the car functions primarily as a technology of motion that is fascinating in its own right, by the mid-1920s the cinematic car's movements, though still of formal interest in a self-reflexive way, have also become intertwined with questions of social mobility and sexual traffic.

Slapstick Comedy and the Automobile Function

The automobile is so central to slapstick comedy that in Donald Crafton's incisive examination of the interaction between the narrative device of the chase and the anti-narrative device of the pie or gag, the automobile, its mishaps, and its infrastructure appear not just as frequently encountered figures, but as metaphors for the genre itself: "It is enough for our purposes to say that the narrative is the propelling element, the fuel of the film that gives it its power to go from beginning to end. (To continue the automotive metaphor, one would say that the gags are the potholes, detours and flat tires encountered by the Tin Lizzie of the narrative on its way to the end of the film.)"[22] This conflation of the car with slapstick is hardly surprising, given its ubiquity and the sheer variety of comic possibilities it offered. Both *Get Out and Get Under* (Hal Roach, 1920) and *Perfect Day* (James Parrott, 1929), for example, demonstrate the comic possibilities of a car that simply won't start. *Get Out and Get Under* also features the mischievous car saboteur in the form of the African American child star Earnest "Sunshine Sammy" Morrison. The potential of the accidental or systematic destruction of the automobile's body, its driver, or both is further explored in films like *The Non-Skid Kid* (Del Lloyd, 1922) and *Perfect Day*, and such gags find their most elaborate and temporally extended form—at least until Jean-Luc Godard's *Weekend* (1967)—in *Two Tars* (1928), where James Parrott assertively "tops the topper."[23] Disrupted traffic patterns structure a series of related jokes around unfit drivers, traffic cops, and the rules of the road in Laurel and Hardy's *Leave 'Em Laughing* (Clyde Bruckman, 1928); this film, like *Two Tars*, adapts to Laurel and Hardy's own rhythm and paces the

FIGURE 16 Car on a train. Still from *Get Out and Get Under*.

chaos familiar to earlier audiences from Mack Sennett's Keystone comedies, which, as we see in *Lizzies of the Field* (Del Lloyd, 1924), are prone to escalate into the total destruction of a demolition derby. Strange hybridizations of the automobile occur through accidental encounters with other modes of transport—with a train in *Get Out and Get Under* (Harold Lloyd, 1920), a film Ford Motors wanted to use for advertising purposes (figure 16); and with streetcars in *Hog Wild* (James Parrott, 1930).[24] These collisions both offer fantastical variations on existing technologies, and participate in a wider strategy of comic reversal that results in moving vehicles bringing each other to a halt while simultaneously animating, as if by contagion, the realm of static objects around them. In this world of irrational and infectious motion, a grand piano can be driven like a car, using the sustain pedal as brake, and a bathtub can be yoked to a horse and driven down the street, or so it seems in Charles Parrott's *Sold at Auction* (1923).

The mechanical variations that emerge out of the ill-functioning or disaster-prone automobile (or driver) certainly belong in a category with the other "mischievous machines" Gunning identifies as persisting from the "cinema of attractions" into slapstick, machines he sees, in their destructive effects, as working against, or at least in tension with, narrative's impulse to "put things back together."[25] Henry Jenkins has argued that early sound comedy often separates linear narrative elements from disruptive gags through the development of a double plotline that shows a conventional romantic couple ultimately triumphing in their love over and against the operations of a transgressive clown. But in silent slapstick, where many of the plotlines are still very thin, the triumph of romance is not guaranteed. Rather, the automobile, unlike other exploding or malfunctioning machines, seems to embody comedy's own paradoxical embrace of *both* motion and stasis, narrative and gag, in that it simultaneously suggests linear progression toward a goal in the form of a journey *and* inertia, in the form of the accident or mechanical failure.[26] Perhaps because of its structural affiliations with the comedy's paradoxes, the automobile in these films works against those critical paradigms that view all narrative as politically regressive and all disruption as necessarily radical, and instead offers a figure through which to think about the relationship between narrative and its counterforces in more nuanced, less two-dimensional ways.[27] To note the slapstick car's doubling of comedy's own paradox is to heighten our awareness of individual films' negotiations of the tension between motion and stasis, and of how the star comedians' performances, in conjunction with other performances, narrative developments, camera movements, and visual gags, may either contain or unleash the car's disruptive or "progressive" potential.

While we cannot simplistically align the disruption of narrative progress with any particular political or ideological position, it is clear that in the 1920s, the cinematic automobile was indissolubly linked to contemporary public concerns about modern space and mobility, and about the impact of transportation technologies on the individual, the couple, and the family. Though Harold Lloyd becomes a victim of automobile mishaps in *Get Out and Get Under*, the film ultimately demonstrates comedy's ability to shift the car's affiliation from clown to couple as Lloyd and his girl drive off into the distance, with Ernest Morrison running ahead, trying to escape from the car's path (figure 17). By contrast, the silent films of Laurel and Hardy resist this resolution of the car's clownish and mischievous aspects into the narrative space of coupling. Although Charles Barr claims that Laurel and Hardy "essentially . . . are, or aspire to be, respectable bourgeois citizens," their varied but almost always disastrous use of the car across a

FIGURE 17 Harold Lloyd driving away with his girl, as Ernest Morrison dodges. Still from *Get Out and Get Under*.

number of films aligns them with a series of possible alternatives to a notion of bourgeois progress that is repeatedly aligned with capitalism, adulthood, heterosexuality, the couple, and the car's forward motion. For Laurel and Hardy, the car was not just something to be exposed or destroyed; it also had to be repeatedly remade and reimagined. Stan Laurel illustrates this when, asked how many Model T Fords he had, he replies, "Oh, we had them specially made. One in a half-circle that would go around and around, then we had one that was squashed up between two cars. It was tall, we were sitting high up in the air, up in the front seat. Then we had one that went into a railroad tunnel, and a train would come through at the other end, and we came out with the four wheels practically in line. . . . There were no motors in them, you know, they were just break-aways; and we had one that was all fitted together, and you pulled wires and everything collapsed, at one time! [Stan laughs uproariously.]"²⁸

This insistent quality of Laurel and Hardy's aesthetic of variation, combined with the temporal quality these variations produce and the narrative frame that contains them, makes Scott Allen Nollen's insistence on these two comedians as "a couple" seem quite wrong, in spite of the seeming obviousness of his claim. Missing the difference a letter can make, Nollen opens his chapter "The Boys as Couple" with a quotation from Stan in *Sons of the Desert* (1933): "We're just like two peas in pot."[29] In a pot, not a pod, their relationship is not one of peas organically bound together and contained, but rather one of open and chaotic collision. Though these random movements of Laurel and Hardy are often highly kinetic, their insistently varied interactions with each other, as well as with the bodies and machines around them, ultimately creates an effect of stasis and inertia that is intimately linked both to the temporality of their comedy and to the critical perception of their comic personas as regressive, infantile, asexual, slow, and retarded. Their films are never progressive in the way we can think of "Speedy" Lloyd's encounters as generally moving toward the goal of a coupling resolution. A comparison of these two respective uses of the comic automobile might challenge critical assumptions about the ideology of velocity in slapstick films.

Gender and Genre

In the critical literature on slapstick one discovers a fairly consistent narrative of gendered preferences about the genre that aligns female audiences with those comedians who, like Lloyd and Charlie Chaplin, value women and marriage, and posits them against those comedians who, like Laurel and Hardy, make a career out of their opposition to marriage and wives. William K. Everson represents the earliest and most assured of the critical voices attempting to account for a gender-differentiated reception of slapstick comedy. He opens *The Complete Works of Laurel and Hardy* (1967) with a lengthy treatise on why women don't like them: "Men like Laurel and Hardy not just for their own sense of superiority, but for their virility and direct physical action in confronting everyday problems. Women, as a group, like Laurel & Hardy not at all. Asked why, they will usually dismiss them as 'silly' and comment on the pain and cruelty in much of their slapstick. But this is undoubtedly a subterfuge, for women must sense the perennial battle against their sex that Laurel & Hardy carried on in their films."[30] In *American Silent Film* (1978), Everson expands on this theory by including women's likes as well as dislikes: "Laurel and Hardy, with their constant vendetta against women, and wives in particular, W. C. Fields, with his perennial battle against nagging wives and mother-in-laws, and Keaton, with his usually helpless and rather stupid heroines, undoubtedly alienated a large percentage of the female audience, whereas Lloyd, Chaplin, and Langdon attracted and embraced them by their attitudes toward women, which consisted of putting them on pedestals and worshipping them."[31] In *The Boys: The Cinematic World of Laurel and Hardy* (1989), Scott Allen Nollen builds on this reductive tradition of the hostile female viewer, adding a new (if anonymous) feminist reference: "Women as characters in the Laurel and Hardy films are never treated very well, which may explain some of the aversion to the team that female viewers have experienced over the years. Feminists have accused Stan and Ollie of being misogynists, and, after a cursory viewing of their films, this conclusion would not be difficult to formulate."[32]

While these historical preferences may continue to be useful as we think about the genre's reception history, the interpretive models used in the discussion of gendered reception patterns, sexuality, and misogyny need revising. Compared with other film genres, slapstick comedy has attracted relatively little attention from feminist and queer film theorists; a discussion of the sexual ideology of the car might therefore simultaneously push back against what seem like assigned, mandatory critical positions (e.g., feminists against the comedian who is against his wife) within the discourse on slapstick. Although particular characters' misogyny may continue to invite feminist critique, a particular focus on the malfunctioning machine may productively loosen our critical grip on a character-driven paradigm in order to move us beyond the identity-bound politics of comedy to consider other questions, such as the alternative experiences of time, space, and objects that a particular film might allow.[33]

Lucy Fischer jokes that feminist film scholars have steered clear of comedy as though "the topic of misogyny were too grave to consider with a jocular light," while Kathleen Rowe attributes the paucity of feminist critical attention to comedy in part to "the powerful hold of melodrama on the female imagination," and goes on to note that romantic comedy in particular may offer "a sympathetic place for female resistance to masculine authority and an alternative to the suffering femininity affirmed by melodrama."[34] Moving away from a character-centered critical approach to slapstick also encourages a critical paradigm less focused on individual star comedians, which, as Douglas Riblet argues, brings the significance of ensemble performance within the genre into clearer view: "Traditional histories of slapstick generally divide the subject into units on each major comedian's career. This model assumes, however, that slapstick was a highly comedian-centered genre across the course of its history, with slapstick films constructed mainly as vehicles for particular star comedians (or occasionally comedian teams, such as Laurel and Hardy). While this characterization applies readily to most 1920s slapstick, both shorts and features, Keystone (and many other early slapstick producers) initially employed a more ensemble form of comic performance."[35] By recognizing the historical limitations of the comedian-centered paradigm in this way, we not only bring critically marginalized films like those of the early Keystone studios into focus, but also bring the neglected contributions of women in the film industry into clearer view, as feminist critiques of auteurism have demonstrated.[36]

Recognizing the limitations of a critical tradition rooted in auteurism and male performers, Rowe finds in Northrop Frye's writing on comedy and romance a useful alternative for feminist critics thinking about comedy. Yet while Frye's narrative paradigm enables Rowe to highlight the gendered dimension of gags' meaning, as well as the centrality of sex, empowered women, and social change to the comic genre, her focus on the figure of the "woman on top," as well as on romantic comedy in particular, tends to result in a conflation of "sex" and "heterosexuality," and a heteronormative equation of the "celebration of bodily pleasure" with "the space of family and the time of generation."[37] Furthermore, this quest to recover the absent female comedian seems to lead inadvertently to a confirmation of the longstanding association of misogyny and homosexuality, which is in itself problematic.[38] In a footnote to the "largely unexamined" "cultural and institutional reasons for that absence," for example, Rowe writes, "Most studies of comedian comedy, such as Seidman's, note the hero's 'sexual confusion' but give scant attention to larger issues of gender. Frank Krutnik acknowledges the misogyny and latent homosexuality in the male comedy team, but does not develop his suggestive remark that the 'sexual specificity' of comedian comedy is 'most blatantly indicated by the veritable absence of *female* comedians.'"[39] Over the last two decades, the critical writing on film comedy has certainly shifted toward a more complex view of individual comedians, as we see, for example, in Fischer's exploration of the maternal in silent film comedy, or in William Paul's essay on Chaplin's anality, which directly revises an existing critical tradition that has usually only acknowledged the "vulgar sources of [Chaplin's] material . . . to point out how much he transcends them."⁴⁰ Henry Jenkins similarly intervenes in earlier paradigms in *What Made Pistachio Nuts?* by using the category of genre to shift the critical discussion of performance away from character-centered and biographical approaches. These gradual changes within genre criticism are further enabled by the increased participation of feminist scholars in early film studies, exemplified by the Women Film Pioneers Project, directed by Jane Gaines, and by important volumes like *A Feminist Reader in Early Cinema* (2002), and it is in this spirit of revision that I introduce speed and stasis as an alternative frame within which to consider the genre.⁴¹

"Speedy"

Though no one better embodied the American fascination, in the 1920s, with speed, mobility, and the technological accident than the silent film comedians, these comedians engaged the multiple velocities of the automobile age in very different ways. Of Lloyd and Keaton, for example, Simon Louvish writes, "Keaton and Lloyd . . . were quintessentially American: their need for problem resolution through action—Keaton's tremendous chases; Lloyd's rush through life's perils to win true love—are defining icons of 1920s America, the urgent social climb, the necessity of speed. These are also individual values, the core of the American Dream."⁴² While Louvish sees the image of Lloyd "hanging by the clock arm above seething traffic" as "a perfect metaphor of the times," he sees Stan Laurel's "problem" as rooted in the fact that "as a foreigner, an Englishman in America, he was slow to grasp these underlying themes, which seem so obvious to us in hindsight, eighty years down the line."⁴³ Laurel and Hardy, Louvish suggests, are out of synch with the time of modernity: "Speed is not of the essence—there is little point in rushing if one can proceed more sedately, and with the proper dignity, towards inevitable disaster."⁴⁴

Of course Lloyd, like Laurel and Hardy, used the automobile as a comic prop, a "mischievous machine," and in his films, too, some kind of technological failure is almost always inevitable. Yet while Miriam Hansen attributes to slapstick comedy in general an "antisentimental, antiauthoritarian, and anticonsumerist appeal," the destruction of commodities may not always signify in an ideologically coherent way.⁴⁵ Two of the most elaborate "automobile destruction" comedies of the decade—*Hot Water* (1924) and *Two Tars* (1928)—serve to highlight these differences.

HOT WATER

Silent slapstick's treatment of the car often functions as an index of a film's relationship to social order, marriage, and the law, and yet this index falters, for the social and sexual values of the car remain ambiguous. *Hot Water*'s opening shot of a bridal car parked outside of a church wedding, however, immediately asserts an affiliation between the car and heterosexual coupling, an impression confirmed at numerous occasions throughout the film, as when "Hubby's" neighbor asks him, "Did the new car come yet?," and Lloyd replies, "It's coming this afternoon—a surprise for the wife!," or when, on the arrival of the car, he beamingly declares to "Wifey" (Jobyna Ralston), "—and just think, dear, fifty-nine more payments and it's ours! Let's take it out for a trial spin—just you and I!" Although this vehicle, so aligned with the institution of marriage, will share the same fate as the cars featured in Laurel and Hardy's *Two Tars*—total destruction—the social and sexual resonance of these spectacles of auto-destruction cannot be generalized across the two films. Rather, in this period marked by a radically intensified public debate about the impact of automobiles on the life and identity of the United States, the symbolic function of auto-destruction emerges within each film through the way the car is diegetically positioned in relation to public and private space, consumerism, the rules of the road, and the family unit.

After the opening shot of the bridal car before the church, the film cuts to a series of shots of the bridegroom running to his wedding, accompanied by his best man (played by Lloyd), who is busy trying to dissuade his friend from marriage by telling him, "You were born a bachelor—why not let well enough alone?" This scene, which lasts almost exactly a minute, is remarkable for the way the camera, by traveling alongside and then in front of the two dapper young men, inducts the film spectator into the runners' mobility. Yet though the bachelors run toward the camera, there is a propriety to their speed as established by the straightness of their path, the symmetry of the frontal shot of them side by side, and the moving camera's maintenance of a steady distance from them as they run, which contains the potentially disruptive effect of this scene of speed (in contrast, for example, with the transgressive experience of movement that defines Hepworth's *How It Feels to Be Run Over*) (figure 18). Though the speed and duration of the camera's motion, combined with Lloyd's protestations against marriage and his declaration "I'll never give up my freedom for a pair of soft-boiled eyes!," may seem to position running, the street, and the camera's tracking movement against the confinements of marriage, Lloyd's assertion of independence is immediately and ironically followed by a collision with a lady who stops Lloyd in his tracks. Though the male characters and camera announce a breathtaking mobility in this early scene, ultimately, no variation of movement seems possible: their path to the church seems inevitable; characters and camera are locked in a coupling embrace with each other; and the encounter with Wifey confirms this immobility with static close-ups of her eyes and ankles, as though both physical and visual mobility had suddenly drawn to a halt (figures 19–20).

Following these scenes of men running into the arms of their wives, *Hot Water* then turns its attention to a second scene of public mobility, the streetcar. In the first shot of married life, Wifey instructs Hubby (Lloyd) over the phone to purchase a few groceries for dinner. The shopping list fills the entire screen (figure 21). Subsequent shots show Hubby, not only laden with groceries, but also in possession of a live turkey (won in a raffle), struggling to stand, walk, and cross the road to get to the streetcar. Blocked by a traffic jam, he takes a detour through a vehicle occupied by two wealthy old ladies in order to access the streetcar, which will gradually emerge as the film's most perverse and mobile space (figure 22).

The streetcar scene begins by emphasizing the proximity of strangers, as Harold steps on toes, gets poked by umbrellas, stumbles into people, and drops his packages on them. Following this, Harold takes a seat next to two young boys. The gag that ensues does more than give "a hand-me-down a new shape," as Walter Kerr suggests, but rather constitutes a crucial sequence in which the film associates the proximity of strangers in the streetcar with perversion and (homo)sexual contagion. The gag goes like this: one boy takes a worm, the other a tiny crab, out of a can. A close-up shows the crab moving first from one boy's lap into the other's, and then on to Hubby's lap, unnoticed by Hubby (for he is tending his turkey) (figure 23). A woman drops her handkerchief over the crab, and Hubby, mistaking the handkerchief for his own shirt, stuffs it, along with the crab, into his pants (figure 24). The discomfort produced by the crab's presence causes him to stand, jiggle about, and scratch inappropriately, much to the annoyance of the male passenger beside him. This annoyance is rewarded when, after the crab descends down Hubby's trousers onto his shoe, Hubby smoothly

FIGURE 18
Bridegroom running, accompanied by best man. Still from *Hot Water*.

FIGURE 19
Wifey's ankles. Still from *Hot Water*.

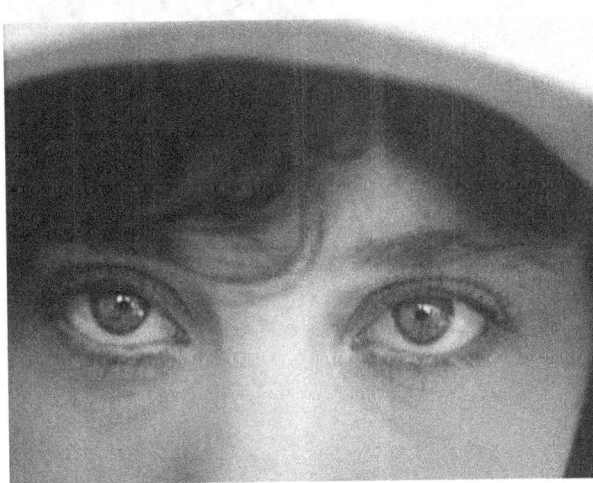

FIGURE 20
Wifey's eyes. Still from *Hot Water*.

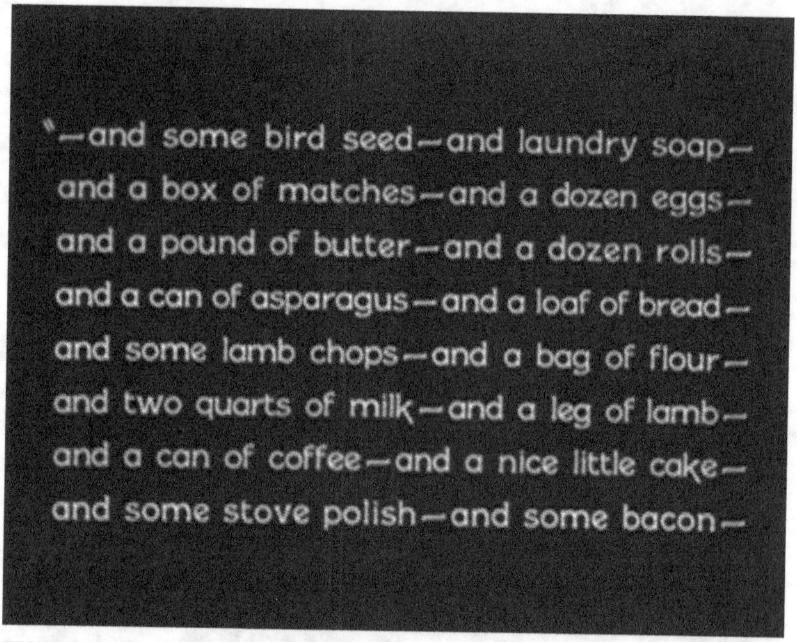

"—and some bird seed—and laundry soap—
and a box of matches—and a dozen eggs—
and a pound of butter—and a dozen rolls—
and a can of asparagus—and a loaf of bread—
and some lamb chops—and a bag of flour—
and two quarts of milk—and a leg of lamb—
and a can of coffee—and a nice little cake—
and some stove polish—and some bacon—

FIGURE 21 The shopping list, as dictated by Wifey. Still from *Hot Water*.

FIGURE 22 Hubby detouring through an automobile to reach the streetcar. Still from *Hot Water*.

reaches his foot toward that of his scornful neighbor, and the compliant crab happily ascends the new leg (figure 25). As though infected by Hubby's own strangely mobile body, the crab's new victim begins to wriggle and squirm.

Though Lloyd repeatedly emerges within the critical discourse on slapstick comedy as emblematic of modernity's speed, this scene can be read as participating in the early-twentieth-century anxieties surrounding "traffic" and speed, and the dangers they pose both to sexual norms and public health. Kristen Whissel discusses these concerns at length in her reading of *Traffic in Souls* (George Loane Tucker, 1913), noting, among other things, that "once the female traveler becomes the object of apparently legitimate traffic, she also risks becoming an object with a dangerously illegitimate traffic."[46] Whissel further notes "the degree to which the 'diseased,' 'subversive,' and threatening elements formerly outside of modernity's circulating systems had become all the more dangerous for having been absorbed into its traffic patterns."[47]

In spite of the generic differences between these two films, one might usefully consider the comic crab scene described above on a continuum with *Traffic in Souls*'s concern for the threat that the "rhizomatic structure of everyday modernity," embodied by ordinary "traffic," poses to female innocence and health.[48] In the 1920s anxiety regarding the link between the spread of (invisible) disease and ever-expanding transportation networks would have been reinforced both by the immigration acts of 1921 and 1924 and by the rise of public-health and science-education films, like the *Science of Life* series of 1922–24, which used microcinematographic techniques to depict bacteria and map the spread of invisible disease.[49] Though the crab sequence may on one level be a familiar gag that uses the well-known comic device of the extreme close-up, seen earlier in *Hot Water*'s depiction of Wifey's ankles and "soft-boiled eyes," the comic close-up of the crab also visually resembles the scientific visual exposure of the microscopic agents of disease. Read in the context of the scientific films of the same period, this cinematic joke seems to revolve around an obscene reference not to any old crab, but in particular to *Pediculosis pubis*, the sexually transmitted disease commonly known as "crabs."[50] While the comic extreme close-up singles out an object of desire through the isolation and freezing of a single feature—eyes, ankles, or lips, for example—the microscopic view reveals an unseen world of infectious life, teeming with entropic movement that

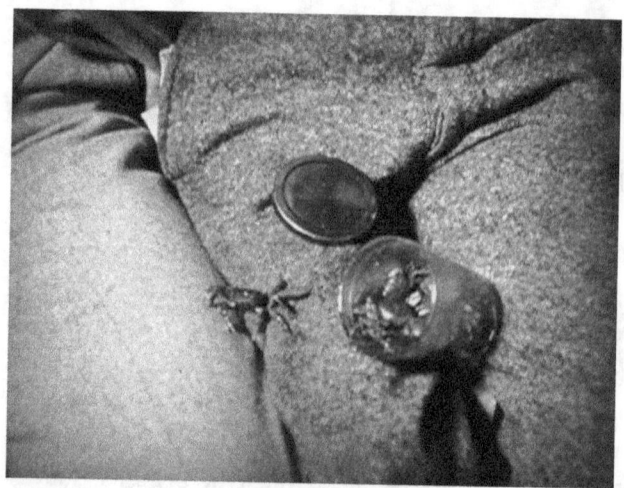

FIGURE 23
The crab changes laps. Still from *Hot Water*.

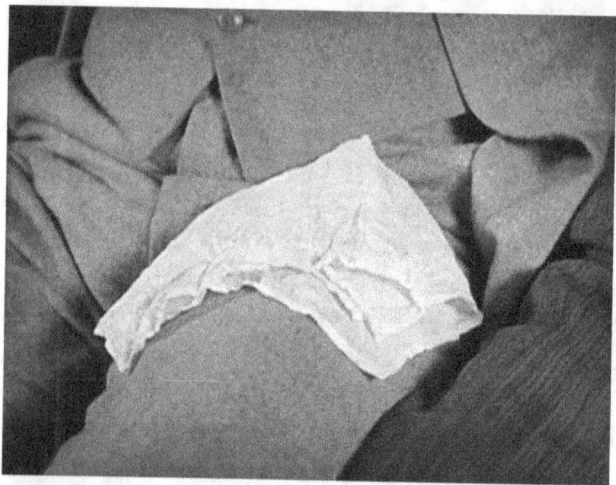

FIGURE 24
A woman's handkerchief covers the crab. Still from *Hot Water*.

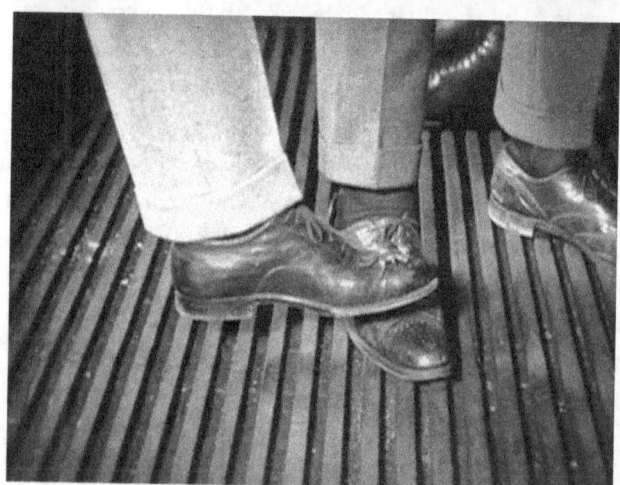

FIGURE 25
Hubby surreptitiously transfers the crab to another passenger's foot. Still from *Hot Water*.

evokes the chaos and contingencies of the modern urban street from which the comic heroine's body parts are extracted. Yet through the intense visual focus of the extreme close-up, the film leaves us gazing in the same way at both Wifey's irresistible eyes and at the crab's rapid movement across little boys' crotches.

If *Traffic in Souls* and the many other white-slavery films of the silent period focus on the threat of traffic networks on female innocence, *Hot Water* portrays the world of the streetcar as a space of male anxiety and homoerotic contamination. Yet public transportation emerges in the film not only as a place where the male body is exposed to both the infectious desires and diseases of other men and boys, but also as a place of social transparency, where a cinematic, almost microscopic, gaze will simultaneously render contamination visible and enable illicit longings and movements of the eye. Indeed, this streetcar sequence notably lacks the kind of smutty heterosexual jokes that are so prevalent in earlier transportation-based comedies.[51] Even when Harold interacts with women in this perverse space, their interactions tend toward phallic and homoerotic rather than heterosexual humor, as when his prize turkey disappears under the skirts of an elderly lady, only to reveal itself by sticking its head out from under the skirt like a third "leg" (figure 26).

While scenes of social disaster often provoke irrepressible laughter in Laurel and Hardy films, Lloyd's film takes little pleasure in Hubby's perverse transgressions. The shots that follow the comic streetcar sequence suggest that the perverse space of public transportation is no place for this married man, an impression that is confirmed when Hubby gets home and his neighbor asks him whether his new car has arrived yet, to which he replies, "Mum's the word—it's coming this afternoon—a surprise for the wife!" Yet though Hubby imagines the car as a perfect vehicle for the modern couple, he discovers on the arrival of his vehicle the extent to which *mum* is indeed the relevant word, for in the course of the film the car will be repeatedly associated neither with the marital couple, nor with masculine flight, but with his mother-in-law, who is introduced by an intertitle as a woman with "the heart of a traffic cop."

Though this link between Hubby's new car and his mother-in-law constitutes an interesting departure from the stereotypical alignment of femininity and stasis, it rapidly becomes clear that within the world of "hubby" and "wifey," it is not only the streetcar, but in fact *all movement* that emerges

FIGURE 26 A turkey peers from under an elderly woman's skirt. Still from *Hot Water*.

as dangerous, deviant, and threatening to the stasis aligned with marriage. In contrast to the popular image of Lloyd as a man of motion, *Hot Water* depicts the transformation of Hubby into an agent of inertia and immobilization, while movement, which the film aligns with repressive female agency (Wifey's mother is also a leader of the temperance movement) and sexual perversion, becomes increasingly uncanny. While it may be correct to view Laurel and Hardy's systematic destruction of the motorcar throughout their films as an example of the anti-authoritarianism and anticonsumerism that both Hansen and Pearl Bowser associate with early slapstick comedy, the car's destruction in *Hot Water* ultimately participates in a rather conservative sexual ideology that seems to advocate the withdrawal from public space and the undoing of strong women.[52]

While Laurel and Hardy repeatedly and actively oppose the structural mechanisms that underlie consumerism and capitalism—as when, in *Thicker than Water* (1935), Hardy takes Laurel's advice (against his wife's) and withdraws their life savings to free themselves of debt and therefore from having to work to meet the demands of loan-payment schemes—

Hubby expresses delight, albeit with ironic comic resonance, at the possibilities for property ownership that such loan schemes afford, telling Wifey, "—and just think, dear, fifty-nine more payments and it's ours!" Though *Hot Water*'s comedy centers around the destruction of Hubby's new car, these destructive gestures neither critique the ideology of the accumulative couple nor challenge the newly emerging rules of the road, for Hubby's loyalty to both, like the film's, never seems to waver. This loyalty is visible not only at the level of plot, where neighbors gather excitedly to view and photograph Harold's new car, but also in the mise-en-scène, which, in the manner of the industry films produced by the car companies themselves, casually reveals an image of America as a landscape defined by the automobile, for the action takes place against a world of car-rental dealers, repair shops, gas stations, "moving about men," autoparks, traffic cops, and suburban homes and families. Though the film certainly reveals the irony of these fantasies surrounding property ownership and upward mobility, it is a gentle irony that suggests affection for the character Lloyd plays, as well as some degree of shared values with him on the part of the audience, and the film's wry observations about consumerism never harden into outright critique. For Lloyd, auto-disasters arise not from a playfully aggressive resistance to the law, as is often the case with Laurel and Hardy, but rather from his excessive obedience to that law, an obedience that, for some, is part of his charm. We see this when he strays from the road while trying to put on the tie he is ashamed to be seen without, and again when, mistaking a soldier's helmet for an awkwardly placed traffic button, he finds himself maneuvering his car onto the sidewalk in an attempt to obey the traffic cop's earlier instruction that such buttons must always be driven *around*, not over (figure 27).

Throughout the film, the tension we encounter between the newly pedantic "rules of the road," embodied by the traffic cop, and the modern freedom of the car are played out through the figure of Hubby's mother-in-law, Mrs. Stokes, who the film paradoxically associates with both the traffic cop's legalistic and repressive attitude (she throws Harold's pipe in the trash can on arrival at his home) and with the freedom and flight of the car. The film underscores its initial association of the mother-in-law with the automobile—"Mum's the word"—by visually echoing an extreme close-up of the car's emblem, "Butterfly Six," with a close-up newspaper photograph of Mrs. Stokes wearing a butterfly necklace (figures 28–29).

FIGURE 27 Hubby drives onto the sidewalk to avoid a soldier's helmet, which he mistakes for a traffic button. Still from *Hot Water*.

And if the body of the car may metonymically stand in for Mrs. Stokes, its destruction takes on a potentially misogynist, rather than liberatory and anticonsumerist, resonance. The film's resistance to Mrs. Stokes as a figure of female movement is further emphasized by a newspaper article, shown in close-up so that viewers can read the text that appears beneath her photograph. Entitled "Women's Club President Delivers Lecture Against Drink," the article notes that "Mrs. Stokes is widely known as a leader of feminine movements." Even if viewers were to miss the film's double invocation of the butterfly, the link between two figures of movement, both of which will be immobilized—the car and the feminist—is emphasized by the fact that both appear as still photographs within the film, the only two photographs to appear in *Hot Water* (figure 30). As the film aligns Hubby's "Butterfly Six" with the feminist Mrs. Stokes, so the catastrophes the car suffers—including a series of collisions that result in a complete disruption of the city's traffic, an accidental stop on a street elevator that results in the car moving vertically, and a collision with a streetcar that decimates the car—can all also be read as the systematic immobilization of female agency, figured simply as "movement" (figures 31–32).

FIGURE 28 Emblem of Hubby's new car. Still from *Hot Water*.

Women's Club President Delivers Lecture Against Drink

"Purity of Prohibition" is Subject of Mrs. Stokes' Stirring Address

One of the most interesting lectures that the Wilton Women's Club has offered to their members was delivered last night when Mrs. Winnifred Ward Stokes told her views on the subject of "The Purity of Prohibition." Mrs. Stokes is widely known as a leader of feminine movements.

Mrs. Winnifred Ward Stokes

a perishable commodity and the contract calls for delivery in installments at regular and distinctly

MADAN

The pup erty from wearing t and their which goe by Mrs. A tried it, I fine. Mrs dental. and mayt and sleev cording to He compe child wer feeling he When a d mistake, principals for leader enjoyable begin.

FIGURE 29 Mrs. Stokes wearing a butterfly necklace. Still from *Hot Water*.

FIGURE 30
Photograph of Hubby's new car. Still from *Hot Water*.

FIGURE 31
Traffic chaos following a series of collisions. Still from *Hot Water*.

FIGURE 32
Hubby's new car accidentally ends up on a street elevator. Still from *Hot Water*.

Once Hubby and his extended family are towed home with the remains of the vehicle, Mrs. Stokes becomes increasingly associated with the uncanny movement of the dead, as though her body's living on in the wake of the car's destruction were itself strange or ghost-like, and in the second part of the film, Hubby is haunted by, and resistant to, the strange and threatening movements she introduces into the domestic space. He first attempts to immobilize his mother-in-law by offering her a napkin doused in chloroform; after she passes out, he believes—wrongly—that he has killed her. Consequently, when Mrs. Stokes begins to sleepwalk around the house, Harold takes her for a ghost, a belief reinforced by his discovery of the reading material under her bed—*Do the Dead Return?* As though infected by the cumulative effect of the queer and feminine movements of the streetcar, the automobile, and the not-quite-dead mother, the house's inanimate objects start to spring to life in increasingly uncanny ways, as when a plate flies across the table, or a glove (inhabited by a mouse) seems inexplicably to creep across the carpet toward an already terrified Hubby (figure 33). Eventually, Hubby decides to exorcise the house of his in-laws by himself adopting the appearance of a ghost, but Wifey, misrecognizing him, hits him over the head with a "Home Sweet Home" tapestry, and he slumps to the ground. The film finally resolves itself in an image of the happily immobilized couple, seated together on the threshold of their private home, to which no roaming compares (figure 34).[53]

RALLENTANDO

If *Hot Water* depicts a man's journey toward the static space of domesticity along the straight-and-narrow path of marriage shown in the opening shot, a path which requires the continuous suppression of errant desires and erratic movements, in *Two Tars* the car becomes a central figure in Laurel and Hardy's transformation of a linear and orderly world into a place of entropic movement and insistent variation. Although early film histories have tended to conflate the various instances of auto-destruction within the slapstick genre, closer attention to the differences between the uses of this familiar device may help to dislodge some of the overly broad critical generalizations about these comedies and enable a more nuanced understanding of the differing social and ideological work individual films within the genre may do.

As with Lloyd, biographical critical paradigms have often established

FIGURE 33 A seemingly animate glove terrifies Hubby. Still from *Hot Water*.

FIGURE 34 The tapestry Wifey uses to hit Hubby over the head. Still from *Hot Water*.

Laurel and Hardy's comic identities through recourse to a vocabulary of velocity; yet while Lloyd's association with speed has led critics to align him with modernity, progress, and the American dream (a wife and a car and a family), the slowness and inertia that for many critics defines the comic duo suggests a different and at times contradictory series of technical and social associations. Charles Barr, responding to a *Guardian* critic's comment that Laurel and Hardy films now seem "gruesomely slow at times," correctly identifies this supposed shortcoming as one of the central technical accomplishments of their performance, stating, "To criticise Laurel and Hardy for their films' slowness is like saying Keaton is funny despite not having a very mobile face."[54] Barr links this essential slowness both to Hardy's on-screen persona and to the practical need for film comedy to find a way to allow the audience to finish laughing before the next action begins, and he describes how "Stan would go with his collaborators to watch the new film with a preview audience, and adjust the length of some of Ollie's camera-looks in accordance with what was needed; sometimes, too, if a particular comedy routine went well they would extend it by further shooting."[55] Nollen confirms Laurel's involvement with this deceleration of the fast pace that was by this point integrally associated with the genre of slapstick comedy: "Laurel created this tempo by using a technique which he called 'holding,' or timing the laughs of an audience at a sneak preview of one of his films. . . . In *Mr. Laurel and Mr. Hardy*, John McCabe states that Laurel felt that 'his earlier directors took the pictures along at too great a speed. He discussed the idea of "holding" with [Clyde] Bruckman and other directors.'"[56] While Barr and Nollen emphasize Laurel's interventions in the cutting room, Walter Kerr describes Hardy, whom he saw as possessing the rhythm of a "Southern gentleman," as not only performing more slowly than Laurel, but also as slowing down both Laurel, rendering him "almost inanimate," and the genre itself: "Silent film comedy may be said to have begun as ragtime. Laurel and Hardy turned it back into a stately quadrille. Once again, rather unexpectedly, it was the lesser of the two zanies, the courtly and formerly upstaged Oliver Hardy, who was most responsible. For it was he—composed, like a child's drawing, almost entirely of circles—who was most responsible."[57]

Though the critical engagement with the question of speed and slowness initially emerged in the context of technical discussions of the timing of gags, Laurel and Hardy's slowness rapidly became interwoven with these same critics' anxious and defensive discussions of the two performers' relationship to homosexuality, adulthood, modernity, progress, and women. Barr himself notes that, "In the slow build-up and the slow run-down, technique and content are indistinguishable," and one could argue, following Barr, that we need to further emphasize the proximity between form and content as we explore the role of sexuality in these films if we are to avoid reducing the critical engagement with sexuality in slapstick to overly literal statements about the identity and psychological makeup of performers and their characters.[58] This tendency, which Lee Edelman describes as "revealing an 'identity' encoded in the text," has to date dominated the discussions of sexuality in Laurel and Hardy's films.[59] The danger of adopting this approach seems particularly prevalent in the case of silent-film comedians, where performers and their fictionalized characters often bear the same name, and where the primary critical approach is character-based. The limited outcomes of this critical strategy can, of course, easily and strategically be used as a rationale for dismissing the question of sexuality altogether. Therefore, one must search for alternative critical approaches to the question of sexuality within the comic context.

Inhibited Progress

Laurel and Hardy's resistance to speed, reflected in their close association with the figure of the slowed, stopped, crashed, or dismantled automobile, has been repeatedly associated with a series of related terms, including backwardness, retardation, regression, autism, automatism, presexuality, asexuality, precivilization, premodernity, circularity (in contrast to linearity and progress), and the South (which seems implicitly aligned with many of the aforementioned traits).[60] Though critics try to frame these "abnormalities" in the adult male as distinctly nonsexual deviations, Laurel and Hardy's embodiment of what one might call "comic timing" frequently raises the specter of homosexuality. Critical attempts to desexualize Laurel and Hardy's slow and destructive behavior frequently invoke the figure of the child, presenting their childlike destruction of machines (of which the car is one example) as evidence of the characters' mischievous, but ultimately innocent and asexual nature. Yet as Edelman has demonstrated in another context, the figures of the machine and the man-child are both intimately tied to historical and cultural constructions of (homo)sexuality that are inseparably bound to the death drive and that understand the sexual as mechanical, anti-life, antisocial, frenetic, and repetitious.[61] While a normative paradigm that emphasizes the reproduction, forward motion, and futurity promised by "offspring" may seem to separate the child from the "suspended animation" and mechanistic repetition associated with what Edelman (via Lacan) calls the "sinthomosexual," a "subject of the drive" associated with the "radical refusal of meaning," Edelman illuminates the extent to which the historical construction of childhood and sinthomosexuality increasingly overlap.[62] Rather than rejecting this construction of a negative homosexuality, Edelman adopts the more radical position of embracing the negativity of the death drive with which homosexuality is often associated, a drive that persistently exceeds and marks the limits of politics in and of the Symbolic, politics which take the form of a coherent narrative and which must exile those illegible bodies and drives that render that narrative incoherent.[63]

For some readers, the introduction of Edelman's discussion of the child, sinthomosexuality, and the drives into the realm of slapstick comedy will seem out of place, particularly as Edelman's theoretical insights, which emerge through close readings of films such as *North by Northwest* (Alfred Hitchcock, 1959) and *The Birds* (Hitchcock, 1963), as well as of Lacanian psychoanalysis and queer theory, may inspire anxiety about the resuscitation of psychoanalytic film theory within the context of early film texts, recalling an era when, as Charles Musser states, "film scholars often used [theory] as a hammer to bludgeon historians into silence."[64] Yet even as we recognize the justified critiques of psychoanalytic approaches to preclassical cinema, Edelman's exploration of the relationship between the child and the sinthomosexual can usefully help us disrupt the normative sexual paradigms of silent-slapstick criticism that insistently frame the destructive, mechanistic, and antisocial behavior of Laurel and Hardy as childish but asexual. Edelman's *No Future* illustrates how these negative markers, which are often aligned with stasis and the resistance to progress, reveal sexuality's inherent relationship to violence, inhumanity, and the death drive. While this negativity has historically emerged in opposition to the reproduction- and progress-centered sexual paradigms that undergird every future-oriented, "positive" political narrative, Edelman suggests that it is only by rendering visible those elements that, like the gags of slapstick comedy, thwart narrative "progress" that time and space emerge for radically reimagining the social order.

Eternal Children

Charles Barr's 1967 study of Laurel and Hardy begins by asserting the absence of sexuality in these films.[65] After first noting that although Stan will often dress up as a woman, "these scenes have no sexual overtones," he then goes on to describe the disappearance of Stan's early "pansy quality" from 1927 on: "In general, the effeminacy of Cuthbert Lamb becomes absorbed into the flat, asexual meekness of 'Stan.'"[66] As sexual deviance is repressed, temporal deviance or belatedness emerges in its place to describe the strange position these comic characters inhabit. Barr remarks that Ollie's miming of the act of writing in the midst of *Leave 'Em Laughing*'s traffic chaos takes us back to "a pre-writing stage of civilization," then adds, "The pre-literate, 'hunting' past of the race has its equivalent in the ruthless solipsism of the child. Looked at another way, Stan and Ollie are children in dodgem-cars: this is what they evoke as they gleefully intercept or back into others."[67] This resistance to progress and delight in destruction, reversal, and collision, Barr concludes, suggest not only "primitive violence against ordered society," but also "childhood against maturity," revealing the key to their "all-inclusive character": childishness.[68] Barr's early emphasis on the childishness of Laurel and Hardy has profoundly influenced other critics like Kerr and Nollen; but for them, as for Barr, the discourse of childishness, initially invoked to assert the innocence of the pair's slow and destructive behavior, becomes increasingly unwieldy as it persistently collapses into a suggestion of abnormal masculinity that leaves critics constantly returning to the specter of homosexuality in the hope of exorcising it.

While Barr does recognize the temptation to read "veiled homosexuality" into Laurel and Hardy's relationship, citing André S. Labarthe's claim that *Liberty* "offers, to anyone who can read, the unequivocal sign of an unnatural love," he invokes this possibility only to reject it, constructing in its place an elaborate linear scheme of normal sexual development.[69] Yet in spite of his best efforts, the temporality of Barr's arguments becomes increasingly contorted as a result of an uncomfortable over-proximity between the "natural" young boy and the adult homosexual, historically constructed as immature and failing to progress. Prefacing his comments about sexuality with the disclaimer that "there is something rather absurd about discussing this seriously at all," Barr states, "Laurel and Hardy's world is presexual, a nursery world. It can in turn be argued that there is no such state really as the pre-sexual, that homosexuality itself consists of a fixation at a certain level of immaturity, but this isn't to establish much, for there is so much that is childish about Laurel and Hardy that their sexual 'backwardness' is consistent with their psychic age, therefore natural. Since their mental processes, particularly Stan's, are those of nursery children, one takes it for granted that they should share a bed as in the nursery."[70] The contours of Barr's argument, which requires the reader's complete suppression of Laurel and Hardy's adult male bodies, reflect the difficulty of using childhood to negate the specter of homosexuality.[71] But the relationship between homosexuality and childishness is no less contorted in other critical contexts. Kerr, for example, commenting on Laurel's behavior at the tailor's in *Putting Pants on Philip*, states, "The fact that the assault is taken as homosexual and Laurel doesn't even know what homosexuality *is* is simply an indication the once knowing and aggressive Laurel is becoming as childlike as Roach envisioned and Hardy already looked."[72] They are, for Kerr, "extraordinarily passionless creatures," and though he allows that a few of their gags are sexual, he qualifies this by stating that the jokes are usually about the sexuality of other characters, for they are "overgrown lads who have arrived at some neutral ground."[73] Kerr introduces this absence of passion as evidence of Laurel and Hardy's asexuality, yet he nevertheless recognizes that it is this absence of passion, "the time-lag, the unemotional patience" that separates them from normal men: "Normal men, real men, have much shorter tempers."[74]

As Kerr defends Laurel's loyalty to Hardy as "sexless boyishness," we see him, like Barr, framing Laurel's relationship to his companion in terms of a paradoxical description of movement: "He would always step forward, resolute in the same retarded rhythm, to shatter an oppressor's windshield."[75] Kerr repeatedly aligns Laurel and Hardy with stasis, or with a discrepancy between their velocities and those of the world, as when he notes how their pace would give audiences "an opportunity not only to catch up with the joke but to get well ahead of it."[76] But ultimately, for Kerr, it is this lack of progress, synonymous with a lack of heterosexual desire and the absence of narrative development, which limits their commercial success: "Their work was in some senses limited; it always would be. The absence of passion, for women or for other goals, would deny them the extended narrative base on which feature films generally depend."[77]

Critical discussions of Laurel and Hardy's queer behavior try to manage and naturalize the comedians' perversity by disavowing their adult male bodies, conflating strange adult performances of childishness into childhood itself. At times this results in what one might describe as a mimetic or transferential criticism that, in its refusal to acknowledge the difference between boys and men, produces (unintentionally) the comic effect of a film like *Brats* (1930), in which Laurel and Hardy play their own children. Consequently, Barr creates the impression that a critical engagement with Laurel and Hardy's sexuality is "absurd," in that the sexual reading seems either to destroy the space of comedy or to render criticism laughable. But this "absurd" situation only comes about if sexuality is invoked as a narrative known in advance, if the disruptive force of sexuality is reduced to flat-footed questions of sexual practice, the pairings of genitals, and male or female object choice. Therefore, rather than trying to combat these readings' dismissal of sexuality by offering counter-examples that "prove" how the queerness of Laurel and Hardy actually exceeds the "norms" of childish affection, I instead suggest that if the critical discussion of slapstick sexuality is itself to be anything other than a one-liner, we need to reframe our approach to the question of sexuality altogether. We might begin by considering what would be involved in moving away from critical paradigms in which a sexual identity has to be "outed" in a given text, a psychoanalytically inflected approach to aesthetics that Leo Bersani in *The Culture of Redemption* calls "an argument for the regressive nature of art," in order to move towards a more expansive understanding of sexuality that emphasizes, following Bersani, the idea of the aesthetic object as an act of repression-free sublimation, not simply a "recycling of oral and anal energies," but a "nonspecific type of sexual activity—that is, sexual activity no longer attached to particular acts."[78]

But if we reject both Barr's view of Laurel and Hardy as "a pair of overgrown babies, who, in Freudian terms, have not grasped the 'reality principle,'" and Kerr's view of their "backwardness" as a sign of their sexual failure and immaturity, how then are we to interpret their slowness, their use of repetition, variation, and destruction?[79] Kerr suggests the pleasure Laurel and Hardy take in destroying things reflects the innocent but ultimately fruitless logic of children: "They are young yet, not concerned with permanence. They like patterns, and broken things make new patterns, surprising ones."[80] Though we need to challenge Kerr's placement of pattern and variation within a paradigm of sexual belatedness and regressive behavior, and his assumption that the concern with the permanence of things is a necessary trait of maturity, the link he suggests between aesthetic repetition, variation, and pleasure nevertheless provides a good place to start.

In addition to moving away from an identity-bound discussion of sex, the focus on the intersection between slapstick aesthetics and a more expansive conceptualization of sexuality may usefully disrupt the critical caricature of female viewers as somehow structurally opposed to both nonromantic forms of slapstick humor and male homosexuality, and may also open up ways of thinking about comedy as a place for imagining alternative forms of community. The social possibilities I identify here need to be distinguished from those offered by the more familiar critical view that comedy is a progressive genre because of its ability to use the anarchistic energy of sex and desire in order to effect social transformations that allow for the restoration of social order to a previously unsettled community.[81] The distinction requires first that we shift our frame away from a restorative or redemptive model and reject, as Bersani puts it, "the critical assumption in the culture of redemption . . . that the work of art has the authority to master the presumed raw material of experience in a manner that uniquely gives value to, perhaps even redeems, that material."[82] To adopt this stance would involve retaining Henri Bergson's claim that laughter (which is, he notes, "something beginning with a crash") "must be . . . a sort of *social gesture*," while rejecting his understanding that laughter pursues the utilitarian goal of improving "a certain rigidity of body, mind and character that society would still like to get rid of in order to obtain from its members the greatest possible degree of elasticity and sociability. This rigidity is the comic, and laughter is the corrective."[83]

Though the pursuit of radical social change via Laurel and Hardy will seem ridiculous to some, Giorgio Agamben, in his exploration of what a sociality that does not demand the destruction of singularity might look like, privileges comedy's proliferation of examples, one after another, each in its singularity, as the radical space for imagining a community without essence: "Tricksters or fakes, assistants or 'toons, they are the exemplars of the coming community."[84] Indeed if, as Agamben suggests, an ethical relation to community needs to be thought through the singularity of the example, which is neither particular nor universal in nature, there might be no better place to start—at least within the world of film history—than with slapstick comedy's at times unresolved proliferation of laughs: "gags, gags,

gags, and then more gags, and nothing more than gags."[85] And if by this point our conception of sexuality as repetition and variation in temporality, velocity, and movement seems to have abandoned sexuality altogether, we might recall that for Michel Foucault, the most radical aspect of gay culture lay not in a particular configuration of gendered bodies but rather in its innovative generation of endlessly varying modes of social relationality, of "unforeseen kinds of relationship."[86]

For Bergson, comedy is marked by a "progressive continuity," a "driving force" that renders the audience, through the laughter that erupts in the face of the comic's serial exposures of "something mechanical encrusted on the living," human, flexible, and mobile once again for society's greater good.[87] By contrast, the slow timing of Laurel and Hardy's comic performances invoke the passionless conditions of stasis, waiting, reiteration, and repetition, not to rehumanize or animate the inanimate moments Bergson identifies, but rather to render them visible as experiences. In this sense, the temporality of Laurel and Hardy's comedy can be seen as analogous to the temporality of masochism, the aestheticism of which, as Jean Ma has pointed out in a different context, mirrors precisely Adorno's insistence that "art enunciates the disaster by identifying with it."[88] The leap between disaster and comedy seems like a precarious one to make; yet for Deleuze, it is precisely this leap—over the Death Instinct and into the realm of the pleasure principle—that masochism's "terrible force of repetition" enables.[89] Whereas one might think that masochism's dependence on repetition reflects a conservative investment in the reproduction of the same, Deleuze argues that the coldness and desexualization associated with masochism (qualities that have also been associated with Laurel and Hardy) "[make] repetition autonomous," allow it to "[run] wild and [become] independent of all previous pleasure."[90] Resisting the violence of the law without any promise of redemption, the subversive potential of masochism's repetitious and "frozen scenes" does not oppose, but rather works through, the comic force. These scenes, Deleuze argues, enact, in their overly zealous adherence to the law, a temporally extended "downward movement of humor which seeks to reduce the law to its furthest consequences," thereby revealing its absurdity.[91] As I now turn my attention to *Two Tars* (1928), which William K. Everson identifies as "about the funniest and most representative of all the Laurel and Hardy silents," I offer masochism's aesthetic of delay, repetition, waiting, and stasis as an alternative frame to the linear temporality of the normative psychological narrative of heterosexual progress and homosexual regression through which to explore Laurel and Hardy's relation to speed, stasis, movement, repetition, time, sexuality, and laughter, all of which come together around the figure of the crashed car.[92]

Two Tars

In spite of the significant place *Two Tars* occupies among Laurel and Hardy's oeuvre, most critical discussions of the film skip over its opening scenes in order to focus on the final traffic-jam sequence, in which Laurel and Hardy immobilize or destroy almost every car in sight. The biographer Simon Louvish describes the pre-traffic jam scenes as being "merely flapdoodle to bring us to the grand part two of the two-reeler," and William K. Everson describes the early scenes as "a trifle forced, but perhaps only because we know what lies ahead, and are eager to be at it."[93] Yet the film's early scenes play an important role in establishing Laurel and Hardy's relationship to cars, movement, women, repetition, variation, and the machine aesthetic, and therefore merit a closer look.

After the first title announces "Our Navy," the film opens with documentary footage of U.S. battleships slicing through the water, shot by a camera mounted on the front of a vessel that moves rapidly in the opposite direction (figure 35). This shot establishes an association among power, speed, vision, and technology, and the Navy's global reach and mobility is confirmed both by the second title, "Japan, China, the Philippines.—And now, the good old USA," and by subsequent shots of sailors climbing rapidly up to land from the dinghy that has brought them to shore. Yet the film asserts this militaristic and cinematic dynamism, with battleship and camera sweeping past each other, only to undermine it through a bathetic cut to a shot of Laurel and Hardy, rigidly upright, driving in sailor's uniform through the streets of a town. In contrast to the sailors of the previous shot, these two "tars" immediately strike us as oddly amphibious creatures, out of place on land, their strange or alien quality communicated both by the uneasy combination of naval uniform and automobile, and by the fact that their car explicitly does not belong to them (a sign hanging off the vehicle's side states, "For Hire, U-Drive Auto Co."). A rapid traveling shot from the point of view of the drivers recalls the assertive opening shot of the camera gliding through the ocean past a spectacle of American speed and might, but the effect of motion evoked by the alignment of car and camera move-

FIGURE 35 U.S. battleships. Still from *Two Tars*.

ment is again undermined by the duo's complete lack of involvement in the experience of movement. Traveling shots are intercut with shots of their chatting faces turned toward each other, rather than the road. Furthermore, the camera's distance from the car they drive is fixed, like their rigid driving bodies—the camera moves either parallel to or fixed on the car, quite unlike the dynamic relationship established between the camera and the battleships moving against each other in the opening shot. After a near miss with a lamppost and a pedestrian, the pedestrian emphasizes our sense of Laurel and Hardy as fish out of water by asking, "What do you guys think you're doin'—? Driving or rowing?"

Hardy takes over the wheel, but drives straight into a lamppost (figure 36), and the timing of this first collision exemplifies the importance of delay and waiting to their comedy. Before the crash, Hardy tells Laurel, looking him straight in the eyes, "The first rule of the road—Always keep your eyes straight ahead—." After they hit the lamppost, we see a long shot of the car, the two tars, and the bent post; a cut to a medium shot of their perplexed faces; a title in which Laurel asks, "What's rule number two?"; and another medium shot of the unhappy pair in the car. Only after this drawn-out

FIGURE 36 Laurel and Hardy crash into a lamppost. Still from *Two Tars*.

visual follow-up to the first collision does the film cut to a close-up of the glass globe on top of the post falling, as though the force of gravity itself had up to this point been suspended. The sequence concludes with a shot of the glass globe finally crashing over Hardy's head, but Stan's response to this delayed falling object is also worth noting. First he looks up to the sky and traces with his finger the vertical path of the surprising missile, emphasizing the unexpected vertical axis that so often erupts in the wake of the cinematic car crash's halted horizontal mobility. But his tentative upward glance after the fall also implies a fear that more may follow, that this falling object, and perhaps by extension each contingent event, might only be the first of a series, might give way to masochism's autonomous and wild repetition. Though Laurel's susceptibility to the idea that each contingent event potentially belongs to a pattern or law may seem naïve or even mad, in some ways the film affirms his logic, as flying circles and ruptured spheres recur throughout *Two Tars*, from kick-dropped headlights to exploding gumball machines, balloons, and inner tubes. Indeed, the halted linear motion of the crashed car appears to be redirected into the production of random and nonlinear movements that share an affinity with non-narrative experimental film practices that foreground formal innovation over narrative progress. Furthermore, this energy surplus and the variations it provokes extend from the aesthetic into the social dimension of the film, as these aesthetic innovations give form to contingent and unfolding, rather than predetermined, modes of encounter.

While critics have largely caricatured Laurel and Hardy's relationship to women in terms of either disinterest or hostility, *Two Tars* quickly establishes the two main female characters, Thelma (Thelma Hill) and Rubie (Ruby Blaine), as playful and equal participants in the film's aesthetic of repetition, delay, and destruction—a departure from Laurel and Hardy's frequent casting of women as nagging wives and mothers. The agile comic variations that emerge within the frozen spaces of collision make visible the inertia that paradoxically inhabits the status quo's idea of progress, and proliferates, within the space of jammed cars, alternative movements and interactions among people and objects.

Thelma and Rubie are no strangers to amphibious sailors, the havoc they cause, or their preference for proliferation. These two characters actively refute both the exclusive logic of the couple—a title explains, "One has a sweetheart on the Arizona—The other has five on the Massachusetts"—and the commonly held critical views that "women as characters in the Laurel and Hardy films are never treated very well" and that they never "[tolerate] the childlike activities of Stan and Ollie."[94] Throughout the film, Thelma and Rubie not only encourage Laurel and Hardy, wildly cheering each antisocial blow, but also actively participate in the social havoc they wreak. As a former female wrestling champion, Ruby Blaine possesses a tall, strong body that forges a particularly commanding screen presence and that is, throughout the film, always on the side of Laurel and Hardy. While the masculine woman may be a standard trope of slapstick in the form of the prohibiting and punishing wife, the character of Rubie, who is herself a little amphibious, rearticulates this type within the sexual economy of the genre, for her body is explicitly marked as sexually interesting to both Laurel and Hardy from the moment they lay eyes on her.

After the men are distracted from their driving by the sight of Rubie and Thelma on the sidewalk, they pull their car over, and we see a series of variations on the shot-reverse shot that, with each reiteration of the movement back and forth between different faces, disrupts the shot-reverse shot's intended coupling gesture and stretch the temporality of this romantic form until it opens out onto a comic space through an excessive articulation of possible visual exchanges. Suspending the moment of "love at first sight," the film offers serial exchanges that move among the characters in the following way: Thelma and Rubie (figure 37); Laurel and Hardy; Thelma and Rubie; Hardy; Thelma; Laurel; Rubie; Laurel; Laurel and Hardy; Hardy; and Thelma and Rubie. When Thelma breaks the spell of serial variation by requesting help with a gumball machine that is stuck, like the film itself (an intertitle tells us, "—We put a penny in this chewing gum gimmick, an' the doodad won't work!—"), Laurel and Hardy rush to their rescue, and, after an equally confused and potentially unending exchange of handshakes—between Rubie and "Ensign Laurel"; Thelma and Laurel; Laurel and "Secretary Wilbur" (Hardy)—the two men set to work on "fixing" the film's second incompliant machine. As Laurel bends down to fiddle with the blocked gumball machine (the opening of which is suggestively aligned with Rubie's genitals within the frame), Hardy approaches Laurel enthusiastically from behind and bumps him out of the way (figure 38). Hardy wiggles his index finger perversely before sticking it into the machine, where, not surprisingly, it gets stuck (figure 39). Building the sexually suggestive potential of the gumball machine, Hardy picks it up, puts it between his legs, and shakes it violently until the gumballs explode all over the sidewalk, bouncing around in random patterns (figure 40). If the machine first functions as a site of unspecified erotic activity in the first part of this sequence, the second part of this sequence evolves as a variation on the first exploding gumball-machine gag. To begin, Hardy, whose physical shape resonates with the film's formal preoccupation with spheres, proceeds to transform himself into a human gumball machine by gathering up the candies from the ground and stuffing them down his shirt. While Laurel, Rubie, and Thelma take refuge in the car at the appearance of the angry storeowner, the storeowner, like Laurel and Hardy before him, pokes and fiddles with the human machine's "button" until Hardy's tickle induced laughter ejects the gumballs all over again. Rubie instructs Laurel to defend Hardy against the shopkeeper's wrath: "You crash him!" Though Laurel tries to do so, warning the shopkeeper, "You're flirtin' with death, my son!," the gumballs prevent his forward motion and bring him to the ground. To top this gag, Thelma and Rubie then swap places with Laurel and Hardy, who return to the vehicle. While Rubie

FIGURE 37 Thelma and Rubie notice Laurel and Hardy. Still from *Two Tars*.

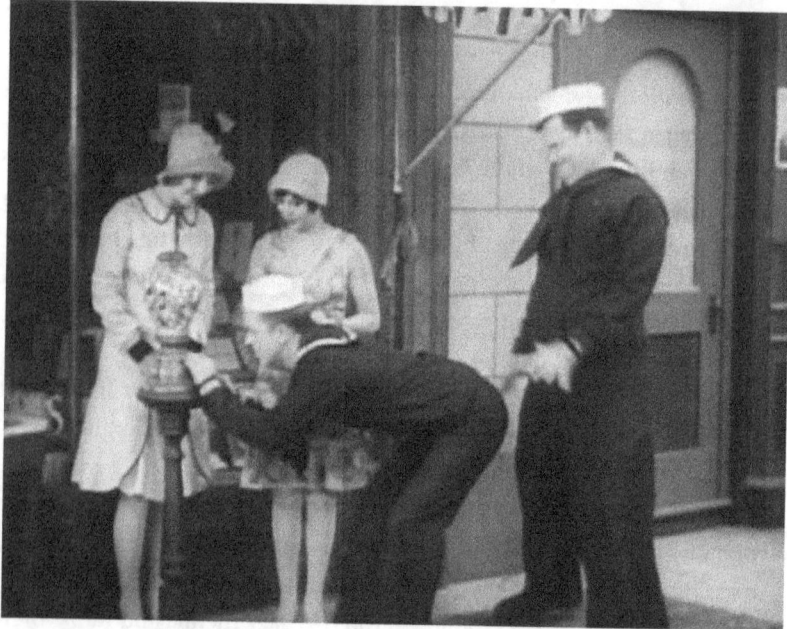

FIGURE 38 Hardy approaches to bump Laurel out of the way. Still from *Two Tars*.

FIGURE 39 Hardy's finger gets trapped in the gumball machine. Still from *Two Tars*.

FIGURE 40 The gumball machine explodes. Still from *Two Tars*.

gives the shop owner a good hiding, Thelma, like Laurel, is brought to the ground by the gumballs, but Rubie helps her up, and the four reunite in the space of the car.

This scene's extended play on gender ambiguity and erotic, nonlinear mobility within the foursome is further emphasized in the opening shot of the next scene, which takes place at the end of what a title tells us has been "a perfect day" together. Unlike the attempted outing of the following year's *A Perfect Day* (James Parrott, 1929), which resembles Harold Lloyd's disaster-ridden spin with his extended family, this outing, which is not depicted at all, seems to have been quite a ride. The four appear—Rubie and Hardy in front, Laurel and Thelma in back—with the women sporting sailors' hats and the men wearing the hats of their female friends, implying an erotics of swapping, reversal, and circulation that is heightened by the presence of four, rather than two, lovers, by the androgyny of Rubie, by the amphibiousness of landed sailors, and by the fact that the space of sex is a rented automobile (figure 41).

The sequences that follow are first of all defined by their spatial confinement within the boundaries marked by the beginning and end of a traffic jam (figure 42). At the front of a long line of cars exists a double block: on one side of the road, a man's car has run out of gas, while on the other side, a construction roadblock prevents other cars from overtaking the static vehicle. A line of immobilized cars and a narrow, blocked road: such are the formal rules of this comedic game, and the scenes that follow systematically explore the possibilities for visual and cinematic interest within this static space. After Laurel and Hardy realize they cannot move forward within the line of cars, they signal to the cars behind them to back up so that they can leave the line and drive down the middle of the road, between the traffic jam and the opposing traffic. Though the cars they pass remain immobilized, the line is animated by a sea of flailing arms that protest through windows at the passersby. After tracing an alternate and prohibited parallel path within the linear space of the road, Laurel and Hardy's vehicle then becomes involved in a second series of gags, all built around the concept of collision within the compressed space of the line. Unlike the spectacular car crashes of the Sennett studios, whose demolition-derby aesthetic persists in the car chases and smash-ups of contemporary action cinema, these scenes of destruction are notable for the impossibility of speed in the space of such limited mobility, and for the smallness and slowness of the bumps, which

FIGURE 41 Laurel and Hardy switch hats with Thelma and Ruby. Still from *Two Tars*.

FIGURE 42 A line of traffic. Still from *Two Tars*.

serve less as ends in themselves than as catalysts for further, and more intimate, interactions between constantly varying configurations of people. Although critics have tended to stress the all-out destruction of this scene, it is primarily a battle of wits and innovation, and the pleasure of the comedy arises at least as much from the ingenious variety of things that can be done with a car as from the comic violence of the battles themselves. Further pleasure arises from the carefully ordered use of time and space within this scene of collision, which delays the escalation of violence and chaos almost until the end of the film. The first collisions take place within extremely small spaces. Laurel and Hardy drive into a barrel, back up, and are then bumped by the driver behind (played by Edgar Kennedy). This gives way to a repetitious back-and-forth sequence in which Hardy, egged on by Thelma ("Are you gonna let that bozo bump our car?—"), inches forward in order to be able to bump the car behind in return, after which Kennedy reverses and moves forward again, Hardy repeats his same maneuvers, and Kennedy repeats his forward bump a third time. A close-up shot of a leaking radiator seems to punctuate this gag, but the next shot offers yet another, only slightly escalated version of the same exact gag: Kennedy bumps Hardy, Hardy moves forward and reverses to bump Kennedy.

This final bump pushes Kennedy's car into the car behind him, and the involvement of a third driver shifts the scene into its second series of gags, all based around drivers physically attacking their opponents' vehicles. Kennedy first steps forward and kicks Laurel and Hardy's car. Laurel solemnly rips off the headlight of the car behind, and then kicks it through the windshield of the third car in line. Retaliation comes in the form of Kennedy popping the foursome's balloon, which is in turn repaid with a mud pie on Kennedy's head. Producing a formal variation on the film's numerous exploding spheres, Kennedy slices the rental car's tire, allowing its inflated inner tube to ooze out strangely before popping (figure 43). The tit for tat continues, cheered on by Rubie and Thelma, gradually spreading outward to infect the rest of the traffic until a policeman arrives on the scene and brings the chaos to a halt.

If the beginning of this traffic-jam sequence presents a line of completely indistinguishable production-line cars, the ending proudly displays the transformation of these standardized products into a series of highly unique examples that parade before the camera, one after another: a car without front wheels (figure 44); a car stuck on the end of a log that is at-

FIGURE 43 An inner tube protrudes from a slashed tire. Still from *Two Tars*.

tached to a truck (figure 45); a car, having no body or floor, with a "walking" driver; a car being towed upside down (figure 46); a car with bat-like wings (figure 47); and a car that bounces its passengers up and down through its roof as it moves along. Each new example is punctuated by the laughter of Laurel and Hardy, who by this point have been placed under arrest, and this laughter renders the law helpless. As for Rubie and Thelma, they bunk off together up the embankment as soon as they catch sight of the traffic cop, but the film has never led us to believe that they would stick around (figure 48). While the other drivers, in pursuit of Laurel and Hardy, are run out of a tunnel, backwards, by an oncoming train, Laurel and Hardy manage to squeak by, thanks to the remarkable flexibility of their rented wheels, the image of which leaves us wondering what further configurations might be possible (figure 49).

FIGURE 44 Car missing its two front tires. Still from *Two Tars*.

FIGURE 45 Car impaled on a log. Still from *Two Tars*.

FIGURE 46 Car flipped upside-down. Still from *Two Tars*.

FIGURE 47 Car with wings. Still from *Two Tars*.

FIGURE 48 Rubie and Thelma leave the scene. Still from *Two Tars*.

FIGURE 49 Laurel and Hardy make it safely through the train tunnel. Still from *Two Tars*.

chapter three

DOING DEATH OVER

Industrial-Safety Films,
Accidental-Motion Studies,
and the Involuntary
Crash Test Dummy

"Houses go up in flames, walls cave in, trains derail, car brakes fail, and suddenly someone is hanging on the big hand of a tower clock. Slapstick films provoke mortal danger and deny death, because everything always turns out all right. There is absolutely no risk. No one is going to die in a slapstick film. And by assuming the improbability of death, slapstick elevates the difficulties of life."—HARTMUT BITOMSKY, "CINEMA AND DEATH"

"Exposure to all kinds of elements can diminish your drive. The need for speed is a common desire. Most of us balance our safety with our desires, each determining our own behaviors according to what makes life worthwhile."—GREGG BORDOWITZ, "THE EFFORT TO SURVIVE AIDS CONSIDERED FROM THE POINT OF VIEW OF A RACE-CAR DRIVER"

After the demise of slapstick, it was not until the 1960s that the frequent intersection of car crashes and visual culture recurred, and when the trope did return, it did so across a variety of media and genre: in the Road Movie and European art cinema; in the work of artists such as Ant Farm and Andy Warhol; and in the mass media. By 1966, as U.S. involvement in Vietnam continued to escalate, President Johnson went so far as to designate highway safety as "the gravest problem before the Nation next to the war in Vietnam."[1] On August 29 of the same year, the front page of the *New York Times* declared, "Traffic accidents are now being seen not as isolated events, but as manifestations of an epidemic which—like other diseases—can be studied in public health terms."[2] Yet how do we move between the disaster images of the 1960s, which cut across the mass media, art, and film, and are marked by their resonance with a culture of revolution, war, and public protest, and the comedies of the 1920s and 1930s? Does the generative relationship between film and the automobile accident disappear between the 1930s and the 1960s, or does it migrate to less visible spaces? Working against the narrative that offers nothing but the dehistoricized risky 1960s and the paralyzed present, I explore how, where, and with what consequence accidents intersect with the media of film and photography between the 1930s and the 1960s, focusing in particular on the complex ways in which the films and the discourse surrounding them within this interstitial period engage and shape the concepts of risk, responsibility, and citizenship in relation to the technological accident.

While at the aesthetic level I provide a more nuanced visual and historical context for the later proliferation of car-crash images in the 1960s and 1970s, at the theoretical level I attempt to engage and challenge some aspects of the auto-cinema paradigm offered by the "High Priest of Speed," Paul Virilio, without disregarding the important issues he raises about the ethics of mobility and speed. Neither embracing nor condemning speed per se, I turn to a hybrid auto-media space that includes mass-education campaigns, military-funded scientific research, and industry-sponsored films to explore how the private car becomes a figure though which to engage the complex question of individual and collective responsibility in the face of uncontrollable and sometimes antisocial drives, addiction, and sexual desire.

Cinema, Citizenship, and the Technologies of Speed and Safety

Blind both to the complexity of the paradigms opened up by the industrial encounter with the enigma of the drives, and to the creative potential of cinema and the automobile, Virilio completely and reductively aligns speed and cinema first with each other, and then with the straight line of progress, with violence, war, "desocialization," and the disappearance of neighbors and citizens: "Between the audiovisual media and the automobile (that is, the dromovisual), there is no difference; *speed machines*, they both give rise to mediation through the production of speed, both are as one since the functions of the eye and the weapon have come to be confused, linked up, since the transportation revolution."[3] "The progress of speed," for Virilio, is "nothing other than the unleashing of violence"; speed is only "an extermination."[4] Polemically, he links the "liquidation of the world" and the "extermination of the passenger" to the "violence of the first camera dollies," and presents the urban motorway as not "a pathway of transmission, but the concentration camp of speed," a space in which Time is administered and speed comes to replace invasion as "the foundation of the law."[5] Technology emerges completely outside Virilio's conception of "the human," and the intersection of the two seems only capable of producing a fascist manifestation.[6]

In the midst of this critique of the violence of speed and movement, encapsulated by technologies of transportation and cinema, the collision emerges in two slightly contradictory formations. On the one hand, Virilio employs the French term *téléscopage* to portray collision as "the disappearance of one vehicle into another." Playing on the two meanings of the term—to "examine what is at a distance" and to "mix indiscriminately"—Virilio offers the crash as a "*mirror of speeds* that reflects back the violence of the trajectory on the object and the subjects of the movement."[7] Here the crash functions as a vengeful return of violence to its perpetrators; gradually, the distinction between speed and its termination (the collision, the *téléscopage*), between the car and *téléscopage* as collision, disappears: "The optical illusion of the telescope consists of approaching what is distant in order to examine it, and that of the automobile of mixing indiscriminately what is close and what is distant."[8] Eventually, both are folded into the image of the "contraction-collision."[9]

Prior to this conflation of the crash, the speeding automobile, and telescopic vision, however, Virilio offers another version of the collision in which the crash emerges as a brief (because potentially fatal) movement from passivity to activity, a laying bare of the ideological operations of the apparatus of security, designed less to keep traveling bodies safe than to hide from the passengers' senses the violence of speed: "So long as the dromoscopic simulation continues, the comfort of the passengers is assured, on the other hand, when the illusion comes to its brutally violent cessation in a collision, it is as if the voyeurs-voyagers are projected like Alice through the looking-glass windshield, a death jump but above all a jump into the truth of their trajectory where the gap between theater hall and the stage collapses, the spectators become actors: it is this *fleeting insurrection* that the seat belt is designed to prevent."[10] The local security that begins with the "corporeal 'packaging' [*l'emballage*] of the passenger" and the mummifying effects of car-safety design result, for Virilio, in a loss of the sense of touch and localization, a hiding of "solid reality" under the padding of surfaces.[11] And as the ideology of speed permeates every aspect of life, the discourse of security, which begins with transportation, replaces all concrete "enemies" so that *"pacification replaces nationalism,* the final *citizen* becoming less active than passive," leaving the new citizen as "a kind of 'zombie' inhabiting the limbs of a devalued public life."[12]

Undoubtedly Virilio captures in this apocalyptic vision something of our contemporary sense of a collective "crash" and disorientation that has persisted in the wake of the euphoric liberation movements and antiwar protests of the 1960s and 1970s. Furthermore, he astutely pinpoints the politically paralyzing effect of the contemporary ideology of security, usefully encouraging an attitude of skepticism toward "safety measures" as seemingly harmless, or even harm-preventing, as the seatbelt, identifying the collision as one potential, if neither permanent nor guaranteed, rupture in the State's security blanket. Yet however suggestive his ideas—such as the link he establishes between car safety and citizenship, or the potential of the crash for theories of subjectivity, citizenship, and visual technology at a time of great hybridity and rapid change—his line of thought can only productively be explored if one highlights some of its fundamental limitations.

First, Virilio's reduction of "cinema" to a singular and homogenous ideology drastically underestimates its capacity, as a complex system of sounds, images, and institutional structures, to create, as well as annihilate, experiences of time and space, to function in critical opposition to, as well as in collaboration with, the war machine he describes. Though his exhibition of disaster images, *Unknown Quantity* (2002), does attempt to mobilize the aesthetic of the crash for critical purposes, his Goldilocks-like paradigm of too much, too little, and just right is built on vast generalizations both about how images have functioned within particular ideological contexts and about how they will function in the present, claiming that liberalism "overexpose[d] the viewer to the incessant repetition of tragedies," that totalitarianism "opted for underexposure and the radical occultation of any singularity," and that in "these early years of the twenty-first century" we will be able, through an idealized notion of "exhibition," "to take what is happening ... and analyse it wisely."[13] Second, Virilio's teleological and nihilistic narrative proceeds from the assumption that human subjectivity is separable, rather than fully intertwined with, technology.[14] His is a narrative of loss: of lost senses, lost citizens, lost agency, lost touch, and lost bodies; his nostalgic story tells of the ever-deepening disorientation of a once whole, active, and fully present, and located, man. While for

Virilio, the separation of the subject from the world on-screen or through the car window, is fully alienating and negative, David Rodowick's recent work serves as a useful counterpoint to this position. Thinking alongside Stanley Cavell, Rodowick insists that the virtual quality of film constitutes one of the essential aspects of the medium's ethical possibilities, through the unfulfilled desire for touch and presence it provokes: "Film presents to me a world from which I am absent, from which I am necessarily screened by its temporal absence, yet with which I hope to reconnect or join."[15] Furthermore, within Virilio's nostalgic narrative, there is, of course, no Eve in Eden, for Virilio's woman is, from the moment of man's birth, part of the problem, being "the first means of transportation for the species, its very first vehicle."[16] And finally, though the translator's introduction to *Negative Horizon* ironically opens with an epigraph from Nietzsche—"We are unknown to ourselves"—the inherent human opacity and ontological blindness and dislocatedness suggested here is nowhere to be found in Virilio's writing.[17] Women-as-technology and technology-as-woman bear the burden of man's blindness, and having located in these two figures an essential violence (in which both cinema and the automobile participate), Virilio stretches backward in search of the responsible, located, active, and fully present man. While Virilio's passionate fear of the total annihilation of the species may work effectively as a call to responsibility, in refusing to allow the opacity and absence of the self as inherently human, rather than as a technologically enforced disappearance, he ultimately negates the very space that makes responsibility and citizenship both necessary and possible in the first place.

Responsibility, Blindness, and Passivity

Judith Butler's remarkable rethinking of the concept of "responsibility" through her creatively intertwined readings of Levinas, Laplanche, Adorno, and Foucault, provides a useful counterpoint to Virilio's paradigm, for it begins with the assumption that "the very meaning of responsibility ... cannot be tied to the conceit of a self fully transparent to itself."[18] In contrast to Virilio, for whom the once oriented and actively responsible citizen has gradually been rendered disoriented, foreign, and passive by the violence of a speed he locates in transportation, women, and audiovisual technologies, all of which gradually converge, Butler (following Levinas) detaches responsibility from the concept of agency altogether, and suggests instead that ethical interpellation derives not from an active, but rather from a "passive relation to other beings [that] precedes the formation of the ego," a relation that is inflicted on us by the other.[19] For Virilio, the crisis of the contemporary moment emerges as a result of the disappearance or disorientation of citizens who are rendered passive by visual and transportation technologies; yet for Butler, agency and the possibility of responsibility arise precisely out of an ontological space of passivity: "Something drives me that is not me, and the 'me' arises precisely in the experience of, and as the effect of, being driven in this way."[20] Within this formulation, responsibility for the other is not something we choose to enact, against violence, but is rather a condition into which we are unwillingly, passively, enigmatically, and indeed violently born. Yet, in what seems like a paradox, passivity functions in multiple ways. So, for example, acknowledging the passivity at the heart of responsibility would still involve refusing earlier models of citizenship founded on the expectation of what Étienne Balibar describes as "the passive enjoyment of formal rights" by individuals belonging to exclusively entitled historical communities.[21] "Passive" responsibility, in Butler's formulation, emerges not as a given, but as a zone of ongoing translation, a borderline between self and other, a space of constant encounter between the familiar and the foreign. To live the self as such is constantly to put the known self at risk, but in doing so, to participate in the forging of a space for a community "of a nonexclusive belonging," a space that demands of its participants an endless engagement with the work of translation and mediation, and in which the existence of conflicting and foreign values, desires and beliefs is not perceived as a threat to, but as the condition of collective freedom and security.[22]

And it is for this reason that responsibility, born of passivity but at odds with passive citizenship, also cannot be understood as a banal and moralistic trait of the one Maurice Blanchot calls "the successful man of action."[23] Rather than redeeming a technologically imposed disappearance and disorientation of the human, responsibility, Blanchot suggests, "separates me from myself... and reveals the other *in place* of me, requires that I answer for the impossibility of being responsible."[24] I am foreign to myself not because, as Virilio suggests in his reading of the contemporary culture of accidents, the body has been denied by the technologically enforced disappearance of space, but rather because I was never, and can never be, fully present or accessible to myself in the first place. Driven, occupied, by the other, a condition experienced by the subject in the form of enigmatic drives, the responsible subject does not set out to redeem its losses, but rather recognizes that the work of ethics begins by acknowledging that the responsible subject "has not made the map it reads, does not have all the language it needs to read the map, and sometimes cannot find the map itself."[25]

For Butler, desire and responsibility emerge from the same unidentifiable place, with the pulsations of the drive alerting us to our enigmatic and "unwilled susceptibility" to the other, even, or perhaps especially, in those moments when, enthralled or overwhelmed by desires and drives, we act "irresponsibly."[26] Yet for Virilio, who has exiled speed and drive from the heart of the human, desire—always accident prone—must also be banished. The "woman-of-burden" embodies "all the desires of conquest and penetration."[27] The spool of film, the prostitute, the highway, desire: each of these, for Virilio, constitute "fossils of violence" in the way they drive the subject to movement and confusion.[28] Though Virilio is not wrong to identify an affinity between violence and desire, his error, perhaps, lies in attempting to build an ethical system around a subject framed solely as threatened by, rather than also forged out of and enabled by, these primary violences. Displacing sexuality onto a technologized realm of violence, cinema, and transportation in his efforts to maintain the integrity of the (male) self, Virilio is left not only without cinema and technology, but also, nihilistically, without sexuality, too. And in discarding sex Virilio may throw away what Leo Bersani goes so far as to describe as "our primary, hygienic practice of nonviolence, and even as a kind of biological protection against our continuously renewed effort to disguise and to exercise the tyranny of the self in the prestigious form of legitimate cultural authority."[29]

As we consider Virilio's critiques of the capitalist desire for speed, cinema, "progress," and sex alongside Bersani's understanding of desire and sexuality, which have the self-shattering, masochistic experience of *jouissance* at their core, important questions about the relation between individual and collective desire, risk, and security begin to emerge. While recognizing that our desires may lead us to act unconsciously, irresponsibly, and at times even disastrously, we need nevertheless to insist on a place for desire in order to maintain, in the face of the inevitable inaccessibility of the other, a call. As Blanchot writes, "Desire, pure impure desire, is the call to bridge the distance."[30] This desire-as-call is itself, for Blanchot, a kind of "dying," and it is intimately linked to the repetitious logic of masochism.

The reimagination of the concepts of community, responsibility, and relationality necessarily involves recognizing the inherent risk of these encounters between the self and other, yet not all risks are equal, and we need to find ways of reflecting more carefully on the differences among various kinds of risk. Jean Laplanche, for example, suggests that there may be mechanisms through which to distinguish psychic from physical risks, and he critiques the term "death drive," noting, "I have called it a sexual death drive, with more emphasis on 'sexual' than on 'death.' . . . And more than death, I would point to primary masochism. I see more of a sense of the sexual death drive in masochism or in sado-masochism than in death."[31] Yet as Tim Dean points out in *Beyond Sexuality*, the psychic risks taken as a result of Laplanche's "sexual death drive" can fall easily into physical risk within the context of the AIDS epidemic, creating an urgent need for sex education to foreground the risk inherent in sexuality, to emphasize "the question central to negotiated safety—*How much risk do you consider acceptable?*"[32] Although my response to this difficult question is, perhaps necessarily, indirect, I propose that one might usefully begin to explore how the concepts of safety, risk, and responsibility have been negotiated and disseminated through the intersection of the auto-accident, car-safety education, and the medium of film, focusing in particular on the period between the 1930s and the 1960s. Attempting to dislodge Virilio's sexual moralism and teleological technophobia, I go in search of more nuanced vehicles through which to think about risk and responsibility, and explore the complex network of relationships that knit together modern transportation technologies, moving images, and the psychic drives.

"And Sudden Death": The Autopsy Effect

Though the auto-disaster had already been established as a self-reflexive figure for the medium of film within early cinema and slapstick comedy, in the mid-1930s, it emerges as a way to explore the possibility of ever more direct modes of communication and subjective experience. Mimicking the car crash's own transgression of spatial boundaries, car-crash images from this period suggest film's capacity to collapse the distance between self and other, and to offer the viewer direct, unmediated access to the thrills and sufferings of others. This confusion of subject-object distinctions is symptomatic of the representations of the car crash that begin to emerge in a variety of cultural texts in the 1930s: films, photographs, scientific research, and journalism. Just as the force of the collision literally displaces the human bodies contained within the car's structure, throwing, opening, and dismembering them, so representations of the crash are particularly susceptible to fantasies and anxieties that involve blurring the boundaries between self and other, inside and outside, human and technological, public and private. Though these zones of risk and transgressed boundaries at times abound with erotic and utopian political potential, their destabilization of limits also renders the subject in question vulnerable to the violent occupation of or by the other, and to death itself.

The gory aesthetic of the driver-education films produced by the Highway Safety Institute of Mansfield, Ohio, in the late 1950s and 1960s, which now circulate as cult films through the distributor Something Weird Video—films like *Signal 30* (1959), *Mechanized Death* (1961), *Wheels of Tragedy* (1963), and *Highways of Agony* (1969)—had no place in the highway-safety films of the period between the 1930s and the 1960s.[33] Yet the potential of this kind of gruesome cinematic "autopsy" (or "seeing for oneself"), which seemed full of cautionary pedagogic value, had already been at least imagined in relation to the car crash within the mass media as early as 1935, most notably within a *Reader's Digest* article, by the historian J. C. Furnas, entitled "—And Sudden Death," which would become the most reprinted *Reader's Digest* article ever.[34]

The documentary historian William Stott claims that "—And Sudden Death" exemplifies the documentary mode of representation that emerged in the 1930s in response to the Great Depression, central to which was the readers' ability to experience in a direct way the truth of the topic under discussion: "By the time the Great Depression entered its third (and worst) winter, most Americans had grown skeptical of abstract promises. More than ever they became worshippers in the cult of experience and believed just what they saw, touched, handled, and—the crucial word—felt. While driving through the Midwest in the early thirties, Louis Adamic picked up a girl tramp who had the 'facks,' as she said, about everything. Adamic, somewhat startled at her brazenness, asked, 'How do you feel?', and the girl gave him the tag answer of the time: 'With my fingers.'"[35] For Stott, Furnas's article, a "documentary reconstruction of what a car accident does to 'you,'" offers a prime example of Dale Carnegie's "dramatization" of the truth, a direct address to "you," the reader, enabling an experiential, bodily knowledge of facts.[36]

Furnas's article is designed to provoke physical sensation in readers. A prefatory and enticing editorial statement warns readers, "Like the gruesome spectacle of a bad automobile accident itself, the realistic details of this article will nauseate some readers. Those who find themselves thus affected are at the outset cautioned against reading the article in its entirety, since there is no letdown in the author's outspoken treatment of sickening facts."[37] In the essay's opening paragraphs Furnas rejects motoring statistics and "a passing look at a bad smash" as inadequate to the task he aims to accomplish in this article, that is, to induce the "vivid and *sustained* realization that every time you step on the throttle, death gets in beside you."[38] This sustained attention, he believes, could only be achieved "if you had really felt" the horror of another's crash for yourself, and the essay attempts to transmit this experience of both duration and intensity.[39] Having rejected statistics and personal witnessing as incapable of conveying the subjective experience of the car crash, Furnas goes on to dismiss both the attempts of artists to represent "in full detail" the scene of the accident and the sentences of judges who send reckless drivers "to tour the accident end of a city morgue," claiming that "even a mangled body on a slab, waxily portraying the consequences of bad motoring judgment, isn't a patch on the accident itself."[40] In trying to convey what a car crash feels like Furnas invokes film as his medium of choice, and he attempts to give his words cinematic force through graphic description.

As he instructs his readers to take "a good look at the picture the artist wouldn't dare to paint," he imagines a truly effective safety poster, which "would have to include motion-pictures and sound effects, too—the flopping, pointless efforts of the injured to stand up; the queer, grunting noises; the steady, panting groaning of a human being with pain creeping up on him as the shock wears off. It should portray the slack expression on the face of a man, drugged with shock, staring at the Z-twist in his broken leg, the insane crumpled effect of a child's body after its bones are crushed inward, a realistic portrait of a hysterical women with her screaming mouth opening a hole in the bloody drip that fills her eyes and runs off her chin."[41] Conflating the description of a man, anesthetized by shock, looking with detachment at his injured leg with the presentation of that same leg to the reader for inspection, Furnas blurs the distinction between subjective and objective viewing positions, just as later highway-safety films will collapse the distance between spectator and driver, leaving readers hovering uncertainly between reading and looking, witnessing and experiencing.[42] Furnas further inducts the reader by persistently shifting from third- to second-person descriptions: "Each type of accident produces either a shattering dead stop or a crashing change of direction, and, since the occupant—meaning you—continues in the old direction, every surface and angle of the car's interior immediately becomes a battering, tearing projectile, aimed squarely at you."[43]

Even as Furnas tries to combat the abstracting effect of statistical reports by asserting the individuality of specific crash victims, regaling the reader with images of "each shattered man, woman and child who . . . had to die a personal death," bodies repeatedly lose their limits, turn inside out, and merge into each other, as with the old lady "who had been sitting in back, lying across the lap of her daughter, who was in front, each soaked in her own and the other's blood indistinguishably, each so shattered and broken that there was no point whatever in an autopsy."[44] Confounding temporal as well as subject-object distinctions, "—And Sudden Death" conjures up a split and self-hating reader-driver, one simultaneously at the edge of and already past death, pulled back from the limit after a cinematic look at her own corpse in preparation for a more cautious present and future: "But the pain can't distract you, as the shock begins to wear off, from realizing that you are probably on your way out. . . . You're dying and you hate yourself for it. That isn't fiction either. It's what it actually feels like to be one of that 36,000. . . . Take a look at yourself as the man in the white jacket shakes his head over you, tells the boys with the stretcher not to bother, and turns away to somebody else who isn't quite dead yet. And then take it easy."[45]

At the center of this popular essay stands the disturbing fantasy of living on in the wake of having looked not just at but also through one's own dead eyes. Indeed, what Furnas dramatizes is the modern subject struggling to find an appropriate relationship to two intertwined technologies that promise the transcendence of subjective limits, a transcendence that links cinema and the car with both a state of ecstasy and the body in pieces. In this sense, "—And Sudden Death" captures something of the complex and at times paradoxical nature of the subject who emerges in the realm of the cinematic car crash. On the one hand, the cinematic crash seems to offer viewers the same thrills, views, and transcendence of bodily and subjective limits as the careening car itself; yet on the other hand, it emerges as the car's antidote, a safety device promising to inoculate spectators against the thrill of technologically enabled speed by allowing them subjectively to experience the thrills and subsequent death of the other without personal risk or consequence.

The car crash serves to render visible, and thereby provoke a negotiation with, an internal tension between the responsible subject and the risky, irresponsible, and inexplicable self that the subject experiences as a technologically introduced foreign other. The scene of the crash emerges as a complex site for grappling with, unleashing, and regulating these opaque drives. Though these drives are, as Laplanche and Butler argue, fundamental to the condition of the human, technology often emerges as a partial culprit, perhaps because this aspect of the human expresses itself in mechanical, automatic, unwilled, and driven ways. But what role does cinema play in this exploration of modern responsibility, good citizenship, mechanical failure, and highway safety?

Auto Safety and the Industrial Sponsored Film

The increased prominence of car safety as a topic for public discussion in the 1930s was preceded both by international conversations about modernity and risk, particularly in regard to the question of who was responsible for the safety of the modern industrial worker, and by the rapid increase in automobile ownership in the United States, which was facilitated by extensively expanded advertising and credit campaigns.[46] Yet both the car and cinema seemed to offer alternative, albeit related, modes of engagement with technology to the factory, modes largely framed by consumption and pleasure rather than by production and labor. From the early 1930s, acutely aware of cinema's capacity to influence the public's reception of the automobile and of the affinities between the two technologies within the landscape of modernity, car manufacturers funded a variety of film shorts—cartoons, travelogues, newsreels, and educational films about a variety of issues, including engine design, the search for oil, driver safety, and other car-related matters—and these neglected films become rich sites for exploring the emerging relationship between the two technologies and the way this relationship forges modern conceptions of responsibility, risk, pleasure, and safety.[47]

Sponsored films often had little or nothing to do with the question of safety, as in the bouncing-ball sing-a-long cartoon *In My Merry Oldsmo-*

bile (1932) — produced by Fleischer Studios, with funding from General Motors — in which two villains, their Oldsmobiles, and a lady, Lucille, become the site for sexually inflected visual play. Yet by 1935, perhaps in response to the publication of Furnas's *Reader's Digest* article, the question of safety had explicitly entered the promotional-film genre, in spite of the fact that car manufacturers throughout the first half of the century argued vociferously, "Safety doesn't sell." While Furnas imagines cinema in its documentary mode as the medium most capable of diminishing the gap between experience and representation, of offering the American public the "facks," the industrial-safety films made between 1935 and 1959 seem caught between the industry's need to assuage consumers' growing anxieties about danger of the automobile and the playful aesthetic that can be traced back to the intersection of the car and the camera in cinema's early years, an aesthetic that demonstrates greater affinities with slapstick comedy, experimental film practice, animation, and fantasy than with the documentary realism and the phenomenological experience of the car crash that Furnas imagines cinema conveying. Though we might expect these industrially sponsored films to reflect an oversimplified company line that unambiguously reassures consumers of the automobile's safety, in the films I consider the stated goal of using motion pictures to advocate against contingent, irregular, irresponsible, and thrill-seeking behavior works in tension both with the films' playful "auto-visual" aesthetic and with the underlying goal of these industrial films — to sell the fantasy of the car, in which speed, risk, and the contingency exemplified by the accident are all central ingredients.

THE SAFEST PLACE (1935)

In 1935 Chevrolet offered a counterpoint to Furnas's nightmare vision of auto-death with a six-minute film, *The Safest Place*, produced by the Detroit-based Jam Handy Organization, which was founded in 1917.[48] The film opens by constructing not the car, but the home as the preeminent space of danger, reminding viewers that 4 million accidents had taken place in American homes during the previous year, a statistic that is visually complemented by three comic scenes of domestic near-mishaps caused by a bar of soap on the bathroom floor, toys on the stairs, and a missing step on a ladder. While the domestic space is established as accident prone, Chevrolet pronounces the car to be "the safest place on earth": a "solid steel" living room with a "turret-top roof and a rigid steel foundation[,] . . . dependable brakes . . . and . . . safety glass all around." Yet having established the car as a space of safety and invulnerability, the film goes on to lament the car's real weakness: the fallibility of the driver.

Even as *The Safest Place* constructs a fantasy-mobile that liberates the driver from the dangers of domestic space, rendering him free to enact his desires through a technologically enabled impenetrable shield, it simultaneously eradicates the desiring human agent through the introduction of what the film calls the "automatic driving mechanism." As the camera shoots from the car's backseat, we see a steering wheel moving of its own accord and empty cars moving in an orderly manner through the streets, while a voice-over celebrates the automatic driving mechanism's obedient adherence to the rules of the road at stoplights, road signs, and corners. Prefiguring the newly secure space of Washington, D.C., today, the film constructs safety as the disappearance of the human from a landscape populated by machines that never, unlike the human drivers the film bemoans, "make secrets of what [they're] going to do." Straddling the competing consumer desires for safety and danger, these advertising films make visible the struggle to formulate psychologically compelling and commercially effective auto-film fantasies. Made at a moment before the cinematic fantasy of the road had yet to find its generic form, these films oscillate between complex and at times contradictory fantasies that include the male subject's escape from both domestic and industrial space; his subsequent domination of the private technology of the car; and his complete submission to or even disappearance within the technological superiority of the impenetrable car-cocoon.

Yet if automatism appears on one level as a solution to the problem of human irresponsibility in *The Safest Place*, it is also a certain automatism that produces the condition of insecurity and danger in the first place at those times when the human driver himself seems driven, internally, by desires and impulses which "make secrets of themselves" even to the subject whose psychic landscape they inhabit. More than simply promoting particular brands of cars, these industrially sponsored films also put irreconcilable fantasies about automatism on display, and thus constitute important sites for historicizing a social, political, and corporate engagement with the question of how to regulate (and exploit) the relationships among human responsibility, technology, automatism, and desire.

THE OTHER FELLOW

Two years after the production of *The Safest Place*, Chevrolet returned explicitly to the problem of the illegible or split subject as driver in another Jam Handy short entitled *The Other Fellow* (1937), a visually complex engagement with the permeability of the self and other to which driving, like cinema, seems to give rise. From the outset, *The Other Fellow* announces its affinity with slapstick comedy by casting Laurel and Hardy's slow-burn sidekick Edgar Kennedy (a notorious on-screen car wrecker, and a crucial figure in *Two Tars*'s disastrous traffic-jam sequence) as the film's only actor. Kennedy plays the part, as the opening titles note, of five different drivers: "Edgar Kennedy (played by . . . Edgar Kennedy; Farmer Driver (the same Edgar Kennedy); Sport Driver (Edgar Kennedy again); Truck Driver (and again Edgar Kennedy); and Newlywed Driver (Edgar Kennedy again)." In the course of the film, Kennedy has near run-ins with the four other drivers, and each time he blames "the Other Fellow." The film states its earnest didactic message in authoritative tones on a number of occasions—that, in the philosophical words of the judge who will ultimately sentence Kennedy, "we will all only improve driving conditions when we see in ourselves the other fellow." Yet this film is most interesting for the way it visualizes the difficulties and sites of confusion embedded within its central proposition of rendering the other legible. First, *The Other Fellow* makes explicit, in ways that later driver-safety films won't, the fact that safety exceeds the control of the self, always being intricately bound to a negotiation between self and other. Yet by casting Kennedy in multiple roles, the film responds to the problem of the other's illegibility by attempting to erase the other completely; it posits safety as synonymous with sameness, and presumes the total transparency of the self to the self. While the film stages examples of the problems that arise from the other's illegibility in slapstick comic scenarios, an earnest voice-over instructs viewers on how to use hand signals developed to allow drivers to signal their intentions to each other. Yet even as *The Other Fellow* works to eradicate the difference and obscurity of the other in the name of safety, contradictory impulses persistently interrupt these efforts.

Rather than emphasizing the universal legibility of Kennedy's multiple selves, as the didactic voice-over would have us do, however, *The Other Fellow* repeatedly contradicts its own verbal message at the visual level by adopting an increasingly kaleidoscopic, almost surrealist, aesthetic that fragments both the urban landscape and the drivers' subjectivities and bodies, eliciting in viewers the kind of fractured and multiplicitous vision that the analyst L. Pierce Clark identified in 1907 as one of the pathological effects of driving: "The constant glancing by of objects, the sub-conscious dread of accidents, the manipulation of the machinery, conversation with the rest of the party, and a hundred other things make the automobilist's mind a regular kaleidoscope, and he may soon find that all his thoughts come in as jumbled a state as do the colors in a childish toy."[49] Counteracting the film's stated goal of avoiding the disastrous effects of driving by rendering visible the other's every move, the car's intersection with cinema produces bodies and modes of vision that are decentered, abstract, illegible, and polysemous.

Throughout *The Other Fellow*, the absence of a clear point of view is emphasized through the use of fractured screen space. Even the film's opening traveling shot emphasizes the driver's divided vision as the film is shot through Kennedy's windshield, which is split in two by a vertical bar. The film further reinforces a sense of the driver's split and multidirectional vision in a later scene where the divided windshield forms the backdrop for the rearview mirror in which we view the car behind (figure 50). After a three-car collision in which Kennedy shouts at alternative versions of himself, his face appears inside the frame of a General Motors service and travel record plaque, and is subsequently surrounded by four other faces (figure 51). Following this kaleidoscopic image of five superimposed faces, the film cuts back to a close-up, through the windscreen, of Kennedy, who stresses the accident's fragmenting impact on his identity by whistling and muttering the incomplete phrase, "Well I'll be a. . . ." After Kennedy is arrested, he promises the judge that he will put himself in "the other fellow's place," and as he returns to his car, the split identity to which he has committed himself as a driver is visually registered in a pronounced shadow on the side of the car (figure 52).

Once Kennedy returns to his car, a voice-over articulates the problem of safe driving as a problem of internal foreignness and obscurity, announcing in a confusing formulation that confounds subject-object distinctions, "All of us are the other fellow. And when we all realize that we are the other fellow to everybody else, we'll all keep out of trouble by letting him know what we're going to do next." The subsequent shots illustrate a series of hand sig-

FIGURE 50
Looking through the rearview mirror. Still from *The Other Fellow*.

FIGURE 51
The split subject. Still from *The Other Fellow*.

FIGURE 52
The driver and his shadow. Still from *The Other Fellow*.

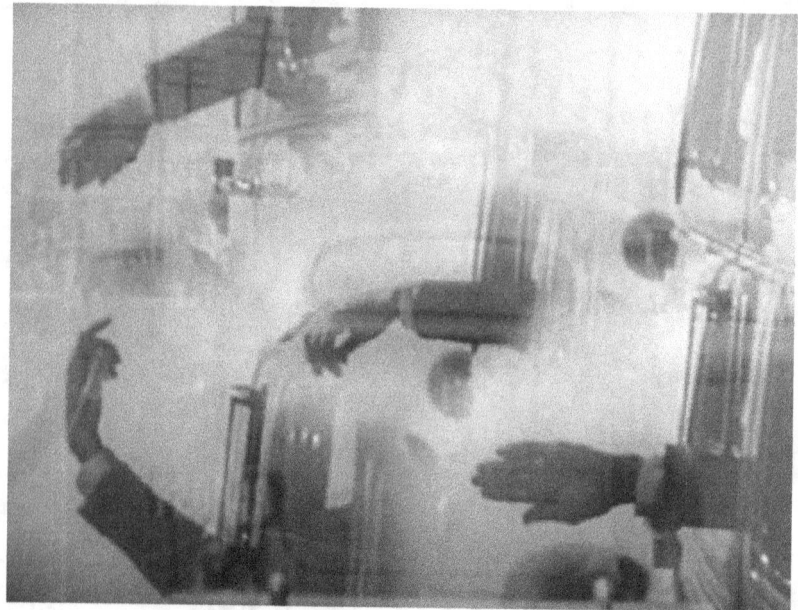

FIGURE 53 Hand signals superimposed over street scenes. Still from *The Other Fellow*.

nals, yet the clarity of each signal, demonstrated by a single hand stretched out of a window, exists in tension with the complex geometrical wipes that overlay each individual signal with diamonds, rectangles, and other signals. This abstract series of framed hands gives way to a montage of five free-floating hands, all moving slightly differently in different parts of the frame, devoid, in their multiplicity, of their symbolic meaning. Eventually these hands are superimposed both together and individually over a series of shots of cars in the street (figure 53). The strangely detached movements of the film's severed hands evoke nothing so much as the mouse-filled glove that crawls before Harold Lloyd's eyes in *Hot Water*, or the surreal severed hand in the street that attracts the attention of passersby shortly before another car accident in Luis Buñuel's and Salvador Dalí's *Un chien andalou* (1929). Just as *The Other Fellow*'s uncanny proliferation of selves and body parts recalls the slapstick multiplicity of a film like Laurel and Hardy's *Brats* (James Parrott, 1930), in which the comedy duo play both themselves and their own children, so the film's central safety message of seeing oneself in the other leads to a kind of visual schizophrenia in which the unified body of Kennedy fragments not only into a series of roles, but also into a series of parts that fracture the space they inhabit as well as the space of the screen, and act independently of the body to which they belong, seeming utterly unaware of the other parts around them. While the film's didactic voice-over works to eradicate the element of risk, difference, and illegibility, *The Other Fellow*'s visual landscape offers a divided and fragmented self, one whose right hand seems literally not to know what the left hand is doing. And as such, the film stages driving and responsibility as a double problem for the car industry—that of regulating drivers who are at times not in the driver's seat, opaque to themselves and not always capable of signaling what they will do next, and of interpellating consumers under the banner of a safety that is not always desired.

LIVE AND LET LIVE (1947)

Continuing the logic of *The Other Fellow*, Aetna Casualty and Surety Company's postwar safety film *Live and Let Live* (1947) similarly engages the contradictions of automobile safety, again through a disjunction between word and image, and through an equally lighthearted approach to form. While the film's voice-over condemns the careless, the impatient, the reckless, the illegible, and the thrill seekers, and aligns virtue with a state of permanent awareness ("You must never, not even for a moment, relax your vigilance while at the wheel"), visually it employs stop-motion animation and toy cars and figures, presenting the road as a scene of play, imagination, and mechanical experimentation, a scene devoid of all human life. Prefiguring the experimental auto-aesthetics of Ernie Gehr's *Shift* (1972–74) by a couple of decades, *Live and Let Live* offers views of the road from a variety of angles that distract attention from the question of road safety. Instead, *Live and Let Live* employs an aesthetic more familiar to us from the early years of cinema, inviting viewers to participate in the kind of topographic approach to film spectatorship celebrated by Noël Burch and, from a feminist perspective, by Guiliana Bruno, that is, to participate in less hierarchized and more decentered modes of viewing.[50] Burch writes,

> In contrast with the linear model, it is striking how many tableaux and even whole films were shot in all the major producing countries up to 1914 . . . which demanded a topographical reading by the spectator, a reading that could gather signs from all corners of the screen in their quasi-simultaneity, often without very clear or distinctive indices im-

mediately appearing to hierarchise them, to bring to the fore "what counts," to relegate to the background "what doesn't count." ... The regular spectator before 1910 surely learnt to be more alert to the screen than the modern spectator, more on the look-out for the surprises of a *booby-trapped surface*. The commercial failure of Jacques Tati's Playtime, whose images frequently share this primitive topographism, confirms that we have lost the habit of "keeping our eyes open" in the cinema.[51]

Although *Live and Let Live* attempts to direct our viewing through the use of a didactic and repetitive voice-over, the pleasure of this film, as with Gehr's *Shift*, lies in the random mechanical movements of automated vehicles around the space of the screen; in the deviations from predictable movements—the accidents; and in the juxtaposition of seemingly proximate sound effects (screeching tires, horns, etc.), which seem to place us inside of one of the toy vehicles, with distant and high-angle images of moving vehicles that appear remote, thereby creating multiple potential viewing positions for the spectator. Because the camera captures the miniature vehicles' frantic movements from various positions, the film refuses to establish a stable relationship among the plane of the screen, the plane of the road, and the viewing subject's position. Instead, in a manner that recalls the nonlinear movement of early cinema, it offers viewers a series of shots that trace changing pathways of brightly colored toy cars across the space of the screen—vertical, curved, diagonal, horizontal, circular. As toy cars and trains careen around the miniature roads on which only a single humanoid toy driver is visible (a drunk driver leaving a toy bar), the sounds of real collisions accompany scenes of miniature disaster to comic effect, and the question of crash prevention gives way to a cinematic exploration of crash aesthetics, including juxtapositions of speed and stasis, variations of camera distance and the direction of movement, and contrasts between the linearity of the road and the (supposedly) contingent movement of colliding vehicles (figure 54). Though these films clearly emerge within the developing discourse of American "auto-safety," they simultaneously participate in and draw on what Steve Kurtz describes as "crash humor," which he links to the self-reflexive practices of artists such as Duchamp, Rauschenberg, Johns, and Warhol.[52]

FIGURE 54 Two vehicles colliding. Still from *Live and Let Live*.

Passive Safety: Hugh De Haven and the Cornell Injury Research Project

While the sponsored films I have discussed so far grapple with the problem of the irresponsible driver and his unpredictable drives, Hugh De Haven (1895–1980), an engineer who headed the Crash Injury Research Project at the Cornell Medical School from 1942 to 1954, and the primary collaborator with Ben Kelley on the production of almost twenty car-safety films between 1968 and the late 1980s, disregarded the problem of human subjectivity altogether in his accidental-motion studies in order to focus exclusively on how to render the human body invulnerable. Although De Haven is now almost unknown, we live today more than ever in the wake of the paradigm of human safety he developed. As Robert Lindsay wrote in 1970, in a *New York Times* article about the effect of Ralph Nader's *Unsafe at Any Speed*, "Nader did it. He was the catalyst . . . but the real hero of this story is a guy few people have heard of, Hugh De Haven."[53] The Hugh De Haven archive of letters, newspaper cuttings, research reports, and films reveals the extent to which automobile safety functioned in the twentieth century as a discourse of escalating importance for the United States as it grappled with questions of individual and collective rights, public and private space, passive and active security, risk and desire, deviance and agency, freedom, responsibility, and citizenship, and the limits of human tolerance.

Within the field of crash-injury research, De Haven is largely notable for shifting the emphasis of research from accident prevention to accident survival, an emphasis he traces back to the fact that in 1917, after enrolling as a cadet pilot in the Canadian Royal Flying Corps, he emerged as the only survivor of a mid-air collision in Texas: "I hit the ground, and I, well, the thing just rolled up in a ball of wire, fabric and splinters—there's nothing left, very little. I broke both legs, and I ruptured my liver, I ruptured my pancreas, I ruptured my gallbladder, I ruptured my kidneys, and they disentangled me from the plane and took me into the hospital. They didn't even bother to set my legs. They just . . . left me to die . . . but I just didn't die."[54] Following this experience, De Haven developed a lifelong interest in what he called "the Jesus factor"—the human ability to survive ostensibly fatal collisions, suicide jumps, and free falls—in measuring the limits of human tolerance for force, and in finding ways to expand those limits.[55] As he worked toward his fantasy of human invulnerability, his research, not surprisingly, became of immediate interest to the military as well as to the automobile and aviation industries.[56]

Although De Haven had retired in 1933, at the age of thirty-eight, to live off income from his patents and inventions, his interest in transportation safety was reignited in 1936, when some casual domestic experiments with eggs became the catalyst for the foundation of the Cornell Crash Injury Research center, dedicated to rendering Americans in motion "deathproof." As he explains in a letter to his mother, dated 2 June 1936, "Dear Mother, While fooling around with one thing and another having bearing on the general thought, I took an egg and dropped it in a series of tests onto a soft sponge rubber mat. . . . Imagine my surprise when I found the height could be increased to TEN FEET without fracture. I don't know how much further it could be increased—the ceiling was the limit. So far as I know there is no engineering thought to cover this phenomenon."[57] By 1942, De Haven's research on the human body's capacity to sustain force had attracted the interest and support of the military, the National Research Council, the Civil Aeronautics Board, the Cornell University College, and the Office of Scientific Research and Development; by 1947, his egg-dropping had become a topic of national, not just maternal, interest. In a front-page article entitled "Eggs Just Bounce in 100-Foot Drop," the *New York Times* reports on De Haven's public display of ovular invulnerability: "It all seemed very foolish at first. A perfectly sane man with two perfectly sane assistants went to the top of a building 100 feet above the street yesterday and began dropping eggs off the roof. . . . Passersby stood agape as the fresh eggs came plummeting down, struck the mat, and went bounding up above the third floor of the eleven-story building. . . . A research group that is studying the mechanical factors that cause injuries in aviation accidents took part in the show. The group is headed by Hugh De Haven."[58]

The research De Haven and his ironically named collaborator Edward Dye pursued under the title "body kinematics" constitutes a continuation both of the early motion studies of Marey and Muybridge, and of Charles Babbage's self-inscribing apparatus, a precursor of the black box, which was designed to graphically record the events preceding a train accident.[59] Yet while Babbage's apparatus, as Greg Siegel has recently argued, was intended to protect "passengers of the future" by recording what Babbage described as the "immediate antecedents of any catastrophe," De Haven's crash tests are not interested in addressing the question of technological failure.[60] Rather, the films and photographs produced in his laboratory document and measure a series of staged propulsions of the living but passive body, using a variety of "actors" in an effort to render select bodies not actively, but "passively safe" under ever more disastrous conditions.

While Marey and Muybridge measured, recorded, and represented active, animate bodies—the walking, running, and jumping bodies of animals and humans—De Haven and Dye were interested measuring the inert body as it was involuntarily moved or thrown by technology; and, as with Muybridge and Marey, the drive to measure the body's involuntary motion led to technological innovation.[61] Researchers in De Haven's lab developed high-speed film (of up to 1,500 frames per second) as well as increasingly sophisticated automatic high-speed film-analysis technology to measure the displacement versus time relationship of thrown bodies in technological collisions.[62] In addition, crash-test researchers called on cinematic stuntmen to learn from them both how best to film high-speed collisions and how to help the body withstand the collision's force, creating a situation where real future disasters were being rehearsed, choreographed, and filmed by the anonymous showmen of Hollywood.[63] The filmic traces of these experiments, found in the Cornell Medical Archive in various forms—mostly as film stills and photographs in scientific reports and some fragments of reels—constitute an important and relatively unexplored component of film's involvement not just in representing but also in imagining and enabling the acceleration of the human body and the construction of a newly expanded frame of safety for American citizens on the move, an acceleration that was exacerbated by the military needs of both the Korean War and the Vietnam War.

As they trace the development of a visual and linguistic rhetoric of what came to be called "passive safety," the apparently benevolent safety studies, films, and press releases relating to Dye's and De Haven's investigations project into the future an image of American citizens as high-speed projectiles which, rather than being slowed down, have the right to be carefully packaged so that they can move uninhibited throughout the world at their desired velocity without sustaining any personal injury. Although this vision of physical invulnerability resonates with the individual automobile consumer's fantasies of unlimited personal freedom, it is important to remember that Cornell's Crash Injury Research Project was funded primarily by a military interested in preventing its soldiers' peacetime death-by-automobile so that they could die fighting instead.[64] The images that measure the thrown body therefore bear witness to the rise of a society in which power would increasingly be determined by the uneven distribution of access to technologies of invulnerability.

Though these scientific tests or "pre-enactments" of disaster-to-come seem inextricably bound to a temporality of futurity, the crash-test films and stills that document and measure the movement of the technologically thrown body bring the insistently deferred temporality of the test into contact with the complex qualities of past and presentness that we associate with photographically based media. As if these contradictions are not already complex enough in the way they document "past performances" of accidents to come, our temporal sense of these strange technical films is thrown into further crisis by some of the actors who play the role of driver. Though variations on the inorganic crash test dummy we know today were developed at least as early as the 1920s, including sandbag dummies, the two-dimensional Thin Man (from the 1940s, named after W. S. VanDyke's 1934 film), and early humanoid models, these dummy actors ultimately failed to satisfy the needs of the crash-test directors because they could not register the subjective experience of pain (figure 55). While some of the crash-test researchers who followed in De Haven's wake—such as Colonel J. P. Stapp,

FIGURE 55 The Thin Man crash test dummy. Courtesy of the New York Weill Cornell Medical Center Archives, Hugh De Haven Papers, Box 6, "The Elmer Spery Award for 1967" (pamphlet), p. 17.

chief medical officer of the National Highway Safety Bureau, and Lawrence Patrick, of Wayne State University—dealt with the epistemological limits of dummies by filming themselves and, incredibly, their students in hundreds of rapid deceleration tests between 1947 and 1975, it was clear that they had to find more adequate and sustainable sources of organic material which could be repeatedly and increasingly forcefully thrown and measured.[65]

Surprisingly unable to recruit human volunteers, De Haven and Dye went in search of what De Haven calls "involuntary volunteers," which eventually took four forms:[66] (1) the dead and injured from car and plane crashes, whose images appeared in the mass media and in police reports;[67] (2) the crash test dummy (figures 56–57);[68] (3) anesthetized animals—including pigs, rhesus monkeys, baboons, and chimpanzees (which General Motors, like many other car companies, continued to use until 1993) (figure

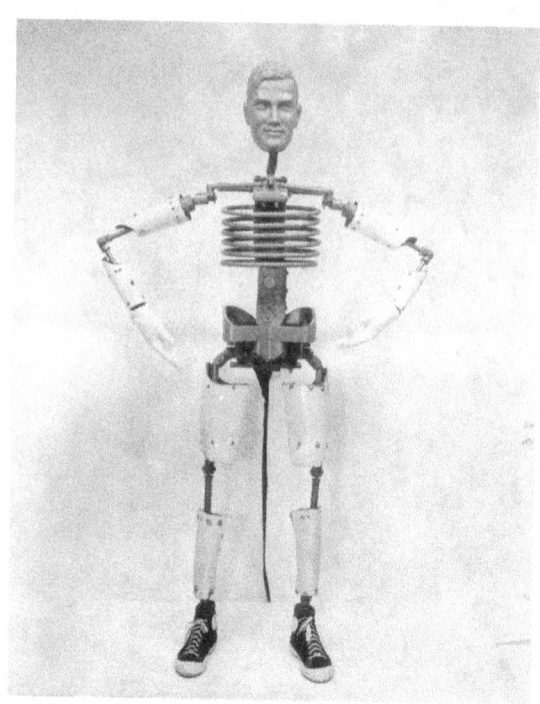

FIGURE 56 Crash test dummy. Courtesy of the New York Weill Cornell Medical Center Archives, Hugh De Haven: Photographs, Box 1, "Equipment Folder," Negative #2142.

FIGURE 57 Crash test dummy. Courtesy of the New York Weill Cornell Medical Center Archives, Hugh De Haven: Photographs, Box 1, "Equipment Folder," Negative #2143.

58);⁶⁹ and (4) unembalmed cadavers, which, before being subjected to their second death, would usually be "dressed in two layers of tight fitting leotards to simulate clothing," and would be subject to collisions, at up to fifty miles an hour, that would be recorded with high-speed film (figure 59).⁷⁰

Pre-enacting the Accident

But what is the effect of casting corpses in cinematically documented "pre-enactments" of future technological disasters? What is the status of the information that is contained within these macabre scientific rehearsals, which, like veritable *ballets mécaniques*, reanimate the dead on film as passively driven drivers, forcing them to undergo a second death, presumably more traumatic than their first, for the first had to have left no physical mark if the cadavers were to be useful for the purpose of measuring the injury inflicted on the body by the test collision. As these "crashes" are rehearsed and recorded within the walls of the laboratory on specially constructed rapid deceleration tracks, these pre-enactments show no trace of the source of the other accident victims; indeed, these films conjure up a world in which there are no human consequences to the creation of indestructible bodies, as if we crashed only with ourselves. As Avital Ronell argues in *The Test Drive* (2005), in the no-place of the laboratory, outside of legible geographic and political space, the test exceeds the temporal and geographic coordinates we need to be able to register anything like a sense of place or history, and this evasion of our epistemological frame contributes to the crash test's ability to register a kind of moral neutrality. The true experiment is slippery, belonging, Ronell argues, "to the future of its elaboration and, being wed to novelty, cannot be said to fall on this or that side of a divide determining good or evil."⁷¹

In recent years, the safety test has arisen as an increasingly visible figure not only in contemporary art and films that engage the escalating prominence of the discourse of risk, safety, and security, but also in popular cultural experiences like Disney World's "Test Track" ride, which opened in 1999. It invites passengers to "experience life as a crash test dummy.... Become a vehicle test dummy for the ride of your life," and puts General Motors's safety archive on display for those waiting in line.⁷² The ride is located in Future World, as if the human occupation of the role of the crash test dummy were yet to happen, instead of being the current condition for many people, particularly those unmarked bodies existing outside the realm of

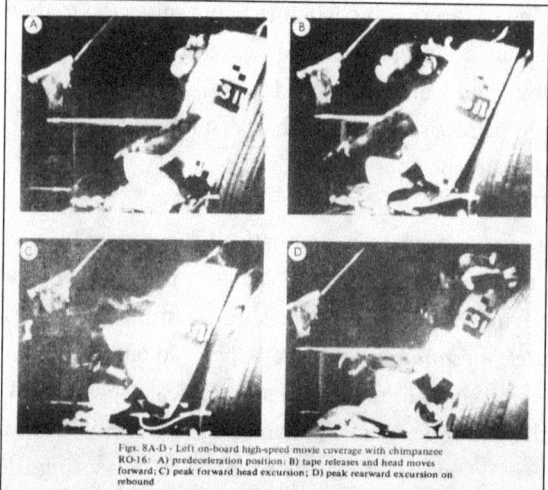

FIGURE 58 Crash test with chimpanzee. *Proceedings of Nineteenth Stapp Car Crash Conference* (1975), p. 334.

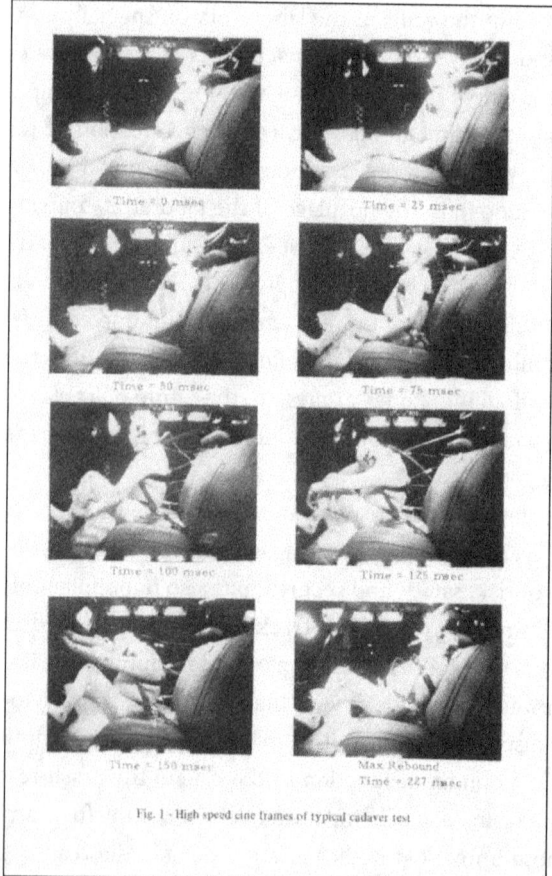

FIGURE 59 Crash test with cadaver. *Proceedings of Nineteenth Stapp Car Crash Conference* (1975), p. 9.

the citizenry, and it only serves to confirm Jean Baudrillard's reading of Disneyland as a "digest of the American way of life": "Disneyland is here to conceal the fact that it is the 'real' country, all of 'real' America, which *is* Disneyland (just as prisons are there to conceal the fact that it is the social in its entirety, in its banal omnipresence, which is carcereal."[73] This rise in the visibility of the technology and discourse of safety is not simply a response to a specific event, such as the attack on the World Trade Center, but is rather a symptom of broader insecurities that emerge within the context of globalization, marked by a new awareness of what Ulrich Beck calls the "world risk society."[74] While the perception of "world risk" has the potential to forge new paradigms of global citizenship that exceed nation-based paradigms and hierarchies, as Beck argues, the self-reflexive and future-oriented paradigms of a risk society also put pressure on the frame of realism. Beck writes, "The definitional power of realism rests upon exclusion of questions that speak more for the interpretive superiority of constructivist approaches. How, for example, is the borrowed 'self-evidence' of 'realistic' dangers actually produced? Which actors, institutions, strategies and resources are decisive in its *production*? These questions can be meaningfully asked and understood only within an anti-realist, constructivist perspective."[75]

What makes risk particularly resistant to ideological critique, and difficult to engage using the documentary form of filmmaking, is the speculative dimension of this concept. Film scholars have long recognized that the reenactment of an event after the fact may not always appear as a diversion from "the truth," and that such dramatic instances can play an important and politicized role in documentary practice. But even if dramatic reenactment offers documentary filmmakers a means to represent elusive or repressed historical events, how can documentary theory and practice begin to grapple with those catastrophes imagined by the discourse of risk that, though they have not yet, and may never, come, potently shape the reality of the present? What is the status of (p)re-enactments such as those that occur within the context of the crash test not as past-, but as future-oriented performances, repetitions of events in advance of their occurrence? And how might such performances bear down on our understanding of documentary film's relation to the concept of truth?

Though the speculative performance of imagined catastrophes may seem to belong squarely in the space of science fiction, not documentary, we might begin to read the scientific safety-test film as a future-oriented documentary film paradigm that allows us to contemplate the political and ideological consequences of the discourse of risk *before* disaster strikes, making them images to which we need to pay greater attention. While television, as Mary Ann Doane argues in "Information, Crisis, Catastrophe," shifts the temporality of the catastrophe from the photographic time of "that-has-been" to the instantaneous time of "this is going on," a time in which it is always too late to intervene, the scientific safety-test film constitutes a temporally oracular, but still documentary form, catching on film not the catastrophe itself, but the ideological fictions that, through repeated rehearsal and performance, shape the form of the disasters to come: the technical test film tells us, "This will be."[76]

Ronell reminds us, through her readings of Nietzsche, of the longstanding affinity that exists between testing and torturing. Testing both reveals a desire for total knowledge and prohibits it through the interminability of the possibility of further experimentation, and it is this insatiable desire for more knowledge that produces the conditions of torture. Yet if, for Nietzsche, the experiment, with its commitment to the not-yet-known, liberates us from the constraints of referential truth, how can we begin to articulate the implications of the test for documentary and for indexical media like film and photography more generally, which are so very invested in precisely that which the test leaves behind? For while documentary photography and film rely in part on the witnessing effect of the this-has-been, made to work in tandem with other signs of authenticity, the scientific test or experiment is, as Ronell argues, "monopolized by non-presence" and "runs on deferral."[77]

Conclusion

Although the timing of our political attunement to the social and political violence of the test may, perhaps by necessity, always be belated, contemporary video artists and filmmakers are increasingly turning to the crash test as they explore what it is that has been pre-enacted for us and that has led us into the situation we are now in, as well as what we are currently rehearsing for the future. In 2006 the intricately intertwined ideologies and industries of testing, security, citizenship, and globalization were brought into sharp focus by "Crash Test Dummy: The New European Self in a Biopolitical Crash Test," a series of performances, happenings, film screenings,

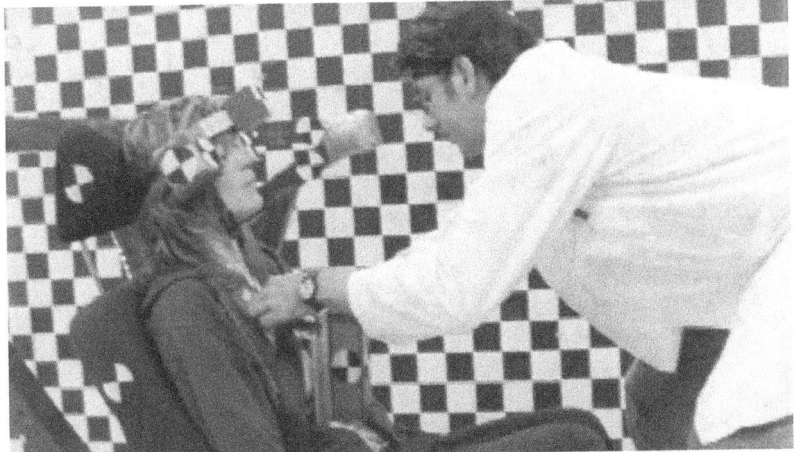

FIGURE 60 Human crash test dummy. Still from *Crash Test Dummies* (Jörg Kalt, 2005).

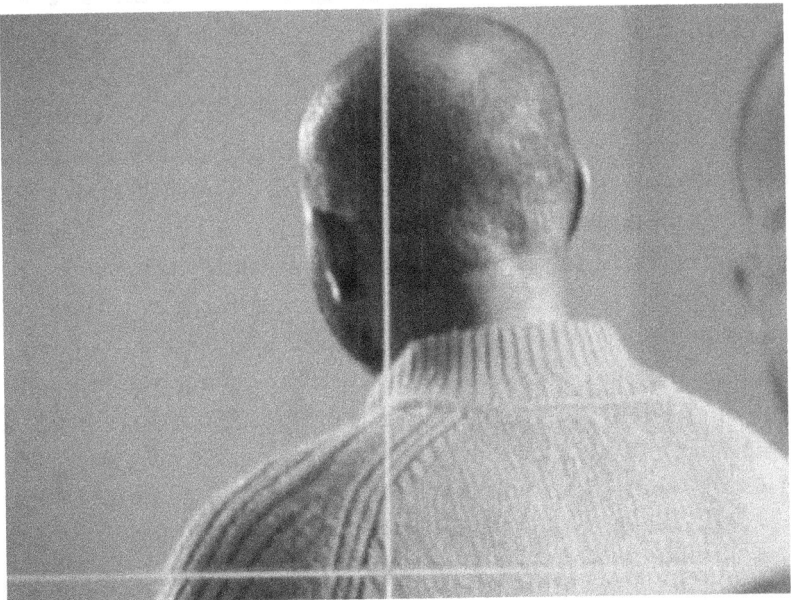

FIGURE 61 Interview with asylum seeker. Still from Alexandra Weltz's *Munich Express*.

FIGURE 62 A car crashes through a brick wall. Still from Du Zhenjun's *Crash*.

and video installations that took place in Munich, Budapest, Prague, and Ljubljana between May and July. This "test" featured a wide range of film and video works, including a screening of the late Austrian filmmaker Jörg Kalt's *Crash Test Dummies* (2005), made shortly before his suicide, a film which follows the fate of Eastern European migrant workers and socially anonymous bodies in Austria, some of whom make livings as human crash-test dummies (figure 60); Alexandra Weltz's video installation *Munich Express* (2006), which documents interviews with asylum seekers cast in the role of "crash test dummies" by the regulations governing their existence in Munich (figure 61); and Du Zhenjun's spectacular public video installation *Crash* (China/France, 2006), which depicts a car crashing through a bright red brick wall (figure 62).[78] Directly echoing the words of Hugh De Haven, the organizer of this series, Dietmar Lupfer, explained, "In the current social and political situation nobody knows where we are heading.... *Crash test dummy* picks up on this uncertain situation, where we, as *involuntary test persons*, find ourselves in a transition phase.... One can take the situation of refugees as a paradigm. Refugees are the current-day 'dummies.'"[79] How we respond to the role of involuntary test person in which some have now been cast—a role formerly reserved for pigs, chimps, and cadavers—will help us answer the questions: Are we really dummies? Are we dead yet?

chapter four

DISASTER TIME,
THE KENNEDY
ASSASSINATION,
AND ANDY WARHOL'S
SINCE (1966/2002)

The interaction of visual culture and the automobile evolved constantly during the 1950s, 1960s, and 1970s in both the European and American contexts, yet the specific histories that shape the relationship between these two technologies is often reductively framed by a narrative that simply recognizes the proliferation of cars and car accidents on-screen or in the art museum as symptomatic of the rise of cultures of speed and spectacle. In France the situationists' attention was not focused on critiquing cars in general; indeed Guy Debord explicitly states, "It is not a question of combating the automobile as an evil in itself."¹ Rather, in his "Situationist Theses on Traffic" (1959), Debord engages the relation between architecture and the automobile, arguing specifically against the reduction of free time by the daily commute, urbanism's overemphasis on the automobile at the expense of "life itself," an approach to urban design that treated automobiles as if they were "eternal," and the demolition of housing in Paris for freeway construction. Two years later, in "Critique of Urbanism," the situationists continued to argue against the spatial reconfiguration of urban space in which the automobile played a central role, resisting in particular attempts to "lubricate" or "improve," rather than overturn, regressive models of this auto-urbanism, and condemning the construction of suburbs whose only function was the "organization of everyday life" through the exportation of working people (and car workers in particular) out of Paris.²

On the other side of the Atlantic, Jack Kerouac's *On the Road* (1957), Robert Frank's *The Americans* (1958), and Ed Ruscha's *Twentyseven Gas Stations* (1963) all reflect the centrality of the automobile and the ever-expanding freeway system to postwar American identity, and this association of the car with the nation was only reinforced when John F. Kennedy was assassinated while riding in a Lincoln convertible.³ At the same time, Ralph Nader, in collaboration with Cornell researchers, was busily engaged in exactly the kinds of ameliorative activism that the situationists opposed. He celebrated Cornell's "experimental car," which included "over sixty safety concepts," arguing that speed was largely an irrelevant factor in car safety if vehicles were properly designed, and declaring, "In a word, the job, in part, is to make accidents safe."⁴ Nader's safe car, introduced in 1959 in his article "The Safe Car You Can't Buy," resonates differently, however, after Kennedy's assassination in 1963, and we need to understand the success of his bestseller, *Unsafe at Any Speed: The Designed-In Dangers of the American Automobile* (1965), in the context of this modern condition of auto-vulnerability. But while Nader lobbied on behalf of a model of responsibility that ultimately served to reinforce parallel paternalistic relationships between governments and citizens on the one hand, and corporations and consumers on the other, helping to produce a passive citizen-consumer, J. G. Ballard explored the new affective landscapes discovered by characters at the intersection of media technologies and car crashes in both *The Atrocity Exhibition* (1970) and *Crash* (1973). At the same time, the radical architecture group Ant Farm drew attention to the affinities between transportation and media technologies through their staged collision of an automobile into a pyramid of television sets in *Media Burn* (1975), and through their reenactment, in collaboration with T. R. Uthco, of the Kennedy assassination in *The Eternal Frame* (1975) (figures 63–66).⁵ Yet, though these works illuminate the affinities between television and automobile culture within the "society of the spectacle," the shift of emphasis from the car's movement and the roadscape in the late 1950s and early 1960s to the car accident from the mid-1960s throughout the 1970s reflects a changing relationship between these two technologies.

In "Eclipse of the Spectacle," Jonathan Crary argues that the car and television depart from each other in the 1970s, and that this diversion helps to illuminate the difference between Debord's "spectacle" and Jean Baudrillard's "hyperreal." Crary writes, "Up through the 1960s television collaborated with the automobile in sustaining the dominant machinery of capitalist representation: in the virtual annexation of all spaces and the liquidation of any unified signs that had occupied them. The TV screen and the car windshield reconciled visual experience with the velocities and discon-

FIGURE 63 A car crashes into a pyramid of televisions. Photo by Ant Farm. Courtesy of the Berkeley Art Museum and Pacific Film Archives.

FIGURE 64 Artist-President John F. Kennedy (Doug Hall) makes his first public appearance during this media event and video, 4 July 1975. Photo by Chip Lord. Courtesy of the Berkeley Art Museum and Pacific Film Archives.

FIGURE 65 *Eternal Frame* 076. Photo by Chip Lord. Courtesy of the Berkeley Art Museum and Pacific Film Archives.

FIGURE 66 *Eternal Frame* 068. In this shot, Ant Farm and T. R. Uthco seek to match the Zapruder film and key frames from *Life* magazine. Photo by Diane Andrews Hall. Courtesy of the Berkeley Art Museum and Pacific Film Archives.

tinuities of the marketplace."⁶ Yet, he continues, "beginning in the 1970s, this vehicular space began to lose its predominance. Television, which had seemed an ally of the automobile in the maintenance of the commodity-filled terrain of the spectacle, began to be grafted onto other networks. And now the screens of home computer and word processor have succeeded the automobile as 'core products' in an on-going relocation and hierarchization of production processes."⁷ While television's alliance with the automobile had tended, as Crary argues, to normalize subjects, regulating both their relation to objects and their affective landscapes, the transitional period *between* television's early alignment with the linearity of the road and its later mapping onto the computer's networks, codes, and flows of information seems unusually rich with images of technological breakdown, vulnerability, and crisis, and these images generate a wide range of non-normative subjectivities and affects. While Crary faults Baudrillard's theorization of the hyperreal for helping to maintain "the myths of the same cybernetic omnipotence he intends to deplore" by failing to pay attention to breakdowns, "faulty circuits," "systemic malfunction," or "a body that cannot be fully colonized or pacified," I focus here on a film in which the alignment of cars, film, and television goes awry, and explore how this disruption is catalyzed at the site of the auto-accident.⁸

The little-known final two reels of Andy Warhol's seven-reel film, *Since* (1966), depict the assassination of John F. Kennedy, an event described by Ballard as a "special kind of car crash," within the space of the Factory, Warhol's New York studio.⁹ The unfinished film, which premiered posthumously in 2002, collapses the distinction between being driven (in an automobile or by one's drives) and watching television, and this collapse produces not normative, but distinctly queer subjects, affects, and experiences of time.¹⁰ Just as Crary advocates opposing the demands of digital culture "by inducing slow speeds and inhabiting silences," so Warhol brings critical attention to the auto-visual effect through a radical disruption of film time, television time, and the velocity of the automobile.¹¹ While Barthes in "The Third Meaning" sees film time, in contrast to reading time, as lacking a certain freedom, as incapable of making multiple velocities and temporalities of viewing available to the spectator "since the image cannot go faster or slower without losing its perceptual figure," Warhol challenges this presumption about the medium, stretching out the temporality of the film by staging the reenactment and revision of a very particular strip of film:

Abraham Zapruder's footage of the Kennedy assassination, the temporality of which had already been radically fractured as a result of being first published as still, not moving images.[12]

Warhol casts his characters as independent bodies that respond to the assassination as media spectacle not by gawking, but by mimicking the actions they see, as if they somehow inhabited the cinematic memory of the event, yet without being fixed by it. Consequently, the filmstrip seems to emerge not only as the material base of the medium, but also as a metaphorical social space of film spectatorship that encourages viewers to mimic and improvise on the content of the strip. Through its double emphasis on the space of spectatorship and on the space of the event via reenactment, *Since* allows us to recognize multiple possible interactions with the repetition of the media event, and challenges us to think differently about the fantasy structures surrounding the act of watching. In *Since* watching and rewatching emerge not as passive experiences, but as a kind of doing, as forms of imaginal and imaginative living through which alternative narrative forms, power relationships, and subjectivities begin to take shape. As such, the film offers a space for thinking about both the relationship between spectator and media event and the formation of queer media communities that are forged by idiosyncratic "inhabitations" of and variations on media experiences. From critical discussions of star and fan culture, we may be familiar with imitation as a queer mode of watching, and the celebrity status of both Jacqueline Kennedy and John F. Kennedy means that in *Since* we are not completely out of the terrain of impersonation.[13] Yet in the case of *Since*, the primary focus is less on identifying with, "getting inside," or reworking a particular star persona—indeed the film persistently disavows the possibility of staying in character—than on the traumatic event itself. The media communities that emerge are queer not only because *Since* explicitly sexualizes the scene of politics; or because of its cross-gender performances; or because of the excess of affect that distinguishes this reenactment of the assassination. Rather, this film seems queer also, and perhaps primarily, because the characters in *Since* refuse to adhere to the time, casting, and chronology of this mass-mediated historical event.

While discussions of contemporary theory and politics frequently emphasize the present's failure to mobilize in comparison with a nostalgic view of the 1960s, giving little attention to the failures of the previous generation,

Since, like (however unlike) *Weekend* (Jean-Luc Godard, 1967), in fact reveals a pre-1968 engagement with arrested auto-mobility, compulsive repetition, and the seeming inability of its characters to act effectively or progress.[14] Though today, our dominant critical paradigms repeatedly highlight the failure of contemporary artists, theorists, and activists to develop clear paradigms in comparison with the paradigms that emerged in the 1960s, I ask how a film like *Since*—in its comic treatment of the very serious, its sexualization and aestheticization of the political event, and its embrace of confusion, repetition, improvisation, stasis, and incoherence—might help those of us united only by our uncertainty as we think about theoretical, political, and aesthetic paradigms for the present that could establish a potentially more productive, differentiated, and complex relationship with the 1960s. Following Elizabeth Freeman's brilliant engagement with intergenerational feminist and queer relationships, I argue that Warhol's *Since*, in its temporal resonance with the stuttering landscape of the present, destabilizes the paradigm of the "post-," and offers instead an opportunity to investigate the stasis and immobility that has been underemphasized—perhaps to our detriment—in historical accounts of the "movement" generation, a chance, as Freeman puts it, to "imagine the future in terms of experiences that discourse has not yet caught up with, rather than as a legacy passed on between generations."[15] As a member of a generation that is constantly chided for failing to live up to its predecessors' abilities to act up and move on, I offer this reading of *Since*, in conversation with the work of Heather Love, Homay King, Lee Edelman, and Judith Halberstam, all of whom have challenged the linear temporality of progressive political rhetoric. Of these, King's work is particularly relevant to my discussion, for, in her essay on three of Warhol's Edie Sedgwick films, she also asserts a resonance between Warhol's queer film time and Freeman's concept of "temporal drag," linking both to Parker Tyler's use, in 1967, of the polarized terms "dragtime" and "drugtime" to describe the temporal quality of Warhol's films.[16] King does acknowledge, however, that though the temporality described in Tyler's essay works "against the conventional temporality of film spectatorship," it is "not precisely queer"; but how do we distinguish, then, between unconventional film times that seem distinctly queer from those that don't?[17]

Tyler's essay on Warhol's time is not without a sexual dimension, but at times it works to neutralize some of the more radical aspects of Warhollan film time. Tyler does describe Warhol's act of "pasting the camera eye on a limited field of vision" in films like *Empire* and *Sleep* as "perverse," and the "charm" of such films as "more than a trifle masochistic."[18] For Tyler, the "drag" of these films stems from Warhol's stretching out of the experience of film viewing, which he frames as "the most passive psychological state of all the arts because the theater seat itself is habit forming, and because while watching plays, on the contrary, one shares a tension with the live performance."[19] He writes, "Whatever value, market or aesthetic, may be placed on Warhol's pop paintings, they do not demand the passive attention of a fixed (that is, seated) spectator in a film theater. This is what makes the viewing time required for his films into a drag exquisitely nuanced or excruciatingly redundant."[20] Yet, repeatedly, the essay seems to cancel out the radical potential of Warhol's temporal expansions. "Watching a man eat a mushroom," for example, makes spectators feel "chic and restful," Tyler claims, and he attributes the feeling of peace that Warhol's films supposedly elicit in viewers to "the ultra-passivity of the pre-conditioned, relaxing filmgoer."[21] For him, Warhol's "experiments in dragtime" also "logically predicted an inoculation of the unwinding reel with drugtime," with drugtime emerging as "the other pole of dragtime," filling the emptiness of dragtime with "magic beauties."[22] Though Douglas Crimp has recently argued that we might find radical possibilities for reimagining relationality outside of paradigms of identification and disidentification in the narcissism of Warhol's films, for Tyler, drugtime pacifies spectators and redirects "the sadistic impulse, like the erotic impulse" suggested on-screen by the presence, for example, of "Leather Boys," into a form of "narcotized narcissism" that he sees, in what is presumably a derogatory dismissal, as being "best suited to Lesbian delusions of grandeur."[23]

Since—which Warhol shot in 1966, only one year before Tyler published his essay—offers an interesting space through which to think these generalized comments about passive spectatorship, gender, sexuality, and time in relation to Warhol's films more specifically, because while Tyler's entire argument about time is founded on an essentialized model of passive film spectatorship, *Since* foregrounds the alternative spectatorial behavior made possible by the private viewing space of television (a brightly lit couch rather than a darkened auditorium seat) while simultaneously opening out this private behavior onto a public space by casting the couch in a second role: the Kennedys' Lincoln convertible.

The Catastrophic Time of *Since* and Cinema

Since disrupts habitual modes of perceiving and experiencing mediated time by inhabiting and internally disrupting the contemporary mediated landscape. While cinema's temporality is often aligned with narratives of progress and uninterrupted forward motion, *Since* stages multiple, at times contradictory temporal experiences, simultaneous experiences of suffering and witnessing, remembering and imitating, performing and improvising. Through his representation of a particularly formative auto-media-disaster, the assassination of JFK, Warhol stages cinema's capacity to represent competing, not singular or linear, time frames and modes of experiencing the historical event caught on film, but he also explicitly links this temporal multiplicity to the question of sexual identity.

August Lumière once famously declared that cinema was "an invention without a future," presciently capturing the way that cinema would always be haunted by the specter of its own obsolescence.[24] The medium's engagement with its own finitude, its necessary embrace of its structural obsolescence (made manifest in the inevitability of the film's end), stands in tension with assumptions about the progressive linearity of filmic time, which might also connote a conservative politics in which film is equated with the idea that the record of the past is fixed, that history is unchangeable. Warhol's filmic reenactments of the Kennedy assassination engage directly the media spectacle of American politics; they also address how the mass mediation of political events shapes the temporality of personal and political subjectivity. *Since* does this not by occupying a position that claims to be outside of the media, but rather by transforming media time from within.

Temporal confusion is immediately foregrounded by the film's title, *Since*, for which the *Oxford English Dictionary* offers several definitions, including (1) Then, thereupon; immediately afterwards; (2) At some time between now and then; subsequently, later; (3) Before now; (4) Ever or continuously from a specified time till now; (5) From the time when; and (6) Because; seeing that. In short, the word encapsulates something of the ruptured time of trauma, a temporal confusion suggested by Freud's notion of *Nachträglichkeit* (translated by Jean Laplanche as "afterwardsness"), and resulting in a proliferation of competing temporalities that trouble the status of the event, narrative, and subjectivity, and leave the subject shuttling around in unanchored temporal landscapes.[25]

Automobile Disasters and the Visual Culture of the 1960s and 1970s

While in the films of the 1920s, the automobile still functioned as a somewhat experimental technology, prone to breakdown and accident, during the 1950s and 1960s, the cinematic car, continuing in the path of earlier travel genres, gradually became aligned with fantasies of uninhibited motion toward as-yet unrealized dreams of the future, of liberation from domesticity and the constraints of postwar society. Yet even in its heyday, the automobile struck some as an obsolescent technology, as a technology less of movement than of stasis, entrapment, and social control. For Roland Barthes in 1963, the advent of space travel had already punctured the dream of "auto-mobility" and rendered it obsolete: "It's normal that the car loses all heroic fables, because today, adventure has been entirely absorbed by the exploration of space; in the face of these cosmic engines, the car can't possibly fulfill a single fantasy of movement into the unknown; from now on, it's an immobilized object."[26] Disrupting the Road Movie's perpetual fantasy of the car as vehicle for escaping the feminized space of the home, Barthes declares simply, "The car is a house," reinforcing Guy Debord's earlier claim, in 1959, that the private automobile is less a means of transportation than a vehicle for restructuring social space and human relations according to models of developed capitalism.[27] Though the car's emergence as an immobile object may signal its mythological demise, for some filmmakers and artists, this coming to a halt marks the technology's moment of greatest interest.[28]

The assassination of Kennedy in his Lincoln Continental on 22 November 1963 marked a turning point in the way automobiles appeared in art and film, unleashing not only the largely repressed figure of the accident, but also, perhaps surprisingly, the comic tone that had been associated with the accident at an earlier cinematic moment. Kennedy's assassination disrupted the dream machine's promise of unrestrained forward mobility, physical invulnerability, and access to a better life, and replaced this image with one of vulnerability, stasis, and death-as-media-spectacle.[29] Nineteen sixty-three, the first year in which vehicular suicide was the subject of psychiatric research, perhaps as a result of despairing people hoping at least to die in presidential style, was the year of the car accident.[30] In the assassination's wake appeared a series of disaster images, including the publication of thirty-one small black-and-white frame enlargements from Zapruder's film of Kennedy's assassination in *Life* magazine on 29 November 1963, followed, in 1964, by the magazine's publication of nine 8" × 5" color frame enlargements alongside a text by Gerald Ford; Warhol's *Death and Disaster* series; Bruce Conner's film *Report* (1963–67) and his installation *Television Assassination* (1963–64/1995); John Waters's 1968 reenactment of the assassination, *Eat Your Makeup*, starring Divine as Jackie Kennedy; and later, Ant Farm's and T. R. Uthco's reenactment of the assassination, in *The Eternal Frame* (1975).[31] In addition to these works, which openly engage the assassination, are less explicit responses, like Wolf Vostell's *Car Crash* (1965–67); the increasingly graphic depiction of death on the road in films like *Bonnie and Clyde* (Arthur Penn, 1967), *Easy Rider* (Dennis Hopper, 1969), and *Medium Cool* (Haskell Wexler, 1969); the proliferation of highly artificial, staged "accidents," so common in the 1960s work of Jean-Luc Godard, who, in films such as *Contempt* (1963), *Pierrot le fou* (1965), and *Weekend* (1967), created landscapes littered with the bodies of wrecked cars and drivers; and finally, J. G. Ballard's exhibition of crashed cars at the New Arts Laboratory in London in 1970, and the publication, also in 1970, of his *The Atrocity Exhibition* and, in 1973, of his novel *Crash*. The worlds of art and film seemed to confirm the government's sense that the car crash was some form of epidemic, and traces of the special car accident permeate the culture, in spite of, or perhaps because of, the fact that the Zapruder footage was not shown on television until March 1975.[32]

In his detailed account of visual responses to JFK's assassination, Art Simon makes several distinctions among the artists most frequently associated with this event, distinguishing, for example, both the "collage aesthetic" of Bruce Conner's *Report* and the "textual appropriations that characterize the Warhol silkscreens" from the Ant Farm's and T. R. Uthco's "more parodic gesture" in their video *The Eternal Frame*.[33] Simon further remarks on the difference between Warhol's and Conner's treatments of the body: "In Warhol's work from the early sixties, the body appears an artificial surface, distanced through repetition and the poses of the publicity still. It is a replacement body, a bloodless copy.... Conner's relationship to the body (almost always female) appears less detached, a fascination founded on attraction and horror which results in representations of texture and a greater sense of corporeality."[34] Finally, in his transition between a discussion of Warhol's silk-screened disaster images and Conner's films, Simon notes, "For all their rich encounters with the contours of the case,

DISASTER TIME | 147

the work of Warhol, Kienholz, and Paschke was confined by its stasis. Silkscreen, sculpture, and painting were somehow not elusive enough, unable to fully challenge perception and therefore rehearse the problems of camera vision."[35]

What is missing from this discussion of Warhol's depictions of the assassination as bodiless and static is, of course, an awareness of his films, which have recently become more familiar to contemporary audiences as the restorations are gradually made available, as well as through Callie Angell's outstanding catalogue raisonné.[36] David M. Lubin, in his discussion of the visual ramifications of Kennedy's death, *Shooting Kennedy*, begins to address the importance of Warhol's films to the media coverage of the assassination by drawing attention to the aesthetic affinities that exist between Warhol's *Sleep* and *Blow-Job* (1963) and Zapruder's footage, but we need to extend this discussion to include Warhol's actual cinematic restaging of the assassination in *Since*.[37] Yet it is necessary first to address some key questions about the works that exist in closest proximity to *Since*. First, what are the spectatorial and political paradigms suggested by Warhol's silkscreened disaster images? Second, how does Bruce Conner activate repetition and comedy in his two assassination works, and how does his use of these two effects compare with Warhol's? And finally, what is the nature of the Ant Farm's and T. R. Uthco's use of comedy and reenactment in *The Eternal Frame*?

While Susan Sontag, in a passing mention of the disaster images, denounces Warhol as "that connoisseur of death and high priest of the delights of apathy," Hal Foster, in his essay "Death in America," argues for the inadequacy of both the postmodern reading of Warhol's disaster images as simulacral and impassive, and Thomas Crow's reading of Warhol as a politically engaged truth-teller.[38] As an alternative, Foster introduces the term "traumatic realism" in order to highlight the disaster silk-screens as at once referential and simulacral, as works that activate the repetition compulsion in order both to defend against affect in the face of traumatic images and to produce it in opening out to the trauma of those images.[39] Yet while Foster locates the silk-screens' "punctum" effect in the "popping" of reproduced press images through technique, "especially through the 'floating flashes' of the silkscreen process," that is, in the minor deviations from exact repetition, in *Since*, a film in which the actual photographic images of the assassination never appear, repetition emerges less as the recurrence of exactly the same than as a symptom of the film's nonlinear temporality.[40] Reenactment emerges as an alternative to reproduction, less a copy of a familiar mediated image than an attempt of individuals to capture, through performance, an "open" or incomplete media experience that has both a collective and an individual dimension, to convey simultaneously a particular event mediated by images and the evolving experience of those images as images over time. Although *Since* operates under an aesthetic of repetition, its recursive temporality never returns to a familiar place. Instead, the film suspends both "actors" and viewers in a perpetual state of having just begun again, but in a slightly different place and manner. If the silk-screens address a mass subject forged in the face of the media spectacle of technological disaster, as Foster suggests, *Since* disavows any coherence of this mass subject and represents instead a loosely affiliated group of people who, though they at times seem on the threshold of getting together, never quite accede to being assembled, and whose repetitions of "the event" are constantly undermined by their flawed memories of that event, by their misunderstandings of their roles and what is expected of them, by their relative states of consciousness, and by the disruptive "noise" of other parallel conversations and events.

Warhol's silk-screen disaster images may invoke suspicions of aloofness and impassivity, but they are never funny in the way Conner's *Report* and *Television Assassination*, Ant Farm's and T. R. Uthco's *The Eternal Frame*, and Warhol's *Since* all are. And yet, in considering these last four works alongside each other, it is important not to collapse the differences between their respective uses of comedy. While the comic element consistently emerges out of the structural repetitions in each of the media's representations of the assassination, death and comedy interact differently in each example. Unlike *The Eternal Frame* and *Since*, which reenact the mediated event, Conner's *Report* and *Television Assassination* both use actual footage shot off the television from around the time of the assassination.[41] As Conner juxtaposes footage of Kennedy's death with commercial images—of "Mrs. Middle Majority" and her refrigerator in *Report*, of high-heeled shoes superimposed over Kennedy's head in *Television Assassination*—the resulting humor satirizes the commodification of both the Kennedys and the assassination, and unveils the collusion of consumer capitalism, the culture of spectacle, violence, and death. David Mosen, in his review of *Report* from 1966, defends Conner's "welding of death and comedy" as satire, and celebrates the film's unprecedented "sense of horror, humor and truth," stating,

"Conner's film loop makes some of us indignant for his apparent irreverence to one of the sacred moments of our time. (He treats a more authentic martyr similarly, with his large awful blood-dripping assemblage of a crucifix.) But who can watch *Report* to the end without realizing that Conner is as serious as Jonathan Swift in *Gulliver's Travels* and that his brand of social consciousness in its expression must transcend conventional morality?"[42] Conner is certainly no stranger to the aesthetics of early film comedy and its penchant for comic automobile disasters. Indeed, as Bruce Jenkins has noted, the "gags" in *A Movie* (1958), which include some spectacular car crashes, hark back to the Marx Brothers's *Duck Soup* (Leo McCarey, 1933), although Jenkins claims that Conner's editing renders this style of comedy "far more transgressive."[43] But the laughter evoked by *Report* is not that of the slapstick audience's response to technological disaster. Instead, Conner describes it as "nervous" and "suppressed," because of its proximity to Kennedy's death, its implication of audiences in that death, and its quality of what Mosen describes as "alien detachment."[44]

If *The Eternal Frame*, Ant Farm's and T. R. Uthco's much later, on-location reenactment and video recording of the assassination, lacks the quality of detachment found in Conner's filmic responses to the assassination, these two works nevertheless share, in spite of their differences, an intimate relationship to Zapruder's documentary recording of the event and that recording's indexical claims. Yet their respective relationships to the documentary emerge in radically distinct ways. Conner, denied access to the Zapruder footage, edits together television footage of the Kennedys' time in Dallas, with appropriated sound and commercial images, thereby retaining a direct—but defamiliarized—indexical link to the event in spite of the film's experimental use of montage, which disrupts the temporality and sequence of the original footage. Ant Farm instead conjures up precise memories of the Zapruder film through a meticulously choreographed reenactment in which fidelity to Zapruder's film plays a central role. As the *Village Voice* reported, in 1975, "They researched every photograph of the original event they could find for spatial relationships. They obtained a copy of the Zapruder film and studied it for hours. 'Then we consulted make-up artists so each of us could play the necessary parts, such as JFK, Connally, and Secret Service agent Hill,' says Michels, who portrayed Jacqueline in the recreation. 'We practiced and timed the event like a ballet. We made it look exactly like the original.'"[45] Indeed part of what is interesting about *The*

Eternal Frame is its ability to conjure up a memory of the indexical record of the film in a videotaped reenactment of it, in spite of its parodic tone and the fact that Jackie Kennedy is played by a man (a variation on this use of cross-dressing was deployed in *Since*, and Jim Dine's earlier happening, *Car Crash* (1960), featured a man-woman and a woman-man, suggesting a certain pattern of gender-crossing within the space of the car accident). *The Eternal Frame*'s complexity also lies in its juxtaposition of the temporality of Zapruder's film, made with a medium of indexical traces, which offers, as Philip Rosen points out, "no possibility of liveness," with their own recording of the reenactment on video, which offers the possibility of "live" indexicality, but which has failed to capture the actual assassination, only its reenactment.[46]

The comedy of *Since* and its relationship to the indexical record of Kennedy's assassination differ from the abovementioned examples, yet we can usefully begin to approach some of these differences via Bruce Jenkins's comments on Conner's *Report* and *Television Assassination*: "In contrast to *Report*, then, *Television Assassination* focuses on the reception of the assassination and its impact on the home front rather than in its mythic construction. A less iconic work than *Report*, it chronicles, as Brakhage has suggested, Conner's 'immediate capturing of his immediate feelings.'"[47] While Warhol never turns completely away from the iconic images that play a central role in his work, *Since* focuses less on those images than on the way the mass-mediated disaster leaves viewers suspended between a public event and the private space in which that event is received. The film provokes us to reflect on the relationship between the time of the event and the time of watching by evoking the mass-mediated images of the Kennedys only through acts of mimicry; and as on-screen viewers enact these couch performances, they leave open the possibility that the supposedly passive viewers of *Since* might in turn start imitating what they see on-screen, touching or even switching identities with the people around them.

The Politics of the Couch: Spectatorship, Performance, and Confusion

David Lubin notes, in passing, the disparity between Warhol's own description of his reception of the news of Kennedy's death and the account offered by John Giorno, and this difference resonates with Warhol's cinematic depiction of the assassination three years after the event.[48] Warhol states, "When President Kennedy was shot that fall, I heard the news over the radio while I was alone painting in my studio. I don't think I missed a stroke. I wanted to know what was going on out there, but that was the extent of my reaction.... I'd been thrilled having Kennedy as president; he was handsome, young, smart—but it didn't bother me that much that he was dead."[49] By contrast, Giorno, who ran over to Warhol's home on hearing the news, offers the following narrative: "We sat on the couch watching the live coverage from Dallas.... I started crying and Andy started crying.... Andy kept saying, 'I don't know what it means!'"[50] In the former account, Warhol experiences the news of the assassination alone and aurally, on the radio, in the space of the studio, and the experience seems devoid of both images and affect. In the latter account, however, the assassination emerges as an emotional, televisual viewing experience shared by Warhol and Giorno over an extended period of time on the intimate space of the couch, during which Warhol characteristically responds by repeating himself. Though it might be useful to remember Thomas Crow's comment that "it would be difficult to name an artist who has been as successful as Warhol in controlling the interpretation of his own work," and to maintain a certain skepticism regarding Warhol's own descriptions of himself, *Since* mirrors these apparently contradictory responses to the assassination—the persistent, almost affectless, production of images on the one hand, and emotional, traumatic spectatorship on the other.[51]

The last two reels of the unfinished film *Since* were made in the autumn of 1966, after *Hedy* (February 1966) and *Chelsea Girls* (summer 1966), both of which marked radical shifts in Warhol's film practices. *Since*, however, was never released in Warhol's lifetime, the final two reels premiering only in November 2002 at Princeton University as part of a conference focusing on "the first pop age," giving the film an additional quality of belatedness that supplements its inherent preoccupation with indexical media's production of "temporal drag," its ability to render us present to a past event.[52] The film's suspended temporal and spatial coordinates—in the time of "since," in the time between the event and its reenactment, in the time between the film's production and premiere, and in the space between private and public, between the Factory couch and Dealey Plaza—not only foreground the issue of temporal between-ness, of then and now, but also prepare the ground for discussion of Godard's *Weekend* and the contemporary interest in that film's figures of "stuckness": the traffic jam and the car crash. *Since* (1966/2002) constitutes, along with Conner's *Report* (1963–

67), one of the earliest cinematic responses to the assassination and to *Life* magazine's subsequent publication of stills from the Zapruder film.[53] *Since* seems to be less a critique of the media coverage of the assassination than an exploration of the interconnected temporal, spatial, spectatorial, and sexual possibilities opened up by the rupture those images enact. Perhaps the most important of these ruptures involves the blurring of the distinction between the profilmic space and the space of the viewing subject, resulting in a situation where watching emerges as a kind of mimetic action that responds to the mass-mediated images being viewed.[54] Yet even though this mimesis at one level functions as a form of traumatic repetition, this repetition also generates a kind of excess that produces a particular form of comic energy, allowing the film increasingly to depart from the primary images with each reenactment, and improvisations and on-screen interactions gradually take on their own momentum. While, as Bill Nichols notes, multiple reenactments within the context of documentary filmmaking can offer filmmakers representing historical events an opportunity to register "the subjective processes by which we each construct a history that corresponds to present needs," *Since*'s reenactments do not function in this way.[55] Rather, the on-screen performances explore, through repetition and variation, the crisis of personal and political subjectivity ushered in by the experience of witnessing mediated death. As it confuses the profilmic space (the Lincoln convertible) with the space of television viewing (the couch), *Since* performs the possibility of a different kind of cinema, a corporeal cinema that emerges less as explicit critique than as dramatization of the excesses (spectacularization, commodification, and repetition) and absences (the Zapruder film) of the media culture highlighted by the other contemporaneous assassination works discussed above. Though the paradigm of absorption may be inescapable here, *Since* disrupts the trajectory by reversing the direction of the mass media's receptive flow; instead of the spectator disappearing into the mass spectacle of disaster, the spectacle of Kennedy's assassination seems, in *Since*, to have been absorbed and transformed by the bodies on the couch. When it reappears through performance, "the event" has multiplied and become inextricable from the singularity of each individual's performance.

These two reels of *Since*, shot on color stock, loosely depict two primary events: the assassination of JFK and the murder of Lee Harvey Oswald, each event occurring in a different space of the Factory, with different cast members, and with some significant variation in shooting style. The assassination scenes take place on the Factory couch—a piece of furniture that had been thoroughly sexualized since its starring role in *Couch* (1964)—which stands in for Kennedy's Lincoln convertible and is located in a part of the Factory where the walls are painted red, yellow, and silver (as opposed to the uniformly silver décor of the Silver Factory of 1964–65). Yet if the couch is a sexualized space, it functions, like the car's backseat, which it doubles, as a "transitional" or adolescent sexual space, one that belies the sanctioned and plotted narrative that leads to the concluding destination of the marital bed. Indeed, perhaps Warhol's most significant departure from other responses to the assassination lies in his decision to restage the event in the space of the Factory in a way that brings together the site of the event (the Lincoln Continental) with the site of the public's private and affective reception of the event (the couch), emphasizing not the television set itself, as Conner does, but the affective and physical experience of living in the vicinity of the set's images. By conflating these two spaces within this film, Warhol not only links the surprise of the back-seat assassination to unscripted sexual encounters, but also offers an alternative way of imaging the relationship between the victims of disaster and those who watch them die. But how does the film move between these two arenas of event and spectatorship?

In each reel, early psychedelic scenes loosely depicting Kennedy's assassination give way to scenes of Oswald's assassination, which are staged in a part of the Factory where the walls are still painted silver and which feature an almost exclusively male cast. Ondine, one of Warhol's film stars, takes center stage as Lyndon Johnson in the Kennedy assassination scenes, and, as Callie Angell has suggested, some of the temporal confusion of *Since* arises from Ondine's own uncertainty about his character's relationship to time. He is unsure, for example, of whether or not he is president as he sits on a swivel chair located next to the couch, verbally emphasizing his chronological and character confusion with asides like "Looking back . . . I'm president, but not president yet" and, in the second reel, "I was sure I was Kennedy." But the uncertainty of assigned roles extends beyond issues relating to the chronological confusion surrounding Johnson's inauguration as president within the film. (We must surely be forgiven for confusing American history with a Ballard novel—as one president dies in a car, another is sworn in on a plane, the former president's wife by his side, at Love Field Airport.) Ondine is not just confused about the identity of himself and other characters—saying, for example, to Ingrid Superstar, who plays the role of Lady Bird Johnson, "Ingrid, I mean Lady Bird . . ." and, more aggressively, "Oh Ingrid! I'm sorry, but you just look like Ingrid. Ingrid! Look like Lady Bird!"—for he is also quite frustrated at a more fundamental level by the general inability of the group to establish *any* sense of character. As a voice announces, "All right, we're going to roll it—we're going down that avenue," Ondine (as Johnson) declares, "We weren't there!" a realization confirmed by Ingrid Superstar (as Lady Bird Johnson), "Ahh—that's right, we weren't there." Ultimately Ondine concludes, "I hate to be the announcer of this, but I think we're all lacking in character. I mean . . . I have one, shaky as it is. I'm trying to maintain mine."

Ondine, moving in and out of the character of President Johnson, expresses some of his frustration in the form of misogynist comments muttered mainly in the direction of Ingrid Superstar as Lady Bird Johnson: "You just be quiet now"; "You had better be my first lady—Now! C'mon, I'm the new president and I don't like it. . . . Anyway, I want you to take your place at my side on the floor"; "Shut up!"; "I can't work with this set of people . . . they're all boring, even the French one"; or "Boredom! . . . You dreary housewife—What's wrong with you people?" Yet we should be wary of extending Ondine's misogyny to the film itself, for his dismissive comments stand in tension with the film's casting of female "actors" in a number of prominent roles, including cross-gender roles. Mary Woronov, perhaps the first female president on film, plays JFK; Ingrid Superstar, of course, plays "Looney Bird" Johnson; and Susan Bottomly (or International Velvet) plays Jackie Kennedy, first lady to a female president in drag.[56] However, just as Ondine has trouble staying in his role, the rest of the cast is similarly at liberty to move in and out of character. Indeed, an off-screen voice at the opening of the first reel emphasizes this fluidity, telling the actors that they "don't have to maintain character designations" and that "one individual can assume another's role." Consequently, characters from the assassination find themselves pairing up with characters from the Factory (Ondine and Lady Bird Johnson; Ingrid Superstar and JFK), just as characters from the Dealey Plaza scenario meet each other in unexpected ways through chance encounters on the couch, as when Lady Bird Johnson and JFK start messing around with each other halfway through the first reel.

While a voice off-screen declares that it's "marvelous being in Dallas with the President," the camera suddenly gives way to rapid and frenetic movements—zoom out, zoom in, wild pan right, zoom out, zoom in; and in the midst of this nauseating camerawork, a sheet of red construction paper is violently crumpled before the camera. The Zapruder film's indexical image of the presidential wound is replaced by a piece of red paper, and Ondine further disrupts any possibility of realism by discussing rehearsals for the scene and by reading his lines (as LBJ) stiltedly from a paper: "This is a sad time for all people.... This is a lot that cannot be weighed... erm." He looks not at the camera, but at the shotgun mike that enters the frame, highlighting the disparity between sound and image that constitutes one of the film's other strategies for representing the experience of ruptured meaning and confusion. In the wake of his words, the camera begins again to zoom in and out of focus on the red piece of paper, until the color fully fills the screen. As the camera cuts back to Ondine, Ivy Nicholson, wearing bright-red fishnet stockings, sits behind him, her legs becoming visually aligned with the red paper that the film associates with Kennedy's wound, as though these disaster images might actually be contagious.

While Warhol depicts the rupturing effect of Kennedy's assassination in the first part of each reel through the abstract use of color and wild camera movements, he depicts Oswald's assassination using quite different aesthetic strategies. First, stark lighting combines with the silver background of the Factory walls to create a sense of intense flatness and two-dimensionality, an effect reinforced by calmer camerawork and by the way the "actors" tend to line up horizontally within the frame, rather than cluster in groups around the Factory (on the couch, behind Ondine), as they do in the Kennedy assassination scenes. Again, the phallic "weapon" of choice is the banana, which characters in this scene proceed to peel and consume, recalling the faux fellatio of Mario Montez in Warhol's film *Mario Banana* (1964).[57] But this banana eating (which, like the reference to *Couch*, only further reinforces our sense of shuttling between different temporal and cinematic moments) marks only the beginning of the homoeroticism that suffuses the depiction of Oswald's assassination.

As the camera cuts between the act of banana eating and the crotches of the men, we hear the words "Bang-ow-bang-ow." These "bangs" and cries of pain, however, seem only loosely bound to the site of the assassination, which increasingly gives way to a sexualized, sadomasochistic space. While the assassin bends over suggestively with his hands against the silver wall, ready to be searched, other male actors wander around the space of the frame, cracking leather whips on the ground. Unlike the couch sequences, these erotic performances seem to be directed neither at other actors nor at the (often disinterested) camera, each person existing largely in isolation from the others. Addressing exactly the sense that each of Warhol's actors appears to be "lost in his own narcissistic space" in an earlier film, *Horse* (1964), Douglas Crimp compares the actors' behavior both with the cruising style known as "stand-and-pose" and with the narcissism he attributes to Warhol's camera: "The quality of narcissism adopted by the actors begins to be assumed by Warhol's camera itself, which enacts its own self-sufficiency as it moves in and around the actors and set independent of the storyline, of who is speaking, or even of where within the mise-en-scène the actors' activities are taking place."[58] For Crimp, this narcissism is only one of many aspects of Warhol's films that work to effect the "complete dissolution of relationships and stories as we know them" and to offer "a radically new scene in which the self finds itself not through its identification or disidentification with the other, but in its singularity among all the singular things of the world that it can 'inhabit.'"[59] Furthermore, the ability to "maintain both the self and other in fundamental distinctiveness" is, for Crimp, "the radical meaning of queer," a distinctiveness on which "an ethical sociality might depend."[60] While the distinctiveness that Crimp locates in *Horse* also exists in the silver scenes of *Since*, the Kennedy-assassination scenes in which women play a major role offer an alternative, more confused relation to the figure of the other than the one outlined by Crimp, and the tension between these two modes of being, performed in parallel within the Factory, constitutes an important dimension of *Since*'s engagement with the question of the subject and its relationship to mediated political spectacle.

In the wake of the (first) assassination, the camera focuses on Jackie Kennedy (Susan Bottomly), smoking and wearing a black hooded mini dress and long black boots, as she begins the first of several crawls along the back of the sofa, imitating Jacqueline Kennedy's crawl across the back of the Lincoln Continental, before the camera returns once again to zooming in and out on the red paper (figure 67). After a fast and dizzying 360-degree pan, we return to the red paper again, which we have begun to equate with John F. Kennedy's death. But just when we think that the "assassination" is over, an off-screen voice declares, "All right, we're going to roll it. We're going down that avenue," reminding us that we have seen nothing but improvisations and that the "real event" is yet to come—and will perhaps always be "to

FIGURE 67 Jacqueline Kennedy crawls across the trunk of the Lincoln Continental following the shooting of John F. Kennedy. Still from the Zapruder film.

come" in the strange time of *Since* and cinematic death. Once again the camera swings around wildly, and as the paper rustles, the camera alights on various out-of-focus faces. As "Jackie" lights another cigarette, the assassins approach the car-sofa with their murder weapons: bananas and giant inflatable Baby Ruth bars, which highlight the comedic and queer potential of excessive masculinity as they frame the phallic weapons as sweet, edible, and, in the case of the Baby Ruth bar, comically inflated.[61] We try hopelessly to follow the distorted soundtrack, on which we hear comments that range from "He's dead, laying there in his own blood" to discussions about the rehearsals and what did or did not happen at the actual assassination, but the camera again begins to zoom in and out in stuttering, steplike increments. After more rustling of the paper, a page of a calendar is shakily held up before the camera—"Friday November 22"—foregrounding the question of what it means to cinematically represent or reenact an event, to make a historical film.

Callie Angell has suggested that we might view the wild camera movements of this film as representing the view from the car, and this seems like a plausible interpretation. But in order to distinguish the conflation of car and camera we see in *Since* from the very different conflation of car and camera in the Road Movie's traveling shots taken by a camera mounted on the side of the car, it is important to note that in *Since* the swirling pans and the nauseating zooms are all shot from a relatively static subject position, and they all resist the linearity and inevitability of progress that views from a moving car imply. In *Since* the simultaneity of camera movement and auto-stasis resonates with the parallel relationship evoked by Bottomly's embodied performance of a subjectivity that shifts chiasmically between Jackie Kennedy and the viewing subject, and that by extension offers the viewer a traumatic crossing of experiences, rather than a full identificatory dissolve. Warhol's frantic filming of Bottomly's crawl along the back of the Factory couch-car captures the response of a physically empathetic viewer of on-screen disaster to a subject of disaster who also emerges as both subject and spectator. For Bottomly's repeated crawl not only mimics the crawl of Jackie Kennedy, but also seems to imitate the medium's ability to go back and redo the event. Though this quality of the medium usually implies film's conservative aspect, the performances of Warhol's cast suggest that the repetitions of the mass media also have the potential to produce an evolving, and potentially critical, sense of the historic event, and in this sense Bottomly's performance resists the petrification of history. The couch's stasis, doubled by the relatively fixed position of the camera, which seems to "gaze" around wildly without moving forward or backward within the physical space of the Factory, suggests something more complex than a simple collapsing of the difference between the space of the event (the Lincoln Continental) and the space of its reception (the couch), between Jackie Kennedy and Susan Bottomly as spectator. When Bottomly mimetically doubles the actions of Jackie Kennedy, she refuses the position of the mass subject described by Hal Foster: "Now even as the mass subject may worship an idol only to gloat over his or her fall, so too it may mourn the dead in a disaster only to be warmed by the bonfire of these bodies.... [T]he mass subject reveals its sadomasochistic aspect, for this subject is often split in relation to a disaster: even as he or she may mourn the victims, even identify with them masochistically, he or she may also be thrilled, sadistically, that there *are* victims of whom he or she is *not* one."[62] In contrast to both the mass subject Foster describes and the isolated narcissistic subject of the Oswald assassination scenes, Bottomly's performance neither embraces the sadistic "not me" position of the mass subject who willingly sacrifices his or her own distinctiveness in order not to be the subject of disaster, nor masochistically dissolves into the role of Jackie Kennedy. Instead, she performs a relation to the traumatized subject of disaster by falling in and out of her different roles, experiencing herself in close corporeal proximity to Jackie Kennedy, "crawling nearby," without either becoming her or disavowing her presence. Like Warhol's other actors, who are never compelled to "maintain character designations," Bottomly is never fully or hysterically absorbed into the role of Jackie Kennedy, a fact made visible by her interactions with other actors between crawls and by the way she pauses midcrawl to light another cigarette. Yet by refusing to fully distance herself from Jackie Kennedy, by actively embodying or trying out the traumatic "backwards" behavior of the mediated subject of the disaster, Bottomly also asserts a subjectivity that acknowledges its investment in an other whose relationship to her remains somewhat opaque.

chapter five

FILM FALLS APART

Crash, Semen, and Pop

While the media spectacle of auto-disaster sends the characters in Warhol's *Since* in search of new experiences of spectatorship, time, identity, and relationality, in J. G. Ballard's novel *Crash* (1973), auto-collision provides vocabulary and a backdrop for exploring the affinities between non-normative sexual encounters and the attempt to translate one medium into another. Although the critical turn toward medium-specific questions is often enacted as a corrective to, or turning away from, social and cultural questions, in *Crash* sexual encounters become inextricably bound to the novel's efforts to translate the materiality of film into words.

Crash follows the lives of some strange people in London, all of whom have been involved in at least one car accident and have subsequently become obsessed with the idea that car crashes have the potential to unleash a new sexuality. At the heart of the novel stands Vaughan, a mad scientist who obsessively stages, photographs, and films the scenes of car wrecks. He is particularly driven by his vision of dying in a car crash with Elizabeth Taylor, who happens to be in London at the time the novel is set. The three other major characters in the book are a fictionalized James Ballard, who directs automobile advertisements for television; his wife, Catherine, a pilot-in-training whose sexual interest in her husband is revived after he becomes involved in a crash; and Dr. Helen Remington, whom Ballard meets in the head-on collision that kills Remington's husband.

Hal Foster describes *Crash* as Ballard's "great pop novel" and the "best complement to Warhol in fiction," and he links these two figures through their shared interest in the breakdown of outside and inside, which Foster equates with trauma.[1] While Warhol says of pop, "It's just like taking the outside and putting it on the inside, or taking the inside and putting it on the outside," Ballard writes in his introduction to *Crash*, "In the past we have always assumed that the external world around us has represented reality, and that the inner world of our minds, its dreams, hopes, ambitions, represented the realm of fantasy and the imagination. These roles, it seems to me, have been reversed."[2] This suggestive classification of *Crash* as a pop novel has not been explored as fully as it might have been, perhaps because the novel's "pop" elements have hitherto been regarded as distinct from its representations of sex, which have dominated *Crash*'s reception history to date. Jean Baudrillard, for example, angered some readers with his controversial essay "Ballard's *Crash*" (1991), primarily because of what was perceived as an uncritical and "obscene" celebration of the sexual possibilities opened up through the (usually feminized) site of the wound: "Every gash, every mark, every bruise, every scar left on the body is an artificial invagination.... And these few natural orifices which we are accustomed to associate with sex and sexual activities are nothing in comparison to all these potential wounds ... to all these openings through which the body turns itself inside out and, like certain topologies, no longer possesses an inside or an outside.[3]

Problematic as Baudrillard's essay may be in its too easy disregard of the body's pain, it does usefully insist that we read the traumatic movement between inside and outside, the movement *Crash* shares with pop art, in a sexual context. The *Pop Out* volume of 1996 has played a key role in opening a sexualized space in which to think about pop in new ways, as has the recent work of Douglas Crimp, but in spite of this new space, feminist concerns remain largely absent from the scholarship on pop art.[4] How, then, can we usefully think of *Crash* in relation to pop art, not in order to turn away from questions of sexual difference and sexuality toward a (desexualized) discussion of pop's engagement with issues of medium specificity, but rather to fold these two questions in on each other in the hope of animating both?

As long as our readings of "sexual difference" in *Crash* remain essentially grounded in the biological specificity of male and female bodies, and as long as the pleasure of reading for feminists depends on the novel's ability to represent male and female sexual practices and desires in new and equally satisfying ways, *Crash* will always seem woefully inadequate.[5] Men in *Crash* do quite well, at least at first glance. They produce prodigious quantities of bodily fluids, and Ballard generously reimagines and reconfigures their seminiferous bodies accordingly. The head of Vaughan's "powerful hose of a penis" comes equipped with a "sharp notch, like a canal for surplus semen," a run-off the man does indeed seem to need.[6] The "fresh-scent of his well-showered body" is immediately overlaid "by the tang of [his] semen moistening in his trousers" as soon as he passes his first car wreck, and his body emits a permanent and not unpleasant "dank odor" of semen and rectal mucous combined with engine coolant.[7] The female characters generally lack this pungent animal magnetism, and the descriptions of female sexual bodies seem clichéd and derogatory by comparison: Catherine's "vulva," we are told, is "like a wet flower," and James describes his wife's masturbation as "fingers groveling at her pubis as if rolling to death some small venereal snot."[8] The severely injured body of Gabrielle is no better off with its "inert nub of a clitoris."[9]

In spite of the sexual limitations of *Crash*'s female bodies, I remain reluctant to dismiss the novel's feminist potential, even at the level of the material body. In addition to the possibility that Ballard acknowledges, through his recourse to clichés, language's consistent failure to represent female sexuality, we should also note that his representation of the male body is far from simple. While Ballard appears to revel in descriptions of Vaughan's "hard groin" and "jutting" penis, such moments are juxtaposed with passages that show this same organ's capacity to make women gag when they have it shoved down their throats, and through such juxtapositions, which I interpret as critical representations of this mode of masculinity rather than as misogynist scenes of pleasure, Ballard complicates the novel's relationship to the phallocentrism of which the "male" avant-garde is so often accused.[10] Further complicating the representation of male sexuality, Ballard presents the penis in a variety of forms. At one point Vaughan "stares down at his half-erect penis, looking back at [James] in a muddled way as if asking [James] to help him identify this strange organ."[11] James's own penis is no less unreliable. The prostitute he hires to fellate him has to search his groin for "an errant penis," inviting the reader to associate this wandering organ with a noble, gentle knight, or perhaps with the more traditional wandering organ, the uterus.[12] Kathy Acker finds in David Cronenberg's cinematic representation of Vaughan's flaccid penis an important alternative to the "dominant and always rigid phallus of the old king-must-not-die world," an alternative that, for her, makes the future imaginable.[13] To the novel's credit, however, *Crash* ultimately resists the simplistic notion that a soft penis alone can provide an adequate foundation for a new vision of sexuality and sexual difference. While Vaughan's "muddled" attitude toward his "strange organ" seems like a promising point of departure, we should remember that his flaccid penis appears in one of the novel's most violent and distressing scenes: "Catherine cried out, a gasp of pain cut off by Vaughan's strong hand across her mouth. He sat back with her legs across his hips, slapping her with one hand as the other forced his flaccid penis into her vagina. His face was clamped in an expression of anger and distress."[14] Functioning less as the harbinger of the postpatriarchal age than as a participant in a violent and misogynist sexual world founded on the suffering of female characters like Catherine and Gabrielle, the soft penis here seems to warn us against reducing the problem of sexual difference to the simple mechanics of male and female bodies.

The question of what a feminist reader should make of the ubiquity of semen is as complicated as the challenges offered by the novel's mutating members. As numerous feminist theorists have argued, fluids and tacky bodily substances are traditionally aligned with femininity, marking women as the baser sex. Vaughan, however, with the "tacky texture" of his anus, a "tacky navel," "unsavoury armpits," and semen-stained clothes, is by far the novel's most viscous character.[15] As with the soft penis, we should be wary of automatically understanding his viscosity as a radical reconfiguration of gender hierarchies, for as Elizabeth Grosz has warned, semen differs from other viscous bodily substances, like vomit or menstrual blood, in that it "is understood primarily as what it makes, what it achieves, a causal agent and thus a thing, a solid: its fluidity, its potential seepage, the element in it that is uncontrollable, its spread, its formlessness, is perpetually displaced onto its properties, its capacities to fertilize, to father, to produce an object."[16]

Read alongside this caution, semen in *Crash* remains interesting precisely because it resists resolving itself into solid form and withstands a logic of fertilization, choosing instead to trace the possibility of moving in and out of one's own and other bodies. Even after ejaculation, semen continues to move, primarily in the form of gravitational drips and leaks: James comes inside of Helen, and she lets the semen fall back onto his crotch; Catherine allows James's semen to run out of her vagina into James's hand; and Vaughan allows James's semen to "leak" from his anus "across the fluted ribbing of the vinyl upholstery" of his car.[17] But does all this dripping semen have anything to offer feminist theory? Does it belong to a more general attempt to rethink sex and gender, and their relationship to representational practices, in radically new ways, or does this new seminal fluidity leave patriarchal hierarchies fundamentally unchanged?

Addressing the general difficulty of feminist encounters with "male avant-garde" texts, Susan Rubin Suleiman advocates a type of feminist doublespeak. Suleiman recognizes the "potentially positive results" of a "formal allegiance" between feminism and the avant-garde, and so recommends: "One may—one must—criticize the misogyny of male avant-garde sexual and cultural politics, and still recognize the energy, the inventiveness, the explosive humor and sheer proliferating brilliance of such male avant-garde 'play.'"[18] Given the apparent ubiquity of misogyny within "male" avant-garde writing, this type of approach might seem unavoidable, but it also raises a number of challenging and potentially productive questions for feminist theory.

1. Can we separate the male avant-garde's sexual and cultural politics from its formal inventiveness, and if not, does its misogyny prevent us from recognizing its "inventiveness" as such?
2. Might the feminist separation of misogyny and inventiveness foreclose productive interactions between (male) avant-garde texts and feminist theorists, freezing the terms of the debate unnecessarily?
3. How useful is it always to fix the male avant-garde as "male"? Does the perpetuation of this division between male and female avant-garde practices limit the possibilities of feminist reading practices, and how can we resist such limitations without abandoning feminist concerns?

While Suleiman is clearly a pioneer in facilitating more productive exchanges between feminism and the (male) avant-garde, could this invitation-turned-imperative to "criticize the misogyny" leave feminists in the position of being always obliged to list (again) the familiar critiques of the avant-garde's manhandling of the female body? While such repetitions are often important, even when they open feminists to charges of being boring and predictable, does not feminism lose its vitality if the gender identity of a given set of practices ("male" avant-garde ones) remains permanently and unquestionably fixed? To separate sexual difference from formal innovation potentially forecloses the possibility that feminist critics might read against the grain of these texts, might discover ways in which the formal innovations and play that seem useful and "brilliant" to feminists could *internally* challenge or destabilize a given work's ostensibly misogyny? Thinking sex and sexual difference *alongside* innovation, form, and medium within avant-garde works may allow us to suspend an automatic critique of misogyny in order to allow the possibility that there might be other ways of understanding avant-garde representations of sexual difference. This is not to say that many of the texts in question would not, or should not, continue to trouble us; nor should this approach de-emphasize the importance for feminism of engaging "female" avant-garde practice.

Just as Warhol explored film's relationship to television and photography in *Since* through a very specific car accident, so *Crash* probes the limits of literary form and language in relation to the adjacent media of photography and film; and, as Warhol does in *Since*, Ballard employs the language of collision to describe a movement between media that becomes intricately intertwined with the language of sexual difference and desire. Consequently, the novel might interest a feminist reader for at least three reasons.

1. It sexualizes the discussions of medium specificity, particularly in relation to pop art, formal discussions that often stand as alternatives to feminist readings of "purely social" or cultural issues.
2. It expands the space of sexual difference beyond the limits of the material body, imagining movements and intersections that a biologically based conception of sexual difference might foreclose.
3. It allows the possibility of folding the newly imagined movements and intersections of mediums back onto the body, perhaps transforming the seemingly fixed limits of that body in the process.

"The Best Complement to Warhol in Fiction"

Andy Warhol's game was, according to Wayne Koestenbaum, "to transpose sensations from one medium to another—to turn a photograph into a painting by silkscreening it; to transpose a movie into a sculpture by filming motionless objects and individuals; to transcribe tape-recorded speech into a novel."[19] Within these transpositions, however, it is remarkable that the realms of the visual and the literary remain largely separate, untransposed or untranslated in relation to each other. Warhol's *a: a novel*, for example, transcribes the almost already linguistic text of audiotape recordings done in and around the Factory.[20] Furthermore, *a* does not necessarily provoke the question of what it means to talk of a "pop novel," to translate visual pop into literature, because the presence of "a by Andy Warhol" on the novel's original stark, white, Warhol-designed cover makes redundant the question of why this work belongs within the pop world.[21] By contrast, *Crash* might be classified as a pop novel primarily because it obsessively engages the question of what it means to translate the visual landscapes of pop—its paintings, its photographs, and particularly its films—into the form of a novel. Warhol and Ballard share a language of the movement between inside and outside, and though this movement might speak of trauma, as Foster suggests, it also speaks of translation, and specifically of translations across different media that work against normative categories of desire.

Ballard never specifies the time setting of his futuristic novel (written in 1973), but the landscape of *Crash* is littered with clues that transport us back a decade to the early 1960s. Liz Taylor constitutes the most explicit of these temporal signposts. An early casual mention of the actress implies, through the juxtaposition of her name with that of the director with whom she is associated, that we should be thinking of Taylor in her Egyptian role. The character James Ballard reports, "On the afternoon of my accident I had attended a conference with Aida James, a freelance director we had brought in. By chance, one of the actresses, Elizabeth Taylor, was about to start work on a new feature film at Shepperton."[22] A little later in the novel Ballard states that he spends hours in the production offices "discussing the contractual difficulties blocking the car commercial, in which we hoped to use the film actress Elizabeth Taylor."[23] The combination of Taylor in London with Egyptian references and contractual difficulties recalls the disastrous production history of Joseph Mankiewicz's *Cleopatra*, released in 1964. Taylor, whose physical and emotional disasters prolonged the completion of *Cleopatra* so extensively as to destabilize the financial security of Fox Studios, becomes a perfect emblem for a novel that is endlessly fascinated with the representational possibilities offered up by the medium of film in the moment of its disintegration. When we first encounter Taylor, in the opening scene of the novel, she has just witnessed the death of Vaughan in his last crash and has only narrowly escaped death herself: "Holding the arm of the chauffeur, the film actress Elizabeth Taylor, with whom Vaughan had dreamed of dying for so many months, stood alone under the revolving ambulance lights. As I knelt over Vaughan's body she placed a gloved hand to her throat."[24] James's description of Taylor under the blue revolving lights of a British ambulance, holding "a gloved hand to her throat," recalls not only Taylor's near death by tracheotomy during the shooting of *Cleopatra*, but also, through the scene's implied blue lighting, Andy Warhol's *Blue Liz* (1963). This oblique reference points to a historical moment that marks Warhol's most intense experimentation with the limits of film stasis and motion in works like *Sleep* (1963), five hours and twenty-one minutes of the poet John Giorno sleeping (when projected at sixteen frames per second), and *Empire* (1964), a stationary eight-hour shot of the Empire State Building (also to be projected at sixteen frames per second). These are the pop images and rhythms toward which Ballard and his novel longingly turn their gaze.

Jonathan Crary, another critic who has explicitly discussed *Crash* in terms of pop, claims the novel has its roots in the "general mechano-morphic eroticism of British Pop" and tells us to "remember Ballard's association in the late 1950s and 1960s with art circles in Britain that included Richard Hamilton, Eduardo Paolozzi and Reyner Banham."[25] One could certainly consider *Crash* as a pop novel simply by association with people, images, and even colors. (Like Warhol's "death and disaster" series, for example, the novel repeatedly juxtaposes vivid colors with dying or dead bodies, as when the body parts of a retired prostitute, thrown through a car windscreen, are removed by a policeman, wrapped in a gaudy "yellow plastic shroud."[26]) Ballard himself explicitly highlights his work's proximity to pop art at the thematic level. The subject matter of science fiction, he suggests, "is the subject matter of everyday life: the gleam on refrigerator cabinets, the contours of a wife's or husband's thighs passing the newsreel images on a colour TV set, the conjunction of unique postures of passengers on an airport escalator—all in all, close to the world of pop painters and sculptors, Paolozzi, Hamilton, Warhol, Wesselman, Ruscha, among others."[27] Ballard aims, however, not simply to represent this visual pop world from the outside but to contribute a linguistic dimension to it: "The great advantage of science fiction," he claims, "is that it can add one ingredient to this hot mix—words." And he ends the essay with the imperative, "Write!"[28] Science fiction is, he asserts, "the only form of literature which will cross the gap between the dying narrative fiction of the present and the cassette and videotape fictions of the near future."[29]

Just as J. G. Ballard fictionalizes himself into the character James Ballard, an ad man (an interesting shift into a realm that includes both writing and image production), so we might also read Vaughan as a fictionalized version of Andy Warhol. Although Warhol's name appears explicitly only once, in passing, as part of a list of celebrities who have sex in cars, Vaughan's distinctive physical traits and obsessions repeatedly evoke Warhol's own body. While Vaughan cannot simply be reduced to Warhol, the resonance between these two characters encourages us to read *Crash* as a pop novel, situates Ballard's literary crash explicitly in relation to other modes of "crash" art, and recognizes at a very early stage the complex sexual nature of Warhol's film work. Aside from Vaughan's endless fascination with dying stars like Liz Taylor, aside from his pleasure in collecting and photographically reproducing the automobile accidents of his age (often with a Polaroid camera, a cine-camera, and a tripod), aside from his strange, "self-cut hair," Vaughan has a "scarred face," "a pock-marked face," recalling Warhol's wandering pimple and his answer to the question "'What's your problem?'": "'Skin.'"[30] Vaughan's pale face, like his body, gets paler in the course of the novel, until James Ballard describes it as being "whiter than I had ever seen it," evoking Warhol's descriptions of his own "chalky, puckish mask," "pale ... presence," "bleached arms and albino-like chalk-skin."[31] When Vaughan at one point removed his shirt, "the falling light picked out the scars on his abdomen and chest, a constellation of white chips that circled his body from the left armpit down to his crotch," recalling Richard Avedon's photographic portrait of Warhol's torso from 1969, *Andy Warhol, artist, New York City 8/20/69*, which displays a similar constellation of white chips that mark a zigzagging path from the armpits down to the crotch.[32]

Kathy Acker reads *Crash* as James Ballard's love letter to Vaughan, but we can also read the novel as a somewhat jealous love letter from J. G. Ballard to Warhol, from fiction to film, one that repeatedly expresses the desire of one to get inside of and simultaneously incorporate the other, conveyed primarily through James's excruciating sexual longing for Vaughan, which remains unfulfilled for most of the novel, and through the dominant metaphor of colliding cars.[33] As we track the relationship between James and Vaughan, then, we are simultaneously tracking the encounters between the linguistic and the visual, between fiction and film, and this complex intertwining of bodies and media becomes crucial to the novel's efforts to think differently about the interaction of sexuality and form.

When James does finally penetrate Vaughan's anus, the care he articulates for the site of entry is striking. Throughout the novel, the word *care* grows out of *car* and *scar*; it is produced by the same supplemental *e* that turns *motion* into *emotion*, suggesting that the novel's words, like its characters, find their meaning only by moving in and out of each other.[34] James begins "crouched behind Vaughan," and though this position might seem to signal a hierarchy of James over Vaughan, even of fiction over film, the position of being "crouched behind" aptly describes Ballard's own somewhat anxious relationship with the pop artists.[35] Like his fictionalized self, always trying to catch up with Vaughan's level of inventiveness and perversity, Ballard looks back longingly to the early 1960s, trying to get inside pop's "hot mix" with his words—not to colonize images through the superior power of language, but rather to revivify the "dying narrative fiction" through a process of mutual and simultaneous translation.

This is how James enters Vaughan: "With my right hand I parted his buttocks, feeling for the hot vent of his anus. For several minutes, as the cabin walls glowed and shifted, as if trying to take up the deformed geometry of the crashed cars outside, I laid my penis at the mouth of his rectum. His anus opened around the head of my penis, settling itself around the shaft, his hard detrusor muscle gripping my glans. As I moved in and out of his rectum the light-borne vehicles soaring along the motorway drew the semen from my testicles. After my orgasm I lifted myself slowly from Vaughan, holding his buttocks apart with my hands so as not to injure his rectum. Still parting his buttocks, I watched my semen leak from his anus across the fluted ribbing of the vinyl upholstery."[36] This scene of penetration disorients the reader with its shifting body parts, locations, and agents. As the fictional body of James moves inside of Vaughan, each body is transformed by the touch of the other, while the rectum's mouth seems actively to consume the penis's head, which has been placed before that mouth like an offering. As James moves in and out of the Warholian Vaughan, a movement marked by James's lightness of touch and care, the sexual act also transforms their surrounding space, thoroughly confusing any sense of where the inside is in relation to the outside. The men begin inside Vaughan's car, but as the penis lies passive and still at the mouth of Vaughan's vent, the walls of the car's interior begin to move, trying to embody the exterior and damaged walls of the crashed cars outside. Relentless in its disturbance of the relationship between inside and outside, the passage then describes James's ejaculation in what might be the novel's most profound moment of dislocation. Rather than independently spurting out of the penis in search of a receptacle, James's semen sits passively inside his testicles, waiting to be drawn by "light-borne vehicles" down the motorway that marks a passage that begins in Ballard's testicles, moves through his penis, then out into the body of Vaughan. What we have assumed up until now to be the space that constitutes the novel's "outside," the space of the motorway, now appears to exist inside James's genitalia, which, far from being impenetrable, at least momentarily seem to contain the entire world.[37]

"Cinema Is the Art of Destroying Moving Images"

If Ballard does play Warhol's game of trying to give the sensations of pop's visual world literary form, he seems particularly interested in the question of how to transpose the stasis and motion of a film like Warhol's *Empire*, which itself plays with translations of one medium into others.[38] For Koestenbaum, for example, *Empire* becomes a type of sculpture, while for Callie Angell, the film moves toward painting: "The image, shot from a tripod-mounted camera, never moves; projected at the slow motion speed of 16 fps and immobilized within the stationary frame of the movie screen, the film becomes equivalent in physical presence to a painting on the wall."[39] Yet this new painting cannot simply contain film; rather, as film enters into the space of the still image, it imbues the idea of the painting with film's temporal dimension, recognizable in spite of the image's stillness through the visible disintegration of the moving strip of film. Angell writes elsewhere, "By presenting an unmoving image of a motionless building in slow motion, Warhol simultaneously alters our perception of time and monumentalizes the ephemeral nature of film itself: passing light flares, watermarks, and other transient phenomena of the medium occur as spectacularly as meteor showers in the minimal scenery of Warhol's films."[40] These acts of translation trouble the limits of the media in question, disorienting our sense of where, if anywhere, the borders of film, painting, sculpture, and literature might lie.

In "The Task of the Translator" Walter Benjamin quotes the following passage from Rudolf Pannwitz's *Die Krisis der europäischen Kultur*: "The basic error of the translator is that he preserves the state in which his own language happens to be instead of allowing his language to be powerfully affected by the foreign tongue. Particularly when translating from a language very remote from his own he must go back to the primal elements of language itself and penetrate to the point where work, image, and tone converge. He must expand and deepen his language by means of the foreign language."[41] Yet as Ballard tries to produce in *Crash* a literary translation of Warhol's film work of the early 1960s, he faces the difficult question of how to begin translating a foreign medium like film into language when it has already been stripped down to its bare bones by Warhol. Ballard does not want simply to be an outside commentator on pop; he wants his words to be part of the movement's "hot mix." We could begin to think about the novel's relationship to film by examining Vaughan's fascination with various forms of visual technology, and several critics have explored *Crash*'s relationship to film from this perspective, noting the way the landscape of this novel is littered with old cameras, tripods, photographs, newspaper images, films, and film stars.[42] This approach, however, risks getting lost in the literal mentions of film and photography in *Crash*. A more interesting approach might be to delineate how Ballard, through his endlessly complex metaphorical web of roads, cars, fluidity, and sex, explores the nature of film movement as well as the possibility of what, having imagined that movement into words, a literary cinematography might look like. Freed from the material, chemical, and perceptual constraints of the medium, Ballard's translation of film takes it well past the point of projectability, well beyond Warhol's reduction of the medium to a single moving strip, allowing film to fall apart into language so that he might examine its otherwise inseparable components in relation to one another.[43] He begins by considering the relation of the moving filmstrip to the static frame through the parallel relation of the road to the car. But then, in a manner typical of the novel's endless twists and inversions, the surface of the car transmutes into the celluloid base of film, allowing Ballard to explore the chemical affinity between this base and the layer of light-sensitive emulsion made up of silver salts suspended in gelatin that adheres to the base.

Through this extended and intricate metaphor, which transforms the medium of film into a system of interconnecting highways, cars, and human bodies, Ballard linguistically engages the philosophical questions of movement and time suggested by *Empire*: How does the still frame relate to the moving filmstrip? How does a body inhabit the individual frame? How slow can film go before it disintegrates? What is the relationship between illusions of stasis and illusions of movement? How might a writer incorporate these temporal and spatial relationships into literature, and what effect on writing would those incorporations have? And if these movements between media are inseparable from the sexual movements between bodies the novel repeatedly represents, how are we to think the two simultaneously?

Still Frames and Moving Strips

Soon after James has returned home from the hospital, he sits on the balcony looking over the London motorways ten floors below and explicitly links his aerial view of the road to the experience of watching American avant-garde film. This sole mention of avant-garde film is framed on one side by the presence of liquid and on the other side by the idea of cinematically induced sexual improvement, a careful placement that clues us in to the importance of both sex and fluidity to Ballard's translation project: "Our own apartment house at Drayton Park stood a mile to the north of the airport in a pleasant island of modern housing units, landscaped filling stations and supermarkets, shielded from the distant bulk of London by an access spur of the northern circular motorway which *flowed past us on its elegant concrete pillars. I gazed down at this immense motion sculpture*.... The houses of our friends, the wine store where I bought our liquor, the small art-cinema where Catherine and I saw American avant-garde films and German sex-instruction movies, together realigned themselves around the palisades of the motorway."[44] Though we usually think of roads as stationary pathways for moving vehicles, the motorways of *Crash* are always in the process of a paradoxically static motion, resonating with Koestenbaum's earlier description of Warhol's films as moving sculptures. The road in this novel is not inert, but rather "an immense motion sculpture" and, later, a "motion sculpture of concrete highway."[45] Furthermore, while the road moves, cars, and the bodies contained within them, seem stuck and unmoving in relation to the road. They are triply fixed like the Empire State Building: first, by their solid form, which contrasts strikingly with the fluidity of the motorway; second, by their stasis; and third, by their entrapment between other stationary vehicles, such as the frame fixed between a series of other static frames on a strip of film. An acid-soaked sugar cube allows James to perceive this relation between the road and its vehicles more clearly, and through his description, the road emerges as a complicated layered structure embodying both movement and stasis, while the cinematic referentiality of the passage becomes increasingly clear: "Two airport coaches and a truck overtook us, their revolving wheels almost motionless, as if these vehicles were pieces of strange scenery suspended from

FILM FALLS APART | 173

the sky. Looking around, I had the impression that all the cars on the highway were stationary, the spinning earth racing beneath them to create *an illusion of movement.*"[46]

While James and Catherine are swept along passively by the road's currents, Vaughan's transgressive driving, like that of Michel in Jean-Luc Godard's *Breathless* (1960), seems to offer extreme possibilities of cinematic motion, some of which are perhaps only thinkable in a space outside of cinema itself.[47] Godard uses driving primarily to explore the new possibilities of the camera's motion as Michel overtakes other cars wildly, crossing the road's white lines with abandon, the camera, already moving with the car, simultaneously pans widely from one side of the road to the other. By contrast, Ballard's cinematic driving verbs point less to the camera's movement or the mobile view from the road than to the movement and manipulation of the strip itself, and they derive directly from the world of film editing and projection. In just one page Vaughan "cuts in" to traffic lanes, and "takes up" a watchful position, "winds" through roundabouts and intersections, and "jumps" a set of traffic lights.[48] The "rules" of this road (or film) are marked by gutters, bollards, and white lines, all of which perforate the unbroken "strip" of the road's surface like sprocket holes, holes that seem complicit with the singular, mechanical, and unidirectional motion of the road that the novel resists. As the surface of the road becomes a centrally perforated filmstrip, we find ourselves moving beyond film as we know it through a backwards utopian leap to an earlier historical moment when, prior to the regulation of film gauge, speed, and perforation, projection practices as well as the size of the image were constantly in flux.[49]

When Vaughan eats his acid-soaked sugar cube, the regulatory white lines of the road suddenly awaken, as though refusing to participate in the smooth transportation of the strip of road or film, no longer willing to bear passive bodies along in mechanical motion. Although for once Vaughan is not ejaculating as he drives wildly against the movement of the road, his transgressive passage over the road's surface seems to animate and liquefy these lines into a wiggling mass of bodies, all celebrating their own aquatic mobility: "The marker lines diving and turning formed a maze of white snakes, writhing as they carried the wheels of the car crossing their backs, as delighted as dolphins."[50] Rather than disciplining the movement of cars, which function here like single frames moving in line on the moving strip of road, the white lines create a maze that requires each car-as-frame to devise an independent path across the strip; and, in what seems to be a reversal of the aforementioned image of James's semen being drawn out of his testicles by the light-borne vehicles, these fluid white snakes now enable cars to move freely and independently of one another by carrying them on their backs.

"A Huge Pool of Cellulose Bodies"

Throughout the novel the road serves as a fluid metaphor for the strip of film. The cars that hover above the strip's surface evoke unmoving frames, while the relationship between the cars and the road seems to be utterly illusory. Yet as a metaphor, the car, like film itself, emerges as semantically and chemically unstable, at times collapsing into the film base from which it at other times seems quite distinct. Nowhere is Ballard's treatment of the car-as-film more visible than in his repeated play with the linguistic and chemical proximity between car "varnish" (a word that repeatedly threatens to slip into "Vaughanish" or "vanish"), which is composed of cellulose, and celluloid, which is the substance of film; motor-body-building handbooks, for example, describe "cellulose lacquer" as "a finishing material containing cellulose nitrate" for car varnishing, cellulose nitrate being the material used to make the base of film until 1951.[51] As though unsure that readers will make the connection, Ballard insistently draws attention to the chemical makeup of the car's coating. James looks out from his apartment at an "immense corona of polished cellulose."[52] In the northbound motorway traffic jam, "the sunlight burn[s] on the overheated cellulose."[53] Similarly, the novel's worst traffic jam suddenly liquefies into "a huge pool of cellulose bodies," a meltdown that produces a state of hypermobility for Vaughan.[54] Utopian images of fluid cinematic motion repeatedly emerge in the moment of the medium's material meltdown. Film, at a distance from itself through its entry into language and densely packed metaphors, emerges in *Crash* as a yearning that strains the border between literature and film because of their interaction with each other in this text.

As if the melted cellulose of the car were not fluid enough, Vaughan and Ballard also inscribe the interior and exterior surfaces of cars with their own liquidity. Vaughan marks his presence by urinating on a radiator grille and, as James will later learn to do, uses his semen to map "the corridors of this future drama."[55] In another autographic moment, Vaughan outlines his penis in chalk on the surface of a dead female dentist's black crashed car, perhaps a direct reference to Jim Dine's happening, *The Car Crash* (1960), in which Dine, dressed as a silver car man, draws the outline of a car with a face on a chalk board.[56] Initially, the idea of writing directly on cellulose invokes figures like Len Lye, Norman McLaren, and Harry Smith much more than any of the pop artists.[57] Yet Ballard's gesture here is pop not because his characters inscribe the filmstrip directly but because this writing on film resonates with the novel's persistent attempts to translate this mode of cinematography into language. Vaughan's and James's inscriptions also "pop" in a way that those of Lye, McLaren, and Smith do not, because the materials the former use to write or paint on black—semen and urine—recall Ed Ruscha's *Stains* (1969) and foreshadow Warhol's *Piss and Sex Paintings* from the late 1970s.[58]

James inspects the fluidly inscribed exterior of Vaughan's Lincoln (the same style car in which Kennedy died) to discover that the fender and wheel housing are marked with "streaks of a black gelatinous material," which he identifies as the blood of a dog they had hit earlier. As the characters set off for the car wash to remove all traces of the blood, Vaughan's camera suddenly, as though independently mobile, "lands on the front seat."[59] James explains, "Its invisible silver memories of pain and excitement distilled themselves on their dark reel, as, behind me, Catherine's most sensitive mucous surfaces quietly discharged their own quickening chemicals."[60] Moving again between the car's exterior and interior space, Ballard juxtaposes the blood on the wheels with both the camera's "silver memories" and Catherine's "quickening chemicals," linking together the gelatinous material on the surface of the car, the emulsion coating on the cellulose base of film, and Catherine's bodily fluids. But while the emulsion's tacky substance elicits "quickening" chemicals from Catherine's body, suggesting some kind of animation and life, this substance simultaneously implies film's own sticky end. Evoking Vaughan's disruption of the road's punctuating lines, his tangy odor, and the viscosity of car surfaces throughout the book, Paolo Cherchi Usai describes the degeneration of celluloid: "The film shrinks, and the distance between perforations decreases. . . . There is a strong pungent smell. . . . The emulsion becomes sticky. . . . Then eruptions of soft dark matter form on the surface of the reels."[61]

The sticky remnant of the dog on the surface of the car's reels or wheels is inseparable not only from the disintegrating matter of film and the moistening body of Catherine, but also from the smells and leaks of Vaughan's scarred body (remember that Vaughan deliberately picks his scabs to keep his blood flowing from the inside to the outside).[62] In the previous chapter James describes his longing to "take [Vaughan's] body in his hands, *like that of some vagrant dog*, and anneal its wounds."[63] James thinks the word *anneal*, so proximate to *anal*, while staring down at the "cleft between Vaughan's buttocks" and imagining the "penetration of his rectum."[64] This anal fantasy of healing, however, is rooted in the Old English word *onaelan*, "to set fire to," linking anal sex with the ultimate vulnerability of cellulose nitrate: its flammability. Indeed, the novel repeatedly offers instances of the fluid movement between inside and outside that produces new pleasure and healing on the one hand and destruction on the other. Throughout *Crash*, however, James tends to transgress boundaries through the penetration of the wounds of others while his own body remains largely intact. The boundaries of female bodies, of Vaughan's body, and, by extension, those of the medium of film often seem more porous and fluid than those of James's body and perhaps of fiction itself. While Ballard explores film beyond its own ostensible limits by allowing it to disintegrate through its interpenetration with fiction, the language of fiction never really undergoes an equivalent transformation, and the reader is left to wonder whether the "dying narrative fiction of the present" actually engages the possibilities offered by pop's aesthetics of translation or simply incorporates the visual in order to assert authority over it.

It seems undeniable that *Crash*, at least to some extent, repeats a "male" avant-garde tendency to discover "the new" through a rhetoric of penetration and fragmentation that is rarely reciprocal. But though the novel in some ways fails to fulfill its own radical dream of mutual translation, it remains interesting in the ways it makes its failures visible. We know from the beginning that Vaughan will eventually die trying to bring about the death of Elizabeth Taylor, yet toward the end of the novel James explicitly articulates his care for Vaughan through his desire to offer his own real wounds in place of the imaginary ones Vaughan tries to inflict on Taylor: "Caring for him, I wanted to stroke his scarred thighs and abdomen, offering him the automobile injuries carried by my own body in place of those imaginary wounds he wished upon the actress."[65] While we might read this moment as a fantasy of the complete displacement of women, a desire for a "new sexuality" that belongs exclusively to the novel's male characters, other readings are also possible. As James imagines a different kind of care and desire, one never quite realized within the novel, he seems less interested in erasing female presence than in transforming the sadistic gaze of the male filmmaker-spectator through a new tenderness, intimacy, and vulnerability with Vaughan. Although the novel offers no sense of the female subjectivities and sexualities that would be enabled by such a transformation, *Crash* does at least recognize the need to let go of the "female" image as we know it—albeit with "sentimental regret"—if the keys to "a new sexuality" are ever to be found.[66] Neither James nor fiction per se make themselves vulnerable enough for the novel to fulfill its radical potential, but the fact that Ballard foregrounds this failure, however minimally, makes *Crash* a useful point of departure for thinking about future dialogues between feminism and pop.

In *Crash*, bodies and mediums imagine themselves differently as they reach to be simultaneously penetrating and penetrated, giving a foretaste of Irigaray's vision of double desire, where the desiring two establish "a chiasmus or a double loop in which each can go toward the other and come back to itself."[67] For Irigaray, this double desire "excludes disintegration or rejection, attraction and decomposition," and "makes possible speech, promises, alliances."[68]

In Ballard, however, there are no such guarantees. Indeed, the possibility of "the new" seems inevitably to involve some degree of disintegration and decomposition, but the embrace of this threatened immolation, the willingness to be transformed by a mutual encounter with another, even at the risk of death, becomes the precondition for the possibility of both motion and emotion. The alternative, Ballard suggests, is to sit stationary in a locked car that hangs immobile above the moving highway below.

chapter six

CRASH AESTHETICS

Amores perros
and the Dream of
Cinematic Mobility

In contrast to early cinema's use of the crash, recent cinematic crashes recall the more complex, self-reflexive use of the figure seen in early cinema and slapstick. While early cinema and slapstick had explored the modern subject's relationship to technology through comic images of exploding machines, by the 1960s, though the comic element had not completely disappeared, this relationship was also being reassessed through the lens of the traumatic but widely circulated images of the body torn open—by the Vietnam War, by political assassins, and by police conflict with protesters representing social-change movements.[1] If on the one hand these images give rise to sexual and spectatorial remappings of a newly gaping body, on the other hand the crash also becomes intertwined with questions about reproducible media, about the relation of these media to politics, about public and private viewing spaces, and about individual and mass subjectivity. But what are we to make of the current resurgence of cinematic car crashes? Not all of them are noteworthy—indeed, as Joshua Levin argues in "Movie Car Crashes: A Primer," the figure has been used so extensively, especially in opening footage, that it risks being regarded as nothing but a cliché, a useful narrative device for introducing contingent events or unexpected encounters.[2] For Levin, the appeal of the crash is obvious: it is an immediate "attention grabber," a useful and efficient narrative device for introducing surprising plot twists (although, as he points out, the ubiquity of this device also works against its surprise element); moreover, it has strong and distinct resonances in a variety of genres, including horrors, thrillers, and comedies.

Beyond this overused narrative shorthand, however, the car accident has also emerged in recent years as a privileged trope in films that engage, with varying levels of complexity, the interrelated issues of global media, global citizenship, and migration or immigration. For example, "Crash Test Dummy: The New European 'Self' in a Bio-Political Crash Test," the series of happenings, installations, film screenings, lectures, dance performances, and architectural interventions that took place in Munich, Ljubljana, and Budapest between May and July 2006, began with the following premise: "Processes of social transformation, surveillance and control scenarios, the disappearance of the social welfare safety net, the challenge of global migration: occidental society is turning into a crash test scenario without any predictable outcome. And within this scenario the social individual is becoming the dummy, the body the site of impact."[3] The film screenings (compiled by the German filmmaker Alexandra Weltz, whose own work *Munich Express* was also featured in the form of an installation) included *Luukkaankangas—Updated, Revisited* (Dariusz Krzeczek, 2005), *Destrukt* (Aline Helmcke, 2005), *Magnetic Identities* (Matei Glass, 2004), *Border* (Laura Waddington, 2005), *War at a Distance* (Harun Farocki, 2003), *The Catalogue* (Chris Oakley, 2004), s-77ccr *Vienna* (2004), and the video files archived at the web site for World-Information.Org (2000–2005). To these films, we might add, among others, Alex Rivera's *The Sixth Section: A Documentary about Immigrants Organizing Across Borders* (2003), in which the car becomes a risky vehicle that enables members of a community to commute back and forth between Mexico and New York State; Jörg Kalt's *Crash Test Dummies* (2005), in which migrant workers make a living as human crash test dummies; and Paul Haggis's Academy Award–winning film *Crash* (2005), a clichéd and sensational depiction of racial tensions in Los Angeles, which seem to be resolved by a miraculous snowfall. While mainstream films in the United States (especially Road Movies and Gangster films) have often mythologized the freedom that supposedly lies just south of the Mexican border, *Amores perros* (2000), by the Mexican filmmaker Alejandro González Iñárritu, activates some of the tropes of these genres—the car and the accident as central "characters," as self-reflexive cinematic tropes for considering the hybrid medium of film within a "globalized" Mexican context, and as potential vehicles of liberation and transformation—to explore questions of mobility and stasis below the border.

On its release, *Amores perros* drew international attention to the state of Mexican cinema and to Mexico itself. It was the first Mexican film to be nominated for an Academy Award for Best Foreign Film in twenty-six years; it won awards at Cannes, Flanders, Bogotá, Sao Paolo, Tokyo, Moscow, and many other international film festivals; and it was repeatedly praised for capturing the "reality" of modern Mexican urban life. *Variety* named González Iñárritu as one of the top ten new directors to watch, and Lynn Hirschberg, in a *New York Times Magazine* article entitled "A New Mexican," described *Amores perros* as "the most ambitious and dazzling movie to emerge from Latin America in three decades."[4] Yet, in spite of the fact that *Amores perros* was the most successful film at the Mexican box office in 2000, domestic responses were clearly ambivalent. On the film's release in Guadalajara, Patricia Torres San Martín found that while for most middle-class viewers the film unleashed a surge of national pride—one commented, "We've had enough of gringo shit and now Mexican cinema is giving us great stuff"—some working-class spectators found the film "disgusting," "sadistic," and "sad," claiming "they always put Mexico down."[5] Jorge Ayala Blanco, an established film critic and scholar, criticized the film's exploitation of "shock," calling it a "success prefabricated by the technomarketing, Fox-style strategy, a tridramatic soap opera." Blanco describes the handheld camerawork as "nauseating," the moral banal, the characters stereotypical, and the representation of Mexico City "grotesque."[6] Finally, the longstanding Mexican filmmaker Arturo Ripstein, asked to comment on *Amores perros* at Cannes, stated simply, "I don't make films for idiots."[7]

The mixed critical reaction to *Amores perros*—the celebration of its innovation, the critique of how it exposed a degraded Mexico to the international arena, and the condemnation of its commercial success—establishes a resonance between this contemporary film and Luis Buñuel's first Mexican film, *Los olvidados* (1950).[8] Like *Amores perros*, *Los olvidados* depicts Mexico City as a place of violence, poverty, and crisis; it, too, won an award at Cannes (in 1951) and enjoyed major success at festivals while being widely condemned by Mexican critics for offending the "honor" of Mexico and for constructing "a viciously negative, false, and 'dirty' image of Mexico."[9] But, more importantly, Buñuel's work prefigures González Iñárritu's attempt both to represent the complexities and contradictions of Mexican national identity by explicitly invoking the complexities and contradictions of the medium of film, and to make the knotty problems emerging from these mutually illuminating phenomena available to commercial audiences. Rita González and Jesse Lerner position Buñuel as a "perverse elder statesman for the subsequent generations of Mexperimentalists," noting in particular his ability to create experimental spaces within, rather than in necessary opposition to, a commercial context: "Stressing the need for a more poetic cinema, Buñuel advocated a flexible filmmaking that could function within the strictures of the system, and yet subtly deconstruct the very terms of narrative. His choice to work within the industry may have been predominantly of economic necessity, but Buñuel did take offense at exclusionary or isolationist practices of the avant-garde that discounted the potential commercial audiences."[10] For González Iñárritu, as for Buñuel, aesthetic, industrial, and national crises are deeply intertwined, which makes it impossible to view *Amores perros* within simplistic paradigms. Rather, as this film refuses fully to embrace or reject either American commercial culture or Mexican nationalism, it challenges us to consider how the idea of the nation inflects González Iñárritu's exploration of the medium of film and its capacity to reflect the complexity of temporality, movement, history, and the contemporary traffic of images at the level of both form and content.

Set in Mexico City, *Amores perros* skillfully interweaves the lives of three separate groups of people and their dogs through the device of a brutal car crash that tangles the fates of these otherwise unrelated characters. The film is divided into three sections. In part 1, "Octavio y Susana," the young and poor Octavio falls in love with Susana, the wife of his brother Ramiro. He enters his brother's Rottweiler, Cofi, into dogfights to make money, with which he plans to head north to Ciudad Juárez with Susana, but he ultimately ends up losing Susana, his dog, his brother, his hair, his money, and, almost, his life. When Susana runs off with her husband and the money, Octavio decides to make more money through dog-fighting, in order to be able to head north with his friend, Jorge. However, Jorge is killed in a car crash, Ramiro is shot dead, and both Susana and Octavio end up back where they started. At Ramiro's funeral, Octavio invites Susana to join him on a bus ride to Ciudad Juárez, but she fails to show up, reinforcing the claustrophobia of the film, in which characters try to play out the familiar Mexican film narrative of heading north for the border, only to find themselves trapped in the space of Mexico City, their dreams of mobility thwarted.

Part 2, "Daniel y Valeria," tells the story of an advertising executive who leaves his wife and daughters to move in with Valeria, a Spanish supermodel who is the poster girl for the perfume *Enchant*. He buys a dreamy apartment, for the two of them, that looks out onto a giant billboard displaying Valeria's ubiquitous *Enchant* ad; but the dream becomes a nightmare when, in the wake of a car crash—with Octavio, as it turns out—Valeria loses one of her legs. To make matters worse, her little white dog, "Richie," her "son," gets stuck under the floorboards of the apartment where he is chewed by rats. In this second part of the film, the fantasy of mobility, deeply tied to the world of images, is again violently punctured. Daniel, in search of the dream woman, leaves his home life for a supermodel who is "all legs," only to find himself stuck with the crippling medical costs of Valeria's amputation, and Valeria loses all her mobility, both professional and physical.

The final section of the film, "El Chivo y Maru," depicts the transformation of El Chivo, the "Billy-goat," a schoolteacher-turned-guerrilla-fighter who had been imprisoned twenty years before and who had become, on his release, a private hit man. El Chivo wanders the streets with a pack of dogs, and he rescues Octavio's dog, Cofi, from the scene of the crash. Once recovered, Cofi proceeds to massacre all of El Chivo's stray dogs, provoking a change of heart in the old goat. El Chivo decides to reestablish contact with his estranged daughter, Maru, who believes her father to be dead, but he plans to do so only after he returns from a voyage of self-discovery, on which he embarks in the film's final image. "El Chivo y Maru" constitutes the only section of the narrative in which mobility remains a possibility, but this option is open exclusively to the man who walks, the man who, in the course of the film, will actively dismantle automobiles, and who is persistently aligned with the medium of photography, not film. Paradoxically, the possibility of change, indeed of futurity itself, seems to exist in a fantasized space between stasis and motion, and it is in this between-space, characterized by a quality George Baker describes as "not-stasis," that the film, and perhaps by extension contemporary Mexican cinema, seeks to find a place for itself.[11]

Amores perros problematizes the critical tendency automatically to align speed, movement, and capitalism with cinema through specific stylistic and formal gestures of resistance. First, as the film consciously evokes the images of the New York–based photographer Nan Goldin, its effort to create a New Mexican Cinema is complicated by the haunting visual presence of this North American photographic aesthetic that is itself already haunted by the specter of cinema. Second, the film's nonlinear narrative is structured around multiple (but changing) depictions of the same car crash. As we repeatedly return to this instant of collision, it becomes clear that if *Amores perros* does create an image of Mexico's present, it is an endlessly traumatic present in which forward narrative movement can only be achieved paradoxically by moving backward to an already lived instant. Third, while commercially successful film might be associated with the velocity of images, in *Amores perros* the possibility of forward motion, of movement aligned with "progress," is constantly troubled by competing movements within the shot. Just as at the diegetic level speeding cars are brought to a halt by encounters with other cars moving in different directions, so at the formal level we repeatedly experience what might be called "competing vectors," movements within the frame that, pulling in other directions, seem to peel images open, disrupting their flow. Finally, these narrative and formal manifestations of interrupted or strained motion are reinforced by the intrusion of a phenomenal number of still photographs into the mise-en-scène of the film.

While we might assume that a commercially ambitious film like *Amores perros* would try to repress the conflict, inherent within the medium, between the moving strip and the static photogram, a conflict that avant-garde filmmakers have productively exploited and exposed, *Amores perros* highlights the confrontation of motion and stasis that defines film, and uses it to explore the difficulty of cinematically representing Mexico's urban present. In one of the most useful recent contributions to contemporary film theory, *Between Film and Screen: Modernism's Photo Synthesis*, Garrett Stewart shows that although film practice has traditionally tried to repress the incursion of the single unmoving image into the illusion of movement, film's "optical unconscious" repeatedly disturbs this illusion through the eruption of freeze frames and still photographs within various film narratives. Stewart asks, "When this automatically suppressed single integer of screen illusion is lifted to view . . . to what extent does it drag with it the historically forgotten or overcome?"[12] *Amores perros* explores this question. Using various devices—including crashing cars, a circular narrative (which begins in the middle, then moves backward and forward in time), an attention to gravity (a constant tension between the downward and horizontal movement of objects), and an obsessive interest in still photographs—the film highlights the medium's conflicted relation to movement and stasis, not to foreground aesthetic over cultural and historical questions, but rather to reflect the complexities of nation, gender, class, and historical narrative through the encounter of cinema and photography.

George Baker describes such encounters at the interstices of mediums as a kind of redemptive "sharing" that can potentially enable old and tired mediums to reinvent or reanimate themselves without simply becoming formless, without losing a sense of the limits that are being contested. In a discussion of James Coleman's films *La tache aveugle* (1978–90) and *Untitled: Philippe VACHER* (1990), for example, Baker writes, "Photography now moves, and cinema freezes. . . . An interstice between mediums has not been 'crossed'; forms can only share themselves around that which they lack. Forms can only (truly) share themselves around an absolute limit, a limit that must be respected, and yet this limitation is a gift. For this limitation also means that forms have an outside through which they can—or perhaps even must—become other. It is in the interstice where film can become photographic, where not only 'shots' and 'frames' collide irrationally, but where image becomes extrinsic, extroverted, profligate."[13] Baker's work on the redemptive possibilities of "sharing" offers a useful paradigm for understanding *Amores perros*'s complex engagement with the limits of film. Yet the extension of Baker's work beyond the realm of artists working with or influenced by film to the sphere of commercial cinema requires a revision of Baker's idea of the "merely cinematic."[14]

Ballad of Aesthetic Dependency

Contrary to Frederic Jameson's suggestion that "whenever other media appear within film, their deeper function is to set off and demonstrate the latter's ontological primacy," photography emerges in relation to film within *Amores perros* in the form of a mutual yearning, akin to the model of "sharing" Baker's outlines.[15] *Amores perros* metaphorically reflects the potentially destructive effect of this encounter through the narrative and visual trope of the crash, which instantaneously transforms moving vehicles into static frames for dying bodies. But the mediums of film and photography also "meet" each other more literally through González Iñárritu's incorporation of Nan Goldin's photography at the level of mise-en-scène, an encounter that in turn metaphorically parallels the complex human relationships depicted within the narrative. In an interview with Bernando Pérez Soler in *Sight and Sound*, González Iñárritu traces his decision to allow Goldin's work such a central role back to a somewhat mythological moment: "I like Nan Goldin's photographs very much, so for my first meeting with director of photography Rodrigo Prieto I took in a book by Goldin to exemplify what I wanted to achieve in terms of coloration, grain, visceral appeal. Curiously enough, he brought the same book with him, so from the very beginning, we had a similar vision."[16] Whether or not this fateful moment actually occurred, Goldin's photographs ultimately play an important role in shaping *Amores perros* as a film capable of taking itself to its own limit, to the border of the medium, as though endlessly in search of transformational encounters.

In order to attain the same level of color saturation in *Amores perros* as Goldin achieves in her photographs, González Iñárritu and Prieto had to use a processing method that literally prevents the preservation of film. In an interview with Travis Crawford, González Iñárritu explains: "We began to make experiments in the lab, and our conclusion was to use this Vision 800 color stock, with a silver-retention process in the negative. It was the second time in the world that anyone had used this. In the United States they say they don't want you to do that because it's very risky. But it gave us those electric earthtones, and it was terrific. I think it really helped the movie—it has something you cannot explain, but it makes it different. Maybe we lost our negative, but we'll have it on DVD."[17] Here, the film's mimicking of photography does more than unveil cinema's repressed proximity to the still image; in recreating the look of Goldin's images, *Amores perros* willingly embraces its own chemical implosion, the limits of its existence as film, flipping the work into yet another proximate medium, reinforcing the film preservationist Paolo Cherchi Usai's recent claim that "cinema is the art of destroying moving images" while allowing that such destruction can mark the revitalization, as well as the end, of what we know as cinema.[18]

Paul Julian Smith remarks on González Iñárritu's debt to Goldin's photographs at the level of mise-en-scène, from "the saturated color, grainy texture and tight composition, the exploitation of mirrors and claustrophobically darkened exteriors," yet at times the film's scenes of empty bedrooms, religious kitsch, photo bulletin boards, fluorescent green hospital interiors, and open caskets also seem so close to Goldin in terms of what we might call "narrative content" that they produce an uncanny effect, as though Goldin's photographs had been strangely transformed into tableaux vivants.[19] While Smith, highlighting the difference between Goldin and González Iñárritu, asserts that "*Amores perros* shows no interest in Goldin's subcultures of drag queens and junkies," the film may not be quite as disinterested in the content of Goldin's images, in subcultures and sexual politics, as Smith suggests.[20] Indeed, Goldin and González Iñárritu share more than a visual style, for both photographer and filmmaker also have in common a way of interweaving this visual style, a style that grows out of the encounter between photography and film, with depictions of borders between nations, genders, classes, and subcultures.

Although Baker sees photography's confrontation of cinema and cinema's "look toward photography" as "absolutely linked... but absolutely different, as if their intertwining was actually a chiasmus," in *Amores perros* these interstitial yearnings are never so cleanly separated, as the Mexican film evokes cinematic photographs that in turn evoke photographic films. Though Prieto and González Iñárritu describe Goldin as a "still" photographer, her photographs are familiar to us not only from their gallery and publication contexts, but have been exhibited as early manual slide shows, accompanied by ever-changing soundtracks; as sophisticated museum installations, in which the slides' relation to the soundtrack becomes fixed; and finally, within the context of Goldin's film *I'll Be Your Mirror*, which has been shown both on television and within the museum context.[21] Furthermore, as J. Hoberman points out, her photographs have "a lot in common with what, in the late 1960s, used to be called the New American Cinema," and Goldin has acknowledged the influence of a wide range of film on her work, including the glamour of Classical Hollywood, the eroticism of the European New Wave films, and the experimentalism of Jack Smith and Andy Warhol, whose films repeatedly invoke a photographic stillness.[22] Her aesthetic grows out of an initial desire to "make Warholian films like *Chelsea Girls*," and she even goes so far as to say that she "never cared about photography too much" and that "film has been [her] number one medium all [her] life."[23]

Resisting the notion of an absolute limit, this intertwining of Goldin's cinematic photography and *Amores perros*'s photographic cinema blurs the line dividing these overly proximate mediums as a result of what looks like a case of over-identification or hysterical mimesis. Though Baker asserts that the absolute limit between photography and cinema "must be respected" in order for forms to truly share themselves, a sharing that depends on the existence of a recognizable "outside," perhaps the lack of respect shown to these aesthetic boundaries by Goldin, González Iñárritu, and the encounter of their work in some ways stages at the formal level the psychic struggles depicted within the narrative, where desire at times refuses to recognize social borders, even when this refusal has destructive effects.[24] While an ethical relation to the other may well depend on the subject's capacity to recognize the limits between self and that other, the complex and often unconscious operations of identification and desire repeatedly trouble or confuse either that boundary or the subject's capacity to recognize it. If the "sharing" that emerges between mediums in the work of artists and filmmakers, to which Baker attributes the medium's capacity to "become other," can be thought of within the paradigms of identification (and the language of "self" and "other" used to discuss the relation between mediums suggests that this paradigm can, even should, be invoked), then it follows that this "sharing" has the capacity to disrupt or dissolve the "absolute" status of the limits that initially make sharing possible or desirable in the first place.[25] For identification, as Diana Fuss suggests, is "a process that keeps identity at a distance, that prevents identity from ever approximating the status of an ontological given, even as it makes possible the formation of an *illusion* of identity as immediate, secure, and totalizable."[26] To raise these questions is not to refute the need to pay attention to the question of "the medium" as it becomes increasingly visible in contemporary art and film, or to claim that because the borders separating mediums from each other are mobile and provisional, all distinctions are meaningless. Rather, these questions, emerging out of a consideration of a particular encounter between cinema and photography, challenge us to be more explicit about what motivates our attempts to explore or regulate the encounters between different mediums, to clarify the difference between analysis and prescription, and to be attuned to the complexities that arise when the discourse on the medium becomes, as it inevitably does, a discourse on human relationships.

Through her work, Goldin has stretched the temporal and spatial implications of the photograph, and has linked the shifting, mimetic nature of photography to the expanded, provisional, and at times destructive views of gender, family, desire, love, and community depicted in her images, establishing a continuum between form and content that at least in part illuminates our investment in regulating the distinctions between one medium and another. While it might be tempting to argue that the social grittiness and poignancy of Goldin's images has merely been incorporated by *Amores perros* as glamorized urban chic (a critique that has also been leveled at Goldin's images), what interests me about González Iñárritu's visual referencing of Goldin's work is the way it invites the specter of her preoccupation with the temporal, spatial, and social possibilities of photography's exposure to film to haunt *Amores perros*. By embracing this expansion of a single medium through its encounter with another, González Iñárritu underscores the difficulty of representing contemporary Mexican urban identity at a moment when that identity is caught between a geographical specificity and the no-place of global capitalism. From Warhol to Goldin to González Iñárritu, though we are never outside of the space of capitalism, we are always in a space where the tension between still and moving images refuses to resolve itself, as the two mediums, mimicking each other in a compulsive dance of desire, identification, and rejection, seem unable either fully to incorporate each other or to let each other go.

While Baker asserts that the "dual articulation" he finds in Coleman's work is not about "a collision of mediums as opposed 'essences'—the inherent stasis of photography, for example, proclaiming war upon the flux of cinema," this space of encounter, the idea of collision nevertheless emerges, as Baker describes the way shots and vectors confront each other in Coleman's work.[27] Though the distinction between destructive and productive collisions would be hard to uphold in any absolute way, we might usefully remember that collisions and crashes function in multiple, sometimes even contradictory ways. With this in mind, I look more closely at how *Amores perros*'s narrative develops around a series of interrelated animating collisions: the repeated car crash, the collision of vectors, and cinema's collision with various forms of the still image.

Octavio y Susana

Amores perros opens with a breathtaking car chase that comes quickly to a dramatic and violent end. The sound of zooming cars first cues spectators to expect the onslaught of rapidly moving images that will soon follow. The black screen gives way to the black road, with movement across the space of that road signaled by the rapid passing of white divider lines across the horizontal screen. "This is a Road Movie," the opening shot seems to say, and yet *Amores perros* departs dramatically from this genre, which is visually identifiable by its recurrent use of panoramic shots that align the freedom of the road with the horizontal space of the cinema screen, and by the repeated employment of traveling shots produced by mounting the camera on the edge of a moving vehicle.[28] Although the film's framing techniques frequently emphasize the concept of horizontality, *Amores perros* questions the possibility of moving freely across these cinematic planes through a juxtaposition of horizontality with competing vertical images and vectors. Similarly, though González Iñárritu often employs a car-mounted camera, as he does in this opening scene, the fluid alignment of cine- and automobility is disrupted by the choppy editing style, multiple points of view, and the sudden termination of the car's motion at the moment of violent collision, all techniques that resist spectatorial equation of the car's movement with cinematic freedom.

As the camera points down at the ground, the surface of the road evokes nothing so much as the early practice of sprocketing filmstrips in the center, hinting that a self-reflexive consideration of the medium's mobility, as well as the possibilities of that medium's transformation in time, will play a central role in the film. Within seconds, however, Rodrigo Prieto's handheld camera moves from this vertical, downward-pointing position to a horizontal position to depict the high-speed movement of Octavio's car through the space of Mexico City. The tension between horizontal and vertical camera positions is further reinforced as the camera pulls our attention schizophrenically between the car's horizontal flight through Mexico City and the slow gravitational slide down of the dying dog Cofi on the backseat of the car.

The tension between high-speed, technological horizontality and the slow, downward animal fall works, like the tension between cinema and photography, to establish two competing temporalities and vectors within the frame, and to prefigure the accident, which, as Paul Virilio has argued, is embedded within the ideology of speed.[29] Like Walter Benjamin's historical materialist, the crash that ends this sequence seems to "blast open the continuum of history," making available, if only momentarily, the possibility of at least imagining a present in which time stands still long enough for thought to happen, in spite of the endlessly rolling film.[30] After a disoriented camera briefly attempts to capture the impact and aftermath of the crash, allowing us a glance of the bloody Valeria pawing at her side window, we face the first of many black screens, as though the film had given up on itself within the opening four minutes. In the course of the film, three further variations of this crash seem to insist that the time of this narrative will be, in spite of film's quality of duration, a single, photographic instant. Yet if the encroachment of the photographic instant seems to impinge on the film's narrative progression, film in turn seems to expose, or traumatize, photog-

FIGURE 68 A car falls from the sky. Still from *Amores perros*.

raphy's singular relation to the present, correcting its ability to represent a moment from only a single perspective as it offers four different views of the same event.

Toward the end of the first section, Ramiro enters his brother Octavio's bedroom to inquire about the dog-fighting profits. But this exchange about capital is preceded by what seems like an inconsequential glance at a close-up shot of the television screen Octavio watches. What we see is actually one of the many car advertisements González Iñárritu produced for Mexican television, but this brief glance at the screen demonstrates not only the way film can appropriate and rework commercial images, but also how commercials themselves might internally resist the capitalist culture in which they participate. This televisual fragment picks up on the film's formal leitmotif in which the horizontal movement of cars across the screen, aligned with cinematic mobility, is challenged by the presence of either a slower downward movement or by a vertical still image. In this instance, a row of stationary, forward-facing cars pointing out toward the viewer is suddenly hit from above by a horizontally aligned car that drops out of the sky, as though forward motion had been completely overtaken by the downward pull of gravity that has hitherto been positioned in opposition to auto-mobility (figure 68). Like the automobile stickers that adorn Octavio's bedroom wall,

all cars in this film will eventually be immobilized. By refusing to allow either cars or time to move forward through the traumatic repetition of the crash, González Iñárritu disrupts spectatorial expectations that the camera must align itself with narrative progress and technological speed, and instead insists that we attend to the proto-photographic instant when competing vectors intersect, opening the question of how, at what pace, and in what direction this new cinema might begin to move.

Daniel y Valeria

Early in the story of Octavio and Susana, we see an unidentified middle-class family driving cautiously through the streets of Mexico City; we will later learn that this is the family of Daniel from the film's second narrative. As the car slows for a stoplight, Daniel's upward gaze creates an eye-line match between the driver of the family vehicle and a giant billboard advertising the perfume *Enchant*, featuring Daniel's paramour, Valeria, the Spanish supermodel. The static, low-angled camera position emphasizes the height and verticality of the image, and creates a tension between the object of Daniel's upward gaze and the forward movement of the family's vehicle. This moment recalls Laura Mulvey's claim that "the presence of woman . . . tends to work against the development of a story line, to freeze the flow of action in moments of erotic contemplation."[31] Yet while Mulvey's critique of the "woman as icon" targets narrative films that exploit such moments of visual arrest for male spectatorial pleasure, in *Amores perros* these static images draw critical attention to the way such images freeze and entrap both male and female subjects. If, as Jean Franco has noted, there is an interchangeability in Latin American cinema of the terms *feminine*, *private*, and *immobile* on the one hand, and *masculine*, *public*, and *mobile* on the other, then *Amores perros* throws a spanner in the tradition of Latin American cinema, and provokes critical reflection on the way Mexican visual culture participates in this gendered ideology of stasis and motion through its excessive accumulation of static images of women and its hijacking of male speed.[32]

After the next representation of the crash, which is followed by a second black screen, a friend takes Valeria to the love nest that Daniel has bought, as a surprise, for the two of them, and in this new space of amorous bliss the immobilizing effect of images on women is triply reinforced. While the apartment window looks out onto another giant billboard featuring Valeria's *Enchant* advertisement, within the apartment two other images encroach on her freedom. First, an enlarged contact sheet, a series of black-and-white photographic images of Valeria arranged in a gridlike structure, reiterates the film's interest in vertical and horizontal vectors, invokes again the specter of the filmstrip's individual static photograms, and creates the impression of an endlessly reproducible Valeria caught inside little boxes. On another wall, a painting of an androgynous figure oppressively encased in a red sheath implicates the "purer" aesthetic object of the painting in the gender ideology so visible in the advertising image while suggesting, through the androgyny of the figure, that the immobilizing effect of images might not only affect women. As the red sheath establishes a visual connection with red circles that are visible on the photo-proofs and with the red background of the billboard poster, these three images seem to intersect with each other across the space of the screen, forming an invisible triangle that traps Valeria in their midst. As though to emphasize these images' gravitational force, their resistance to female mobility, when Valeria walks between them, she falls through the floorboards (figures 69–70).

Given the fact that the love nest turns out to be a claustrophobic collection of frozen female images and floor traps, it's perhaps not surprising that Valeria insists, against Daniel's will, on nipping out in the car to get some champagne, taking her fluffy white dog, Richie, with her. Although Valeria's driving, and the filming of it, differs dramatically in pace from Octavio's driving in the opening scene of the film, here, too, the camera is torn between a traveling shot of the car's movement through Mexico City, represented largely from Richie's point of view, and a static, interior, and voyeuristic shot that lingers on the space between Valeria's crotch and lips. Immediately following the third version of the crash, which ends this scene, represented this time by the black screen alone, we encounter an image of the hospitalized Valeria, who now, rigidly wrapped in neck brace and sheets, resembles nothing so much as the cocooned woman in the painting, albeit now rotated ninety degrees and brought to a strange kind of still life (figure 71).

When Valeria returns home from her first hospital visit, her leg has been heavily pinned, and she can move only in a wheelchair. After Daniel leaves for work the next morning, the difficulty of unimpeded forward motion is again emphasized by establishing a tension between vectors, and between still and moving images. First, as Valeria turns her wheelchair to move left from the center of the frame, a wall mirror catches her reflection, uncannily

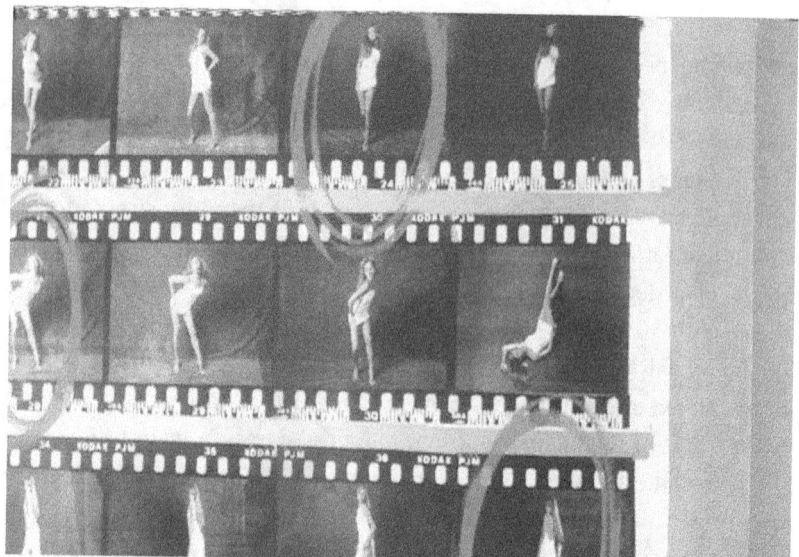

FIGURE 69 Contact sheet with images of Valeria. Still from *Amores perros*.

FIGURE 70 Painting of an androgynous figure wrapped in red cloth. Still from *Amores perros*.

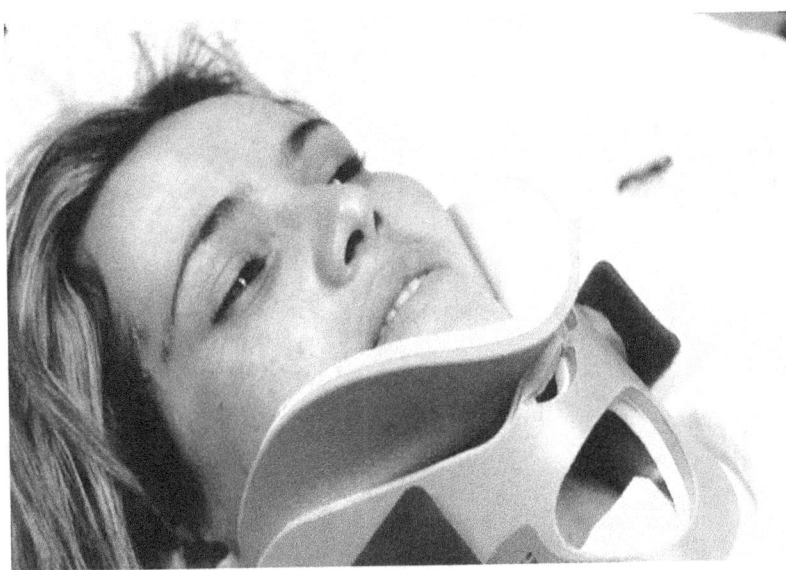

FIGURE 71 Valeria, in a neck brace, following the crash. Still from *Amores perros*.

doubling and dividing Valeria as she moves symmetrically toward the left- and right-hand sides of the frame simultaneously, folding the image out of itself as though exposing it for critical examination. This gesture of doubling is then reiterated as we cut to a shot of Valeria looking through the horizontal slats of the blinds that now cover the "billboard window," which further reinforces the division of this icon of femininity. After seeing a close-up of Valeria, shot from outside the window, her face and the screen horizontally segmented by the blinds, we then cut to a shot, filmed from Valeria's point of view, of her representational double, the billboard image, which is similarly fragmented into thin horizontal strips. In the wake of these visual splits and fractures, Valeria pours over snapshots and magazine images of herself, as though trying to pull her identity together from these fragments of her life (figures 72–73).

Valeria is soon rushed back to hospital, and when she next returns home, it is without her leg. After a brief night-shot of cars moving along the highway, Valeria enters the apartment, and her partial body seems rigid and petrified as the new electric wheelchair moves her through the room as though she is now fully at the mercy of technological motion. She immediately goes to the window, this time wearing a black sweater that visually links her to the mourners at the two funerals that occur in the course of *Amores perros*,

FIGURE 72 Valeria in a wheelchair, along with her reflection in a mirror. Still from *Amores perros*.

FIGURE 73 View of Valeria's *Enchant* billboard advertisement, divided into horizontal segments by the blinds. Still from *Amores perros*.

as well as to the black screens that punctuate the film's multiple depictions of the crash. Looking again through the blinds at the billboard, Valeria finds that her image has now been replaced by a black space on which is imprinted "DISPONIBLE" (SPACE AVAILABLE) and a telephone number. Resonating with the film's repeated use of black screens, as well as with the final shot of Jean-Luc Godard's seminal car-crash film, *Weekend* (1967), in which words on a black screen declare simply, "Fin de cinema," this empty billboard mourns the death of spectacle and announces that there is no image for the present: it has yet to be found. As if to reinforce this gesture, the scene then ends with another fade to black.

González Iñárritu, in his DVD commentary, says of this scene, "I love Goya Toledo [the actress who plays Valeria] here. . . . She's stopped being a doll. Paradoxically, by losing her leg, she gains more inner life and spirituality. She stops being a doll and becomes a woman." Yet, in many ways, at this moment Valeria resembles nothing so much as a doll, specifically recalling one of Hans Bellmer's corporeally fragmented *poupées*. Hal Foster reads Bellmer's *poupées* as an explicit "attack on fascist father and state alike" while recognizing that in choosing to enact political resistance on the site of the female body, they "produce misogynistic effects that may overwhelm any liberatory intentions" and "exacerbate sexist fantasies about the feminine . . . even as they exploit them critically."[33] Foster may too easily separate his two readings of Bellmer's dolls—as sadistic toward women on the one hand, and as representations of the sadistic "armored aggressivity" of fascism on the other—prematurely suspending attention to the former in order to understand the liberatory possibilities of the latter.[34] Yet the space Foster opens, in which he engages the problematic coexistence of radical political and misogynist iconography, is useful for addressing this scene in *Amores perros*. While *Amores perros* clearly at some level participates in a form of misogyny that exhibits and mutilates the glamorous female body, in part justifying this mutilation by positioning Valeria as Spanish, an allegorical figure whose presence destroys Mexican unity and integrity (here figured as Daniel's family), the fact that the film simultaneously works to expose the superficiality, aggression, and misogyny of a wide range of visual images seems to implicate the film in its own critique, and creates a dialectical space around the question of gender that should not be reductively assessed. Though my critical comparison with surrealism may seem farfetched, we can localize this reference by remembering the self-acknowledged influence of Luis Buñuel on González Iñárritu and by recalling the excesses of another female Spanish amputee, as played by Catherine Deneuve in Buñuel's *Tristana* (1970). If the spectacle of Valeria's disfigured body in some ways participates in a Mexican tradition of aligning women with stasis and domestic confinement, it also cites Deneueve's aggressive exposure of her stump to the camera in *Tristana*, which brings the narrative to a halt and forces audiences to reflect on patriarchal culture's aggressive immobilization of women, a disruption of the flow of images that is underscored in both *Amores perros* and *Tristana* by the haunting presence in both films of mournful, solid-black images.

El Chivo y Maru

Although each of the three sections of *Amores perros* engages the tension between stasis and motion, photography and cinema, it is in the third section, "El Chivo y Maru," that the film works hardest to relate these formal tensions to the question of what a New Mexican Cinema might look like. As a former guerrilla who abandoned his family to pursue revolutionary activities, and who subsequently became a private hit man, El Chivo exists on the margins of human society, a fact underscored by his animal nickname: the goat. Though the commercial ambitions of *Amores perros* clearly preclude the film from having any claim to being "guerilla cinema," it is important to note how strongly at the end of the film González Iñárritu's vision for contemporary Mexican cinema aligns itself with the visual perspective of this once radical, but now contaminated goat man and his dog Cofi. Yet what are we to make of this turn to animal vision? In *Electric Animal: Toward a Rhetoric of Wildlife* Akira Lippit identifies the animalistic nature of Eisenstein's vision of cinema in a way that might usefully illuminate the final section of *Amores perros*. Lippit writes, "One senses in Eisenstein's cinema a biomorphic hallucination. Films exist here as complex organisms—they have become animal, or animetaphor. . . . Eisenstein's animetaphor here functions as a technology. . . . Despite the concept of nature it references, the animetaphor is itself profoundly unnatural, prosthetic, pressing the limits of world against the void. . . . The animal projects from a place that is not a place, a world that is not a world. A supplemental world that is, like the unconscious, like memory, magnetic in the technological sense."[35]

So what does El Chivo's animal vision bring to the film's struggle to construct, in the interstices between commercial, technologically reproduced images, a new, authentic way of representing Mexican life? In the early part of the film's third section, El Chivo might seem to represent a kind of purity or naturalism in opposition to the cult of technologically enhanced vision and capitalist mobility that surrounds and undermines the other characters and brings them to a halt. Wandering the streets with a pack of stray dogs and a handcart like a modern-day flâneur, he cannot see clearly, for he willfully refuses to wear glasses, telling one character that if God wants him to see blurry, he'll see blurry. Yet in spite of this apparent rejection of visual technology, El Chivo's world revolves around not only dogs, but also photographs; if his dogs represent a connection to life and movement, photographs repeatedly function as signs of death and loss. He encounters his assassination victims first in photographic form, for example, and only later learns about those he has killed, when he sees their images in newspaper death announcements. Over the course of the final section, however, this narrative becomes increasingly preoccupied with the question of how to animate the photographs that have been so aligned with death, that is, with the project of how to unite dogs and photographs. Cinema is the place where the two eventually meet.

Increasingly unable to cope with his separation from his grown daughter, Maru, who believes him to be dead, El Chivo lingers over photographs of his daughter as a baby, taken prior to his departure from the family for guerrilla life. He steals from Maru's apartment a graduation photograph of Maru with her mother and stepfather, studying them as if wondering how to inscribe himself into the frozen memories of another, how to animate the image and thereby humanize himself. Early in the final section, El Chivo visits a photo-booth, and as the strip of images emerges from the machine—which, like the animal, looks on its subject from no place—we are reminded again of the still photograms which the moving filmstrip represses, and which threaten endlessly to disrupt the illusion, and ideology, of life as motion. El Chivo tears off an image of his own grizzly head and pastes it over the face of Maru's stepfather, visually writing himself back into a story from which he was absent. The effect may be unconvincing, but this rough Eisensteinian collision of two images (staged within the frame instead of within the mind of the viewer) marks the moment when photography seems to start moving toward life. Although photographs never fully lose their gravity within the film, El Chivo's—and by extension, the spectator's—relationship to photography fundamentally shifts after he witnesses, from the sidewalk, the crash between Octavio and Valeria (the film's fourth reiteration of this collision). He loads the left-for-dead dog, Cofi, onto his truck and nurses him back to life, but as soon as El Chivo leaves Cofi alone with his other beloved dogs, Cofi kills them all. Seeing the monstrousness of his own murders in those of the dog, El Chivo refrains from shooting Cofi and decides instead to shift his own relation to the image, and to the world.

Lying back on his bed, El Chivo stretches his neck backward to gaze up at the wall behind him. After a brief close-up of a framed photograph of Maru, which hangs above his bed, followed by various shots of El Chivo stretched out below her picture, the camera moves in for a close-up of El Chivo tentatively reaching for his glasses. Immediately before he puts the glasses on, we see a quick out-of-focus shot of the peeling wall, a reminder of El Chivo's decision to live in a "natural" state of impeded vision, which he now renounces. As the camera cuts back to El Chivo, he licks his lips in anticipation of the clarity of vision that these two lenses will bring him. Then, in one of the most poignant moments of the film, he puts on the glasses as the camera, now in focus, and reflecting El Chivo's point of view, slowly climbs up the peeling wall until it reaches the framed photograph of Maru. In a rare moment when the camera movement within a vertically oriented shot travels up, not down, and is unimpeded by the pull of a competing horizontal vector, we receive the strange impression that Maru's photograph is magically suspended, stopping time and defying gravity, which conveys a sense that this unbearably light cinema has finally been able to catch the present moment, and suggests that perhaps only by adopting new perspectives on the images of what we have lost will the future of cinema reveal itself (figures 74–75).

In the final shots of the film, El Chivo cuts his hair and beard, hacks through his thick toenails and fingernails, and dresses himself in the suit of a businessman who earlier hired El Chivo to kill his half-brother. Instead of killing the half-brother, however, El Chivo ties both brothers up, takes their cars, and leaves them in a room with each other and a gun. Now physically humanized and enabled by his glasses, which are broken but mended with tape, he finds a different photo-booth—this one located beneath another of Valeria's billboards—where he produces four new photographs. Then, in the front seat of one of the stolen cars, he removes the roughly torn photograph he had pasted over the stepfather's head, and sticks on one of the new images with spit (figure 76). At this moment the serial strip of slightly

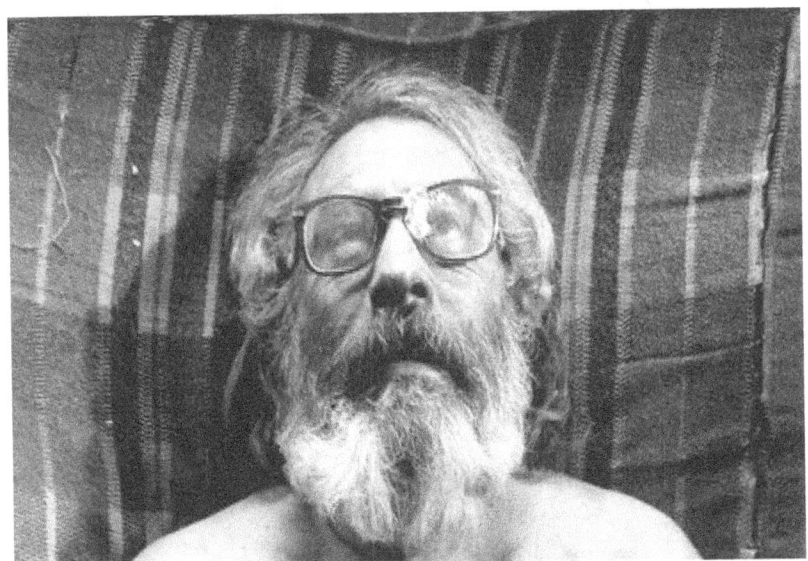

FIGURE 74 El Chivo gazes through his glasses. Still from *Amores perros*.

FIGURE 75 The framed photograph of Maru, seen from El Chivo's perspective. Still from *Amores perros*.

FIGURE 76 El Chivo replaces his own image in the family album. Still from *Amores perros*.

FIGURE 77 El Chivo sets off on foot, accompanied by the dog Negro. Still from *Amores perros*.

changing images combined with the act of carefully cutting the strip and pasting incongruent, nonsynchronous images on top of each other cannot help but again invoke the practice of film editing. But if this is cinema, it is cinema returned to its infancy, with the magical intervals between images that so entranced Eisenstein here being constructed and animated manually, one image at a time.

Before El Chivo drives off in his client's SUV, he glances briefly at Valeria's billboard image descending in the background, reinforcing the overall sense, created by the film, that commercial image culture is at the point of collapse, endlessly having to resist the force of gravity. As El Chivo starts driving the SUV, however, it seems momentarily that his pedestrian, animal cinema is picking up speed as he drives these images off in a bourgeois vehicle. But this is not how the film ends. Once El Chivo has returned his daughter's photocollage, he takes the SUV to a scrap dealer where he sells it for parts, as he had done earlier with the other half-brother's car. As he stands with the dog Cofi in this car graveyard, the dealer asks what the dog is called, and, after a brief pause, El Chivo replies, "Negro." This name, which the subtitles translate as "Blackie," connects the dog to the film's repeated use of black, signifying lost limbs, lost loved ones, and the loss of the image itself; but "Negro" is also, as many of the promotional materials surrounding *Amores perros* note, the well-known nickname of González Iñárritu himself. At this moment, when the director casts himself as a dog, we catch a glimpse of his dream of a cinema that can show us our world from a techno-animal elsewhere, a place that forces us to encounter our own limits by perceiving ourselves, impossibly, through the eyes of an other. Attempting to find a parallel for the human-animal encounter within the visual realm, he takes cinema to the edge of itself by staging its repeated encounters with stasis, photography, and the instant, creating a visual and temporal gap, a pause for thought and imagination. Leaving the detritus of car culture behind him, the bespectacled goat, carrying only a small bag that contains the image of his daughter, sets off on foot, accompanied by Negro, promising to return to Mexico City and his daughter only when he has found himself in the no-man's-land between human and animal, cinema and photography (figure 77).

chapter seven

THE AFTERLIFE OF *WEEKEND*

Or, The University Found on a Scrapheap

I have deliberately postponed analysis of Jean-Luc Godard's *Weekend* (1967), a notorious site of collision, placing it last in order to emphasize a particular aspect of the film that has gone relatively unremarked: its complex relationship to endings. *Weekend* is frequently regarded as one of Godard's most nihilistic films, a film with an utterly terminal logic. For Jean Genêt, writing in 1968 for the *New Yorker*, the lack of creative response to the disasters depicted within the film constituted *Weekend*'s ultimate failure: "All this offers a total evasion on Godard's part of any sane, constructive solution of a situation that started with a weekend bottleneck of cars on a highroad leading out of Paris."[1] But *Weekend*'s scenes of auto-stasis and collision are not simply nihilistic spectacles of disaster, but serve rather as sites for exploring the condition of living on after "the end," and of filmmaking as one form of this living on in the wake of accidents, disasters, uncertainty, and failure.

Weekend is a film in which hyperbolic, apocalyptic visions of disaster repeatedly suggest the end of everything while continually, and often comically, giving way to the next scene. If *Weekend* is a film about disasters and endings, it is also about aftermath, about what happens in the wake of this end, and the next, and the next one after that. This preoccupation with the experience of aftermath, with living on after the disaster, resonates beyond the limits of the film into other works that respond to the film's simultaneous embrace and refusal of "the end," including, in particular, two works that "live on" after Godard's declaration of the end of cinema: Ousmane Sembène's *Xala* (1974), which invokes *Weekend* in its engagement of the condition of living on in Senegal in the wake of decolonization, and Nancy Davenport's *Weekend Campus* (2004), which brings *Weekend* into direct conversation with the challenges facing contemporary North American universities today as they grapple with the role of the arts and humanities within them.

Godard and the Automobile

Few filmmakers have engaged the automobile as extensively, and with such passionate ambivalence, as Godard, particularly within his work of the 1960s. As John Orr argues in *Cinema and Modernity*, *Pierrot le fou* (1965) "shows the centrality of the car in Godard's imagination, that the car indeed is crucial not only to the movie's theme but to Godard's cinematic art itself.... For Godard, the car defines everything. To borrow, wreck and steal is doomed and romantic. To own and be possessive and go on weekend outings is bourgeois. Yet the two are never totally separate.... For Godard's ambivalence over the speed-machine is never exorcized. His love-hate is primordial. The automobile is a work of art but also an agent of destruction."[2] However didactic Godard's films at times become, through the trope of auto-mobility and its accidents emerge his films' more complex engagement with cinema's affinities with capitalism, the limits of and alternatives to narrative cinema, film's relation to other art forms, the relationship between individual and collective freedom, and the (im)possibility of collective movement.

The proliferation of car crashes in *Weekend* is not an isolated phenomenon, but rather a complex culmination of the series of car crashes and thwarted journeys depicted in Godard's earlier films. At the end of *Contempt* (1963)—his most explicit (and frustrated) journey film, in which Fritz Lang plays himself trying, and failing, to translate *The Odyssey* into cinematic form—the characters played by Jack Palance (Jeremy) and Brigitte Bardot (Camille) embark on a road trip to Rome only to find their dreams thwarted by a highly stylized car accident. In order to distinguish his own cinematic crashes from the realism and spectacle of Hollywood smash-ups, Godard limits his viewers' access to the accident scene, substituting the accident itself with the scene of writing. After a shot of the couple's moving sports car, the film cuts to a handwritten letter in which Camille bids farewell to her husband, Paul. The cut forces viewers to shift from the state of being swept along with the car's speed to the slower mode of reading the on-screen text, and we hear the sound of the collision while reading the letter; the scene thus highlights the film's preoccupation with the difficult en-

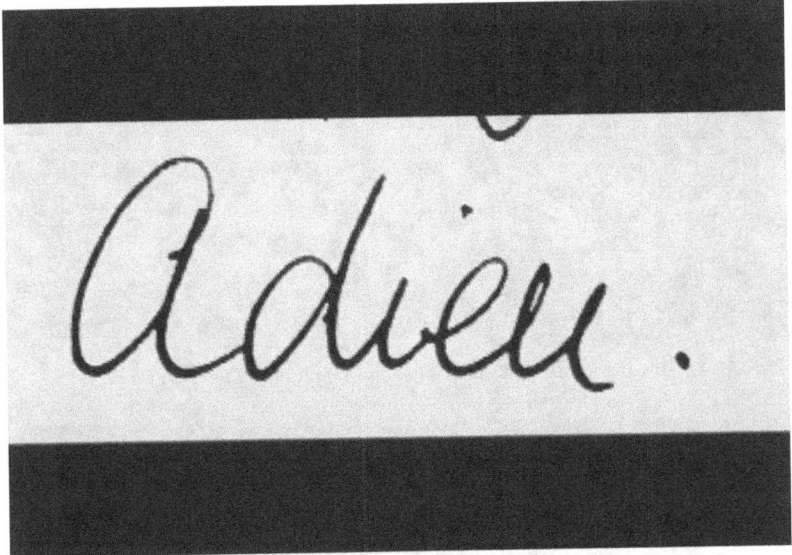

FIGURE 78 Camille's farewell letter. Still from *Contempt*.

FIGURE 79 The scene of the crash. Still from *Contempt*.

counter between literature and cinema to which Godard repeatedly returns in *Weekend*. Only on completion of the text does the film cut to a (highly artificial) tableau of the death scene (figures 78–79).[3] Though David Sterritt has suggested that in *Weekend* Godard transforms "the personal car crash that climaxed *Contempt* into a socioeconomic car clash (Shell vs. citizen)," *Contempt*'s preoccupation with stardom and the studio system ultimately prevents even the accidents in the earlier film from ever occupying a purely personal realm. Indeed, both films explore at some level the extent to which it is ever possible to imagine the personal, sexual relationship outside of the socioeconomic frame.[4]

FIGURE 80 The highly stylized site of a car crash. Still from *Pierrot le feu*.

FIGURE 81 Burning wreckage. Still from *Pierrot le feu*.

While *Contempt* prefigures *Weekend*'s engagement with the difficulty of translation, and with the complex relationship between words and images, *Pierrot le fou* might be read as a testing ground for *Weekend*'s combined use of song, slapstick, pop aesthetics, political critique, and car crashes as sculptural backdrops to acts of cinematic violence, as when the two protagonists stop at the site of a burning car crash in order to dispose of the body of their murder victim within the flames of someone else's (also highly stylized) accident (figures 80–81). For Sterritt, Godard's use of automobiles in his films of the 1960s traces a somewhat linear path that increasingly moves toward cynicism and stasis: "*Weekend* veers even more sharply in this cynical direction, paralyzing cars altogether by cramming them into a self-suffocating gridlock so devoid of action and energy that the movie itself almost stops moving."[5] Yet *Weekend* seems less to move toward paralysis per se than to resist a reductive alignment of cinema with the formal structures, viewing modes, and self-reflexive metaphors offered by the journey motif and narratives of progress.

In the midst of *Weekend*'s serial disasters, film viewers wander unguided through a scrapheap of cinematic and literary references that appear within a nonlinear, nonteleological framework. There are no redemptive figures here; even Hermes, god of road travelers, boundary crossers, and thieves, appears only in the debased form of Corinne's Hermès handbag, and that, too, is lost in the flames of a car accident. Yet to focus on the film's failure to solve the problems it represents, as Genêt does, is to miss its central preoccupation with the experience of living on within the condition of confusion and uncertainty that follows the disaster, refusing either to reassure spectators with fictional solutions or to equate the end of one particular social narrative with the end of everything. As Robin Wood notes, "What makes *Weekend* so much more insupportable is Godard's refusal to see the end of civilisation as final. It is insidiously flattering to the liberal-humanist ego to be able to equate the end of western civilisation with the end of the world—it is simply about the end of *our* world."[6]

The End in *Weekend*

Weekend's well-known traffic-jam sequence, its documentary filming of the slaughter of animals, its characters' turn to cannibalism, and its closing statement ("Fin de conte, Fin de cinéma") all seem to insist on a paradigm of pessimistic finality. Yet if we abandon the linearity of the progressive journey, as the film encourages us to do, *Weekend*'s temporal structure, in conjunction with its activation of the tension between stasis and motion, functions in productive and even comic ways that may resonate with our contemporary sense of living in the wake of disaster. This resonance may in turn prove useful as we consider how to reimagine our relationship to the 1960s and to our own perceived condition of inadequacy, immobility, inertia, and uncertainty. While Warhol's depiction of the Kennedy assassination suspends film viewers in the time of "since," *Weekend* operates under a similar rubric of "afterwardsness" (*Nachträglichkeit*), a psychoanalytic term describing a double movement, as Jean Laplanche has noted, both from present to past, as in retrogressive fantasy, and from past to present, implying "the deposit of something in the individual which will be reactivated later."[7] Central to the film's strange temporality is its almost compulsive re-

FIGURE 82 Stylized repetition of the film's title. Still from *Weekend*.

turn to the problem of endings. Weekend is full of narrative fragments and fictional characters. Stories never develop, being either endlessly disrupted by digression or, as in the case of the Emily Brontë–Alice in Wonderland character, failing to progress because of an inability or unwillingness to produce anything other than nonsensical, paratactically structured poetic images, which ultimately leads to the character's being burned alive.

The concept of "the end" is first introduced, perhaps ironically, at the film's opening. After two dramatic titles—"A film lost in the cosmos" and "A film found on a scrap heap"—which are intercut with short sequences on a balcony, we encounter the film's title printed ten times across the screen in red, white, and blue letters. Because of the layout of the letters, the top line does not read "Weekend," but rather "END WEEK END" (figure 82). If this word order emphasizes the fact that we are at the beginning of the end of something—of bourgeois French society, or of cinema itself, as the final title suggests—it also punningly reminds us that at least in this film, the end is weak, and the repetition of the title institutes a circular and recursive, rather than a linear mode of reading that will persist throughout the film.[8] The weakness of endings is emphasized for the last time by the film's double closure, where the words "End of Story" ("Fin de conte") are followed by a second finale: "End of Cinema" ("Fin de cinema"), suggesting that, at least sometimes, things do come after the end (figures 83–84). Because the film begins with the word *end*, its closing emphasis on the word *fin* (end) operates as a kind of return that institutes an almost circular cinematic form. Yet though the word "fin" returns us to the "end" we found at the film's beginning, it is also important to note that in the process of "returning" we have changed languages, moving from English to French, and the linguistic gap that exists between the opening and closing iterations of "the end" offers translation as a temporal as well as a linguistic practice that traces a path not only between languages, but also among the film's nonlinear temporal points.

A similar intersection of translation and temporal uncertainty occurs when the title "Lumiere en août" appears. When translated into English, this title repeats the title of William Faulkner's novel *Light in August* (1932), but as we play in the space between French and English, we also find an encryption of the French film pioneer Auguste Lumière. Sterritt recalls that Lumière's famous claim that cinema was "an invention without a future" had earlier been inscribed on the projection room wall in *Contempt*, and he sees a resonance between Lumière's and *Weekend*'s terminal world views, stating, "It seems apt that Godard invokes his name in this portrait of what appears to be a society without a future."[9] Yet as Godard evokes the strange, memory-inducing, coppery August light of Faulkner's novel and intertwines it with Lumière's unfulfilled prediction, *Weekend* seems less to testify to the end of film and society than to point to the effect of temporal destabilization and uncertainty inherent to cinema, as film captures the presentness of past moments, allowing those moments to linger on, long after they have past, through the projected beam of light. As they mediate between past and future voices, cinematic images and looks travel across time in search of an other waiting to translate their cryptic messages.[10] Rather than confirming an apocalyptic view of cinema, this title may instead serve as a call for a less linear teleological paradigm through which to understand the experience of living on in the wake of something that feels like the end.

Hal Foster has described our own time as being marked precisely by this sense of "living on" or "coming after"—after modernism, the avant-garde, the 1960s, and postmodernism, and we might read *Weekend* as a film that calls forward to our present condition of uncertainty from the past. Yet, while for Foster, the movements and moments preceding our own possess a clarity of purpose that he contrasts to our present state of confusion,

FIGURE 83 *Weekend*'s first ending: "End of Story." Still from *Weekend*.

FIGURE 84 *Weekend*'s second ending: "End of Cinema." Still from *Weekend*.

Weekend seems strangely ahead of its time in its focus on the difficulty of movement in the late 1960s and its critical reflections on the ideology of movement itself, and this resonance between *Weekend* and the present provides a helpful starting point for reconfiguring our often nostalgic relation to this earlier decade.[11] Indeed, it is perhaps for this reason that contemporary artists, writers, and filmmakers have recently returned to the film with such interest.

In its own time, *Weekend* provoked critical responses that were noticeably preoccupied with questions of aftermath, following, and the film's reception by future generations.[12] Paul Meyersberg, for example, opens his *New Society* review of the film, published in 1968, by noting, "Jean-Luc Godard's latest colour film, *Weekend*, which opens in London this week, is an aftermath movie."[13] Meanwhile, James Roy MacBean begins his *Film Quarterly* review in a similar way: "*Week-end*, in more ways than one, equals 'dead-end:' not for Godard, and not for the cinema, but for a particular type of cinema—the cinema of spectacle—which is pushed to its limit. Future generations (if there are any) may even look back upon *Week-end* as the terminal point of a particular phase in the development—or, more literally, the disintegration of western civilization."[14]

Coming after Godard

Although *Weekend* constantly invokes the temporality of disaster, most explicitly through the proliferation of wrecked car bodies across the French landscape, it would be a mistake to regard this film, which so persistently engages the question of how to develop a nonbourgeois relationship to culture, tradition, and history, and which contains so many homages to other writers, artists, and filmmakers, as simply performing a radical break with the past. The film seems obsessed with the practice of citation and translation as artistic modes of "coming after," and yet no sequence illuminates the film's complex treatment of the difference between "coming after" and simply "following" better than the scene that begins with the title "L'ANGE EXTERMINATEUR" (figure 85). In this scene the character Joseph Balsamo first leads the protagonists Corinne and Roland into a field of wrecked cars, then proceeds magically to transform the field of cars into a flock of sheep (figures 86–87). Both the title and the surrealist appearance of sheep refer to Luis Buñuel's *The Exterminating Angel* (1962), wherein Buñuel momentarily substitutes a flock of sheep for the immobilized bourgeois dinner

FIGURE 85 Title preceding the magical transformation of cars into sheep: "The Exterminating Angel." Still from *Weekend*.

FIGURE 86 Wrecked cars in a field. Still from *Weekend*.

FIGURE 87 The wrecked cars are transformed into sheep. Still from *Weekend*.

guests who seem incapable of thinking for themselves.[15] So while *Weekend* implicitly critiques those who, like Buñuel's sheep-characters, or like the drivers in the traffic jam who, in simply following others, paralyze themselves, this critique itself emerges through a quotation from someone else's film, implying a paradigm of change that retains a relationship to the past.

For those following in the wake of *Weekend*, however, the balance between homage and mimicry seems hard to attain, at least according to Pauline Kael, who in "Weekend in Hell," a review she published in October 1968, offers the most polemic view of the situation.

> At thirty-seven, [Godard] is in something of the position in the world of film that James Joyce was at a considerably later age in the world of literature; that is, he has paralyzed other filmmakers by shaking their confidence (as Joyce did to writers).... Again, like Joyce, Godard seems to be a great but terminal figure.... But when [the most gifted young directors and student filmmakers all over the world] try to follow him they can't beat him at his own game, and they can't (it appears) take what he has done into something else; he's so incredibly fast, he always gets there first.... At each new film festival, one can see the different things that are lifted from him; sometimes one can almost hear the directors saying to themselves, "I know I shouldn't do that, it's too much like Godard, but I've just got to try it." They can't resist, and so they do what Godard has already gone past, and the young filmmakers look out-

of-date before they've got started; and their corpses are beginning to litter the festivals.... You don't have to walk behind Renoir, because he opens an infinite number of ways to go. But when it comes to Godard you can only follow and be destroyed. Other filmmakers see the rashness and speed and flamboyance of his complexity; they're conscious of it all the time, and they love it, and, of course, they're right to love it. But they can't walk behind him. They've got to find other ways, because he's burned up the ground.[16]

For Kael, it is Godard's ability to outpace other filmmakers in a paralyzing way that positions him as one who must not be followed; other critics, however, offer more biting explanations for this same recommendation. Sterritt tends to emphasize the commonalities between Godard and the Situationist International (SI).[17] But the situationists forcefully critique "the directly conformist use of film by Godard" and his "caricature of freedom"; they state, "In the final analysis the present function of Godardism is to forestall a situationist use of the cinema."[18] Furthermore, the situationists object to the affinity between Godard's political "critiques" and "*Mad* magazine humor," and dismiss his work as a paralyzing and obsolescent force that must be rejected.[19] Meanwhile, an article entitled "Cinema and Revolution" (September 1969) asserts, "Godard was immediately *outmoded* by the May 1968 movement, recognized as a spectacular manufacturer of a superficial pseudocritical art rummaged out of the trashcans of the past.... At that point Godard's career as a filmmaker was essentially over, and he was personally insulted and ridiculed on several occasions by revolutionaries who happened to cross his path. The cinema as a means of revolutionary communication is not intrinsically mendacious just because Godard or Jacopetti has touched it."[20] Similarly, for the Italian experimental actor, director, and playwright Carmelo Bene, it is less the overwhelming innovation of Godard seen by Kael than the failure of *Weekend* that makes Godard a figure who must not be followed, leading Bene to declare, in 1969, in an interview published by *Cahiers du Cinéma*, "We have to be done with morality, just like we have to be done with Godard. I repeat this, since it's important if you want to take responsibility."[21]

Yet in spite of the repeated imperatives to "be done" with Godard that emerge in the wake of *Weekend*, few of Godard's films have had as elaborate and extended an afterlife, have been as extensively quoted and reworked, as *Weekend*, and it is primarily to the scenes of crashed cars and the well-known tracking shot to which other filmmakers and artists tend to return. Ironically, one of the very first agents of this compulsive return is Bene himself, who casts Godard's second wife, Anna Wiazemsky (who had appeared in both *Weekend* and *La Chinoise*), in his film *Capricci* (1969), which responds directly to *Weekend*'s scenes of auto-destruction through intensely sexualized demolition derby scenes. While the sexual body rarely appears in *Weekend* after Corinne's account at the beginning of the film of her sexual adventures with two others named Paul and Monique, Bene, prefiguring Ballard's *Crash*, explores the intersection of sex, cinema, and the crashed car throughout the film. In contrast with *Weekend*, condemned by some for throwing didactic ideological monologues and "chunk[s] of theory" at audiences, the words and grunts in *Capricci* can rarely be understood.[22] As Marc Siegel notes, "Bene's films are not political cinema because they stage or represent preconstituted ideas or espouse political ideologies. Rather his films, by deforming the process of representation, allow for new possibilities for conceiving of or even sensing the political."[23]

As we move into the following decade, we find echoes of *Weekend*'s honking horns and congested traffic patterns in *Xala* (1974), Ousmane Sembène's satirical engagement with the aftermath of Senegalese decolonization and the persistent influence of the French, and of Western capitalism more generally, on Senegal. References to *Weekend* permeate the film, but Sembène's invocation of Godard does not represent the kind of passive following that Kael, the situationists, and Bene all warn against. Rather, Sembène develops a dialectical approach in which references to Godard appear as a form of homage, even as these same references to French cinema are implicated in the film's critique of other imported French commodities, such as bottled Evian water and Renault automobiles, that appear throughout *Xala*.

Xala's first reference to *Weekend* appears early in the film, during the opening credits. As the soundtrack puts traditional Wolof singing in competition with a cacophony of honking horns, recalling *Weekend*'s own traffic jamming, we move from a medium close-up shot of the main character El Hadji's third wife-to-be, N'Gone, seated inside a car on the way to her wedding, to a crane shot that sweeps over the roads of Dakar. If this shot reveals the continued economic presence of the French after decolonization by focusing on a Renault building at the roadside, it also does so by making visible the continued postcolonial legacy of the French in African filmmaking through Sembène's use of the expensive technology of the crane (figure 88). In this, too, *Xala* explicitly references the way Godard also quite deliberately drew attention to his implication in capitalist systems of production through use of the crane, and of excessively long tracks, in the traffic-jam sequence. As Harun Farocki notes, "[Godard] often puts the camera on a crane, and the crane on tracks. . . . The crane is more clearly a kind of status symbol, a way of separating *Weekend* from underground filmmaking. It says, 'Look, we have a Mercedes. We're not working with a Deux Chevaux.'"[24] Sembène invokes *Weekend* on numerous other occasions. The procession of French cars approaching the wedding is again accompanied by the referential sound of honking horns. The last vehicle in the procession, a wedding gift, is a small blue car that is facing in the opposite direction to the truck that bears it, which reminds us of a similar use of stasis, opposing directions, and size differentials between vehicles in *Weekend* (figures 89–90). Yet Sembène's reference to Godard, like Bene's, is not uncritical. While in *Weekend* a head-on encounter between a woman's small car and a gigantic Shell oil truck seems to declare the impossibility of individual opposition to corporate power, implicitly reinforcing capitalism's ideology of inevitability and impotence, in *Xala* the small car and the truck are not head-on, but back-to-back, as though to suggest the possibility of simply moving in other directions and at different speeds, a possibility played out by El Hadji's daughter Rama, who decides not to drink bottled water and to ride a moped.[25]

At the wedding reception, two guests chat in French (the film moves back and forth between French and Wolof) about the niece of one of the men, and this conversation once again establishes a relationship between *Weekend*'s disaster-prone cars and the practice of translation.[26] After the friend comments, "You're niece is magnificent. . . . She has such a pretty mouth, I'll give her a Mercedes," the uncle says to his niece, "I'll give you a villa for the weekend." This mention of "the weekend" becomes the catalyst for a linguistic problem. "How do you say 'weekend' in English?," the men ask each other. Eventually, an androgynous servant answers their query directly to the camera: "'Weekend' is 'weekend.'" Though *Xala*'s repetition of the word echoes *Weekend*'s own repetition of its title at the film's opening, and though both cases threaten, through repetition and wordplay, to destabilize the word's meaning and reduce it to jibberish, in *Xala*, the servant's

FIGURE 88 The Renault building in Dakar. Still from *Xala*.

FIGURE 89 A small car faces in the direction opposite to that of its transport truck. Still from *Xala*.

FIGURE 90 A small car collides head-on with a corporate oil truck. Still from *Weekend*.

assertion of the lack of difference between English and French—"'weekend' is 'weekend'"—expands the film's critique of the French legacy in Africa to include both the British legacy in Africa and American neoimperialism, too. Yet while some have critiqued *Xala* for operating within a overly simplistic binary paradigm of African and European, David Murphy rightly suggests that the film approaches the challenges of postcoloniality with far greater complexity than this, and supporting this view are Sembène's ambivalent intertextual references to Godard, which seem to suggest the possibility of more complex and nuanced modes of "coming after."[27]

Nancy Davenport's FAUX-TOGRAPHIE

While *Xala* offers a postcolonial response to *Weekend*'s engagement with issues of failed mobility and aftermath, Nancy Davenport's digital work *Weekend Campus* (2004) returns to the challenge of coming after not only Godard, but also after the 1960s more generally, from within a North American, academic context.[28] The photographer describes her DVD (figures 91–95) in the following way:

> The piece is set along the entrance of a university, the institutional buildings visible beyond a generic campus landscape. In the foreground, there is a seemingly endless line of waiting cars, punctuated by the wreckage of a series of car accidents. As the piece proceeds with horizontal movement, we pass an accumulation of accidents and witnesses—portraits of the student body, faculty and police. Intermittently, there are groups of students gathered at the edge of the road. Some are staring blankly out at the viewer; all are frozen in photographic stasis. In fact, the whole scene is a still image, a digital montage constructed from hundreds of stills I had taken at junkyards and at universities across the country. The montage was then looped and animated so that it moves across the screen like a tracking shot.
>
> In addition to the rubbernecking motion of the image plane, the other element of the piece that counters photographic stasis is the recurring flash of police light. The image comes awake momentarily with the changing light, which generates a transitory cinematic effect.[29]

Like Kenneth Goldsmith in *Traffic* (2007), a literary homage to Ballard, Warhol, and Godard that Craig Dworkin describes as "recall[ing] nothing so much as the extended tracking shot in Jean-Luc Godard's 1967 film

Week-End," Davenport responds from the present to the temporal, political, and aesthetic crises figured by the car accidents in *Weekend* by staging a remake involving not only car accidents, but also collisions among different media.[30] Most explicitly, *Weekend Campus* maps the abrupt shift the car-crash enacts from movement to stasis onto the tense relationship between both cinema and photography, and analog and digital media, inviting us to explore how suggestions of movement and stasis function in each, and how changes in media both participate in and shape our understanding of moments of historical transition. This digital work's reference to an analog film activates competing temporalities that emerge through both the contrasted temporalities of "'old" and "new" media and the historically specific reference from 2004 back to 1967, the year of *Weekend*'s production.[31] A more subtle but equally precise reference to the late 1960s operates through the architectural structures in the background of Davenport's images, which she shot at various college campuses across Canada and the United States, all of which were built around the time that *Weekend* was made.[32] The importance of this architectural backdrop to the looping scenes of wreckage is emphasized by the fact that Davenport has frequently exhibited *Weekend Campus* alongside a second series, entitled *Campus*, that consists of still, digitally manipulated photographs depicting late-1960s college architecture. But what are we to make of *Weekend Campus*'s juxtaposition of still, "still-moving," and remembered cinematic images; of architecture with images; and of the modern university with the junkyard's abandoned vehicles? How do the formal, aesthetic tensions and expansions enacted in Davenport's work relate to the issues of politics, pedagogy, and history that exist at the thematic level?

Davenport's comments on the relationship of *Weekend Campus* to Godard's traffic jam testify yet again to the unusual importance of endings in *Weekend*, as well as to the role that spectatorial fantasy plays in the afterlife of a film.

> I imagine that most people rewind this famous sequence when they watch Jean-Luc Godard's *Weekend*. But in my case, it is not a simple instance of rewind fever, wanting to watch the great scene over and over. I literally do not want this scene to end. I have always fantasized that when we reach the final accident, it would not be the end, but the beginning of another traffic jam, then another accident, then another traffic

FIGURE 91 Original photo by Nancy Davenport. Still from *Weekend Campus*. Courtesy Nicole Klagsbrun Gallery, New York.

FIGURE 92 Original photo by Nancy Davenport. Still from *Weekend Campus*. Courtesy Nicole Klagsbrun Gallery, New York.

FIGURE 93 Original photo by Nancy Davenport. Still from *Weekend Campus*. Courtesy Nicole Klagsbrun Gallery, New York.

FIGURE 94 Original photo by Nancy Davenport. Still from *Weekend Campus*. Courtesy Nicole Klagsbrun Gallery, New York.

FIGURE 95 Original photo by Nancy Davenport. Still from *Weekend Campus*. Courtesy Nicole Klagsbrun Gallery, New York.

jam—continuing on and on. The duration of Godard's shot certainly suggests an endlessness, a progression to more of the same.... The camera movement sets it apart from the rest of the film. In cinematic language, the tracking shot exaggerates an illusion of temporal continuity, a horizontal momentum of history and time. Here this momentum confronts a plugged roadway of wreckage and waiting traffic, an image of interminable delay. It is a scene of excessive continuity which is also relentless in its congestion, its depiction of society at a standstill.[33]

As she foregrounds this moment of transition from analog to digital forms of photography and cinema, Davenport digitally reconstructs a scene from *Weekend* in which, as in several other well-known cinematic sequences (such as the final scenes of *Two Tars* or the opening of Fellini's *8½*), the traffic jam functions as a self-reflexive figure through which to reflect on the formal possibilities and limitations of the strip of film, with its collection of frames lined up in serial fashion.[34]

Yet, however explicit the references to Godard's film may be, Davenport's work feels very different from *Weekend*, and it is only through a close comparison of the relationship among cars, bodies, and the camera in each work that we can begin to understand how these works differ formally, and to what effect. We can take as a starting point the production of *Weekend*'s traffic-jam scene, humorously documented in the *Manchester Guardian* by Peter Lennon, an eyewitness, as a scene less of persistent, linear, and unbroken movement than of frustrated retakes, repetitions, undulations, and distractions.

> A motor horn gave the signal to set everything in motion. Possibly to irritate his new Communist supporters of "La Chinoise" the starting signal was "Algérie Française."
>
> At each take the movement of the camera was precisely the same. Starting with a high, stretched neck to catch the couple roaring into the blocked traffic, it then sank down to drift parallel with their erratic passage through the honking drivers and then rose again to get a bird's eye view of the holocaust at the crossroads as the couple [Corinne and Roland] swung clear out into the deserted grim countryside.
>
> The first time it all went wrong. With his stubborn determination to dictate every frame of a sequence, Godard could not make allowances for slippery human beings coming at him on a kind of conveyer belt. They kept pulling out of the frame while the cameraman was condemned to follow an imaginary line. After haggling, they compromised: the camera would still follow the line but with freedom to swing about to catch what was happening. . . .
>
> He went through this seven times before lunch and four after.[35]

While the traffic-jam sequence is often misremembered in reviews of the film as a single, unbroken, horizontal, unidirectional shot along the edge of a traffic jam, Lennon's description highlights the distracted camera movements that disrupt and resist the perfection of the horizontal line Godard envisioned, and that remind viewers of the various alternatives to the scene's dominant movement along a horizontal line. We might note, for example, the camera's vertical movements when an outsized object like the Shell truck comes into view, or when the camera betrays a momentary interest in the yellow fields behind the road. Just as the camera's movement in this sequence is often selectively remembered, so, too, the soundtrack is often reduced to nothing more than a cacophony of honking car horns, effacing what could be described as delicate flashes of musical optimism, which stand in tension with the scene's audio aggression, as when a few bars of jazz accompany the appearance of schoolchildren, a strange moment of Tatiesque humanism in a sequence frequently regarded as marking the peak of Godard's misanthropy.

While the speed of the tracking shot remains steady during the traffic-jam sequence, the camera, being outrun by the children, pans right as though reluctant to allow them to leave the film frame. At other times, it pans left, seemingly resistant to being carried along by the relentless mechanical motion of the cinematic apparatus, and to the scene's spatialized enactment of film's affinity with what Rodowick calls "the flow of everyday life."[36] The final moments of this sequence, however, invite an ambivalent response. Because of the grating nature of the car horns on the soundtrack and the uncertainty produced by the traffic jam's serial structure, the end of the track, which is punctuated by another car accident, produces a certain sense of relief. Yet as the camera follows Corinne and Roland speeding off into the field, beginning again in a new direction, we are invited to indulge, as Davenport does, in a fantasy of film as a medium without end or repetition, defying both the structure of the linear filmstrip and this indexical medium's necessary relationship to pastness and temporal delay, to its inevitable repetition of a time that has already passed.

Although the seriality of the jam to some extent provokes in Davenport a desire for continuity, we might also read her fantasy of a film without end as a response to Raoul Coutard's final camera movements at the end of the line. As Corinne and Roland zoom past the accident and turn right, the camera, which has reached the end of the track, shifts from linear to circular movement, beginning a lengthy pan that turns almost 180 degrees to the right, until it seems unable to continue further.

Though the camera here fails to complete the circle and return us to the road, leaving the desire for continuity unfulfilled, a later scene, introduced by the title "Action Musicale," revisits this dream of interminable film that emerges at the end of the jam. Here the camera has abandoned linear in favor of circular movement, offering not one but two complete 360-degree counterclockwise pans (followed by a circle in the opposite direction) in a French farmyard, where a pianist performs Mozart for the farmworkers who stand, mannequin-like, in the presence of "art." Both sequences are formally built on the camera's tracing of a horizontal line, but each sequence's distinct use of space creates a different temporal effect. Although the bodies being filmed in both sequences are relatively static, the motion along a line in the traffic-jam sequence creates the effect of a progressive temporal motion, and this in turn mirrors the forward movement of the filmstrip. However, in the "Action Musicale" sequence, the movement of the camera along a circular rather than linear route from a static "fulcrum" creates a sensation not of endlessness, but of a loop, of being caught temporally inside the circle that is being spatially marked. We know that the filmstrip is continuous (i.e., that this is not a loop), because we see changes with each revolution, yet perhaps because of the absence of movement along a straight line, this scene does not imply the same degree of infinite movement that the traffic jam's linear movement through space instills.

Though Davenport stresses *Weekend Campus*'s reference to Godard's traffic-jam sequence in particular, her looping photographic frieze of frozen figures also recalls the earlier film's circular farmyard sequence. Indeed, by considering *Weekend Campus* in relation to the traffic-jam and farmyard sequences in *Weekend*, both of which stand out because of their striking engagement with the horizontal line, we begin to see more clearly how Davenport's use of the space between old and new media allows us to explore our contemporary moment's relationship to the 1960s without adopting an attitude of either nostalgia or pessimism, and provokes us to consider the differences between our phenomenological experience of space and time in film and digital media.

By exploiting the "flat" effect of digital photographic montage and combining it with the illusion of temporal duration created by the flashing light, which, as Davenport points out, tricks viewers into thinking that they are perceiving not only moving images, but also images recorded in real time, *Weekend Campus* paradoxically seems to collapse the progressive horizontal motion of Godard's linear tracking shot with the potential infinity of the 360-degree pan. Davenport, of course, has substituted a temporal digital loop for the physical circle traced in space in continuous time by the camera in *Weekend*'s farmyard, but this substitution, or translation, of space into time creates a work in which viewers experience visually the illusion of moving in one direction along a straight, unbroken, temporal and spatial path while simultaneously encountering over and over again things that "happened" before. And in this way *Weekend Campus* creates a medium for a non-nostalgic encounter with the 1960s, one that resolutely insists on its belonging to the time of the present while simultaneously calling out to earlier figures of inertia and failure. *Weekend Campus* thus does the important work of resisting the notion that recursive encounters are necessarily opposed to the idea of progress, or to an engagement with the present.

Weekend Campus lacks the wandering and subjective gaze of the camera in the traffic-jam sequence, a gaze that acts as a counterpoint to the mechanical precision of the tracking motion, but as the unending digital frieze moves across the screen in imitation of the tracking shot, Davenport relocates the distractable gaze of *Weekend*'s camera in the viewer, as each repetition of the same provides the opportunity to look again and differently at the images that appear, establishing a relationship not only with the cinema of the 1960s, but also with the very earliest film loops and spectatorial pleasures of the cinema of attractions. Furthermore, because even our first encounter with each part of the loop provokes a sense of déja vu through the work's use of iconic film and architectural references, *Weekend Campus* also seems to question the possibility of any "new" encounter with an image. Although looping images has always been possible with analog film, Davenport's use of a digital loop that is purely temporal (there is neither circular filmstrip nor spinning camera) reinforces the paradoxical experience of a looping straight line through which it is possible to conceptualize a continuous process of beginning anew, but with a sense of history, a counterpoint to the nihilistic experience of stasis and repetition without change.[37]

The strange temporal logic of *Weekend* is further confused by the way the frieze of images moves across the screen from left to right, which forces viewers to read backward the words that appear within the work, continuing *Weekend*'s own play with letters, word order, and puns, slowing down the time it takes to "process" the information offered within the image and reminding us of the extent to which seemingly linear activities like reading rely on recursive strategies and memory. In *Weekend Campus* the words we encounter explicitly address the question of temporal deferral and indebtedness in the form of one of the band's slogans that announces, "Taking care of Today Tomorrow" ("Tomorrow Today of care Taking"), and this ominous temporal frame is further reinforced by the presence of a car plastered with ads for student credit cards, suggesting a paradigm of "live now, pay later."[38] But what are we to make of this scene's students, professors, and police, scattered and frozen amid car wrecks, credit-card ads, and college art buildings? How might we interpret this work's stance toward our own moment through its references to *Weekend* and its difference from it? What kind of vision of art, education, and campus life is this?

Davenport resists a cynical interpretation of the figures who populate the landscape she has created, stating, "Unlike the characters in Godard's traffic jam who are all busily engaged with self-involved tasks or futile arguments, indifferent to the carnage around them, everyone in *Weekend Campus* is depicted in the stillness of witnessing and waiting. For me, these witnesses are not blank or apathetic subjects, but rather shocked subjects—shocked by out-of-control forces into an appearance of passivity. They are also shocked into an unwilling collective. The social map of Godard's *Weekend* is impossible now, just as any catalogue of the social is incomplete, inadequate. At this moment of post-feminism, post-identity politics, post-community— what could make subjects cohere as a collective?"[39] Resisting the critical tendency to dismiss contemporary students, academics, and artists as ineffectual in their opposition to the war and as lacking in the political vision and coherence found in earlier generations, *Weekend Campus*'s staging of the collision of cinematic and digital time and space allows us an opportunity to reconceptualize intergenerational relationships through the less linear paradigms that emerge at the intersection of these overlapping media.

Davenport brings into consciousness the extent to which contemporary expectations for political action might be shaped by photographic memories of past conflicts, conflicts that, as Gilles Deleuze argues in his essay on Carmelo Bene, "One Manifesto Less," become immediately "normalized, codified, institutionalized," emerging as "products," rather than destabilizers, of systems of power.[40] Both *Campus*, Davenport's photographic series of deserted, brutalist-influenced college spaces, and *Weekend Campus* feature the stark campus architecture of the 1960s, and Davenport acknowledges that the buildings she shot for *Campus* "were either the sites of very particular Vietnam War protests or they were built shortly after '68" (figures 96–98). As we look at these images, we feel like we have seen buildings, or ones like them, before; but something is missing: they are devoid of the scarf-wrapped students, raised fists, and riot police that made the earlier, iconic photographs that featured these buildings so memorable. While to some, the absence of familiar signs of political activism within the university may suggest a nostalgic longing for a more effective and engaged era, along with a disdain for the contemporary era's passivity, Davenport's

FIGURE 96 "Classroom 1" (C-Print, 50 × 36", 2004), by Nancy Davenport. Courtesy Nicole Klagsbrun Gallery, New York.

FIGURE 97 "Library" (C-Print, 44 × 31", 2004), by Nancy Davenport. Courtesy Nicole Klagsbrun Gallery, New York.

FIGURE 98 "Performing Arts Center" (C-Print, 33 × 25.5", 2004), by Nancy Davenport. Courtesy Nicole Klagsbrun Gallery, New York.

work simultaneously conjures up and counteracts this nostalgic interpretation through its memory of Godard's emphasis on the 1960s' own confusion and failure. If the activists are missing in these photographs, this absence may well operate less as a declaration of failure on Davenport's part than as a more strategic operation of amputation or subtraction, which, Deleuze suggests, may constitute an essential step in the process of becoming-minoritarian: "You begin by subtracting, taking away everything that comprises an element of power, in language and in gestures, in representation and in the represented. You cannot even say that it is a negative operation inasmuch as it already engages and sets in motion positive processes. You will thus take away or amputate history, because history is the temporal marker of power.... You will subtract the constants, the stable or stabilized elements, because they belong to the major use."[41]

The cinematic crash represents ideological and aesthetic impurity, hybridity, and uncertainty. As a self-reflexive figure for the medium of film, it persistently turns our attention toward film's collisions with other media. Its gestures of radical creativity, such as those found in the Futurist Manifesto, exist in dialectical tension with the traumatized flesh and searing pain of the accident victim. And even at its most clearly experimental and critical, the cinematic crash never quite manages to escape its affinity with the capitalist commodity culture of cars, disaster spectacles, and territorial expansion. For some, the instability and impropriety of this trope, its inability to offer a clear paradigm of either cultural redemption or cultural critique will prove frustrating; yet it is precisely this unstable figure's uncertainty, its paradoxical suggestion of high speed and total immobilization, that resonates with the contemporary moment, in which we seem to be both stuck and unable to keep up with an ever accelerating pace, struggling to find a still, reflective place in which to think and from which to act. In Don DeLillo's *White Noise* (1984), Professor Murray Jay Siskind's seminar on car crashes and film produces two polarized, seemingly irreconcilable positions: his own ("I tell them they can't think of a car crash in a movie as a violent act. It's a celebration. . . . Look past the violence. . . . There is a wonderful brimming spirit of innocence and fun."), and that of his students ("What about the sheer waste, the sense of a civilization in a state of decay? . . . Look at the crushed bodies, the severed limbs.").[42] My consideration of cinema's century-long preoccupation with car crashes is more dialectical than Professor Siskind's approach; it neither "looks past the violence" nor fails to recognize that, however proximate, the cinematic body and the physical body are not the same. Film theory is, at least in part, the practice of thinking about, and through, the distance between these two kinds of bodies, which makes this discourse useful not only for our understanding of the ever-changing phenomenology of cinema, but also for our ethical reflections on how to live on in the wake of those disasters that occur at a distance from ourselves.

I have explored how earlier shifts in collective and individual experiences of the temporality and velocity of life that parallel our own both respond to and express themselves through technological transitions and translations, with a particular focus on the transitions, collisions, and mutations that occur when film borders on photography, literature, television, and video. At its best, the bastardized field of cinema studies, with which this book is in conversation, can offer an ideal space in which to think about the challenges currently facing humanities educators in general, and arts educators in particular, not least because, in the increasingly corporate private university, few fields exist in closer and more uncomfortable proximity to the "development" office, whose role often involves trying to elicit money for the pursuit of critical thinking from organizations that might benefit from an absence thereof in their consumers, and attempting to construct a dynamic, glitzy, and "relevant" profile for the humanities, the value of which is hard to calculate in corporate terms.

Film scholars, of course, always have the option of crafting academic programs that structurally react to the commercially minded, antihistorical framing of cinema studies as the more practical or marketable face of the humanities by excluding popular film and media from their curricula in order to focus exclusively on texts that seem somehow less contaminated by film's essential hybridity and commercialism. Yet this approach would miss the opportunity this field offers us to engage with students, colleagues, administrators, and donors in critical conversations about the place of commercial culture in the humanities at what feels like a moment of crisis and change. *Weekend Campus* presents university arts buildings as sites of disaster and stasis. But if such images bear witness to earlier projects that have gone wrong or simply run out of energy, they also challenge us to reflect on the intersections among space, time, and pedagogy we have created for our own time; to see students and teachers as occupying this space together; and to use the confusion that emerges at those places where past and present, old media and new media collide as a vehicle for bringing new modes of thinking, seeing, and feeling into the world.

NOTES

Introduction

1. Frampton, "The Invention without a Future," 70.
2. Rodowick, "Dr. Strange Media," 1400.
3. Ibid.
4. Ibid.
5. Frampton, "The Invention without a Future," 74.
6. Baudrillard, "The Ecstasy of Communication," 127; Virilio, "The Third Window," 180. Both are quoted in Friedberg, *Window Shopping*, 203.
7. Dimendberg, "The Will to Motorization," 107; Corrigan, *A Cinema without Walls*, 146.
8. Although I mention these trajectories together in the context of "embodiment," I do not mean to suggest that these approaches can be equated with each other. Each is quite different from the other, except in the way they move away from psychoanalytic film theory's focus on disembodiment. For examples of these approaches, see in particular the work of Laura Kipnis, Vivian Sobchack, Linda Williams, and Jackie Stacey.
9. At a recent conference entitled "The Art of Projection" (Berlin, October 2006), Mary Ann Doane commented that her doubts about descriptions of embodied and physically mimetic spectatorship stem from the fact that this is not how she watches film. I have found her resistance to a wholesale embrace of "embodied" spectatorship theory extremely suggestive as I have attempted to articulate the ambivalent spectatorial position articulated by the car-crash films I address herein.
10. See Baudrillard, "Two Essays: 1. Simulacra and Science Fiction. 2. Ballard's *Crash*"; Sobchack, "Baudrillard's Obscenity."
11. Self, *Junk Mail*, 348, quoted in Day, "Ballard and Baudrillard," 290. On this same issue, one might also look at Andrew Hultkrans's "Body Work," in which he recounts a conversation he had with Ballard: "He said, 'Well, it must be a cautionary tale.' And I said, 'When you were writing the book, were you thinking: "I

am writing a cautionary tale?"' And he said no. So I said, 'So basically, this is an analysis that you're doing of your book after the fact.' And he said yes.... When the film is being attacked for being pornographic and perverse, it's too easy to fall back on saying, 'No, no, it's a cautionary tale.' And I feel that Ballard—tough as he is—bought into that. I'm trying to be experimental, but not cautionary" (76, 81). Claudia Springer, in her feminist consideration of *Crash*, also turns to Ballard's preface to the French edition of his novel, but her argument is stronger when it locates the moral dimension of *Crash* in the novel's insistence on exploring "the unresolved tension between surface and depth" ("The Seduction of the Surface," 205–6).

12. Gunning, "From the Kaleidoscope to the X-ray," 25. Works that have shaped this field include Schivelbusch, *The Railway Journey*; Crary, *Techniques of the Observer*; Crary, *Suspensions of Perception*; Gunning, "An Aesthetics of Astonishment" and "The Cinema of Attraction"; Friedberg, *Window Shopping*; Bruno, *Streetwalking on a Ruined Map*; and Kirby, *Parallel Tracks*.
13. Kirby, *Parallel Tracks*, 57.
14. Gunning, "An Aesthetics of Astonishment," 37.
15. Schivelbusch, *The Railway Journey*, 166. The language of sacrifice marks Freud's description of the shield: "By its death, the outer layer has saved all the deeper ones from a similar fate" (quoted in Schivelbusch, *The Railway Journey*, 166).
16. Hansen, "Benjamin and Cinema," 317.
17. Ibid.
18. Ibid., 335.
19. Ibid., 334.
20. Gunning, "An Aesthetics of Astonishment," 41.
21. Ibid., 43.
22. Hansen, "Benjamin and Cinema," 325.
23. See Redhead, *Paul Virilio*, 33. I am grateful to Melissa Rangona for pushing me to think more carefully about the role of Virilio's writing on accidents in this project.
24. Virilio, *Unknown Quantity*, 59.
25. Ibid., 27.
26. Ibid., 25.
27. Ibid., 9.
28. *None for the Road*, made in conjunction with the Yale Center of Alcohol Studies, features experiments on rats followed by a teenage bar-scene narrative. *Stop Driving Us Crazy* features a soundtrack by Art Blakey and his band, and tells the story of a Martian who comes to earth in the form of a car, only to discover the brutality of the sinning human race through their reckless driving. As one car exclaims, incredulously, "Some of them even like getting loaded!" These and many other car-safety films from this period can be found in the Prelinger Ar-

chive, which contains ephemeral films from between 1927 and 1987. For more information, see the web site of the Prelinger Archive.
29. Virilio shares Malfetti's association of the emergence of transportation systems with the destruction of the social: "The very notion of a neighbour will at some point disappear for ever, this kinetic addiction to the sudden disappearance of the congener will have the tragic character of a social divorce" (Virilio, *Negative Horizon*, 53).
30. Malfetti, "Human Behavior—Factor X," 98.
31. See Butler, *Giving an Account of Oneself*.
32. Virilio, *Negative Horizon*, 39. For a discussion of the place of deviance in traffic-safety discourse, see Albert, "Primitive Drivers: Racial Science and Citizenship in the Motor Age," 327–51.
33. Virilio, *Negative Horizon*, 40.
34. Ibid., 47.
35. Ibid., 91.
36. Brottman, *Car Crash Culture*, xv.
37. Schnapp, "Crash (Speed as Engine of Individuation)," 3.
38. Ibid., 4.
39. Ibid., 8–9.
40. Ibid., 9.
41. Ibid., 7.
42. Hansen, "Benjamin and Cinema," 321.
43. Schnapp, "Crash (Speed as Engine of Individuation)," 27.
44. Ibid., 26, 27, 28.
45. Ibid., 3.
46. Gunning, "An Aesthetics of Astonishment," 41.
47. Schnapp, "Crash (Speed as Engine of Individuation)," 35, 34.
48. Ibid., 26.
49. Ibid., 7.
50. Schnapp explicitly distinguishes his own work from that of Virilio for two reasons. First, he sees Virilio as reducing "speed's history to that of motorization and mechanization" (Schnapp, "Crash [Speed as Engine of Individuation]," 4), which one would have to admit is not an accurate reflection of a work such as *Negative Horizon*, in which Virilio carefully begins his history of speed with speed's origin, the "woman of burden" (Virilio, *Negative Horizon*, 40), and the domestication and breeding of the war horse (Virilio, *Negative Horizon*, 48). Second, Schnapp sees Virilio's "stimulating (though rarely rigorous) ruminations on velocity and modernity" as being "undergirded by a recurring strain of technological determinism and naïve apocalypticism" (Schnapp, "Crash [Speed as Engine of Individuation]," 4n8).
51. Schnapp, "Crash (Speed as Engine of Individuation)," 5.

52. Ibid., 5, 9, 26.
53. Marinetti, "The Founding and Manifesto of Futurism," 20–21.
54. Ibid., 22.
55. Wolff, "On the Road Again"; Franco, "Beyond Ethnocentrism"; and Coffman, "Woman in Motion."
56. Wolff, "On the Road Again," 193.
57. For a detailed discussion of some of these transgressions in early train films, see Kirby, "Romances of the Rail in Silent Film."
58. Suleiman, "Mothers and the Avant-Garde," 135–46. See also Suleiman, *Subversive Intent*.
59. Hansen, "Benjamin and Cinema," 316.
60. Freud, "Instincts and Their Vicissitudes," 87.
61. Freud, *Beyond the Pleasure Principle*, 32.
62. Ibid., 33.
63. Laplanche, "The Drive and Its Source Object," 129.
64. Ibid., 126.
65. Ibid., 127.
66. Ibid., 132.
67. Freud, *Beyond the Pleasure Principle*, 35.
68. Ibid., 71.
69. Laplanche, "The Drive and Its Source Object," 118.
70. Freud ends his book with a quotation from the last lines of "Die beiden Gulden," a German version of one of the *Maqâmât* of al-Hariri: "What we cannot reach flying we must reach limping.... The Book tells us it is no sin to limp" (Freud, *Beyond the Pleasure Principle*, 78).
71. Kristeva, *Revolt, She Said*, 107–8.
72. Virilio, *Speed and Politics*, 29.
73. Virilio, *Speed and Politics*, 30. bell hooks offers a different critique of feminist movement, claiming that it "lost meaning as the terrain of radical feminist politics was overshadowed by a lifestyle-based feminism which suggested any woman could be a feminist no matter what her political beliefs" (*Feminism Is for Everybody*, 11). Although hooks writes about "new feminist movement" with what seems, at times, like a touch of nostalgia, advocating the revival of feminist consciousness-raising groups in communities, for example, her ongoing commitment to imagining how one might understand both community and pedagogy differently counterbalances this effect.
74. Alexander Laurence, "Avital Ronell Interview" (1994), http://www.altx.com/int2/avital.ronell.html. In the same interview, Ronell states that in her book *Finitude's Score* "there is a suspension between the distinction dividing the mediatic fast-track and the slow, deliberate philosophical trekking through problems.

This is one of the major problems of our modernity, which is the speed as Paul Virilio calls it, and also the need to resist acceleration when thinking about it."

75. Nancy, *The Inoperative Community*, 12.
76. Ibid., 25. I am grateful to Craig Dworkin for introducing me to the intellectual and aesthetic possibilities of cinematic thinking.
77. Butler, *Undoing Gender*, 180.
78. Jakobsen, *Working Alliances and the Politics of Difference*, 155. Hal Foster uses the phrase "paradigm-of-no-paradigm" to describe the contemporary moment in *Design and Crime* (128).

Chapter One. "Jerky Nearness"

1. Benjamin, *Reflections*, 85–86. For a detailed discussion of Benjamin's position in "One-Way Street," as well as Theodore Adorno's critique of that position, see Hansen, "Benjamin and Cinema."
2. Dionysius Lardner, *The Museum of Science and Art*, 196.
3. Woolf, "The Movies and Reality."
4. Ibid., 231.
5. Ibid.
6. Ibid., 233.
7. Ibid.
8. Rodowick, *The Virtual Life of Film*, 84.
9. I am grateful to Tom Gunning for drawing my attention to the prominence of the car crash in early cinema and, in particular, to the relationship between *Two Tars* and Jean-Luc Godard's *Weekend* (1967), a relationship I examine in chapter 2.
10. Hepworth, *Came the Dawn*, 58. For examples of these urban street scenes, see the films of Mitchell and Kenyon, a film company, some of which are included on the DVD *Electric Edwardians: The Films of Mitchell and Kenyon*. Hepworth not only shot many of these local urban films, with his friend A. D. Thomas (a.k.a. Edison-Thomas or Thomas-Edison), in the "grim city" of Manchester, but, as Leo Enticknap points out, he also has a cameo role in M&K 422: *Lord Robert's Visit to Manchester* (1901). See Enticknap, "'A Real Brake on Progress'?," 25; see also Hepworth, *Came the Dawn*, 58.
11. As Jon Gartenberg points out in his discussion of early American cinema, in 1900, when the attempts at panning were still faltering and almost accidental, Edison avoided the two-dimensionality of many indoor scenes in a series of reconstructions of the Boer War made around April 1900 through the use of mise-en-scène alone: "Soldiers charge from the background to towards the foreground, often moving diagonally across the field of vision. (This can be seen as early precursor of the chase films in which characters move diagonally through

the frame.)" (Gartenberg, "Camera Movement in Edison and Biograph Films, 1900–1906," 5).

12. There are some examples of camera movement (mainly pans) in the 1900–1906 period. Gartenberg discusses the variety of movements that emerge in this period in the American context, including pans, forward dollies, and traveling shots, many of which one finds in shots depicting people entering or leaving transportation vehicles. He writes, "Panning seemed inextricably linked to the machine age. In film after film, cars, trains, and trolleys move throughout image after image, and the camera, a machine itself, also engages in the sensation of movement" (Gartenberg, "Camera Movement in Edison and Biograph Films, 1900–1906," 14). For a discussion of camera movements in the British context, including pans (which often led to misframing and shots from moving vehicles as early as 1902, see Enticknap, "'A Real Brake on Progress'?," 23–27. Rachel Low and Roger Manvell also cite a lecture delivered by R. W. Paul, on 3 February 1936, in which Paul says of his Sydney Road studio, built in 1899: "A trolley mounted on rails carried the camera, which could thus be set at any required distance from the stage, to suit the subject. Sometimes the trolley was run to or from the stage while the picture was being taken, thus giving a gradual enlargement or reduction of the image on the film" (Low and Manvell, *The History of the British Film 1896–1906*, 31). For Low and Manvell, this suggests, "that a mobile camera was not entirely unthought of even in the very early period" (ibid.). Hepworth is quite aware of the extent to which the development of transportation technologies provoked and enabled technological developments within film history. For example, as he explored the possibilities of the "phantom ride," he realized that it would be "no use tackling that job in fifty-foot driblets," and so, he states, "I determined to construct a camera big enough to take a thousand feet of film at a time and take no chances. What eventually emerged was a long, narrow, black box, rather like a coffin standing on end" (*Came the Dawn*, 44–45). Similarly, he describes how filmmakers wanting to get their news pictures on-screen on the day of shooting would charter a railway carriage in which to develop footage of, for example, the Grand National on the way back to London, or would hang wet film behind a motorcar to dry it out on the way to the theater (ibid., 63). Though he acknowledges that these stories may be apocryphal, they reveal something of the proximate relationship between the speed of transportation and the developing imagination of cinema as a medium for the almost-instantaneous communication of visual information.

13. In SHaH's description of Hepworth's film, for example, there is no mention of the bicycle ("How It Feels," 23). The invisibility of the camera means that *How It Feels to Be Run Over* differs significantly from *A Photographer's Mishap* (Edison/Porter 1901), another film in which a diegetic man with a camera is run over,

this time by a train. Kirby discusses *A Photographer's Mishap* and its assertion of cinema's supremacy over photography and a hysterical cinematic spectator (*Parallel Tracks*, 71). For another discussion of *How It Feels to Be Run Over*, see Littau, "Eye-Hunger," wherein Littau posits the effects of this film as physiological, rather than purely psychological. Although the bicycle in this instance follows the path of the soon-to-be-obsolescent horse and cart, Hepworth notes that in 1899, only one year prior to this film, "even bicycles . . . were still so new that the riding of them attracted attention and people flocked in quantities to these gymkhanas to see a *Musical Ride by Ladies* and *Comic Costume Race for Cyclists*" (*Came the Dawn*, 43). Yet perhaps the continued presence of bicycles on film has less to do with the vehicle's novelty than with the fact that "the interest in mere movement in screen pictures" had not yet died out (ibid.). Though this film seems to align the bicycle with the seemingly outdated horse and cart, it is interesting to note that at that moment, in Britain, automobile drivers were regarded as being very much in league with, and developing out of, the cyclists' popularization of traveling for pleasure. For a discussion of the cross-class affiliation of motorists with these "cads on casters," in opposition to horse lovers, see Plowden, *The Motor Car and Politics in Britain 1896–1970*, 7, 15.

14. See Michael Brooke's notes on this film, "How It Feels to Be Run Over (1900)," at the web site of Screenonline.

15. See SHaH, "How It Feels," 24. One might also usefully compare films that depict a vehicle's potentially deadly rupture of a material surface with Hepworth's description of the experience of the Royal Polytechnic Institution's "diving bell": "For sixpence you could take your seat with a lot of other boys in the huge diving bell and be completely submerged. Just below your feet there was the surface of the blue water, for the bell was open at the bottom, but as it descended the surface of the water went down too and you didn't get your school boots even wet" (*Came the Dawn*, 16). Like the magic theater, the Royal Polytechnic, which Hepworth describes as providing "the mainspring of [his] future career," revealed the relationship between modern pleasure and terror, and the instability of vision.

16. Ruoff, *Virtual Voyages*, 7. Rachel Low and Roger Manvell do explicitly, if briefly, refer to "motoring trick films" and "the motoring subject." See, for example, Low and Manvell, *The History of the British Film 1896–1906*, 80, 83.

17. Burch, *Life to Those Shadows*, 202.

18. For Tom Gunning's reading of Hepworth's film in relation to Burch, which focuses on the way this film establishes a continuity of framing that is at odds with the continuity devices used to implement a subordination to narrative in the IMR, see, Gunning, "'Primitive' Cinema?," 8–9. Here Gunning also discusses the importance of Hepworth's use of a nontheatrical frame for a trick effect.

19. See Schivelbusch, *The Railway Journey*, 16–32.
20. Burch, *Life to Those Shadows*, 35. On "panoramic perception," see Schivelbusch, *The Railway Journey*, 64.
21. Hepworth himself included the Lumières' film, along with *Explosion of a Motor Car* (Hepworth, 1900) and *How to Stop a Motor Car* (Percy Stow, 1902), in which he acted, and which depicts a policeman being run over by a motorcar, on a compilation assembled to illustrate a lecture he delivered in January 1953. For further information on this program, see the web site of the British Film Institute's National Film Archive, http://ftvdb.bfi.org.uk/sift/title/69119?view=synopsis (accessed 26 January 2007).
22. Gunning, "An Aesthetics of Astonishment," 34, 41.
23. Ibid., 43.
24. Hansen, *Babel and Babylon*, 38.
25. The transcendentalists include Henri Agel, André Bazin, and Roger Munier. The existentialists include Yvete Biró, George Linden, and Sobchack. The third group includes Mark Slade and Parker Tyler. See Sobchack, *The Address of the Eye*, 29nn35–36.
26. Sobchack, *Carnal Thoughts*, 6.
27. Butler, "Sexual Ideology and Phenomenological Description," 98–99.
28. Sobchack, *Carnal Thoughts*, 5; Turvey, "Theory, Philosophy, Film Studies," 116.
29. For an excellent overview of the history of film theory's relationship to phenomenology, see Andrew, "The Neglected Tradition of Phenomenology in Film Theory," in *Movies and Methods*, ed. Nichols, 2: 627. See also Sobchack's important earlier work, *The Address of the Eye*.
30. Andrew, "The Neglected Tradition of Phenomenology in Film Theory," 631.
31. Sobchack, *Carnal Thoughts*, 162.
32. Ibid., 71.
33. Ibid., 72, 71.
34. Ibid., 63.
35. Ibid., 67.
36. Ibid., 66.
37. Bazin qtd. in Andrew, "The Neglected Tradition of Phenomenology in Film Theory," 247; Rodowick, *The Virtual Life of Film*, 63.
38. Sobchack, *Carnal Thoughts*, 65.
39. Ibid., 149.
40. Ibid., 54–56.
41. Ibid., 31.
42. See Deleuze, *Cinema 2*, 200–201, 190.
43. Deleuze, *Cinema 1*, 57.
44. Sobchack, *The Address of the Eye*, 31; Deleuze, *Cinema 1*, 58.
45. Ibid.

46. Ibid.
47. For discussions of this cinematic nostalgia for a direct encounter with a live audience, see Hansen, *Babel and Babylon*, 37–38; and Vernet, "The Look at the Camera," 48–63.
48. This moment prefigures in interesting ways another post-crash scene of cryptic, autocinematic writing, to which I will turn later, in which J. G.Ballard's fictional character Vaughan will outline his half-erect penis with white chalk on "the black cellulose" of an upended car (Ballard, *Crash*, 169). Similarly, my discussion of *Amores perros* (Alejandro González Iñárritu, 2000) will highlight how the scene of the car crash is repeatedly marked by the presence of a black screen, the absence of an image, and the incorporation of "another" medium.
49. Deleuze, *Cinema 1*, 12–13.
50. Deleuze, *Cinema 2*, 7. I understand the interesting possibilities of the blankness of the image and the inaccessibility or shattering of the categories of subjective and objective here as being related to Leo Bersani's and Ulysse Dutoit's exploration, in *Forms of Being*, of cinema's capacity to evoke a condition of immanence, the unfinished or unaccomplished event, and the possibility of new modes of relationality through the erasure of all existing relations in the space of the aesthetic.
51. Woolf, "The Movies and Reality," 233.
52. "The Open" emerges in Deleuze in relation to Henri Bergson's writing on time. As Rodowick explains, "Time is defined by Bergson as the Open: that which changes and never stops changing its nature at each moment" (*Gilles Deleuze's Time Machine*, 10). In *The Movement-Image* the term, although linked to time, comes to stand in for the impossibility of the whole and the inevitability of endless change. Deleuze writes, "Many philosophers had already said that the whole was neither given nor giveable: they simply concluded that the whole was a meaningless notion. Bergson's conclusion is very different: if the whole is not giveable, it is because it is the Open, and because its nature is to change constantly, or to give rise to something new, in short, to endure. . . . If one had to define the whole, it would be defined by Relation. Relation is not a property of objects, it is always external to its terms. It is also inseparable from the open, and displays a spiritual or mental existence" (*Cinema 1*, 9–10). While David Bordwell has emphasized classical Hollywood cinema's ability to absorb and domesticate the variations, transgressions, and innovations of alternative aesthetics, I see Henry Jenkins's resistance to this model of Hollywood as always knowing "in what direction it was moving and what would work best to achieve its goals" as supporting the theoretical credibility of Deleuze's claims about cinema's ongoing variation and unfolding validity within a film-history as well as theoreticial paradigm. See Henry Jenkins, *What Made Pistachio Nuts?*, 18–19.
53. Deleuze, "One Manifesto Less," 219.

54. Hepworth, *Came the Dawn*, 51.
55. Burch, *Life to Those Shadows*, 202.
56. John Barnes writes, "The driver of the car was Hepworth himself and the passengers were H. M. Lawley and his brother" (*The Beginnings of the Cinema in England 1894–1901*, 26). As a source for this information, Barnes cites *British Kinematographic Society Proceedings*, 3 February 1936, 10–11.
57. Eileen Bowser discusses the importance of the explosion in early cinema in "Preparation for Brighton: The American Contribution," in *Cinema 1900–1906*; Tom Gunning explores the function of these exploding machines in "Crazy Machines in the Garden of Forking Paths." I will discuss this issue further in the following chapter.
58. Hepworth, *Came the Dawn*, 51.
59. In the same year as these two car-accident films, Hepworth constructed a camera specifically for "star-gazing" and successfully filmed the solar eclipse of May 1900. See Hepworth, *Came the Dawn*, 48. For a discussion of early train films and the way they shape both space and spectatorship, see Gunning, "An Unseen Energy Swallows Space."
60. For Gilles Deleuze's theorization of cinema's out-of-field spaces in relation to this infinite unfolding, the Open, see *Cinema 1*, 12–18.
61. One finds a similar tension between the inhibited progress of the automobile and the activation of a tension between horizontal and vertical screen space in *Le Brigandage moderne* (Pathé, 1905), as discussed by Burch in *Life to Those Shadows* (173). Burch is also one of the few critics to raise the question of why the vertical axis has historically been neglected. He writes, "Do we refer so much more frequently to left-right binarism than to up-down binarism just because the former is more often *active* on the screen than the latter? In theory, of course, the spectator's 'bodily' centering is a homogeneous whole, and modern practice attaches equal importance to all its axes. But historically the problem was always the left-right relationship, partly because high- and low-angle shots developed belatedly, but mostly, I think, because of the way in which the distinctions between left hand and right hand in the human body are bound up in a whole education process, whereas the up-down relation is an immediately perceivable geophysical datum (gravity)" (*Life to Those Shadows*, 231n11). While Gartenberg notes the use of slight vertical movements of the camera in three American films (1903, 1904, and 1906), he states that unlike pans, "camera tilts were not a frequently used technique, and like the dolly, remained a novelty for the period" ("Camera Movement in Edison and Biograph Films, 1900–1906," 12). Writing about the representation of the fallen woman who exploits her sexuality for economic gain, Lea Jacobs notes how an upward tilt can, by the 1920s, function as a formal device that participates in a "sly and sexually knowing" joke capable of escaping the censors' notice, at least until around 1934, when

nonverbal devices such as camera movement were more heavily regulated. See Jacobs, *The Wages of Sin*, 75, 151.

62. This will obviously change with the development of the Road Movie, which often articulates a desire to escape from feminized spaces. For further discussion of this question, see Wolff, "On the Road Again."

63. Hansen suggests the phantom-ride films as offering another "reverse effect" to Hepworth's film. See Hansen, *Babel and Babylon*, 304n31.

64. In this film Booth is indebted not only to the animated fantasy sequences of Méliès, but also to the surprising shift from horizontal to vertical axes found in Pathé films like *The Ingenious Soubrette* (1902) and *Magic Picture Hanging* (1904?), both discussed by Burch in *Life to Those Shadows*, (228). I use the term *realist* to denote the fantasy of the diegetic world as a three-dimensional space that might be entered by the spectator, and the repression of the flatness of the screen and the images projected onto it.

65. It may be useful to recall Burch's description of Lumière's *Arroseur et arrosé*, in which we see something like an acentric spectatorial subject emerge, neither a subject lost in the world of the film nor an embodied, centered subject firmly located in his or her theater seat. Burch writes, "It is non-linear, non-centered, impossible to grasp on first viewing, true, but it provides, as it were, a sense of closeness to reality, precisely insofar as the latter itself is non-centered, unclosed, non-linear, ungraspable on first viewing" (*Life to Those Shadows*, 33). Burch sees the "surprises of a *booby-trapped surface*" persisting on into, and causing the commercial failure of, the work of Jacques Tati in particular (ibid., 155).

66. Comically, in the scene prior to this substitution trick, we can see the horse in the background, waiting for his cameo appearance.

67. Tom Gunning notes that the single-shot gag films made efficient use of areas of the screen usually ignored in classical film composition out of necessity, and he remarks that "many of these early films are composed with the clarity of the turn-of-the-century comic strips that were their inspiration" ("Crazy Machines in the Garden of Forking Paths," 92). While later multishot shorts are not bound by the same spatial and temporal limitations, these early restrictions, and their solutions, may well have established a comic aesthetic that included the expansive use of the compositional space of the screen that is at work here.

68. Doane, *The Emergence of Cinematic Time*, 184–85. In this passage Doane cites Gaudreault, "Temporality and Narrative in Early Cinema, 1895–1908," 314.

69. Doane, *The Emergence of Cinematic Time*, 258–259n9. This cinema of becoming takes on a political dimension in its potential for activating its audience as a collective subject that is never fully realized but is always, like cinema itself, in a process of unfolding. As Rodowick writes within the context of modern political cinema, "While a collective subject is undesirable as a teleological end, it is nonetheless still desirable as a political goal. The problem is to affirm people in

their collective becoming, to define their potential or their affirmative will to power" (*Gilles Deleuze's Time Machine*, 153). Doane points readers to Rodowick for "a more sympathetic analysis of Deleuze's approach to cinema" (*The Emergence of Cinematic Time*, 259n9), and while Rodowick also describes Deleuze's "historical understanding of primitive cinema" as "terribly remiss," he stresses, in what is a potentially very significant observation for the theoretization of early cinema, that "by [Deleuze's] own criteria one can see elements of the 'time-image' emerging through the early period, especially, I think, in kinesthetic films.... Deleuze's unfamiliarity with the stylistic variety and complexity of early cinema causes him to miss its implications for his own theory" (*Gilles Deleuze's Time Machine*, 214n6).

70. One could argue that the ability to mount the camera on a car can at times limit the cinematic potential of the relationship between the camera and the car, and make the emergence of the true movement-image, in the Deleuzian sense, harder to realize. Already in *Boarding School Girls* (Edison, 1905) we see one example, of girls in a moving car being shot head-on from a car moving in front of them (Gartenberg, "Camera Movement in Edison and Biograph Films, 1900–1906," 8), and while this marks a significant development in the camera's ability to move, it may also initiate the expectation that the moving camera and the moving body be yoked together in a way that may inhibit cinema's ability to unleash utopian visions of becoming through movement in the way that Deleuze describes. The independence of the movement-image from the moving bodies from which it derives its motion might, for example, be regulated by the implementation of codes that would potentially regard such moments of independence as errors or unfortunate accidents. Gartenberg, for example, notes that when, in *Wife Wanted* (Biograph, October 1907), "the vehicle containing the camera moves more rapidly than the characters are able to run on foot," the effect is "a lack of smooth control on the part of the filmmakers over the rate of motion," producing a "distancing effect" and resulting in a film that "fall[s] short of creating new forms of expressiveness" (ibid., 15).

71. Laplanche, "The Drive and Its Source-Object," 118.

72. Burch, *Life to Those Shadows*, 154.

73. Deleuze, *Cinema 1*, 23.

74. Ibid., 25, 24.

75. Quoted in Rodowick, *Gilles Deleuze's Time Machine*, 141. The films of Mitchell and Kenyon demonstrate the almost total absence of cars from British urban centers in the first few years of the twentieth century, a time when cars were primarily used for driving between towns *through* the country rather than within the urban space itself. See Yearsley, "On the Move in the Streets"; Plowden, *The Motor Car and Politics in Britain 1896–1970*, 15–16.

Chapter Two. Car Wreckers and Home Lovers

I would like to thank Jean Ma, Scott Bukatman, Dana Polan, and Paula Marantz Cohen for their helpful suggestions at an early stage of this chapter.

1. For a discussion of these debates, see Plowden, *The Motor Car and Politics in Britain 1896–1970*, 142–213.
2. For a detailed examination of the Ford Motor Company's involvement in the production of a series of educational films entitled *Civics and Citizenship in the United States*, made between 1921–1925, see Lee Grieveson's "Visualizing Industrial Citizenship: Or, Henry Ford Makes Movies," lecture manuscript in the author's files.
3. McFarland, "The Billboard and the Public Highways," 100. McFarland was the president of the American Civic Association.
4. Gunning, "Crazy Machines in the Garden of Forking Paths."
5. Graham, "Safeguarding Traffic," 176.
6. Bright, "The Plan of Philadelphia," 233. The volume also includes studies of the effect of "the Traffic Problem" on Detroit, New York, Chicago, St. Louis, and Los Angeles.
7. See Eno, "The Storage of Dead Vehicles on Roadways," 169. William P. Eno was the chairman of the board of directors for the Eno Foundation for Highway Traffic Regulations.
8. Bright, "The Plan of Philadelphia," 235. Bright imagines the following four layers: a subway; a road for pedestrians and streetcars; and a "two-storied street" above the pedestrian roadway, with each street taking cars in different directions, thereby eliminating the need for cars to stop at intersections. He writes, "At first glance this seems a dreadful thing, but what else is to be done? A horizontal amplification of the corridor is ineffective" (234).
9. Mandel, "The Automobile and the Police," 192, 193.
10. Ibid., 194. E. Austin Baughman discusses the potential for driving to turn the ordinary citizen into a criminal in "Protective Measures for the Automobile and Its Owner" (194).
11. McFarland, "The Billboard and the Public Highways," 100–101. It is interesting to note that accompanying this move toward the ever-increasing visual transparency of the road is a public resistance to the idea of the road as a space of mandatory and commercially directed vision. McFarland complains, "Only the blind man can avoid seeing the billboards along the highways" ("The Billboard and the Public Highways," 96). In *They Live by Night* (Nicholas Ray, 1948), "Bowie" hides behind a billboard after his getaway at the film's opening.
12. Ross, *Fast Cars, Clean Bodies*, 19. Also important here is the article Ross cites: Grazie, "Mass Culture and Sovereignty."

13. Grieveson, "Visualizing Industrial Citizenship; or, Henry Ford Makes Movies," 4.
14. This film is available through the Prelinger online film archive, a database of ephemeral films from 1927–1987. The collection was acquired by the Library of Congress in 2002, and can be browsed at http://www.archive.org/. I discuss the safety films from this collection in the next chapter.
15. Mandel, "The Automobile and the Police," 191.
16. For an outline of the increasing standardization and censorship of films produced in the United States from 1922 through 1934, see Jacobs, *The Wages of Sin*, 27–42.
17. Graham, "Safeguarding Traffic," 179.
18. Koszarski, *An Evening's Entertainment*, 203. Richard Dyer MacCann adopts a similar view of DeMille's relation to the Puritanism of the 1920s: "[DeMille] found that audiences were interested in seeing the shocking sins and occasional sufferings of the rich. It was possible through the medium of the motion picture to watch how scandalously certain accepted values were sometimes put aside. Exploring these departures generally took a lot longer than deploring them—a process of regret which might be briefly wrapped up in the last ten minutes" (*Films of the 1920s*, 5). The film *Manslaughter*, originally made by Cecil B. DeMille in 1922, offers a particularly interesting case study for understanding the strange combination of fact and fiction to which the intersection of car and film culture and morality gave rise. Charles Barton's remake of *Manslaughter*, retitled *And Sudden Death* (Paramount, 1936), combined the plot of DeMille's film with the content of a nonfiction article on car safety written by the historian J. C. Furnas and published in *Reader's Digest* in August 1935. Furnas is listed in the film credits. William Stott lists Furnas's article as a prime example of Dale Carnegie's claim, in *How to Win Friends and Influence People* (1936), that in America in the 1930s "truth has to be made vivid and interesting." See Stott, *Documentary Expression and Thirties America*, 73, 332. I would like to thank Jonathan Kahana for his generosity in drawing my attention to this, and to many other interesting things.
19. Henry Jenkins, *What Made Pistachio Nuts?* 213.
20. Jacobs, *The Wages of Sin*, 67.
21. The tension between the law and the motorist is already visible in the first decade of the twentieth century, but in films like *Explosion of a Motor Car* and *The (?) Motorist*, the policeman in question is still a bobby on his beat, and the humor of these films in part depends on the speed differential between the law and the driver, making law itself seem obsolescent. The traffic cop capable of keeping up with his prey comes later.
22. Crafton, "Pie and Chase," 111.
23. The proximity of these films to each other can be explored through the recycling of gags. In *The Non-Skid Kid*, for example, we see an early iteration of the some-

what uncanny image of an inner tube bulging through a slit in a tire, an image that will recur in *Two Tars*. In the latter, however, the injury is—of course—inflicted not accidentally, but deliberately. "Topping" describes, as James Agee explains through recourse to an automobile example, the step beyond "milking" a gag: "In an old, simple example of topping, an incredible number of tall men get, one by one, out of a small closed auto. After as many have clambered out as the joke will bear, one more steps out: a midget. That tops the gag. The auto collapses. That tops the topper" ("Comedy's Greatest Era," 11). Although Agee bemoans the inability of later comedians to milk or top their gags, we find an example of the queer potential of topping in the contemporary moment in Judith Halberstam's discussion of *Austin Powers* and "comic torture," of taking a joke past the point of being funny "until it becomes funny again" (Agee, "Comedy's Greatest Era," 18; Halberstam, *In a Queer Time and Place*, 144).

24. Lloyd writes, "In *Get Out and Get Under* I was fixing my Ford, and I had the hood up. I had my head inside, then my shoulders went in, then half of me was in the car, and pretty soon my feet disappeared inside the engine.... The Ford people were after me to use that film only about eight months ago. They were *delighted* with it. But I didn't let them have it; not unless I knew how they were going to use it" (quoted in Brownlow, *The Parade's Gone By*, 463).

25. Gunning, "Crazy Machines in the Garden of Forking Paths," 96. In his response to Crafton's essay, Gunning makes the important point that "while most narratives operate so that containment dominates disruption, thus providing closure, it should be emphasized that the forces of disruption *are essential* to even the most conventional narrative" ("Response to 'Pie and Chase,'" 120). For an excellent discussion of the development and destruction of plot in the "anarchistic tradition" of early sound comedy, see Henry Jenkins, *What Made Pistachio Nuts?*

26. For a discussion of the relationship between the clown and the couple in the comic tradition, see Jenkins, *What Made Pistachio Nuts?*, 214–44.

27. I find Ben Brewster's skepticism about the value of thinking of narrative as linear and two-dimensional very suggestive. "Ben Brewster recently pointed out to me the limitations to our conception of narrative as linear. Useful as this two-dimensional metaphor may be in describing the goal-directed aspect of many narratives and narrative's own containment, it also makes narrative appear more simple than I think it is in practice" (Gunning, "Response to 'Pie and Chase,'" 121). David Bordwell and Kristin Thompson usefully point out that the automatic critical celebration of formally radical films as politically radical neglects the fact that formally radical practices cannot, without careful historicization, "reckon a film's political range" ("Linearity, Materialism, and the Study of Early American Cinema," 13).

28. From an interview with Bill Rabe, quoted in Louvish, *Stan and Ollie*, 226.

29. Nollen, *The Boys*, 35.
30. Everson, *The Complete Films of Laurel and Hardy*, 27.
31. Everson, *American Silent Film*, 271n. In a footnote to his excellent chapter on comedy and gender, Henry Jenkins makes the following observation: "Wes Gehring, who has uncovered several previously unpublished scripts from Fields's stage performances, finds that the figure of 'the victimized central male—his leisure time usurped by females, machines (especially cars) and the city' was a key element throughout his early theatrical career" (*What Made Pistachio Nuts?*, 321n22). I draw attention to this footnote only because it suggests that while the genre of the Road Movie will later align masculinity, male leisure, and freedom (from women and domestic spaces) with the motorcar, at an earlier and more technically unreliable moment in the car's history, its relation to received notions of masculinity and femininity may have functioned very differently.
32. Nollen, *The Boys*, 69.
33. I am thinking, for example, of the space Judith Halberstam opens up for feminist theory in her discussion of comic representations of stereotypes of femininity and nonmale and nonphallic masculinities in *In a Queer Time and Place*. For my discussion of how such work challenges feminist theory to open itself to the shifting significance of a given text to feminists across generations, see Beckman, "The Archive, the Phallus, and the Future."
34. Fischer, "Sometimes I Feel Like a Motherless Child," 61; Rowe, "Comedy, Melodrama, and Gender," 41.
35. Riblet, "The Keystone Film Company and the Historiography of Early Slapstick," 181.
36. Doublas Riblet notes, for example, that "Keystone's stock company contained several prominent female comic performers, who often participated fully in the knockabout—another aspect which differentiated the studio's style of comedy from the classic 1920s slapstick" ("The Keystone Film Company and the Historiography of Early Slapstick," 176). See also Gaines, "Of Cabbages and Authors."
37. Rowe, "Comedy, Melodrama, and Gender," 45.
38. Leo Bersani and Ulysse Dutoit, for example, open interesting spaces for thinking about the place of women, and "indifference to women," in relation to male homosexual desire, in the chapter "'Almodóvar's Girls' (*All About My Mother*)," in *Forms of Being* (74–123). It is interesting that the alternative forms of being explored in this chapter are also rooted in a comic sensibility, "everyone's very unsolemn interest in the penis" (120). Although I find their exploration of the comic, dephallicized penis compelling, their reading does leave the reader with a sense that relationships among women *and* between men and women might be impossible without the detached penis as an "enlivening, civilised, and nonobsessive topic of interest" (106). Though it is described as a "passing topic of interest," we never seem to get past it.

39. Rowe, "Comedy, Melodrama, and Gender: Theorizing the Genres of Laughter," 45, 356n16.
40. Paul, "Charles Chaplin and the Annals of Anality," 115.
41. More information on the Women Film Pioneers project is available on its web site.
42. Louvish, *Stan and Ollie*, 223.
43. Ibid., 144.
44. Ibid., 224.
45. Hansen, *Babel and Babylon*, 113. It is important to note the substantial changes that slapstick in the 1920s had gone through since its earlier inceptions. Eileen Bowser points out that while "slapstick was vulgar, amoral, and anti-establishment, and reformers in the post-1908 period wanted it suppressed," by 1912 critics were expecting that, just as Thomas H. Ince had done for the Western, "some wise producer," wearing a "cap of discretion," would "push through the field of darkness and show the field the correct handling of so-called slapstick in pictures" (*The Transformation of Cinema 1907–1915*, 179, 181). Though she notes that after 1909 slapstick "drew on the cheerfully amoral traditions of pre-1909 American film and vaudeville," and that the legacy of the reform period meant that people continued to deplore slapstick as "vulgar, tasteless, and not for refined audiences," by 1920 we find a greater variety in slapstick's relationship to bourgeois consumer values than the tendency she identifies in the early Sennett-Keystone films to burlesque "everything that Americans took seriously, from melodrama . . . and mother love to the Ford car" (ibid., 183, 181).
46. Whissel, "Regulating Mobility," 4.
47. Ibid., 10.
48. Ibid.
49. See Ostherr, "Contagion and the Boundaries of the Visible," 1–39. For a discussion of the rise of the venereal-disease propaganda film in the British context, see Kuhn, *Cinema, Censorship, and Sexuality 1909–1925*, 49–74. And for an outstanding exploration of microcinematography's marking of the "fluid boundaries between science and entertainment in the culture of modernity and modernization," see Oliver Gaycken's unpublished dissertation, "Devices of Curiosity: Cinema and the Scientific Vernacular." A comparison of Low and Manvell's illustrations of Charles Urban's 1903 microcinematography (Low and Manvell, *The History of British Film 1896–1906*, 81) with their illustrations of "Facials" and close-ups in comedy from 1902–1906 (plate 22, n.p.) clarifies the intimate relationship between these two uses of close-up. The authors also stress the importance of recognizing that "the first use of close-ups was for comic and not dramatic effect" (76).
50. In an interesting critical moment that implicitly recognizes this overlap between film comedy and early science films, Ross describes, in the context of French

cinema of the 1960s, her tendency to associate extreme close-ups of moving objects with microcinematography and the comic genre: "Another common film tactic, more associated with comedy or burlesque realism, is the extreme close-up, such that the car, like some enormous insect on a microscopic slide, occupies the whole frame; what little background remains in the frame only heightens the wondrous nature of the object." Ross, *Fast Cars, Clean Bodies*, 30.

51. See Kirby, *Parallel Tracks*, 89–100.
52. See Hansen, *Babel and Babylon*, 113.
53. The tapestry's motto is taken from the John Howard Payne's 1823 lyrics to Henry Rowley Bishop's music (1821). The song ends with the traveler resolving never to leave home again: "No more from that cottage again will I roam, / Be it ever so humble, there's no place like home."
54. Barr, *Laurel and Hardy*, 17.
55. Ibid., 18.
56. Nollen, *The Boys*, 12.
57. Kerr, *The Silent Clowns*, 330, 329.
58. Barr, *Laurel and Hardy*, 19.
59. Edelman, *No Future*, 43.
60. The automobile, and the Model T Ford in particular, plays an important role in establishing the affiliation of the duo with slowness. As Scott Allen Nollen writes, "Almost as important as the bowler hat is the Ford Model T. The Boys' inability to exist within a world of adults is symbolized by the way in which they operate an automobile. Not only do Stan and Ollie inhibit their own progress, but they also prevent others from accomplishing even the most routine of goals. In *Leave 'Em Laughing*, they cause a citywide traffic jam when they stop to laugh at a policeman. *Two Tars* shows them complicating an already existing traffic jam and starting a domino effect of destruction that comprises most of the narrative" (*The Boys*, 51).
61. Edelman, *No Future*, 143.
62. Ibid., 55, 149. For Edelman's discussion of the "sinthomosexual," see ibid., 113. Edelman points to the "uncannily intimate connections" between dangerous unmarried men and the children whose lives they threaten: Scrooge and Tiny Tim; Lord Voldemort and Harry Potter; Captain Hook and Peter Pan (ibid., 21).
63. Ibid., 9–11.
64. Musser, "Divorce, DeMille and the Comedy of Remarriage," 285.
65. The "Eternal Children" references the title of Gian Piero Brunetta's essay on Stan Laurel, "Eternal Child: The Many Meanings of a Mask," available at the web site for *Bright Lights Film Journal* (accessed 14 February 2007).
66. Barr, *Laurel and Hardy*, 12.
67. Ibid., 31.
68. Ibid., 31, 32.

69. Ibid., 56, 57.
70. Ibid., 57, 58. Scott Allen Nollen implies an association between homosexuality and immaturity when he writes, "The Boys literally are just boys, children who attempt to act like mature human beings.... At times, they begin to participate in mature activities (smoking, drinking, contact with the opposite sex, marriage), but do not possess sufficient development to bring them to a successful conclusion" (*The Boys*, 35).
71. The association between temporal regression and queer sexuality does not just apply to male homosexuality, but also marks the historical construction of lesbian sexuality. For a discussion of lesbian identity in relation to "temporal drag," see Freeman, "Packing History, Count(er)ing Generations." See also Love, *Feeling Backward* and "Spectacular Failure." Love writes of the way in which "lesbians and gays, despite the new possibilities that are open to them, continue to be positioned as modernity's others," and she discusses the need to develop a politics capable of accounting for "socially regressive" lesbian desires that fail to fall in line with a politically mandated "forward thinking" ("Spectacular Failure," 129). I am grateful to Heather Love for drawing my attention to the Freeman article.
72. Kerr, *The Silent Clowns*, 327.
73. Ibid., 330, 331.
74. Ibid., 333.
75. Ibid., 332.
76. Ibid., 334.
77. Ibid.
78. Bersani, *The Culture of Redemption*, 34, 31, 32. For a full elaboration of this reading of Freud, see ibid., 31–35.
79. Barr, *Laurel and Hardy*, 58.
80. Kerr, *The Silent Clowns*, 334.
81. For an example of this approach, see Rowe, "Comedy, Melodrama, and Gender: Theorizing the Genres of Laughter," in *Classical Hollywood Comedy*, ed. Karnick and Jenkins, 39–59, especially 47. Here Rowe suggests that in romantic comedy, the couple's marriage constitutes "a sign of the partial suspension of conflict—the tolerance for difference—on which community depends" (47).
82. Bersani, *The Culture of Redemption*, 1.
83. Bergson, "Laughter," 73–74.
84. Agamben, *The Coming Community*, 10, 1. For Agamben, the "rascality" of such characters is explicitly linked to the condition of suspension experienced by the "cartoon-style" inhabitants of limbo, whose actions occur, without perdition or salvation, in a context that is, like the world of Laurel and Hardy, "without a destination" (ibid., 5, 6).
85. Buster Keaton, quoted by John McCabe, in his preface to Nollen, *The Boys*, viii.

86. Foucault, "Sexual Choice, Sexual Act," 153. Tim Dean builds on the work of both Bersani and Foucault in *Beyond Sexuality*, where he discusses how an expanded view of sexuality, one that escapes the inherently gendered dimension of queer paradigms based on object-choice, can enable us to imagine community differently. See especially Dean, *Beyond Sexuality*, 218–28.
87. Bergson, "Laughter," 102, 84.
88. Jean Ma, "Discordant Desires, Violent Refrains," 24. Here Ma quotes Adorno, *Aesthetic Theory*, 19.
89. Deleuze, "Coldness and Cruelty," 120.
90. Ibid.
91. Ibid., 71, 85–89.
92. Everson, *The Complete Films of Laurel and Hardy*, 70.
93. Louvish, *Stan and Ollie*, 226; Everson, *The Complete Films of Laurel and Hardy*, 68–69.
94. Nollen, *The Boys*, 69. Nollen does note that Stan and Ollie do meet other kinds of women, "usually prostitutes, gangsters' mistresses, or everyday women of the man-hunting variety," but states that these women are "very similar to the wives" (74).

Chapter Three. Doing Death Over

1. "Message to the American Trial Lawyers Association Meeting in New York City," 2 February 1966. Available at *The American Presidency Project*, http://www.presidency.ucsb.edu/.
2. "Revolution in Safety," *New York Times*, 29 August 1966, § A, 28.
3. Virilio, *Negative Horizon*, 116. For a discussion of desocialization, see ibid., 53.
4. Ibid., 45, 44.
5. Ibid., 53–54, 59, 60.
6. Ibid., 49.
7. Ibid.
8. Ibid., 113.
9. Ibid., 115.
10. Ibid., 107–8.
11. Ibid., 55.
12. Ibid., 166, 167.
13. Virilio, *Unknown Quantity*, 62–63.
14. For a discussion of the political stakes in refusing this separation of technology and human subjectivity in the work of Walter Benjamin, see Hansen, "Benjamin and Cinema," 325.
15. Rodowick, *The Virtual Life of Film*, 63.
16. Virilio, *Negative Horizon*, 39.
17. Ibid., ix.

18. Butler, *Giving an Account of Oneself*, 83.
19. Ibid., 87.
20. Ibid., 89.
21. Balibar, *We, the People of Europe?*, 162.
22. Ibid.
23. Blanchot, *The Writing of the Disaster*, trans. Smock, 27, 25.
24. Ibid., 25.
25. Butler, *Giving an Account of Oneself*, 110. Butler knits together Jean Laplanche's writing on the enigmatic signifiers of the Other with Levinas's notion of passive responsibility, and it is this relationship that produces responsibility within the context of the drives, and thereby links moral philosophy to the question of sexuality in a fundamental way. For Laplanche on the enigmatic signifiers of the Other, see Laplanche, "The Drive and Its Source Object," 127.
26. Butler, *Giving an Account of Oneself*, 91.
27. Virilio, *Negative Horizon*, 40.
28. Ibid., 90–91.
29. Bersani, *The Culture of Redemption*, 4.
30. Blanchot, *The Writing of the Disaster*, 29.
31. Cathy Caruth, "Interview with Jean Laplanche" (2001), paragraph 92, available at the web site for *Postmodern Culture*; quoted in Butler, *Giving an Account of Oneself*, 141n15.
32. Dean, *Beyond Sexuality*, 165.
33. For a more detailed discussion of these films, see Mikita Brottman's essay, "*Signal 30*," in *Car Crash Culture*, 233–43.
34. Stan Brakhage makes explicit the relationship between the documentary impulse and the desire to confront death itself in his film, *The Act of Seeing With One's Own Eyes* (1971). Thanks to Jonathan Kahana for bringing Stott's reference to Furnas's article "—And Sudden Death" to my attention. A footnote to this article states, "Reprints Available. Convinced that widespread reading of this article will help curb reckless driving, reprints in leaflet form are offered at costs (2¢ each), with a special price of $1.50 per hundred. To business men's organizations, women's clubs, churches, schools, automobile clubs, or other groups interested in public welfare, we suggest the idea of distributing these reprints broadcast" (26). In the wake of the article, *Reader's Digest* was "bombarded by proffered 'follow-ups,'" of which they published only one, "The Aftermath of Sudden Death," by A. J. Bracken, a village embalmer, which the journal describes as "impressive in its photographic directness" (Bracken, "The Aftermath of Sudden Death," 52). We see the widespread penetration of the article in the fact that when Charles Barton remade Cecil B. DeMille's 1922 film *Manslaughter* in 1936, he renamed it *And Sudden Death* and attributed screenplay credits to Furnas. The original *Manslaughter* (Cecil B. DeMille, 1922) was adapted

by Jeanie Macpherson from Alice Duer Miller's sensational eponymous novel, published in 1921, about Lydia Thorne (Leatrice Joy), a high-society and masochistically inclined speed fiend who accidentally runs over a traffic cop. The film was remade by Paramount on at least four other occasions: *Manslaughter* (George Abbott, United States, 1930), starring Claudette Colbert and Frederic March; *Leichtsinnige Jugend* (Leo Mittler, Germany, 1931); *Le réquisitoire* (Dimitri Buchowetzki, France, 1931); and *And Sudden Death* (Charles Barton, United States, 1936).

35. Stott, *Documentary Expression and Thirties America*, 73. Stott mentions Furnas's article in a note to this passage (332n9).
36. Ibid., 332n9.
37. Furnas, "—And Sudden Death," 21.
38. Ibid.
39. Ibid.
40. Ibid.
41. Ibid., 22.
42. This conflation of driving and viewing experiences would later be facilitated by the use of early cinematic driving-simulation machines in driver education, such as the Aetna Driver Trainers, first used to test reflexes, and shown in use in Centron Corporation's film *None for the Road: Teenage Drinking and Driving* (1957), made in cooperation with the Yale Center of Alcoholic Studies.
43. Furnas, "—And Sudden Death," 22–23.
44. Ibid., 24.
45. Ibid., 26.
46. For a discussion of the debates surrounding the industrial accident and workers' accident insurance, and the way these debates shaped modern conceptions of social responsibility, see Rabinbach, *The Human Motor*, 228–34. On the question of credit expansion and car ownership, see Higashi, *Cecil B. DeMille and American Culture*, 176.
47. For a wide variety of these films, see the automotive films available at the web site of the Prelinger Archives.
48. Henry Jamison Handy (1886–1983) made thousands of training films for the military and many different corporations, including Chevrolet. His papers are available at the Burton Historical Collection, Detroit Public Library; for more information, see the web site of the Detroit Public Library. For more Jam Handy films, see the library pages of the Historic Films web site. For information on Jamison Handy himself, see the DVD *History of Motion Pictures: Jam Handy: Genius at Work* (A2ZCDS, 2005).
49. See Clark, "Effect of Auto Speeding," *Minnetonka Record*, 11 January 1907, n.p.
50. See Burch, *Life to Those Shadows*, 154; and Bruno, *Streetwalking on a Ruined Map*.

51. Burch, *Life to Those Shadows*, 154–55.
52. Kurtz, "Black Humor, Crash Humor, and Aesthetic Representation," 285.
53. Robert Lindsay, "Auto Deaths Dip Sharply: Safety Advocates Credited With Largest Decrease Since '58," *New York Times*, 14 December 1970, § I, 1, 47.
54. "Interview with Hugh De Haven," Erich Meyerhoff, Librarian and Assistant Dean of Information Resources, Weill Cornell Medical Center Archives, New York City, Box 6, unpublished. For more on the collision, see Hugh De Haven Papers 1920–1980, 58A/B, archival notes on collection, 3, Weill Cornell Medical Center Archives, New York City. Thanks to Jim Gehrlich and Elizabeth Shepard for their help with my research on De Haven.
55. Ibid., 12. Ironically, after a lifetime of working to prevent death by automobile, De Haven committed suicide by carbon monoxide poisoning in his own car in 1980.
56. See Hugh De Haven Papers 1920–1980, "Photographs" (Box 1 of 1), Weill Cornell Medical Center Archives, New York City; and for De Haven's collection of freefall and suicide survival articles, see Box 5/2.
57. Hugh De Haven Papers 1920–1980, Box 6, CS-36-1, Weill Cornell Medical Center Archives, New York City.
58. "Eggs Just Bounce in 100-Foot Drop," *New York Times*, 5 April 1947, 22. Hen eggs were also used in the Cornell Laboratory, in tests that involved swing-like carriages. See the pamphlet *The Elmer A. Sperry Award for 1967 to Edward R. Dye, Hugh De Haven and Robert A. Wolf* (Detroit, Mich.: 9 January 1968), Hugh De Haven Papers 1920–1980, Weill Cornell Medical Center Archives, New York City. In a further public demonstration of the need to protect the egg-human in motion, De Haven appeared with Walter Cronkite, in 1954, in a special issue of CBS's *The Search* devoted to the question of safety on the "living laboratories" of the American highway. After Cronkite drops and breaks an egg onto a nonrubberized surface, the viewer is told, "If you can save the egg, you can save the human head." Car-safety education has repeatedly returned to De Haven's presentation of the human body as a fragile egg. In 1955, for example, Steven M. Spencer's influential *Saturday Evening Post* article "How to Avoid Sudden Death" ended by describing the prize-winning project of George Sitts, an eighth-grader from Ilion, New York: two miniature cars containing egg shells filled with different colored dyes were propelled into head-on collisions, with only half of the egg-passengers equipped with belts (16 July 1955, 88). Decades later, in 1999, Volvo's safety engineer Nils Bohlin demonstrated the significance of his three-point safety belt, adopted in 1959, by using miniature cars and painted happy and sad egg passengers during the PBS broadcast *Escape: Because Accidents Happen: Car Crash* (aired 16 February).
59. *The Elmer A. Sperry Award for 1967 to Edward R. Dye, Hugh De Haven and Robert A. Wolf* (Detroit, Mich.: 9 January 1968), Hugh De Haven Papers 1920–

1980, Box 6, Weill Cornell Medical Center Archives, New York City, 16. For discussions of Muybridge and Marey's time-movement studies, see Braun, *Picturing Time*; and Doane, *The Emergence of Cinematic Time*. For Babbage, see Siegel, "Babbage's Apparatus."

60. Siegel, "Babbage's Apparatus," 48; Charles Babbage, quoted in ibid., 31.
61. We might find a precedent for De Haven's studies of the technologically thrown body in Muybridge's images of a man driving a horse and cart. See, for example, "Horse galloping with cart. 'Occident,'" 1878, Kingston Museum (M8), available at the web site of Kingston University, London.
62. Col. Stapp discusses the speed of the film used, in *Escape: Because Accidents Happen: Car Crash* (PBS, aired 16 February 1999).
63. For the history of the use of high-speed film technologies in crash testing and kinematic analysis, see Rogers and Van Haaften, "Process Impact Test Data."
64. Steven M. Spencer reports, for example, that "the Air Force, even at the height of the Korean fighting, in 1951, found that more than half of its crash fatalities were in automobiles. And the Navy's statistics showed that during 1952, still in the Korean-war period, 'battle casualties and motor-vehicle accidents were almost equal: 8700 for the former and 8486 for the latter'" ("How to Avoid Sudden Death," *Saturday Evening Post*, 16 July 1955, 88).
65. Hertzberg, "Anthropology of Anthropomorphic Dummies," 203.
66. "Interview with Hugh De Haven," 20.
67. Ibid., 7, 23.
68. Hertzberg, "Anthropology of Anthropomorphic Dummies," 202–3.
69. The engineer Leon E. Kazarian reports the process of one mode of crash-testing primates in "The Primate as a Model for Crash Injury." Experiments were all "conducted according to the *Guide for the Care and Use of Laboratory Animals*" (ibid., 931). A chimpanzee of up to ninety pounds would be anesthetized with pentobarbital, after which its ankles would be tied together and bound to the metal drop cage, its upper limbs suspended from the carriage, and its chest bound with a 1.75 inch strap before it was dropped from a height of fifty-four feet, with results captured by high-speed photography. After impact, the chimpanzee was removed from the cage, radiographs were taken, and "each animal was transferred to the necropsy room and killed with a massive overdose of pentobarbital" (ibid., 936).
70. Patrick and Levine, "Injury to Unembalmed Belted Cadavers in Simulated Collisions," 81.
71. Ronell, *The Test Drive*, 45.
72. Details of this ride, which opened in 1999, can be found at the Disney web site. Thanks to Mara Mills for bringing this to my attention.
73. Baudrillard, "The Precession of Simulacra," 262.
74. Beck, "World Risk Society as Cosmopolitan Society?"

75. Ibid., 5.
76. See Doane, "Information, Crisis, Catastrophe."
77. Ronell, *The Test Drive*, 44.
78. *Crash* can be viewed at web site of Du Zhenjun (accessed 23 June 2008).
79. See the web site for Crash Test Dummy: The New European "Self" in a Bio-Political Crash Test, "Interview/English/Lupfer.doc," 3. http://www.crashtestdummy.net/press/pressimages.htm. (accessed 11 December 2007).

Chapter Four. Disaster Time

1. Debord, "Situationist Theses on Traffic," 57.
2. See "Editorial Notes: Critique of Urbanism." Originally published as "Critique of Urbanism" and translated by John Shepley, in *Internationale situationniste* 6 (August 1961), 3–11.
3. For a detailed discussion of the role played by the car and the road for Los Angeles–based pop artists, particularly in relation to questions of masculinity, see Whiting, "Cruising Los Angeles."
4. Nader, "The Safe Car You Can't Buy," 310, 312.
5. See Scott, "Shouting Apocalypse."
6. Crary, "Eclipse of the Spectacle," 294. Tom McDonough notes the importance of the distinction Crary makes between Debord's spectacle and Baudrillard's hyperreal in his introduction to *October*'s special issue on Debord. See McDonough, "Rereading Debord, Rereading the Situationists," 8.
7. Crary, "Eclipse of the Spectacle," 290.
8. Ibid., 290, 291.
9. Ballard, *Crash*, 130. Vaughan, one of the central characters of Ballard's novel *Crash*, travels, like Kennedy, in a Lincoln Continental, a vehicle in which, like Kennedy, he will meet his death. Kennedy is elided into Vaughan's fantasies of car-crash victims, which include James Dean, Albert Camus, and Jayne Mansfield (see ibid., 15, 135). The deaths of both Vaughan and Kennedy resist the idea of death-by-automobile as necessarily "accidental." Although *Crash* was not published until 1973, Ballard wrote a three-page piece entitled "Crash!" in 1968 that mentions John F. Kennedy three times. See Ballard, *The Atrocity Exhibition*, 97–100.
10. Callie Angell has been incredibly helpful in helping me think about the status of this film and how to frame it, and I want to thank her for her intellectual generosity, as well as for her wonderful work on Warhol's films in general. I choose to call the film unfinished because of an email exchange with her in which she suggests:
    > You might call the film "unfinished," rather than "incomplete." There are seven existing reels, labeled "Ondine I-VII." Some of these reels have no soundtrack, which seems to have been caused by a technical problem and

not done deliberately, since a person holding a microphone can be seen in the footage. I think of *Since* as unfinished rather than incomplete because—although I am not aware of Warhol ever showing any of this footage in public and I don't know how he would have chosen to release it—I have no information indicating that he was planning to shoot additional reels. Warhol was not in the practice of editing footage at this time but usually only exhibited full-length, uncut 1,200 reels. Usually he would shoot several reels, and then decide which to exhibit, and in which format and order. For example, various sequences were shot for *The Chelsea Girls*, and then Warhol selected reels from these sequences and showed them in double screen. The exact combination and order of the reels evolved over time, until a final version was arrived at about 4 months after *Chelsea Girls* was first screened. There is no information about any similar process taking place with *Since*. . . . Only the two reels ("Ondine VI" and "Ondine VII") have been preserved so far. The title *Since* refers to the entire project (all seven existing reels). . . . Apparently the full title of the film was *Since the Assassination*, which I believe to be a reference to the Bertolucci film "Since the Revolution." (Email to author, 9 September 2009.)

11. Crary, "Eclipse of the Spectacle," 294.
12. Barthes, "The Third Meaning," 68.
13. See, for example, White, *Uninvited*; Dyer, *Heavenly Bodies*; and Stacey, *Star Gazing*.
14. For a discussion of how art in the 1960s engages the question of time, see Lee, *Chronophobia*. Her discussion of the dialectical tension in Warhol's films between finitude and the infinite is especially relevant to the questions I address in this chapter. See Lee, *Chronophobia*, 279–88.
15. Freeman, "Packing History, Count(er)ing Generations," 742. For another discussion of Warhol's films and the queer temporality of their nonteleological "action" from a feminist perspective that, like this essay, works to move between the formalist and queer readings of Warhol, see King's essay "Girl Interrupted: The Queer Time of Warhol's Cinema." King relates her sense of Warhol's queer film time to Parker Tyler's essay "Dragtime and Drugtime: Or, Film à la Warhol."
16. Tyler, "Dragtime and Drugtime."
17. King, "Girl Interrupted," 100.
18. Tyler, "Dragtime and Drugtime," 29.
19. Ibid.
20. Ibid.
21. Ibid.
22. Ibid., 30, 87, 30.
23. Tyler, "Dragtime and Drugtime," 88. Also see Crimp, "Coming Together to Stay Apart."

24. For an interesting discussion of how time-travel films restage the primal scene in their depictions of futurity, see Penley, "Time Travel, Primal Scene, and the Critical Dystopia (on *The Terminator* and *La Jetée*)."
25. For further discussion of the concept of Nachträglichkeit, see Faimberg, "Après-Coup"; and Laplanche, "Notes on Afterwardsness."
26. "Il est normal que l'auto perde tout fabuleux héroïque, car l'aventure est aujourd'hui entièrement absorbée par l'exploration de l'espace sidéral; face aux engins cosmiques, l'automobile ne peut plus accomplir aucun rêve de mouvement inconnu: c'est un objet désormais immobile" (Barthes, "La voiture, projection de l'ego," 96). Kristin Ross provides an excellent discussion of the automobile in the context of French culture in *Fast Cars, Clean Bodies*.
27. "L'auto est une maison" (Barthes, "La voiture, projection de l'ego," 96). Also see Debord, "Situationist Theses on Traffic." For a discussion of the complex gendering of mobility in travel narratives, see Wolff, "On the Road Again."
28. In the scholarship on the Road Movie genre, there is a long tradition of conflating the car and the camera, the perforated strip of road with the moving strip of film. These comparisons tend to align film with the car in motion. When characters come off the road, they tend to be aligned instead with the medium of photography. See, for example, *Bonnie and Clyde* (Arthur Penn, 1967), *Badlands* (Terrence Malick, 1973), or *Thelma and Louise* (Ridley Scott, 1991). For recent discussions of film's paradoxical relationship to stasis and motion, see Stewart, *Between Film and Screen*; and Rosen, *Change Mummified*.
29. Within the mass media, the celebrity deaths of figures like James Dean (1955), Albert Camus (1960), and Jayne Mansfield (1967) helped to consolidate the relationship between the automobile and death as a spectacular, collective, and repeatable event.
30. See Macdonald, "Suicide and Homicide by Automobile"; republished in Brottman, *Car Crash Culture*, 91–98. See Brottman also for discussions of a wide range of the celebrity deaths that occurred during this period.
31. Thanks to James Meyer for drawing my attention to *Eat Your Makeup*. For a full discussion of the art and film works that emerged in response to Kennedy's assassination, see Simon, *Dangerous Knowledge*. Other relevant Ant Farm projects from 1975 include *Cadillac Ranch*, *7 Car Pile Up*, *Media Burn*, and *Citizen's Time Capsule*, which included the burial of a 1968 Oldsmobile Vistacruiser. See Lewallen and Seid, *Ant Farm, 1968–1978*. One might also note the fact that between 1972 and 1975, on a ranch near Amarillo (the location of Cadillac Ranch), John Chamberlain was working on his *Texas Pieces*, a group of ten sculptures named after Texas towns and made out of the bodies of discarded automobiles. While Chamberlain's Texas sculptures may serve inadvertently to memorialize in some way the location of the nation's recent "car accident," they do not engage the question of mediated violent events in the way that the aforementioned

works seem to do. Chamberlain's work resonates more obviously with the work of César (Baldaccini), who joined the Nouveaux Réalistes in 1960, after the exhibition of his *Compressions d'automobile*, seeming more concerned with the inherent qualities of the material and the artist's interaction with and transformation of those qualities. One might, however, make a connection between Ballard's exploration of auto-sexuality and the sexual dimension Chamberlain sees in his automobile sculptures. For example, in an unpublished statement on his *Texas Pieces*, available at the Chinati Foundation in Marfa, Texas, Chamberlain writes, "I deal with new material as I see fit in terms of my decision making, which has to do primarily with sexual and intuitive thinking. I am told, to a lesser degree, what to do by the material itself.... With my sculpture the sexual decision comes in the fitting of the parts.... The definition of sculpture for me is stance and attitude. All sculpture takes a stance. If it dances on one foot, or, even if it dances while sitting down, it has a light-on-its-feet stance. What I do doesn't look like heavy car parts laid up against a wall."

32. This first public presentation of the film on national television is included in the documentary *Images of an Assassination: A New Look at the Zapruder Film* (MPI Home Video, 1998).
33. Simon, *Dangerous Knowledge*, 146.
34. Ibid., 132–33.
35. Ibid., 130.
36. The Museum of Modern Art (New York) launched theAndy Warhol Film Project in 1989.
37. Lubin also establishes interesting resonances between the lives of Warhol and Kennedy: both shared a fascination with movie stars (especially Marilyn Monroe), both became "bonafide superstars," and both were victims of an assassination attempt. Lubin, *Shooting Kennedy*, 36.
38. Sontag, *Regarding the Pain of Others*, 100.
39. Foster, "Death in America."
40. Ibid., 73.
41. For an important discussion of NBC's television coverage of the assassination, of the role of indexical media, and of the tension between film's temporal delay, television's lack of images, and the centrality of distorted telephone transmissions on camera during the news reports of the event, see Rosen, "Document and Documentary."
42. Mosen, "Review (untitled)," 54, 56. Similarly, Bruce Jenkins notes in his excellent essay on Conner's films that "multiple ironies begin to emerge as Conner mixes visual humor with social criticism in highly condensed passages" ("Explosion in a Film Factory," 207).
43. See Bruce Jenkins, "Explosion in a Film Factory," 191.
44. Ibid., 208. The laughter here is more akin to the response of audiences to Jim

Dine's happening, *Car Crash* (1960), which was also influenced by early film comedy, and which Judith Rodenbeck describes in the following way: "If for Dine *Car Crash* was not humorous, the laughter it produced had to be understood as the visceral, prelinguistic enunciation of a cognitive disjunction: a register of discomfort masquerading as amusement" ("*Car Crash*, 1960," 105).

45. Howard Smith and Brian Van Der Horst, "Doing It Again in Dallas," *Village Voice*, 3 November 1975, 24; reprinted in "Ant Farm Timeline," in Lewallen and Said, *Ant Farm, 1968–1978*, 88–149.
46. Rosen, "Document and Documentary," 60.
47. Bruce Jenkins, "Explosion in a Film Factory," 211.
48. Thanks to Heather Love for suggesting the phrase, "politics of the couch."
49. Lubin, *Shooting Kennedy*, 258.
50. Ibid., 260.
51. Crow, "Saturday Disasters," 50.
52. Freeman, "Packing History, Count(er)ing Generations," 728. The film premiered on 15 November 2002, as part of Princeton University's "Art, Architecture and Film in the First Pop Age" conference, having recently been restored by the Museum of Modern Art. The film was introduced by Callie Angell, and a discussion of the film was then moderated by P. Adams Sitney. My discussion of this film is indebted to their comments.
53. For a discussion of the Zapruder film itself, see Thoret, *26 Secondes*, 21–38. Thanks to Keith Sanborn for drawing this book to my attention.
54. This mimetic response recalls the phenomenological responses of spectators to the cinema of attractions and of slapstick, described by Miriam Hansen, who writes, "What seems important to me regarding Benjamin's concept of innervation and its implications for film theory is the notion of a physiologically 'contagious' or 'infectious' movement that would trigger emotional effects in the viewer, a form of mimetic identification based in the phenomenon known as the Carpenter Effect." Hansen, "Benjamin and Cinema," 318. See also footnote 38 in Hansens's essay for further discussion of the Carpenter Effect.
55. Nichols, "'Getting to Know You . . . ;'" 179.
56. Mary Woronov's official web site boasts, on its "Cult Film Star" page, "She can wield an intense androgynous power" (accessed 12 June 2008).
57. For a full discussion of *Mario Banana*, see Crimp, "Face Value," 119–122.
58. Crimp, "Coming Together to Stay Apart," n.p.
59. Ibid., n.p.
60. Ibid., n.p.
61. For a discussion of the disruptive potential of this kind of repetitious and excessive performance of gender, see Judith Halberstam's discussion of "comic torture" in *In a Queer Time and Place*, 144.
62. Foster, "Death in America," 80.

Chapter Five. Film Falls Apart

My conversations with Craig Dworkin provoked this essay, and I thank him for them. Thanks to Hal Foster and Branden Joseph for inviting me to present an earlier version of this essay at Princeton. I also thank Branden for his subsequent help with this piece. I'm grateful to Callie Angell, Douglas Crimp, Michael Beckman, and the participants in the Visual and Cultural Studies "rehearsals" at the University of Rochester for their suggestions.

1. Foster, "Death in America," 76.
2. Quoted in ibid.
3. Baudrillard, "Two Essays," 316.
4. See Doyle, Flatley, and Muñoz, *Pop Out*; Crimp, "Face Value" and "Getting the Warhol We Deserve"; and Suárez, *Bike Boys, Drag Queens, and Superstars*, 214–59. For a discussion of Warhol's female stars in particular, see King, "Girl Interrupted."
5. For some of the more interesting critiques of *Crash*'s sexual promises, see Sobchack, "Baudrillard's Obscenity," as well as her later essay on the same subject, "Beating the Meat/Surviving the Text, or How to Get Out of This Century Alive"; Creed, "The *Crash* Debate"; and Grundmann, "Plight of the Crash Fest Mummies."
6. Ballard, *Crash*, 91.
7. Ibid., 168, 148.
8. Ibid., 180.
9. Ibid., 178.
10. Penises repeatedly cause women to gag, as in the following example: "Vaughan lay for ten minutes with his penis in the mouth of a middle-aged, silver-haired prostitute, almost choking her as she knelt across him. He held her head fiercely in his hands to prevent her from moving, until the spit dribbled from her mouth like a tap. . . . She let the semen drip onto the damp vinyl below Vaughan's testicles, gasping for breath as she wiped away the flecks of vomit from his penis" (Ballard, *Crash*, 190–91).
11. Ibid., 169.
12. Ibid., 63.
13. Acker, *Bodies of Work*, 175. As Linda Williams has shown, the flaccid penis played an important role for porn star Candida Royalle's production company, Femme, which used female directors to make new pornography for women. In a film called *Urban Heat*, for example, the male character's penis remains soft for the first half of an elevator sex scene. Williams comments, "The softness of the penis simply permits the rest of the body to perform. . . . We do not sense that the sole goal of the number is for the male organ to perform" (*Hard Core*, 252–53).

14. Ballard, *Crash*, 163–64. In the conclusion to *Hard Core* Linda Williams discusses the temptation for feminist critics of pornography to equate phallic power with the penis itself. In regard to Bonnie Klein's *Not a Love Story* (1982), an antipornography documentary, Williams writes, "The problem with *Not a Love Story* is that it proceeds as if suppressing the 'dick' could solve all the sexual problems of patriarchal power.... The feminist critique of explicit pornography fails, however, precisely in its attack on the literal organ of the penis.... But the tempting conflation of meaning between the two accedes to the impossibility of change. We would do well to remember, therefore, that the phallus is fundamentally not real and not possessed by anyone" (*Hard Core*, 266).
15. Ballard, *Crash*, 212, 210.
16. Grosz, *Volatile Bodies*, 199.
17. Ballard, *Crash*, 81, 188, 223, 202. In the quoted examples the flow of semen transcends the heterosexual paradigm suggested by Grosz, moving both from male to female and from male to male. Obviously, images of lesbian sex are excluded from this economy of seminal flows. On rare occasions female characters show their own capacity to "leak" sexually, as when Catherine's "most sensitive mucous surfaces quietly discharged their own quickening chemicals," but this is exceptional and is not even linked to sexual desire per se (ibid., 158). It is hard to read the novel as offering an interesting sexual program for women if this "program" is defined solely by what male and female bodies do to each other.
18. Suleiman, "Mothers and the Avant-Garde." See also Suleiman, *Subversive Intent*.
19. Koestenbaum, *Andy Warhol*, 134.
20. The voices that make up the novel constantly invoke an awareness of the movement between tape-recorded sound and the idea of a book. For example, in section 11/2, we "hear" the following conversation.

    Drella—But how can I put a piano, a piano in the uh

    Ondine—Very easy

    D—How? I mean in the uh, book.

    O—We can probably scan somebody else's piano. What do you mean, how are we gonna put a piano in the book? All right, let's talk about the book.

    D—We'll talk about uh—

    O—Oh we can talk about the (*Music*) (*Della is talking*) What do you mean transcribe this?

    D—What?

    O—Well why don't we make the book a tape? We can make a tape book, y'know so that, so that you can only play it on a tapere—, yeah you're right. (Warhol, *a*, 257)

    One could argue that *a* at least obliquely contemplates the possibility of transposing moving visual images into the novel at the moment Warhol's "enormous" $15,000 camera arrives (ibid., 40), especially given Paul Morrisey's comparisons of the camera to a tape recorder: "And the picture goes onto the tape and then you push the tape. . . . And you push the tape just like you play back your tape recorder and the tape plays back through a television set" (ibid., 56). The strip of electromagnetic tape could also itself function as a visual filmstrip, so the movement between film and literature is not absolutely absent in *a*, just as the tape is never fully linguistic.

21. Warhol's plan to produce the *Warhol Bible*, a thirty-day-long film in which each page of the Bible would be projected on-screen long enough for the audience to read it would, had he completed it, have made an interesting contribution to this inquiry. See Angell, *The Films of Andy Warhol*, 15.
22. Ballard, *Crash*, 35.
23. Ibid., 54.
24. Ibid., 7.
25. Crary, "J. G. Ballard and the Promiscuity of Forms," 160.
26. Ballard, *Crash*, 14.
27. Ballard, "Fictions of Every Kind," 207.
28. Ibid.
29. Ibid., 205.
30. Ballard, *Crash*, 64, 63; Warhol, *The Philosophy of Andy Warhol*, 8.
31. Ballard, *Crash*, 192; Warhol, *The Philosophy of Andy Warhol*, 7–10. For an excellent discussion of Warhol's whiteness in a queer context, see Sedgwick, "Queer Performativity."
32. Ballard, *Crash*, 150. These scars, which for Vaughan and Ballard represent the collisions and highways of the future, are for Warhol, too, "a roadmap" (Warhol, *The Philosophy of Andy Warhol*, 195).
33. Acker, *Bodies of Work*, 175.
34. For another example of this slippage between *car*, *care*, and *scar*, as well as the relation between *motion* and *emotion* suggested by a parallel relationship between the words *inert* and *emotionless*, we might consider an exchange that occurs between Catherine and James in Ballard's apartment shortly after his crash. The linguistic slippages seem to elicit saliva from Catherine, and this body fluid transforms the scars into sites of pleasure: "happy changes."

    "You won't try to borrow the janitor's car?"

    Her care was touching. Since the accident she seemed completely at ease with me for the first time in many years. . . . She was fascinated by the scars on my chest, touching them with her spittle-wet lips. These happy changes I felt myself. At one time Catherine's body lying beside me in bed had seemed as inert and emotionless as a sexual exercise doll. (Ballard, *Crash*, 51)

Some critics find the novel to be devoid of both emotion and eroticism. Vivian Sobchack, for example, states that "*Crash*'s cold and clinical prose robs the sex acts and the wounds the narrator describes of feeling and emotion and, I would assume in most cases, also of the ability to arouse the living flesh of the reader" ("Beating the Meat/Surviving the Text, or, How to Get out of This Century Alive," 311). In this instance Sobchack actually seems to share some common ground with her opponent, Jean Baudrillard, who also argues for the novel's absence of intimacy: "All the erotic vocabulary is technical: not ass, prick, or cunt, but anus, rectum, penis, vulva. No slang, no intimacy in the sexual violence, only functional language. . . . No sexual pleasure, just discharge, plain and simple" ("Two Essays" 316–17). I find, however, that these linguistic slippages, these transformations of meaning brought about by free-floating letters moving between and bumping up against words, infuse the language of the novel with an erotic tenderness, and provide a pleasurable linguistic parallel for, and enabler of, the "perversion of touching" outlined by Marq Smith in relation to Cronenberg's film: "Against a Freudian hydraulics of sexuality, which seems to necessitate that *Crash* be interpreted, favorably or otherwise, through the violence of vaginal and anal penetration and its reproductive (or 'creative') imperatives, I am interested in the perversion of touching as fore-pleasure" ("Wound Envy," 201).

35. Roy Grundmann criticizes Ballard's "phallic impenetrability" in both the novel and the film: "There is no question that it is Ballard who will do the fucking" ("Plight of the Crash Fest Mummies," 27). Although on one level I agree with Grundmann, the irresolvable confusion of inside and outside that the penetration scene quoted above enacts makes it hard to know whether any character's "insides" remain untouched.

36. Ballard, *Crash*, 202.

37. For the importance of reconfiguring the relationship between the container and the contained to feminist theory, see Irigaray, "Sexual Difference," 10–12. It is interesting to note that, for Irigaray, the figure of the angel becomes the one capable of passing "through the envelope(s) or container(s), [going] from one side to the other" (ibid., 15). Vaughan is described as having "scales of metallic gold," and when James drives with him on the motorway, they are surrounded by "an armada of angelic creatures" (Ballard, *Crash*, 201, 199). These angelic references directly precede James's penetration of Vaughan.

38. "Cinema is the art of destroying moving images" (Usai, *The Death of Cinema*, 7).

39. Angell, *The Films of Andy Warhol*, 16.

40. "Andy Warhol," n.p.

41. Benjamin, "The Task of the Translator," 81. Benjamin describes Pannwitz's work as "the best comment on the theory of translation that has been published in Germany" (ibid., 80).

42. For examples of this approach to the novel's interest in visual technology, one might look at Aidan Day's essay "Ballard and Baudrillard," where he notes, "But *Crash* is not solely about cars. It is at least as much about photography and

film" (280). The essay continues to pursue the relationship between the parallel discourses of cars and visual technology, rather than between visual technology and literature. Jeffrey T. Schnapp's essay "Crash (Speed as Engine of Individuation)" mentions Ballard's novel only in passing, but it explores brilliantly the relationship between high-speed automobiles and film. Paul Youngquist, in "Ballard's Crash-Body," is interested in the triangular relationship between photography, the automobile, and the body, claiming, for example, that "the impact of the automobile upon the organic body is thus to transform it. Literally. The body becomes a surface in relation to the car's stylized cockpit, a surface which, like that of the photographic image, lacks opposable interior and exterior" (n.p.).

43. As David James points out, for many underground filmmakers, "the only response to the hegemony of the industrial practice capable of integrity is the denial of the medium itself. The coherent anti-film includes only as much implication of film-as-such as its negation of it may body forth" (*Allegories of Cinema*, 127).

44. Ballard, *Crash*, 48; emphasis added.

45. Ibid., 48, 166.

46. Ibid., 196; emphasis added.

47. The films Godard made in the 1960s share Ballard's preoccupations in this congested novel. We see this not only in Godard's exploration of the (im)possibility of emotion in late capitalism through metaphors of driving, traffic congestion, and combustion, so visible in films like *Breathless* (1960), *Pierrot le fou* (1965), and *Weekend* (1967), but also in his fascination with the way these metaphors allow him to explore the shifting relation between writing and film. In an interview, in 1963, with Bertrand Tavernier for *Cahiers du cinéma*, he states, "I think of myself as an essayist, producing essays in novel form or novels in essay form: only instead of writing, I film them. Were the cinema to disappear, I would simply accept the inevitable and turn to television; were television to disappear, I would revert to pencil and paper. For there is a clear continuity between all forms of expression. It's all me" (quoted in Thompson, "Godard," 29–30). For a discussion of Godard's movement between cinema and painting, see Vacche, *Cinema and Painting*, 107–34. On Godard's use of cars, David Sterritt writes, "It is interesting to note how the metaphorical meaning of cars has shifted in Godard's value system. In the early *Breathless* they represent a Beat-style dream of liberation via speed, flexibility, elusiveness. They played a more somber role in *My Life to Live*. . . . *Weekend* veers even more sharply in this cynical direction, paralyzing cars altogether by cramming them into a self-suffocating gridlock so devoid of action and energy that the movie itself almost stops moving" (*The Films of Jean-Luc Godard*, 97). Ballard asks us to consider, within the confines of one novel, this wide-ranging metaphorical use of the car in relation to the medium of film.

48. Ballard, *Crash*, 215.
49. These practices were regulated in the second half of the 1920s. For examples of reproductions of early centrally perforated filmstrips that vividly recall the central division of roads, see Usai, *Silent Cinema*, plates 17, 35.
50. Ballard, *Crash*, 196.
51. For a definition of *cellulose*, see the web site for the *Oxford English Dictionary*.
52. Ballard, *Crash*, 50.
53. Ibid., 72.
54. Ibid., 151.
55. Ibid., 169, 172.
56. Ibid., 169. For a discussion of Dine, see Kirkby, *Happenings*, 184–99. See also Lambert, "Documentary Dialectics: Performance Lost and Found"; and Rodenbeck, "*Car Crash*, 1960."
57. For drawing on black, see Norman McLaren's *Hen Hop* (1942); for scratching on black, see his *Blinkity Blank* (1955). See also Len Lye's *A Colour Box* (1935), and Harry Smith's *No. 1* (1950). The description of Vaughan's black car after the crash that causes his death evokes Smith's *No. 2* and *No. 3*, which were both colored by spray paint and dyes applied directly to the film. The death vehicle, Ballard writes, looks "as if the blood had been sprayed on with a paint gun" (*Crash*, 224). For a full discussion of the development of these techniques, see Sitney, *Visionary Film*, 266–312.
58. Ruscha's portfolio *Stains* included painting with blood and semen. Warhol's *Oxidation Paintings* (1978), made by urinating on canvas previously painted with a synthetic polymer medium mixed with metallic powder, provide an interesting parallel to the endlessly fluid surfaces in *Crash*. For a technical discussion of the paintings, see Livingstone, "Do It Yourself." Warhol tells Benjamin Buchloh, "When I showed them in Paris the hot lights made them melt again . . . it's very weird when they drip down. They look like real drippy paintings and they never stopped dripping because the lights were so hot. Then you can understand why these holy pictures cry all the time" (Buchloh, "Three Conversations in 1985," 43).
59. Ballard, *Crash*, 157.
60. Ibid., 157–58.
61. Usai, *The Death of Cinema*, 12–13.
62. "Vaughan picked repeatedly at the scabs running across his knuckles. The scars on his knees, healed now for more than a year, were beginning to reopen. The points of blood seeped through the worn fabric of his jeans. Red flecks appeared on the lower curvature of the dashboard locker, on the lower rim of the radio console, and marked the black vinyl of the doors" (Ballard, *Crash*, 191–92).
63. Ibid., 148; emphasis added.
64. Ibid.

65. Ibid., 184.
66. Mulvey, "Visual Pleasure and Narrative Cinema," 47.
67. Irigaray, "Sexual Difference," 9.
68. Ibid., 9.

Chapter Six. Crash Aesthetics

1. For a more detailed discussion of the images of the exploding body generated by the Vietnam War, see Chong, *The Oriental Obscene*.
2. Joshua Levin, "Movie Car Crashes: A Primer," available at *Slate* magazine's video web site, *Slate V* (accessed 21 July 2008). Thanks to Jim Lastra and Peter Struck for drawing my attention to this.
3. See the "Project" page on the web site for Crash Test Dummy: The New European "Self" in a Bio-Political Crash Test (accessed 22 July 2008).
4. Hirschberg, "A New Mexican," 34.
5. Paul Julian Smith, *Amores perros*, 27.
6. Ayala Blanco, *La fugacidad del cine mexicano*; quoted in Paul Julian Smith, *Amores perros*, 25.
7. *El Universal*, 19 May 2000; quoted in Paul Julian Smith, *Amores perros*, 87.
8. Some critics did briefly compare the content of *Amores perros* with that of Buñuel's work. Edward Lawrensen mentions *The Exterminating Angel* in passing (Lawrensen, Soler, and González Iñárritu, "Pulp Fiction," 28); Claudia Schaefer notes the fact that female characters lose a leg in both *Amores perros* and *Tristana* (*Bored to Distraction*, 92–93); and Michael Wood compares the film with both *Tristana* and *Los olvidados*, the latter of which he describes as "another study of Mexico City as a place of danger and destitution" ("Dog Days," 57).
9. Acevedo-Muñoz, *Buñuel and Mexico*, 74. For a full discussion of the domestic and international reception of *Los olvidados*, see Acevedo-Muñoz, "*Los olvidados* and the Crisis of Mexican Cinema."
10. González, Lerner, and Marmasse, *Mexperimental Cinema*, 43.
11. See George Baker's essay "Photography's Expanded Field." Baker echoes Krauss's use of the terms "not-landscape" and "not-architecture" in her seminal essay, "Sculpture in the Expanded Field" (283).
12. Stewart, *Between Film and Screen*, 226. In the introduction to *Between Film and Screen*, Stewart problematically separates the mechanical eruptions from social questions, stating that the book "must necessarily remain unconcerned in any detail with all the things that may properly be noted about photographic ways of seeing apart from their instituted arrest. Set aside for the most part are social, economic, and psychosexual uses and abuses of the photochemically indexed world, except when certain screen narratives take them up. The book is preoccupied instead with the mechanical fixation of the photography and with

the incursion of its discreteness into the projected film track" (37). We might read this early distinction of the mechanical and the social as symptomatic of Stewart's attempt to reorient film theory away from its late-twentieth-century focus on the psychology of spectatorship toward a more focused consideration of the medium itself, but happily, in the course of the book, Stewart's astute readings demonstrate the impossibility of severing these medium-specific discussions from sociohistorical questions and problems.

13. Baker, "Reanimations (1)," 47–48.
14. Ibid., 41. For a recent example of the reconsideration of narrative film within feminist film criticism, see Fischer, "'Dancing through the Minefield.'"
15. Jameson, *The Geopolitical Aesthetic*, 84n19.
16. Lawrensen, Soler, and González Iñárritu, "Pulp Fiction," 30. Interestingly, Rodrigo Prieto, González Iñárritu's cinematographer, articulates a stylistic debt to the work of Goldin, as well as to other photographers, in his second feature film, *21 Grams* (2003), which posed particular challenges for the cinematographer trying to turn the "look" of photographs into film. John Calhoun writes: "Prieto notes that he and Iñárritu used still photos by Laura Letinsky, Sebasteao Salgado, Nan Goldin and William Eggleston as reference points for their images. 'We emulated all of the defects that occur when you're shooting with available light,' he explains. 'The difference is that in still photography, you don't have issues of continuity. We had to do entire scenes in whatever time it took to shoot them, so obviously I had to light as well'" ("Heartbreak and Loss," 48).
17. Travis Crawford, "Humane Society," *Filmmaker* (winter 2001), available on the web site for *Filmmaker* magazine. In an interview with Jean Oppenheimer, Prieto describes the effects of the bleach-bypass process: "The contrast in general is enhanced with skip-bleach, but so is the contrast of the grain. . . . [The process] desaturates certain hues and colors, such as skin tones, but the reds and blues [are] even enhance[d]" (Oppenheimer, "A Dog's Life," 20, 23; quoted in Paul Julian Smith, *Amores perros*, 77).
18. Usai, *The Death of Cinema*, 7.
19. Paul Julian Smith, *Amores perros*, 76. In this "translation" of extant still images into new moving forms, González Iñárritu's work resonates in interesting ways with contemporary artists whose work seems to hover at the border of movement and stasis. For a recent example of this preoccupation in contemporary art, see Eve Sussman's *89 Seconds at Alcazar* (2004), a tableau vivant of Diego Velázquez's *Las meninas* (1656); Nancy Davenport's *Weekend Campus* (2004); or Adad Hannah's *Stills* (2002). A recent exhibition at the Baltimore Museum of Art, *Slide Show: The Projected Image* (2005), also reflects on this recent interest in the murky border between cinema and photography.
20. Paul Julian Smith, *Amores perros*, 77.
21. *I'll Be Your Mirror* (Nan Goldin and Edmund Coulthard, 1995). Interestingly,

Goldin states that had she had the final cut of this film, she would have excluded the slide show that appears at the end of the film. Goldin and Hoberman, "'My Number One Medium All My Life,'" 143.

22. See Goldin and Hoberman, "'My Number One Medium All My Life,'" for Goldin's discussion of her relation to film culture.
23. Ibid., 136–37.
24. Baker, "Reanimations (1)," 47.
25. Ibid., 48.
26. Fuss, *Identification Papers*, 2.
27. Baker, "Reanimations (1)," 35, 48.
28. Laderman, *Driving Visions*, 14–15.
29. Virilio, *Unknown Quantity*, 27.
30. Benjamin, *Illuminations*, 262.
31. Mulvey, "Visual Pleasure and Narrative Cinema," 41.
32. See Franco, "Beyond Ethnocentrism."
33. Foster, *Compulsive Beauty*, 115, 122.
34. Ibid., 115.
35. Lippit, *Electric Animal*, 195.

Chapter Seven. The Afterlife of *Weekend*

1. Genêt, "Letter From Paris," 81.
2. Orr, *Cinema and Modernity*, 138–39.
3. Sterritt, *The Films of Jean-Luc Godard*, 98.
4. For a discussion of the relationship between sex and capitalism, see Silverman and Farocki, "Anal Capitalism."
5. Sterritt, *The Films of Jean-Luc Godard*, 97. Annie Goldmann, writing shortly after the release of *Weekend*, shares this sense of a movement away from comedy toward cynicism, arguing that while Godard employs tactics familiar to caricaturists, he does so "without any comic intention," and offering Jacques Tati as a comic and optimistic counterpoint to Godard in his use of cars and roads. See Goldmann, *Cinéma et société moderne*, 179–83.
6. Robin Wood, "Godard and *Weekend*," 11. Giorgio Agamben echoes this attitude toward apocalyptic visions, noting that "the life that begins on earth after the last day is simply human life" (*The Coming Community*, 7).
7. Laplanche, "Notes on Afterwardsness," 261.
8. Godard actively encourages reading for puns, as in the title "FAUX-TOGRAPHIE."
9. Sterritt, *The Films of Jean-Luc Godard*, 123.
10. "Afterwardsness," for Laplanche, allows exploration of the temporal lags that may exist between the utterance of messages in the past and our ability to receive or understand them through the figure of translation, which is conceived of as alternating between progressive and retrogressive temporalities: "In my

view, afterwardsness is inconceivable without a model of translation: that is, it presupposes that something is proffered by the other, and this is then afterwards retranslated and reinterpreted" ("Notes on Afterwardsness," 265).

11. This critical perspective toward the supposedly more successful antiwar activism of the 1960s and 1970s emerges in some of the more interesting responses to a questionnaire on the Iraq War that appeared in *October* in 2008, but particularly in the responses of Simon Leung, Coco Fusco, and 16BEAVER. See Leung, untitled; Fusco, untitled; and 16BEAVER, untitled. For a discussion of the prevalence of nostalgia for the 1960s in contemporary art, and of the effacing of history that such nostalgia enacts, see Meyer, "Nostalgia and Memory."
12. Foster, *Design and Crime (and Other Diatribes)*, 139.
13. Meyersberg, "Godard's Last Weekend," 23.
14. MacBean, "Godard's Week-end, or the Self Critical Cinema of Cruelty," 35.
15. This moment may also refer to Chaplin's critique of the regulation of human movement in his juxtaposition of sheep and workers entering the factory in *Modern Times* (1936).
16. Kael, *Going Steady*, 172–74.
17. Sterritt, *The Films of Jean-Luc Godard*, 92.
18. From *Internationale Situationiste #10*; reprinted in Knabb, *Situationist International Anthology*, 175–76.
19. Knabb, *Situationist International Anthology*, 175. It is worth noting that in contrast to the situationists' dismissal of Godard's comic-book humor (which actually has closer affinities with slapstick comedy), Giorgio Agamben argues that "tricksters or fakes, assistants or 'toons, they are the examples of the coming community" (*The Coming Community*, 7).
20. Knabb, *Situationist International Anthology*, 298.
21. Nöel Simsolo, "Carmelo Bene: *Capricci*," 213. For an overview of Bene's work, see Marc Siegel, "Contesting Cinema."
22. Kael, *Going Steady*, 170.
23. Marc Siegel, "Contesting Cinema," 34.
24. Silverman and Farocki, "Anal Capitalism," 99.
25. *Xala* means "impotence," and the film constantly explores the alternatives to impotence in political, sexual, and cinematic contexts.
26. For an important discussion about *Xala* and the role of foreign languages in it, see John Mowitt's essay "Sembène Ousmane's *Xala*: Postcoloniality and Foreign Film Language."
27. See Murphy, "Africans filming Africa."
28. On "Tomorrow's Expanded Cinema University," see Buckminster Fuller's introduction to Youngblood, *Expanded Cinema*, 35.
29. Davenport, "Weekend Campus," 192–93.
30. Goldsmith, *Traffic*, back cover.

31. This linear stretch of immobilized people and vehicles also recalls another iconic moment of late-1960s cinema: the Maysles brothers' aerial shots of the auto-stasis that preceded the Rolling Stones' disaster-ridden performance at the Altamont Speedway in *Gimme Shelter* (Albert Maysles and David Maysles, 1970). There were approximately 50,000 more cars at this event than there were parking spaces.
32. In this sense, Davenport's work does seem to reference not only Godard's *Weekend*, but also *La Chinoise*'s focus on the relationship between radical politics and the university.
33. Davenport, "Weekend Campus," 189, 192.
34. I am grateful to Tom Gunning for pointing out the resonance between the traffic-jam sequences in *Two Tars* and *Weekend*.
35. "La Vie Weekend: Paul Lennon Watches Jean-Luc Godard at Work," *Manchester Guardian*, 27 September 1967, 5.
36. Rodowick, in a discussion of the film theorist Siegfried Kracauer, writes, "The temporality of the projected film sustains us in a given duration that parallels the flux of becoming characteristic of the *Lebenswelt*, or flow of everyday life. In this way film transcribes not only objects, but also the duration wherein they exist and persist" (*The Virtual Life of Film*, 77).
37. In an essay on how movies "solicit and sustain the possibility of ethical thought," David Rodowick invokes a possibility that resonates strongly with the experience of time, space, and return created by Davenport's *Weekend Campus*. He writes, "Deleuze's reading of lyrical abstraction is close to the ethical interpretation of Nietzsche's eternal return. We are not caught by the absolute values of darkness and light, or even the indecisiveness of grey. Rather, the possibility of 'spiritual determination,' indeed what Cavell might call moral perfectionism, is a choice not to be defined by what is chosen, 'but by the power choosing possesses of being able to start again at each instant, to restart itself, and to affirm itself of itself, by putting all the stakes back into play each time'" ("Ethics," 14–15).
38. "Taking care of Today Tomorrow" grammatically parallels "Challenging Minds, Changing Lives," the slogan of Jackson State University, where, in May 1970, policemen killed two students during student protests. Following this, President Nixon established the President's Commission on Campus Unrest, on 13 June 1970. For a discussion of the implications of the expanded presence of credit-card companies on college campuses, see the documentary *Maxed Out: Hard Times, Easy Credit, and the Era of Predatory Lenders* (James D. Scurlock, 2006).
39. Davenport, "Weekend Campus," 193.
40. Deleuze, "One Manifesto Less," 218.
41. Ibid., 211.
42. DeLillo, *White Noise*, 218–19.

BIBLIOGRAPHY

Acevedo-Muñoz, Ernesto R. *Buñuel and Mexico: The Crisis of National Cinema.* Berkeley: University of California Press, 2003.

———. "*Los Olvidados* and the Crisis of Mexican Cinema." *Buñuel and Mexico: The Crisis of National Cinema*, 57–79. Berkeley: University of California Press, 2003.

Acker, Kathy. *Bodies of Work: Essays.* London: Serpent's Tail, 1997.

Adorno, Theodor. *Aesthetic Theory.* Translated by Robert Hullot-Kentor. Minneapolis: University of Minnesota Press, 1997.

Agamben, Giorgio. *The Coming Community.* Translated by Michael Hardt. Minneapolis: University of Minnesota Press, 1993.

Agee, James. "Comedy's Greatest Era." *Agee on Film: Reviews and Comments by James Agee*, 2–19. New York: Beacon, 1958.

Albert, Daniel M. "Primitive Drivers: Racial Science and Citizenship in the Motor Age." *Science as Culture* 10, no. 3 (2001), 327–51.

Andrew, Dudley. "The Neglected Tradition of Phenomenology in Film Theory." *Movies and Methods: An Anthology*, ed. Bill Nichols, 625–32. Vol. 2. Berkeley: University of California Press, 1985.

"Andy Warhol." Exhibition brochure. New York: Dia Center for the Arts, 1994.

Angell, Callie. *The Films of Andy Warhol: Part 2.* New York: Whitney Museum of American Art, 1994.

Ayala Blanco, Jorge. *La fugacidad del cine mexicano.* Mexico City: Océano, 2001.

Baker, George. "Photography's Expanded Field." *October* 114 (fall 2005), 120–40.

———. "Reanimations (1)." *October* 104 (spring 2003), 28–70.

Balibar, Étienne. *We, the People of Europe? Reflections on Transnational Citizenship.* Translated by James Swenson. Princeton, N.J.: Princeton University Press, 2004.

Ballard, J. G. *The Atrocity Exhibition.* San Francisco: Re/Search, 1990.

———. *Crash.* New York: Picador, 1973.

———. "Fictions of Every Kind." *A User's Guide to the Millennium: Essays and Reviews*, 205–7. New York: Picador, 1996.

Barnes, John. *The Beginnings of the Cinema in England 1894–1901.* Vol. 5, *1900.* Exeter: University of Exeter Press, 1997.

Barr, Charles. *Laurel and Hardy*. Berkeley: University of California Press, 1974.

Barthes, Roland. "La voiture, projection de l'ego." *Réalités* 213 (1963), 92–97.

———. "The Third Meaning." *Image-Music-Text*, ed. Stephen Heath, 52–68. London: Fontana, 1977.

Baudrillard, Jean. "The Ecstasy of Communication." *The Anti-Aesthetic: Essays on Postmodern Culture*, ed. Hal Foster, 126–34. Port Townsend, Wash.: Bay, 1982.

———. "The Precession of Simulacra." *Art after Modernism: Rethinking Representation*, ed. Brian Wallis, 253–81. New York: New Museum of Contemporary Art, 1984.

———. "Two Essays: 1. Simulacra and Science Fiction. 2. Ballard's *Crash*." *Science Fiction Studies* 18 (1991), 309–20.

Baughman, E. Austin. "Protective Measures for the Automobile and Its Owner." "The Automobile: Its Province and Its Problems," special issue, *Annals of the American Academy of Political and Social Science* 116 (November 1924), 194–98.

Bean, Jennifer M., and Diane Negra, eds. *A Feminist Reader in Early Cinema*. Durham, N.C.: Duke University Press, 2002.

Beck, Ulrich. "World Risk Society as Cosmopolitan Society? Ecological Questions in a Framework of Manufactured Uncertainties." *Theory, Culture and Society* 13, no. 4 (1996), 1–32.

Beckman, Karen. "The Archive, the Phallus, and the Future." *Camera Obscura* 22, no. 1 (2007), 184–91.

Benjamin, Walter. *Illuminations*. Edited by Hannah Arendt. Translated by Harry Zohn. New York: Schocken, 1968.

———. *Reflections: Essays, Aphorisms, Autobiographical Writings*. Edited by Peter Demetz. New York: Schocken, 1978.

———. "The Task of the Translator." *Illuminations*, ed. Hannah Arendt, 69–82. New York: Schocken, 1968.

Bergson, Henri. "Laughter." *Comedy*, ed. Wylie Sypher, 61–190. New York: Doubleday, 1956.

Bersani, Leo. *The Culture of Redemption*. Cambridge, Mass.: Harvard University Press, 1990.

Bersani, Leo, and Ulysse Dutoit. *Forms of Being: Cinema, Aesthetics, Subjectivity*. London: British Film Institute, 2004.

Bitomsky, Harmut. "Cinema and Death." *Kino wie noch nie / Cinema Like Never Before*, ed. Antje Ehmann and Harun Farocki, 125–40. Vienna: Gernerali Foundation, 2006.

Blanchot, Maurice. *The Writing of the Disaster*. Translated by Ann Smock. Lincoln: University of Nebraska Press, 1995.

Bordowitz, Gregg. "The Effort to Survive AIDS Considered from the Point of View of a Race-Car Driver." *Drive: The AIDS Crisis Is Still Beginning*, ed. Gregg Bordowitz, 72–75. Chicago: WhiteWalls, 2002.

Bordwell, David, and Kristin Thompson. "Linearity, Materialism, and the Study of Early American Cinema." *Wide Angle* 5, no. 3 (1983), 4–15.

Bowser, Eileen. *Cinema 1900–1906: An Analytical Study*. Vol. 1. Edited by Roger Holman. Brussels: Fédération Internationale des Archives du Film, 1982.

———. *The Transformation of Cinema 1907–1915*. New York: Charles Scribner's Sons, 1990.

Bracken, A. J. "The Aftermath of Sudden Death." *Reader's Digest*, December 1935, 52–54.

Braun, Marta. *Picturing Time: The Work of Etienne-Jules Marey (1830–1904)*. Chicago: University of Chicago Press, 1992.

Bright, John Irwin. "The Plan of Philadelphia." "The Automobile: Its Province and Its Problems," special issue, *Annals of the American Academy of Political and Social Science* 116 (November 1924), 231–35.

Brottman, Mikita, ed. *Car Crash Culture*. New York: Palgrave, 2001.

Brownlow, Kevin. *The Parade's Gone By*. London: Secker and Warburg, 1968.

Bruno, Giuliana. *Streetwalking on a Ruined Map: Cultural Theory and the City Films of Elvira Notari*. Princeton, N.J.: Princeton University Press, 1993.

Buchloh, Benjamin H. D. "Three Conversations in 1985: Claes Oldenburg, Andy Warhol, Robert Morris." *October* 70 (autumn 1994), 33–54.

Burch, Noël. *Life to Those Shadows*. Edited and translated by Ben Brewster. Berkeley: University of California Press, 1990.

Butler, Judith. *Giving an Account of Oneself*. New York: Fordham University Press, 2005.

———. "Sexual Ideology and Phenomenological Description: A Feminist Critique of Merleau-Ponty's *Phenomenology of Perception*." 1981. Reprinted in *The Thinking Muse: Feminism and Modern French Philosophy*, ed. Jeffner Allen and Iris Marion Young, 85–100. Bloomington: Indiana University Press, 1989.

———. *Undoing Gender*. New York: Routledge, 2004.

Calhoun, John. "Heartbreak and Loss." *American Cinematographer* 84, no. 12 (December 2003), 38–42, 44, 46–51.

Chong, Sylvia. *The Oriental Obscene: American Film Violence and Racial Transference in the Vietnam Era*. Durham, N.C.: Duke University Press, forthcoming.

Coffman, Elizabeth. "Woman in Motion: Loie Fuller and the 'Interpretation' of Art and Science." *Camera Obscura* 17, no. 1 (2002), 72–105.

Corrigan, Timothy. *A Cinema without Walls: Movies and Culture after Vietnam*. New Brunswick, N.J.: Rutgers University Press, 1994.

Crafton, Donald. "Pie and Chase: Gag, Spectacle and Narrative in Slapstick Comedy." *Classical Hollywood Comedy*, ed. Kristine Brunovska Karnick and Henry Jenkins, 106–19. New York: Routledge, 1995.

Crary, Jonathan. "Eclipse of the Spectacle." *Art after Modernism: Rethinking Repre-*

sentation, ed. Brian Wallis, 283–94. New York: New Museum of Contemporary Art, 1984.

———. "J. G. Ballard and the Promiscuity of Forms." *Zone 1/2* (1986), 159–65.

———. *Suspensions of Perception: Attention, Spectacle and Modern Culture*. Cambridge, Mass.: MIT Press, 2001.

———. *Techniques of the Observer: On Vision and Modernity in the Nineteenth Century*. Cambridge, Mass.: MIT Press, 1991.

Creed, Barbara. "The *Crash* Debate: Anal Wounds, Metallic Kisses." *Screen* 39, no. 2 (summer 1998), 175–79.

Crimp, Douglas. "Coming Together to Stay Apart: Ronald Tavel's Screenplays for Andy Warhol's Films." Unpublished paper, 2005. Files of Douglas Crimp.

———. "Face Value." *About Face: Andy Warhol Portraits*, ed. Nicholas Baume, 110–25. Hartford, Conn.: Wadsworth Athenaeum, 1999.

———. "Getting the Warhol We Deserve." *Social Text* 59, no. 2 (summer 1999), 49–66.

Crow, Thomas. "Saturday Disasters: Trace and Reference in Early Warhol." *Andy Warhol*, ed. Annette Michelson, 49–68. Cambridge, Mass.: MIT Press, 2001.

Davenport, Nancy. "Weekend Campus." *Still Moving: Between Cinema and Photography*, ed. Karen Beckman and Jean Ma, 189–95. Durham, N.C.: Duke University Press, 2008.

Day, Aidan. "Ballard and Baudrillard: Close Reading *Crash*." *English* 49 (autumn 2000): 277–93.

Dean, Tim. *Beyond Sexuality*. Chicago: University of Chicago Press, 2000.

Debord, Guy. "Situationist Theses on Traffic." 1959. Reprinted in *Situationist International Anthology*, ed. Ken Knabb, 56–58. Berkeley: Bureau of Public Secrets, 1981.

Deleuze, Gilles. *Cinema 1: The Movement-Image*. Translated by Hugh Tomlinson and Barbara Habberjam. Minneapolis: University of Minnesota Press, 1986.

———. *Cinema 2: The Time-Image*. Translated by Hugh Tomlinson and Robert Galeta. Minneapolis: University of Minnesota Press, 1989.

———. "Coldness and Cruelty." *Masochism*, 9–142. New York: Zone, 1991.

———. "One Manifesto Less." *The Deleuze Reader*, ed. Constantin V. Boundas, 204–22. New York: Columbia University Press, 1993.

DeLillo, Don. *White Noise*. New York: Penguin, 1988.

Dimendberg, Edward. "The Will to Motorization: Cinema, Highways, and Modernity." *October* 73 (summer 1995), 91–137.

Doane, Mary Ann. *The Emergence of Cinematic Time: Modernity, Contingency, the Archive*. Cambridge, Mass.: Harvard University Press, 2002.

———. "Information, Crisis, Catastrophe." 1990. Reprinted in *The Historical Film: History and Memory in Media*, ed. Marcia Landy, 269–85. New Brunswick, N.J.: Rutgers University Press, 2001.

Doyle, Jennifer, Jonathan Flatley, and José Esteban Muñoz, eds. *Pop Out: Queer Warhol*. Durham, N.C.: Duke University Press, 1996.

Dyer, Richard. *Heavenly Bodies: Film Stars and Society*. New York: St. Martin's, 1986.

Edelman, Lee. *No Future: Queer Theory and the Death Drive*. Durham, N.C.: Duke University Press, 2004.

"Editorial Notes: Critique of Urbanism." Translated by John Shepley. "Guy Debord and the Internationale Situationniste," special issue, *October* 79 (winter 1997), 113–19. Originally published in *Internationale Situationniste* 6 (August 1961), 3–11.

Eno, William P. "The Storage of Dead Vehicles on Roadways." "The Automobile: Its Province and Its Problems," special issue, *Annals of the American Academy of Political and Social Science* 116 (November 1924), 169–74.

Enticknap, Leo. "'A Real Brake on Progress'? Moving Image Technology in the Time of Mitchell and Kenyon." *The Lost World of Mitchell and Kenyon: Edwardian Britain on Film*, ed. Vanessa Toulmin, Simon Popple, and Patrick Russell, 21–30. London: British Film Institute, 2004.

Everson, William K. *American Silent Film*. New York: Oxford University Press, 1978.

———. *The Complete Films of Laurel and Hardy*. New York: Carol, 1991.

Faimberg, Haydée. "Après-Coup." *International Journal of Psychoanalysis* 86 (2005), 1–6.

Fischer, Lucy. "'Dancing through the Minefield': Passion, Pedagogy, Politics, and Production in *The Tango Lesson*." *Cinema Journal* 43, no. 3 (spring 2004), 42–58.

———. "Sometimes I Feel Like a Motherless Child: Comedy and Matricide." *Comedy/Cinema/Theory*, ed. Andrew S. Horton, 60–78. Berkeley: University of California Press, 1991.

Foster, Hal. *Compulsive Beauty*. Cambridge, Mass.: MIT Press/October Books, 1995.

———. "Death in America." *Andy Warhol*, ed. Annette Michelson, 68–88. Cambridge, Mass.: MIT Press, 2000.

———. *Design and Crime (and Other Diatribes)*. London: Verso, 2002.

Foucault, Michel. "Sexual Choice, Sexual Act." *Ethics: Subjectivity and Truth*, ed. Paul Rabinow, 141–56. Vol. 1 of *The Essential Works of Michel Foucault, 1954–1984*. New York: New Press, 1997.

Frampton, Hollis. "The Invention without a Future." *October* 109 (summer 2004), 64–75.

Franco, Jean. "Beyond Ethnocentrism: Gender, Power and the Third World Intelligensia." *Marxism and the Interpretation of Culture*, ed. Cary Nelson and Lawrence Grossberg, 503–15. Urbana: University of Illinois Press, 1988.

Freeman, Elizabeth. "Packing History, Count(er)ing Generations." *New Literary History* 31, no. 4 (2000), 727–44.

Freud, Sigmund. *Beyond the Pleasure Principle*. Translated and edited by James Strachey. New York: Norton, 1961.

———. "Instincts and Their Vicissitudes." 1915. Reprinted in *General Psychologi-*

cal Theory: Papers on Metapsychology, ed. Philip Rieff, 83–103. New York: Collier, 1963.

Friedberg, Anne. *Window Shopping: Cinema and the Postmodern.* Berkeley: University of California Press, 1993.

Furnas, J. C. "—And Sudden Death." *Reader's Digest*, August 1935, 21–26.

Fusco, Coco. Untitled. *October* 123 (winter 2008), 53–62.

Fuss, Diana. *Identification Papers: Readings on Psychoanalysis, Sexuality, and Culture.* New York: Routledge, 1995.

Gaines, Jane M. "Of Cabbages and Authors." *A Feminist Reader in Early Cinema*, ed. Jennifer M. Bean and Diane Negra, 88–118. Durham, N.C.: Duke University Press, 2002.

Gartenberg, Jon. "Camera Movement in Edison and Biograph Films, 1900–1906." *Cinema Journal* 19, no. 2 (spring 1980), 1–16.

Gaudreault, André. "Temporality and Narrativity in Early Cinema, 1895–1908." *Film before Griffith*, ed. John Fell, 316–19. Berkeley: University of California Press, 1983.

Gaycken, Oliver. Devices of Curiosity: Cinema and the Scientific Vernacular. Ph.D. diss., University of Chicago, 2005.

Genêt, Jean. "Letter from Paris." *New Yorker* 43, no. 50 (3 February 1968), 79–82.

Goldin, Nan, and J. Hoberman. "'My Number One Medium All My Life': Nan Goldin Talking with J. Hoberman." *Nan Goldin: I'll Be Your Mirror*, ed. Nan Goldin, David Armstrong, and Hans Werner Holzwarth, 135–45. New York: Whitney Museum of American Art, 1996.

Goldmann, Annie. *Cinéma et société moderne: Le cinema de 1958 à 1968: Godard—Antonioni—Resnais—Robbe-Grillet.* Paris: Anthropos, 1971.

Goldsmith, Kenneth. *Traffic.* Los Angeles: Make Now, 2007.

González, Rita, Jesse Lerner, and Isabelle Marmasse. *Mexperimental Cinema: Sixty Years of Avant-Garde Media Arts from Mexico.* Santa Monica, Calif.: Smart Art, 1998.

Graham, George M. "Safeguarding Traffic: A Nation's Problem—A Nation's Duty." "The Automobile: Its Province and Its Problems," special issue, *Annals of the American Academy of Political and Social Science* 116 (November 1924), 174–85.

Grazie, Victoria de. "Mass Culture and Sovereignty: The American Challenge to European Cinemas, 1920–1960." *Modern History* 61 (March 1989), 53–87.

Grieveson, Lee. "Visualizing Industrial Citizenship: Or, Henry Ford Makes Movies," Lecture presented at the University of Pennsylvania, 19 November 2008.

Grosz, Elizabeth. *Volatile Bodies: Toward a Corporeal Feminism.* Bloomington: Indiana University Press, 1994.

Grundmann, Ray. "Plight of the Crash Fest Mummies: David Cronenberg's *Crash*." *Cinéaste* 22, no. 4 (1997), 24–27.

Gunning, Tom. "An Aesthetics of Astonishment: Early Film and the (In)credulous Spectator." *Art and Text* 34 (spring 1989), 31–45.

———. "The Cinema of Attraction: Early Film, Its Spectator and the Avant-Garde." *Wide Angle* 8, nos. 3–4 (1986), 63–70.

———. "Crazy Machines in the Garden of Forking Paths: Mischief Gags and the Origins of American Film Comedy." *Classical Hollywood Comedy*, ed. Kristine Brunovska Karnick and Henry Jenkins, 87–105. New York: Routledge, 1995.

———. "From the Kaleidoscope to the X-ray: Urban Spectatorship, Poe, Benjamin, and *Traffic in Souls* (1913)." *Wide Angle* 19, no. 4 (1997), 25–61.

———. "'Primitive' Cinema? A Frame-Up? Or the Trick's on Us." *Cinema Journal* 28, no. 2 (winter 1989), 3–12.

———. "Response to 'Pie and Chase.'" *Classical Hollywood Comedy*, ed. Kristine Brunovska Karnick and Henry Jenkins, 120–22. New York: Routledge, 1995.

———. "An Unseen Energy Swallows Space: The Space in Early Film and Its Relation to American Avant-Garde Film." *Film before Griffith*, ed. John Fell, 355–66. Berkeley: University of California Press, 1983.

Halberstam, Judith. *In a Queer Time and Place: Transgender Bodies, Subcultural Lives*. New York: New York University Press, 2005.

Hansen, Miriam Bratu. *Babel and Babylon: Spectatorship in American Silent Film*. Cambridge, Mass.: Harvard University Press, 1991.

———. "Benjamin and Cinema: Not a One-Way Street." "*Angelus Novus*: Perspectives on Walter Benjamin," special issue, *Critical Inquiry* 25, no. 2 (winter 1999), 306–43.

Hepworth, Cecil M. *Came the Dawn: Memories of a Film Pioneer*. London: Phoenix House, 1951.

Hertzberg, H. T. E. "Anthropology of Anthropomorphic Dummies." *Proceedings of Thirteenth S Fondation Cartier pour l'art contemporain Stapp Car Crash Conference* (2–4 December 1969), 201–14. Boston: Society of Automotive Engineers, 1969.

Higashi, Sumiko. *Cecil B. DeMille and American Culture: The Silent Era*. Berkeley: University of California Press, 1994.

Hirschberg, Lynn. "A New Mexican." *New York Times Magazine*, 21 March 2001, 32–35.

hooks, bell. *Feminism Is for Everybody: Passionate Politics*. Cambridge, Mass.: South End, 2000.

Hultkrans, Andrew. "Body Work: Interview with Author J. G. Ballard and Director David Cronenberg." *ArtForum* (March 1997), 76–81.

Irigaray, Luce. "Sexual Difference." *An Ethics of Sexual Difference*, 5–19. Ithaca, N.Y.: Cornell University Press, 1984.

Jacobs, Lea. *The Wages of Sin: Censorship and the Fallen Woman Film, 1928–1942*. Berkeley: University of California Press, 1997.

Jakobsen, Janet R. *Working Alliances and the Politics of Difference: Diversity and Feminist Ethics.* Bloomington: Indiana University Press, 1998.

James, David. *Allegories of Cinema.* Princeton, N.J.: Princeton University Press, 1989.

Jameson, Frederic. *The Geopolitical Aesthetic: Cinema and Space in the World System.* Bloomington: Indiana University Press, 1992.

Jenkins, Bruce. "Explosion in a Film Factory: The Cinema of Bruce Conner." *2000 B.C.: The Bruce Conner Story Part 2,* ed. Peter Boswell, Bruce Jenkins, and Joan Rothfuss, 185–224. Minneapolis: Walker Art Center, 2000.

Jenkins, Henry. *What Made Pistachio Nuts? Early Sound Comedy and the Vaudeville Aesthetic.* New York: Columbia University Press, 1992.

Kael, Pauline. *Going Steady.* New York: Bantam, 1971.

Kazarian, Leon E. "The Primate as a Model for Crash Injury." *Proceedings of Nineteenth Stapp Car Crash Conference* (17–19 November 1975), 931–64. Warrendale, Penn.: Society of Automotive Engineers, 1975.

Kerr, Walter. *The Silent Clowns.* New York: Knopf, 1975.

King, Homay. "Girl Interrupted: The Queer Time of Warhol's Cinema." *Discourse* 28, no. 1 (2006), 98–120.

Kirby, Lynne. *Parallel Tracks: The Railroad and Silent Cinema.* Durham, N.C.: Duke University Press, 1997.

———. "Romances of the Rail in Silent Film." *Parallel Tracks: The Railroad and Silent Cinema,* 75–131. Durham, N.C.: Duke University Press, 1997.

Kirkby, Michael. *Happenings: An Illustrated Anthology.* New York: Dutton, 1966.

Knabb, Ken, ed. and trans. *Situationist International Anthology.* Berkeley: Bureau of Public Secrets, 1981.

Koestenbaum, Wayne. *Andy Warhol.* New York: Viking, 2001.

Koszarski, Richard. *An Evening's Entertainment: The Age of the Silent Feature Picture 1915–1928.* Vol. 3 of *History of the American Cinema.* New York: Scribner, 1990.

Krauss, Rosalind. "Sculpture in the Expanded Field." 1979. Reprinted in *The Originality of the Avant-Garde and Other Modernist Myths,* 276–90. Cambridge, Mass.: MIT Press, 1985.

Kristeva, Julia. *Revolt, She Said.* Los Angeles: Semiotext(e), 2002.

Kuhn, Annette. *Cinema, Censorship, and Sexuality 1909–1925.* New York: Routledge, 1988.

Kurtz, Steve. "Black Humor, Crash Humor, and Aesthetic Representation." *Black Humor: Critical Essays,* ed. Alan R. Pratt, 283–300. New York: Garland, 1993.

Laderman, David. *Driving Visions: Exploring the Road Movie.* Austin: University of Texas Press, 2002.

Lambert, Carrie. "Documentary Dialectics: Performance Lost and Found." *Visual Resources* 16 (2000), 275–85.

Laplanche, Jean. "The Drive and Its Source Object: Its Fate in the Transference."

Essays on Otherness, ed. Jean Laplanche and John Fletcher, 117–32. New York: Routledge, 1999.

———. "Notes on Afterwardsness." In *Essays on Otherness*, ed. Jean Laplanche and John Fletcher, 260–65. New York: Routledge, 1998.

Lardner, Dionysius, ed. *The Museum of Science and Art*. Vol. 7. London: Walton and Maberly, 1859.

Lawrensen, Edward, Bernardo Pérez Soler, and Alejandro González Iñárritu. "Pulp Fiction." *Sight and Sound* 11, no. 5 (May 2001), 28–30.

Lee, Pamela. *Chronophobia: On Time in the Art of the 1960s*. Cambridge, Mass.: MIT Press, 2004.

Leung, Simon. Untitled. *October* 123 (winter 2008), 102–4.

Lewallen, Constance M., and Steve Seid, eds. *Ant Farm, 1968–1978*. Berkeley: University of California Press, 2004.

Lippit, Akira Mizuta. *Electric Animal: Toward a Rhetoric of Wildlife*. Minneapolis: University of Minnesota Press, 2000.

Littau, Karin. "Eye-Hunger: Physical Pleasure and Non-Narrative Cinema." *Crash Cultures: Modernity, Mediation and the Material*, ed. Jane Arthurs and Iain Grant, 35–51. Portland: Intellect, 2003.

Livingstone, Marco. "Do It Yourself: Notes on Warhol's Techniques." *Andy Warhol: A Retrospective*, ed. Kynaston McShine, 63–78. Boston: Bullfinch/Little, Brown/Museum of Modern Art, 1989.

Louvish, Simon. *Stan and Ollie: The Roots of Comedy: The Double Life of Laurel and Hardy*. London: Faber and Faber, 2001.

Love, Heather. *Feeling Backward: Loss and the Politics of Queer History*. Cambridge, Mass.: Harvard University Press, 2007.

———. "Spectacular Failure: The Figure of the Lesbian in *Mulholland Drive*." *New Literary History* 35 (2004), 117–32.

Low, Rachel, and Roger Manvell. *The History of the British Film 1896–1906*. Vol. 1. London: George Allen and Unwin, 1948.

Lubin, David M. *Shooting Kennedy: JFK and the Culture of Images*. Berkeley: University of California Press, 2003.

Ma, Jean. "Discordant Desires, Violent Refrains: *La Pianiste*." *Grey Room* 28 (summer 2007), 6–29.

MacBean, James Roy. "Godard's Week-end, or the Self Critical Cinema of Cruelty." *Film Quarterly* 21, no. 2 (winter 1968–winter 1969), 35–43.

MacCann, Richard Dyer. *Films of the 1920s*. Lanham, Md.: Scarecrow, 1996.

Macdonald, John M. "Suicide and Homicide by Automobile." *Psychiatry* (October 1964), 366–70.

Malfetti, James L. "Human Behavior—Factor X." "Highway Safety and Traffic Control," special issue, *Annals of the American Academy of Political and Social Science* 320, (November 1958), 93–102.

Mandel, Arch. "The Automobile and the Police." "The Automobile: Its Province and Its Problems," special issue, *Annals of the American Academy of Political and Social Science* 116 (November 1924), 191–94.

Marinetti, F. T. "The Founding and Manifesto of Futurism." 1909. Reprinted in *Futurist Manifestos*, ed. Umbro Apollonio, 19–24. New York: Viking, 1973.

McDonough, Thomas F. "Rereading Debord, Rereading the Situationists." "Guy Debord and the Internationale Situationniste," special issue, *October* 79 (winter 1997), 3–14.

McFarland, J. Horace. "The Billboard and the Public Highways." "The Automobile: Its Province and Its Problems," special issue, *Annals of the American Academy of Political and Social Science* 116 (November 1924), 95–101.

Meyer, James. "Nostalgia and Memory: Legacies of the 1960s in Recent Work." *Painting, Object, Film, Concept: Works from the Herbig Collection*, 26–35. London: Christie's, 1998.

Meyersberg, Paul. "Godard's Last Weekend." *New Society* 12, no. 301 (4 July 1968), 23.

Mosen, David. "Review (Untitled)." *Film Quarterly* 19, no. 3 (spring 1966), 54–56.

Mowitt, John. "Sembène Ousmane's *Xala*: Postcoloniality and Foreign Film Language." *Camera Obscura* 31 (January–May 1993), 73–97.

Mulvey, Laura. "Visual Pleasure and Narrative Cinema." 1975. Reprinted in *Feminism and Film*, ed. E. Ann Kaplan, 34–47. Oxford: Oxford University Press, 2000.

Murphy, David. "Africans Filming Africa: Questioning Theories of an Authentic African Cinema." *African Cultural Studies* 13, no. 2 (December 2000), 239–49.

Musser, Charles. "Divorce, Demille and the Comedy of Remarriage." *Classical Hollywood Comedy*, ed. Kristine Brunovska Karnick and Henry Jenkins, 282–313. New York: Routledge, 1995.

Nader, Ralph. "The Safe Car You Can't Buy." *Nation* 188, no. 15 (4 April 1959), 310–13.

Nancy, Jean-Luc. *The Inoperative Community*. Edited by Peter Connor. Minneapolis: University of Minnesota Press, 1991.

Nichols, Bill. "'Getting to Know You...': Knowledge, Power, and the Body." *Theorizing Documentary*, ed. Michael Renov, 174–91. New York: Routledge, 1993.

Nollen, Scott Allen. *The Boys: The Cinematic World of Laurel and Hardy*. Jefferson, N.C.: McFarland, 1989.

Oppenheimer, Jean. "A Dog's Life." *American Cinematographer* 82, no.4 (April 2001), 20–29.

Orr, John. *Cinema and Modernity*. Cambridge: Polity, 1993.

Ostherr, Kirsten. "Contagion and the Boundaries of the Visible: The Cinema of World Health." *Camera Obscura* 17, no. 2 (2002), 1–39.

Patrick, L. M., and R. S. Levine. "Injury to Unembalmed Belted Cadavers in Simulated Collisions." *Proceedings of Nineteenth Stapp Car Crash Conference* (17–19

November 1975), 79–115. Warrendale, Penn.: Society of Automotive Engineers, 1975.

Paul, William. "Charles Chaplin and the Annals of Anality." *Comedy/Cinema/Theory*, ed. Andrew S. Horton, 109–30. Berkeley: University of California Press, 1991.

Penley, Constance. "Time Travel, Primal Scene, and the Critical Dystopia (on *The Terminator* and *La Jetée*)." *The Future of an Illusion: Film, Feminism, and Psychoanalysis*, 121–39. Minneapolis: University of Minnesota Press, 1989.

Plowden, William. *The Motor Car and Politics in Britain 1896–1970*. London: Penguin, 1971.

Rabinbach, Anson. *The Human Motor: Energy, Fatigue, and the Origins of Modernity*. 1990. Reprint, Berkeley: University of California Press, 1992.

Redhead, Steve. *Paul Virilio: Theorist for an Accelerated Culture*. Toronto: University of Toronto Press, 2004.

Riblet, Douglas. "The Keystone Film Company and the Historiography of Early Slapstick." *Classical Hollywood Comedy*, ed. Kristine Brunovska Karnick and Henry Jenkins, 168–89. New York: Routledge, 1995.

Rodenbeck, Judith F. "Car Crash, 1960." *Trauma and Visuality in Modernity*, ed. Lisa Saltzman and Eric Rosenberg, 103–31. Lebanon, N.H.: University Press of New England/Dartmouth College Press, 2006.

Rodowick, David N. "Dr. Strange Media: Or, How I Learned to Stop Worrying and Love Film Theory." *PMLA* 116, no. 5 (October 2001), 1396–404.

———. "Ethics." Unpublished paper, 2008. Author's file.

———. *Gilles Deleuze's Time Machine*. Durham, N.C.: Duke University Press, 1997.

———. *The Virtual Life of Film*. Cambridge, Mass.: Harvard University Press, 2007.

Rogers, R. A., and J. A. Van Haaften. "Process Impact Test Data." *Proceedings: General Motors Corporation Automotive Safety Seminar*, 1–9. Milford, Miss.: General Motors, 1968.

Ronell, Avital. *Finitude's Score: Essays for the End of the Millennium*. Lincoln: University of Nebraska Press, 2001.

———. *The Test Drive*. Urbana: University of Illinois, 2005.

Rosen, Philip. *Change Mummified: Cinema, Historicity, Theory*. Minneapolis: University of Minnesota Press, 2001.

———. "Document and Documentary: On the Persistence of Historical Concepts." *Theorizing Documentary*, ed. Michael Renov, 58–89. New York: Routledge, 1993.

Ross, Kristin. *Fast Cars, Clean Bodies: Decolonization and the Reordering of French Culture*. Cambridge, Mass.: MIT Press, 1999.

Rowe, Kathleen. "Comedy, Melodrama, and Gender: Theorizing the Genres of Laughter." *Classical Hollywood Comedy*, ed. Kristine Brunovska Karnick and Henry Jenkins, 39–59. New York: Routledge, 1995.

Ruoff, Jeffrey, ed. *Virtual Voyages: Cinema and Travel*. Durham, N.C.: Duke University Press, 2006.

Schaefer, Claudia. *Bored to Distraction: Cinema of Excess in End-of-the-Century Mexico and Spain*. Albany: State University of New York Press, 2003.

Schivelbusch, Wolfgang. *The Railway Journey: The Industrialization of Time and Space in the Nineteenth Century*. Berkeley: University of California Press, 1986.

Schnapp, Jeffrey. "Crash (Speed as Engine of Individuation)." *Modernism/Modernity* 6, no. 1 (1999), 1–49.

Scott, Felicity. "Shouting Apocalypse." *Architecture or Techno-utopia: Politics after Modernism*, 209–45. Cambridge, Mass.: MIT Press, 2007.

Sedgwick, Eve Kosofsky. "Queer Performativity: Warhol's Shyness/Warhol's Whiteness." *Pop Out: Queer Warhol*, ed. Jennifer Doyle, Jonathan Flatley, and José Esteban Muñoz, 134–43. Durham, N.C.: Duke University Press, 1996.

Self, Will. *Junk Mail*. London: Penguin, 1996.

SHAH. "How It Feels." *Crash Cultures: Modernity, Mediation and the Material*, ed. Jane Arthurs and Iain Grant, 23–34. Portland: Intellect, 2003.

Siegel, Greg. "Babbage's Apparatus: Toward an Archeology of the Black Box." *Grey Room* 28 (summer 2007), 30–55.

Siegel, Marc. "Contesting Cinema: A Carmelo Bene Project." *CineAction* 47 (1998), 30–35.

Silverman, Kaja, and Harun Farocki. "Anal Capitalism: Weekend/Le Week-End (1967)." *Speaking about Godard*, 83–111. New York: New York University Press, 1998.

Simon, Art. *Dangerous Knowledge: The JFK Assassination in Art and Film*. Philadelphia: Temple University Press, 1996.

Simsolo, Nöel. "Carmelo Bene: *Capricci*." *Cahiers du Cinéma* (1969), 213.

Sitney, P. Adams. *Visionary Film: The American Avant-Garde*. New York: Oxford University Press, 1974.

16BEAVER. Untitled. *October* 123 (winter 2008), 149–60.

Smith, Marq. "Wound Envy: Touching Cronenberg's *Crash*." *Screen* 40, no. 2 (summer 1999), 193–202.

Smith, Paul Julian. *Amores perros*. London: British Film Institute, 2003.

Sobchack, Vivian. *The Address of the Eye: A Phenomenology of Film Experience*. Princeton, N.J.: Princeton University Press, 1992.

———. "Baudrillard's Obscenity." *Science Fiction Studies* 18 (1991), 327–29.

———. "Beating the Meat/Surviving the Text, or How to Get out of This Century Alive." *The Visible Woman: Imaging Technologies, Gender and Science*, ed. Paula A. Treichler, Lisa Cartwright, and Constance Penley, 310–20. New York: New York University Press, 1998.

———. *Carnal Thoughts: Embodiment and Moving Image Culture*. Berkeley: University of California Press, 2004.

Sontag, Susan. *Regarding the Pain of Others*. New York: Farrar, Straus and Giroux, 2003.

Springer, Claudia. "The Seduction of the Surface: From *Alice* to *Crash*." *Feminist Media Studies* 1, no. 2 (2001), 197–213.

Stacey, Jackie. *Star Gazing: Hollywood Cinema and Female Spectatorship*. London: Routledge, 1994.

Sterritt, David. *The Films of Jean-Luc Godard: Seeing the Invisible*. Cambridge: Cambridge University Press, 1999.

Stewart, Garrett. *Between Film and Screen: Modernism's Photo Synthesis*. Chicago: Chicago University Press, 1999.

Stott, William. *Documentary Expression and Thirties America*. 1973. Reprint, Chicago: University of Chicago Press, 1986.

Suárez, Juan A. *Bike Boys, Drag Queens, and Superstars: Avant-Garde, Mass Culture, and Gay Identities in the 1960s Underground Cinema*. Bloomington: Indiana University Press, 1996.

Suleiman, Susan Rubin. "Mothers and the Avant-Garde: A Case of Mistaken Identity?" *Avant-Garde* 4 (1990), 135–46.

———. *Subversive Intent: Gender, Politics, and the Avant-Garde*. Cambridge, Mass.: Harvard University Press, 1990.

Thompson, David. "Godard: That Breathless Moment." *Sight and Sound* 10, no. 7 (2000), 28–31.

Thoret, Jean-Baptiste. *26 Secondes: L'Amérique Éclaboussée: L'assassinat de JFK et le cinéma américain*. Pertuis: Rouge Profond, 2003.

Turvey, Malcolm. "Theory, Philosophy, Film Studies: A Response to D. N. Rodowick's 'An Elegy for Film Theory.'" *October* 122 (fall 2007), 110–20.

Tyler, Parker. "Dragtime and Drugtime: Or, Film à la Warhol." *Evergreen Review* 11, no. 46 (April 1967), 27–31, 87–88.

Usai, Paolo Cherchi. *The Death of Cinema: History, Cultural Memory and the Digital Dark Age*. London: British Film Institute, 2001.

———. *Silent Cinema*. London: British Film Institute, 2000.

Vacche, Angela Dalle. *Cinema and Painting: How Art Is Used in Film*. Austin: University of Texas Press, 1996.

Vernet, Marc. "The Look at the Camera." *Cinema Journal* 28, no. 2 (winter 1989), 48–63.

Virilio, Paul. *Negative Horizon: An Essay in Dromoscopy*. Translated by Michael Degener. London: Continuum, 2005.

———. *Speed and Politics: An Essay on Dromology*. Translated by Mark Polizzotti. New York: Semiotext(e), 1986.

———. "The Third Window." *Global Television*, ed. Cynthia Schneider and Brian Wallis, 185–97. Cambridge, Mass.: MIT Press, 1988.

———. *Unknown Quantity*. London: Thames and Hudson, 2003.

Warhol, Andy. *a: a novel*. New York: Grove, 1988.

——. *The Philosophy of Andy Warhol*. New York: Harcourt Brace Jovanovich, 1975.

Whissel, Kristen. "Regulating Mobility: Technology, Modernity, and Feature-Length Narrativity in *Traffic in Souls*." *Camera Obscura* 17, no. 1 (2002), 1–29.

White, Patricia. *Uninvited: Classical Hollywood Cinema and Lesbian Representability*. Bloomington: Indiana University Press, 1999.

Whiting, Cécile. "Cruising Los Angeles." *Pop L.A.: Art and the City in the 1960s*, 61–106. Berkeley: University of California Press, 2006.

Williams, Linda. *Hard Core: Power, Pleasure, and the "Frenzy of the Visible."* Berkeley: University of California Press, 1989.

Wolff, Janet. "On the Road Again: Metaphors of Travel in Cultural Criticism." *Feminism–Art–Theory*, ed. Hilary Robinson, 184–97. London: Blackwell, 2001.

Wood, Michael. "Dog Days." *New York Review of Books* 48, no. 14 (20 September 2001), 57–58.

Wood, Robin. "Godard and *Weekend*." *Weekend and* Wind from the East*: Two Films by Jean-Luc Godard*, 5–14. London: Lorrimer, 1972.

Woolf, Virginia. "The Movies and Reality." 1926. Reprinted in *Red Velvet Seat: Women's Writing on the First Fifty Years of Cinema*, ed. Antonia Lant with Ingrid Periz, 230–34. London: Verso, 2006.

Yearsley, Ian. "On the Move in the Streets: Transport Films and the Mitchell and Kenyon Collection." *The Lost World of Mitchell and Kenyon: Edwardian Britain on Film*, ed. Vanessa Toulmin, Simon Popple, and Patrick Russell, 180–90. London: British Film Institute, 2004.

Youngblood, Gene. *Expanded Cinema*. New York: Dutton, 1970.

Youngquist, Paul. "Ballard's Crash-Body." *Postmodern Culture* 11, no. 1 (September 2000).

INDEX

a: a novel (Warhol), 166–67, 265n20
accidents. *See* the crash
Acker, Kathy, 163, 169
Act of Seeing With One's Own Eyes, The (Brakhage), 255n34
Adamic, Louis, 113
Address of the Eye: A Phenomenology of Film Experience, The (Sobchack), 36
Adorno, Theodor, 90
Aetna Casualty and Surety Company, 123–25
Aetna Driver Trainers, 256n42
"Aftermath of Sudden Death, The," 255n34
afterwardsness, 145, 209–10, 272n10
Agamben, Giorgio, 89–90, 253n84, 272n6, 273n19
Agee, James, 248n23
Agel, Henri, 242n24
"'Almodóvar's Girls' *(All About My Mother)*" (Bersani and Dutoit), 250n38
Altamont Speedway, 274n31
American Academy of Political and Social Science, 56
Americans, The (Frank), 137–38
American Silent Film (Everson), 65–66
Amores perros (González Iñárritu), 179–203; animal vision in, 198–200, 203; circular narrative of, 183–84; color saturation methods of, 186; competing vectors of movement in, 184, 189–91, 193–94, 200; critical response to, 181–82; interrelated collisions in, 189–91, 193, 200; misogyny in, 197–98; Part One: "Octavio y Susana," 182, 189–92; Part Two: "Daniel y Valeria," 182–83, 192–98; Part Three: "El Chivo y Maru," 183, 198–203; stasis and motion in, 183–85, 189, 192–98, 271n19; still photographs in, 183, 185–89, 199–203, 271n16; women as static icons in, 192–98
Andrew, Dudley, 38
And Sudden Death (Barton), 248n18, 255n34
"—And Sudden Death" (Furnas), 113–17, 255n34
Andy Warhol, artist, New York City 8/20/69 (Avedon), 169
Angell, Callie, 148, 152, 158, 171, 259n10, 263n52
animal metaphors, 198–200
Ant Farm, 105, 138–40, 147–51, 261n31
L'arrivée d'un train (Lumière and Lumière), 30–35, 242n21
Arroseur et arrosé (Lumière), 245n65
art cinema, 2
art per se, 2
Atrocity Exhibition, The (Ballard), 147

audience. *See* spectators
Austin Powers (Roach), 249n23
automatism, 118
"Automobile: Its Province and Its Problems, The" 56
automobiles: early relationship to cinema of, 30–36, 58–60, 241n16; emancipation by the camera of, 47–53, 246n70; frames of movement in, 4–5; Godard's engagement with, 206–9, 272n5; as media spectacle of 1960s and 1970s, 146–51; regulatory challenges of, 55–61, 247n8, 247nn10–11, 248n18, 248n21; slapstick function of, 61–68, 248n23, 249nn24–27, 251n45; unreliable technology of, 28–29, 45, 56, 244n56; in urban design, 137. *See also* movement
avant-garde. *See* futurism and the avant-garde
Avedon, Richard, 169

Babbage, Charles, 127
Baker, George, 183, 185–89, 270n11
Baldaccini, César, 261n31
Balibar, Étienne, 110
Ballard, J. G., 6–7, 38, 138, 235n11, 243n48; Baudrillard's response to, 6–7, 162, 235n11, 266n34; exhibition of crashed cars of, 147; fictional self-portrait of, 161, 163, 164, 167–71; futurist discussions of, 14; mulitlayered London of, 57; on orgasmic aspects of the crash, 17–18, 252n31; on Warhol's *Since*, 141, 259n9. *See also Crash* (Ballard)
"Ballard and Baudrillard" (Day), 267n42
"Ballard's Crash-Body" (Youngquist), 267n42
Banham, Reyner, 168

Bardot, Brigitte, 206
Barr, Charles, 63–64, 83–84, 86–88
Barthes, Roland, 141, 146, 261n26
Barton, Charles, 248n18, 255n34
Baudrillard, Jean: on Ballard's *Crash*, 6–7, 162, 235n11, 266n34; on Disneyland, 133; "hyperreal" of, 138, 141, 259n6; on movement, 4–5
Bazin, André, 39, 242n24
Beck, Ulrich, 133
Bellmer, Hans, 197
Bene, Carmelo, 44, 53, 216–17, 230
Benjamin, Walter, 8–10, 190; on innervation, 14, 15–16, 20; on nearness of mass culture, 10, 25–27, 35; on stimulus shield, 10; on the translator, 171–72, 267n41
Bergson, Henri, 89–90, 243n52
Bersani, Leo, 88–89, 111, 243n50, 250n38
Between Film and Screen: Modernism's Photo Synthesis (Stewart), 184, 270n12
Beyond Sexuality (Dean), 112, 254n86
Beyond the Pleasure Principle (Freud), 21, 238n70
bicycles, 29–30, 240n13
billboards, 58, 247n11
Biró, Yvete, 242n24
Blaine, Ruby, 94–98
Blanchot, Maurice, 110–11
Blanco, Jorge Ayala, 181
Blow-Job (Warhol), 148
Blue Liz (Warhol), 168
Boarding School Girls (Edison), 246n70
body kinetics research, 127–31
"Body Work" (Hultkrans), 235n11
Bohlin, Nils, 257n58
Bolz, Norbert, 11
Bonnie and Clyde (Penn), 147
Booth, Walter R., 29, 42, 47–52, 245n64

290 | INDEX

border crossings. *See* media border crossings and collisions
Border (Waddington), 180
Bordwell, David, 243n52, 249n27
Bottomly, Susan, 155, 157–60
Bowser, Eileen, 251n45
Bowser, Pearl, 76
"Boys as Couple" (Nollen), 65
Boys: The Cinematic World of Laurel and Hardy, The (Nollen), 66
Bracken, A. J., 255n34
Brakhage, Stan, 151, 255n34
Brats (Parrott), 88, 122
Breathless (Godard), 174, 268n47
Brewster, Ben, 249n27
Brigandage moderne, Le (Pathé), 244n61
Bright, John Irwin, 57, 247n8
Brottman, Mikita, 14
Bruno, Giuliana, 123
Buñuel, Luis, 122, 181–82, 198, 213–15, 270n8
Burch, Noël, 30–32, 44–45; on topography of film screen, 48, 52, 123–24; on vertical axis, 244n61, 245nn64–65
Butler, Judith, 12–13, 24, 116; on Merleau-Ponty, 37; on responsibility, 109–11, 255n25; on subjectivity, 39–40

Calhoun, John, 271n16
Campion, Jane, 38
Campus (Davenport), 221, 230–32, 274n32
Camus, Albert, 259n9, 261n29
Capricci (Bene), 217
Car Crash (Dine), 151, 176, 262n44
Car Crash (Vostell), 147
Carnal Thoughts: Embodiment and Moving Image Culture (Sobchack), 36–42

Catalogue, The (Oakley), 180
Catherine (character), 161, 163–64, 173–74, 176, 265n17, 266n34
Cavell, Stanley, 39, 109
Chamberlain, John, 261n31
Chaplin, Charlie, 65–66, 67–68, 273n15
Chelsea Girls (Warhol), 152, 187, 259n10
Chevrolet: Jim Handy production company of, 58–59, 256n48; safety films of, 117–23
chien andalou, Un (Buñuel and Dalí), 122
chimpanzees, 129, 132, 258n69
Chinoise, La (Godard), 274n32
Cinema and Modernity (Orr), 206
Cinema and Painting (Vacche), 268n47
"Cinema and Revolution," 216
"Cinema of Attractions" (Gunning), 16–17
cinema studies, 1–5, 233–34
Civics and Citizenship in the United States, 247n2
Clark, L. Pierce, 120
Cleopatra (Mankiewicz), 167–68
clinamen, 23, 239n76
Coleman, James, 185, 189
collisions. *See* the crash
comedic spaces: autos' embodiment of slapstick in, 61–65, 179, 248n23, 249nn24–27, 251n45; crash humor, 124; in early car-crash films, 47–52, 56; energy of sex and desire in, 84–91, 253n81; in Kennedy assassination treatments, 149–51, 153, 261n31; topping the gag in, 248n23. *See also* slapstick comedies of the 1920s
commercial narrative cinema, 2
Complete Works of Laurel and Hardy, The (Everson), 65
Compressions d'automobile (exhibition), 261n31

computers, 141
Conner, Bruce, 147–52, 154, 262n42, 262n44
Contempt (Godard), 147, 206–8, 211
Cornell Crash Injury Research Project, 125–32, 138, 257n58, 258n61
Corrigan, Timothy, 5
Couch (Warhol), 154
Coutard, Raoul, 227
Crafton, Donald, 61
Crary, Jonathan, 8–9, 32, 138–41, 168, 259n6
crash, the, 8, 11–14, 232–34; aesthetics of, 124; as critical metaphor, 4–5, 233; desire for speed in, 14; driver fallibility discourses in, 21–24; moral discourses of, 12–13, 236n28; as privileged trope of global media, 179–80; as *téléscopage*, 107; trauma thrills of, 15–19. See also traffic jam sequences
crash aesthetics, 124
"Crash" (Ballard) (1968), 259n9
Crash (Ballard) (1973), 38, 138, 147, 161–78, 259n9; Ballard's self-portrait in, 161, 163, 164, 167–71; Baudrillard's response to, 6–7, 162, 235n11, 266n34; feminist potential of, 162–66, 177–78; graphic interpretations in, 243n48; language of collision in, 166; metaphors for film (cellulose) in, 175–78, 269nn57–58; new male sexuality in, 17–18, 161–64, 169–78, 264n10, 264–65nn13–14, 265n17, 266–67nn34–35, 267n37; probing of visual pop culture in, 166–71, 267nn42–43; Sobchack's response to, 266n34; stasis and motion in, 171–75, 178, 268n47, 269n49; temporal setting of, 167–68. See also Vaughan (character)
Crash (Cronenberg), 38, 163, 266–67nn34–35

Crash (Du Zhenjun), 136
Crash (Haggis), 180
"Crash (Speed as Engine of Individuation)" (Schnapp), 267n42
crash-test dummies and involuntary volunteers, 128–36, 258n69
Crash Test Dummies (Kalt), 135–36, 180
"Crash Test Dummy: The New European Self in a Biopolitical Crash Test" (performances), 134–36, 180
Crawford, Travis, 186
Crimp, Douglas, 144, 157, 162
critical distance. See nearness/affective proximity
"Critique of Urbanism" (*October*), 137
Cronenberg, David, 38, 163
Cronkite, Walter, 257n58
Crow, Thomas, 148, 152
Culture of Redemption, The (Bersani), 88–89

Dalí, Salvador, 122
Davenport, Nancy, 7–8, 205–6, 271n19; *Campus*, 221, 230–32, 274n32; on Godard's traffic jam, 221–25, 227; on photographic montage, 220. See also *Weekend Campus*
Day, Aidan, 267n42
Dean, James, 1, 259n9, 261n29
Dean, Tim, 112, 254n86
Death and Disaster series (Warhol), 147
"Death in America" (Foster), 148
Debord, Guy, 137, 138, 146, 259n6
De Haven, Hugh, 125–31, 136, 257n55, 257n58, 258n61
de Lauretis, Theresa, 37
Deleuze, Gilles, 90; on embodied spectators, 40–42; on lyrical abstraction, 274n37; on movement-image and montage, 50–53, 245n69, 246n70; "the Open" of, 44, 243n52; on peda-

gogy of the image, 42–43, 243n50; on political action, 230–32; understanding of primitive cinema of, 51, 245n69
DeLillo, Don, 233
DeMille, Cecil B., 60, 248n18, 255n34
Deneuve, Catherine, 198
depth of field, 32–34, 239n11, 240n12
Destrukt (Helmcke), 180
Die Krisis der europäischen Kultur (Pannwitz), 171–72
digital images, 27–28, 220–21, 228–29, 274n37
Dimendberg, Edward, 5
Dine, Jim, 151, 176, 262n44
Disney World's "Test Track," 131–33, 258n72
Divine (actor), 147
Doane, Mary Ann, 37, 51, 134, 235n9, 245n69
documentary truth, 113–17, 134, 255n34
drive theory, 8, 20–24, 238n70
driving/drivers, 118–23
Duchamp, Marcel, 124
Duck Soup (McCarey), 150
Dutoit, Ulysse, 243n50, 250n38
Du Zhenjun, 136
Dye, Edward, 127–29

early car-crash films, 28–53, 61, 239n9; continuous variation in, 44–47; embodied spectators of, 36–42; encounters with other media in, 42–44, 243n48; multidimensional spaces in, 47–52, 244n59, 244n61, 245nn64–67; visual experience of the accident in, 30–36, 241n15, 242n21
Easy Rider (Hopper), 147
Eat Your Makeup (Waters), 147, 261n31
"Eclipse of the Spectacle" (Crary), 138–41
Edelman, Lee, 84–85, 143, 252n62

Edison, Thomas, 239n11, 240n13, 246n70
educational films: on invisible disease, 73–75, 251nn49–50; safety mission of, 58–60, 247n2, 248n14. *See also* safety discourses
Eggleston, William, 271n16
8½ (Fellini), 225
89 Seconds at Alcazar (Sussman), 271n19
Eisenstein, Sergei, 198, 199, 203
Electric Animal: Toward a Rhetoric of Wildlife (Lippit), 198
embodied spectators, 5–8, 235nn8–9, 242n24; cinematic transcendence of, 7; gendering of, 37; moral gaze of, 6–7; in Sobchack's phenomenological film theory, 36–42
Emergence of Cinematic Time, The (Doane), 245n69
Empire (Warhol), 144, 168, 171–72, 173
"End of Sexual Difference?, The" (Butler), 24
Eternal Frame, The (Ant Farm and Uthco), 138–41, 147–51
European art cinema, 105
Everson, William K., 65–66, 90
existentialism, 36, 242n24
experimental film/video, 2
Explosion of a Motor Car (Hepworth), 29, 44–47, 242n21, 248n21
Exterminating Angel, The (Buñuel), 213–15, 270n8
Extraordinary Cab Accident (Booth), 42
"Eye-Hunger" (Littau), 240n13

fallibility discourses, 21–24
Farocki, Harun, 180, 218
Faulkner, William, 211
feminist perspectives, 18–19, 24, 238n73, 239n78; on Ballard's *Crash*,

INDEX | 293

feminist perspectives (*continued*)
162–66, 177–78; on comedy and
comedians, 66–68, 250nn31–38; on
immobilization of female agency in
Hot Water, 77–82; on male bodily
fluids, 164–66; of phallic power, 163–
64, 264–65nn13–14; on psychoanalytic
film theory, 37; on Sobchack's em-
bodied film theory, 37–42; on topographical readings by spectators, 123
Feminist Reader in Early Cinema, A
(Bean and Negra), 68
Femme production company, 264n13
Fields, W. C., 65–66, 250n31
Finitude's Score (Ronell), 238n74
Fischer, Lucy, 66, 67
Fondation Cartier pour l'art contempo-
rain, 11
Ford, Gerald, 147
Ford Motor Company: advertising in
films by, 62, 249n24; educational
films of, 58, 247n2; Laurel and
Hardy's Model-Ts, 252n60
Forms of Being (Bersani and Dutoit),
243n50
Foster, Hal, 148–49, 159, 161, 167, 197,
211–13, 239n78
Foucault, Michel, 90, 254n86
"Founding and Manifesto of Futurism,
The" (Marinetti), 14, 17, 19
Frampton, Hollis, 1
Franco, Jean, 18–19, 192
Frank, Robert, 137–38
Frankfurt School, media theory at, 8
Freeman, Elizabeth, 143
freeze frame shots, 160, 184–85
French New Wave cinema, 185
French postcolonial legacy, 217–20
Freud, Sigmund, 8; drive theory of,
20–21, 238n70; on innervation, 15,
20; *Nachträglichkeit* of, 145, 209–10;

272n10; on the stimulus shield, 10,
236n15
Friedberg, Ann, 8–9
Frye, Northrop, 67
Furnas, J. C., 113–17, 248n18, 255n34
Fusco, Coco, 273n11
Fuss, Diana, 188
futurism and the avant-garde, 8, 232–
33; feminist potential of, 162–66; in
Foster's "coming after," 211–13; gendered metaphors of, 18–19; male
phallocentrism in, 163–66; thrills
and innervation of, 14–18, 20. See
also *Crash* (Ballard); technology of
motion
Futurist Manifesto, 232–33

Gabrielle (character), 163–64
Gaines, Jane, 68
Gartenberg, Jon, 239–40nn11–12,
244n61
Gaudreault, André, 51
Gehr, Ernie, 123–24
Gehring, Wes, 250n31
gendered approaches, 17–18; to immo-
bilization of female agency, 75–82;
of Merleau-Ponty's universal mas-
culine, 37; to metaphors of stasis
and motion, 18–19, 192–98; to slap-
stick comedies of the 1920s, 65–68,
250nn31–38. *See also* feminist per-
spectives
General Motors, 116–18, 131–33
Genêt, Jean, 205, 209
Get Out and Get Under (Roach), 61–64,
249n24
Gimme Shelter (Maysles and Maysles),
274n31
Giorno, John, 151–52, 168
Giving an Account of Oneself (Butler), 40
Glass, Matei, 180

Godard, Jean-Luc, 7, 61, 239n9; ambivalent engagement with the automobile of, 206–9, 272n5; *Breathless*, 174, 268n47; *Contempt*, 147, 206–8, 211; critical response to, 213, 215–16, 273n19; cynical stasis of, 208–9, 272nn5–6, 272–73nn10–11; exploration of camera motion by, 174, 218, 225–30, 268n47; homage and mimicry of, 215–16; *My Life to Live*, 268n47; *Pierrot le fou*, 147, 206, 208, 268n47. See also *Weekend*
Goldin, Nan, 183, 185, 271n15
Goldman, Annie, 272n5
Goldsmith, Kenneth, 220–21
González, Rita, 181–82
González Iñárritu, Alejandro, 7, 180–82; animal vision of, 198–203; car advertisements of, 191; car-mounted camera of, 190; on Goya Toledo as Valeria, 197; nickname of, 203; use of Goldin's photography by, 183, 185–89, 271n16, 271n19. See also *Amores perros*
Graham, George M., 56, 60
Grosz, Elizabeth, 164, 265n17
Grundemann, Roy, 267n35
Gulliver's Travels (Swift), 150
Gunning, Tom, 8–11, 16–17, 239n9; on Hepworth's nontheatrical framing, 241n18; on "mischievous machines" in slapstick, 56, 62–63, 249n25; on modernity in Lumières' *L'arrivée d'un train*, 32–34; on panoramic perception of train travel, 32; on single-shot gag films, 245n67

Haggis, Paul, 180
Halberstam, Judith, 143, 248n23, 250n33, 263n61
Hall, Doug, 139

Hamilton, Richard, 168
Handy, Henry Jamison, 58–59, 256n48
Hannah, Adad, 271n19
Hansen, Miriam Bratu, 8–9, 263n54; on failed encounters, 36; on innervation, 10–11, 15–16, 20; on slapstick comedy, 76
Hard Core (Williams), 265n14
Hardy, Oliver, 83, 86, 87. *See also* Laurel and Hardy films
Hedy (Warhol), 152
Helen Remington (character), 161, 164
Helmcke, Aline, 180
Hepworth, Cecil, 7, 16; acting roles by, 42, 239n10, 244n56; on diving bells, 241n15; *Explosion of a Motor Car*, 44–47; *How It Feels to Be Run Over*, 29–36, 240nn12–13; lecture of (1953), 242n21; star-gazing camera of, 244n59
Highway Safety Institute, 113
Highways of Agony, 113
Hill, Thelma, 94–98
Hirschberg, Lynn, 181
HIV/AIDS, 112
Hoberman, J., 187
Hog Wild (Parrott), 62
hooks, bell, 238n73
Hopper, Dennis, 147
horse, the, 13
Horse (Warhol), 157
Hot Water (Taylor and Newmeyer), 56, 68–81, 122; heterosexual stasis in, 69–73; homoerotic streetcar scenes in, 70–76; misogynist readings of car's destruction in, 78–81
How It Feels to Be Run Over (Hepworth), 16, 29–36, 42–43, 240nn12–13
"How to Avoid Sudden Death" (Spencer), 257n58

How to Stop a Motor Car (Stow), 42, 242n21
How You See It: How Persistence of Vision Makes Motion Pictures Possible, 58–59
Hultkrans, Andrew, 235n11
"Human Behavior—Factor X" (Malfetti), 12
Husserl, Edmund, 36

I'll Be Your Mirror (Goldin), 187, 271n21
In a Queer Time and Place (Halberstam), 250n33
Ince, Thomas H., 251n45
industrial-safety films, 116–36; by Cornell Crash Injury Research Project, 125–32, 138, 257n58, 258n61; high-speed film analysis in, 127–28, 258n63; *Live and Let Live*, 123–24; *The Other Fellow*, 119–23; playful aesthetics in, 117–18, 119, 123–24; pre-enactment of risk in, 131–36, 258n69; *The Safest Place*, 117–18
inertia, 23, 238n74
"Information, Crisis, Catastrophe" (Doane), 134
Ingenious Soubrette, The (Páthe), 245n64
In My Merry Oldsmobile, 116–17
innervation, 10–11, 14–18, 20
Inoperative Community, The (Nancy), 23–24
Irigaray, Luce, 178, 267n37

Jackson State University, 274n38
Jacobs, Lea, 60, 244n61
Jakobsen, Janet R., 24
Jamaica Street, Glasgow (M&K 186), 32–33, 52
James, David, 268n43

James Ballard (character), 161, 163–64, 167–78, 266n34, 267n35
Jameson, Fredric, 185
Jenkins, Bruce, 150, 262n42
Jenkins, Henry, 60, 68, 243n52, 250n31
Jim Handy production company, 58–59, 256n48
Johns, Jasper, 124
Johnson, Lyndon, 105

Kael, Pauline, 215–16, 217
Kalt, Jörg, 135–36, 180
Kazarian, Leo, 258n69
Keaton, Buster, 65–66, 68
Kelley, Ben, 125
Kennedy, Edgar, 100, 119–23
Kennedy, Jacqueline, 142, 147, 150–51, 157–60
Kennedy, John F., assassination, 138, 146–51; as car crash, 141, 259n9; comedic treatments of, 149–51, 153, 261n31, 262n42, 262n44; Conner's works on, 147–52, 154; reenactment in *Eat Your Makeup* of, 147, 261n31; reenactment in *The Eternal Frame* of, 138–41, 147–51; reenactment in *Since* of, 141–45, 148–49, 151–60; still depictions of, 147–48; television news coverage of, 149, 262n41; Warhol's silk screens of, 147–49; Zapruder film of, 38, 123–24, 140–42, 146–48, 150, 156–59
Kerouac, Jack, 137–38
Kerr, Walter, 70, 83, 86–89
Keystone cop comedies, 62, 67, 250n36
King, Homay, 143, 259n15
Kirby, Lynne, 4, 8–9, 19, 30, 32, 240n13
Kittler, Friedrich, 11
Klein, Bonnie, 265n14
Koestenbaum, Wayne, 166, 171, 173
Krauss, Rosalind, 2, 270n8

296 | INDEX

Kristeva, Julia, 22–23
Krutnick, Frank, 67
Krzeczek, Dariusz, 180
Kurtz, Steve, 124

Labarthe, André S., 86
Lang, Fritz, 57, 206
Langdon, Harry, 66
Laplanche, Jean, 8, 52, 112, 116, 255n25; drive theory of, 20–22; on *Nachträglichkeit*, 209, 272n10
Lardner, Dionysius, 26
laughter, 89–90
Laurel, Stan, 64, 65, 68; childish portrayals of, 87; deceleration of pace by, 83; effeminate guises of, 86
Laurel and Hardy films, 56, 61–62; childishness and pre-sexuality in, 84–88, 122, 253nn70–71; masochistic aesthetics in, 88–104, 253n84; misogyny in, 65–66, 254n94; Model T Fords in, 252n60; out-of-synch timing in, 68, 83–86, 87, 90, 252n60; social spaces in, 63–65. See also *Two Tars*
Lawley, H. M., 244n56
Lawrensen, Edward, 270n8
Leave 'Em Laughing (Bruckman), 61–62, 252n60
Lee, Pamela, 259n14
Lennon, Peter, 226
Lerner, Jesse, 181–82
Letinsky, Laura, 271n16
Leung, Simon, 273n11
Levin, Joshua, 179
Levinas, Emmanuel, 109, 255n25
Liberty (McCarey), 86
Liebig's Real Meat Extract advertisement, 26, 27
Life magazine's Zapruder stills, 140, 146–47, 153

Life to Those Shadows (Burch), 244n61, 245nn64–65
Light in August (Faulkner), 211
Linden, George, 242n24
Lindsay, Robert, 125
Lippit, Akira, 198
Littau, Karin, 240n13
Little Bastard, 1
Live and Let Live, 123–25
Lizzies of the Field (Lord), 62
Lloyd, Harold, 56, 63–64; association with speed of, 68, 83; gendered responses to films of, 65–66; in *Get Out and Get Under*, 62, 249n24; in *Hot Water*, 68–81, 122
Louvish, Simon, 68
Love, Heather, 143, 253n71
Low, Rachel, 240n12, 241n16
Lubin, David M., 148, 151, 262n37
Lumière, Auguste, 30, 145, 211, 242n21, 245n65
Lumière, Louis, 30, 242n21
Lupfer, Dietmar, 136
Luukkaankangas—Updated, Revisited (Krzeczek), 180
Lye, Len, 176

Ma, Jean, 90
MacBean, James Roy, 213
MacCann, Richard Dyer, 248n18
Macpherson, Jeanie, 255n34
Magic Picture Hanging (Páthe), 245n64
Magnetic Identities (Glass), 180
Malfetti, James L., 12, 237n29
Mankiewicz, Joseph, 167–68
Mansfield, Jayne, 259n9, 261n29
Manslaughter (DeMille), 60, 248n18, 255n34
Manvell, Roger, 240n12, 241n16
Marey, Étienne-Jules, 127
Marinetti, F. T., 14, 17, 19

Mario Banana (Warhol), 156
Marx Brothers, 150
masculine approaches. *See* gendered approaches
masochism, 90–91; aesthetic of delay and repetition in, 88–104, 111; sexual death drive in, 112
Maysles, Albert, 274n31
Maysles, David, 274n31
McCabe, John, 83
McDonough, Tom, 259n6
McFarland, J. Horace, 247n11
McLaren, Norman, 176
Mechanized Death, 113
media border crossings and collisions, 3–4, 7–8; in early car-crash films, 42–44, 243n48; in González Iñárritu's *Amores perros*, 183, 185–89, 199–203, 271n16; in Warhol's media transpositions, 166–67, 265n20, 266n21; in *Weekend Campus*, 221
Media Burn (Ant Farm), 138–39
Medium Cool (Wexler), 147
Méliès, Georges, 245n64
meninas, Las (Velázquez), 271n19
Merleau-Ponty, Maurice, 36–37, 40–41
Metropolis (Lang), 57
Mexican cinema, 180–81, 183; animal vision of, 198–200; Buñuel's work and, 181–82, 198, 270n8; gendered stasis and motion in, 192, 197–98; portrayals of identity in, 188–89. *See also Amores perros*
Meyersberg, Paul, 213
Michel (character), 174
microcinematography, 73–75, 251nn49–50
military research, 128–29, 258n64
Miller, Alice Duer, 255n34
misogynist approaches. *See* gendered approaches

Mitchell and Kenyon (M&K), 32–33, 50, 52, 239n10, 246n75
mobility. *See* movement
modernity: desires for speed in, 14–19, 211–13; mobile spectators of, 8–11; stimulus shield of, 10, 236n15. *See also* futurism and the avant-garde
Modern Times (Chaplin), 273n15
Montez, Mario, 156
Morrison, Earnest "Sunshine Sammy," 61, 63–64
Mosen, David, 149–50
Motion Picture Producers and Distributors Association (MPPDA), 60–61
Motorist, The (?) (Booth), 29, 47–52, 245nn64–67, 248n21
movement, 22–24, 61; automobile frames of, 4–5; gendered approaches to, 18–19, 24, 238n73; resistance to (inertia), 23, 238n74. *See also* speed; stasis and motion; technology of motion
Movement-Image, The (Deleuze), 42, 243n52
Movie, A (Conner), 150
"Movie Care Crashes: A Primer" (Levin), 179
Mr. Laurel and Mr. Hardy (McCabe), 83
Mulvey, Laura, 37, 192
Munich Express (Weltz), 135–36, 180
Munier, Roger, 242n24
Murphy, David, 220
museum projections, 2
Musser, Charles, 85
Muybridge, Eadweard, 127, 258n61
My Life to Live (Godard), 268n47

Nachträglichkeit, 145, 209–10, 272n10
Nader, Ralph, 125, 138

Nancy, Jean-Luc, 23–24
narrative cinema: absorption of the spectator into, 9; male spectatorial pleasure in, 192; progressive linearity of film time in, 145
nearness/affective proximity, 25–53; continuous variation in, 44–47; in early car-crash films, 29–36; encounters with other media in, 42–44; failed encounters in, 36; multidimensional/fantastical perspectives in, 47–53; Sobchack's embodied film theory on, 36–42
Negative Horizon (Virilio), 109, 237n50
New American Cinema, 187
New Mexican Cinema, 183, 198
"New Mexican, A" (Hirschberg), 181
New Wave cinema, 187
Nichols, Bill, 153
Nicholson, Ivy, 156
Nietzsche, Friedrich, 109, 134
Nixon, Richard, 274n38
No. 2 (Smith), 269n57
No. 3 (Smith), 269n57
No Future (Edelman), 85
Nollen, Scott Allen, 64–65, 83, 86, 253n70, 254n94
None for the Road: Teenage Drinking and Driving, 12, 236n28, 256n42
Non-Skid Kid, The (Lloyd), 61, 248n23
Not a Love Story (Klein), 265n14
not-stasis, 183, 270n11
Nouveaux Réalistes, 261n31

Oakley, Chris, 180
Los Olvidados (Buñuel), 181–82, 270n8
Ondine, 154–56, 265n20
"One Manifesto Less" (Deleuze), 230–32
"One-Way Street" (Benjamin), 26
On the Road (Kerouac), 137–38
Open, the, 44, 243n52
Orr, John, 206
Oswald, Lee Harvey, 153–54, 156–57
Other Fellow, The (Handy), 119–23
Oxidation Paintings (Warhol), 269n58

Palance, Jack, 206
Pannwitz, Rudolf, 171–72, 267n41
Paolozzi, Eduardo, 168
Parrott, Charles, 62
Parrott, James, 61
passengers, 14–15
Patrick, Lawrence, 129
Paul, R. W., 240n12
Paul, William, 67
Payne, John Howard, 252n53
Penn, Arthur, 147
Pérez Soler, Bernando, 185
Perfect Day, A (Parrott), 56, 61, 98
personal computers, 141
phenomenological film theory, 36–42, 242n24
Photographer's Mishap, A (Edison/Porter), 240n13
Piano, The (Campion), 38–39
Pierrot le fou (Godard), 147, 206, 208, 268n47
Piss and Sex Paintings (Warhol), 176
Playtime (Tati), 124
pop art. *See* visual culture of the 1960s and 1970s
Pop Out (Doyle, et al.), 162
postcolonial challenges, 217–20
post-9/11 era, 11–12
Prieto, Rodrigo, 185–86, 187, 190, 271nn16–17
primate victims, 129, 132, 258n69
psychoanalytic film theory: disembodied spectator of, 5–6, 36, 38, 235nn8–9; feminist scholarship on, 37; *Nachträglichkeit* in, 145, 209–10; in sexual

INDEX | 299

psychoanalytic film theory (*continued*) readings of Laurel and Hardy, 84–91; theorizing drive of, 8, 21–24
Putting Pants on Philip (Bruckman), 87

queer spaces: imitation of media experiences in, 142; intimations of contagion in, 70–75; sexualized political space of *Since*, 142–44; temporal regression (childishness) in, 253n71

railroad films, 9, 30–36
Rauschenberg, Robert, 124
reckless drivers, 60
regulation of driving, 56–61, 247n8, 247nn10–11, 248n18, 248n21
Report (Conner), 147–52, 262n42, 262n44
responsibility discourses, 109–12
Riblet, Douglas, 66–67, 250n36
Ride on the Tramcar though Belfast (M&K 183), 32–33, 52
Ripstein, Arturo, 181
risk society, 131–36
Rivera, Alex, 180
Road Movies, 28, 47, 105, 146, 245n62; masculinity and freedom in, 250n31; panoramic shots in, 189; traveling shots in, 158–59, 260n28
Rodowick, David: on Bergson's "the Open," 243n52, 245n69; on the flow of everyday life, 227, 274nn36–37; on medium specificity, 2–3; on the virtual quality of film, 28, 39, 109
Rolling Stones, 274n31
Ronell, Avital, 23, 131–34, 238n74
Rosen, Philip, 151
Ross, Kristin, 58, 251n50, 261n26
Rowe, Kathleen, 66–68, 253n81
Royalle, Candida, 264n13

Ruoff, Jeffrey, 30
Ruscha, Ed, 137–38, 168, 176, 269n58

safe car, 138
"Safe Car You Can't Buy, The" (Nader), 138
"Safeguarding Traffic: A Nation's Problem—A Nation's Duty" (Graham), 56
safety discourses, 12–13, 105–36, 236n28; agency and responsibility in, 109–12; in car-company films, 58, 60, 248n14; documentary modes of truth in, 113–17, 134, 255n34; driver-education films, 113; driver fallibility in, 118–23; driver-simulation machines, 256n42; in industrial-safety films, 116–36; markers of risk and deviance in, 13; on passive safety and survival, 125–31, 138; Virilio's views on car-safety design, 107–8
Salgado, Sabasteao, 271n16
San Martín, Patricia Torres, 181
S-77CCR Vienna, 180
Schaefer, Claudia, 270n8
Schivelbusch, Wolfgang, 4, 8–10, 14, 30, 32
Schnapp, Jeffrey, 14–19, 267n42; on cultures of transportation, 14–15; on thrill-based accidents, 15–17, 237n50
Science of Life series, 73, 251n49
"Sculpture in the Expanded Field" (Krauss), 270n8
Sembène, Ousmane, 7, 205, 217–20
semiotic understandings of photography, 37–38, 183, 185–89. *See also* psychoanalytic film theory
Senegal, 205, 217–20
Sennett, Mack, 62

"Sexual Ideology and Phenomenological Description" (Butler), 37
sexual possibilities, 17–19; Bersani's views on non-specificity in, 88–89; of cross-dressing, 151, 155, 157, 263n56; of death drive, 84–85, 112; of heterosexual stasis, 69–73; in *Hot Water*, 56, 68–81; of immobilized female agency, 75–82; in Laurel and Hardy's childlike resistance to progress, 84–88, 253nn70–71; of masochistic delay and repetition of Laurel and Hardy, 88–104, 253n84; of new male sexuality in Ballard's *Crash*, 17–18, 161–64, 169–78, 264n10, 264–65nn13–14, 265n17, 266–67nn34–35, 267n37; in political spaces of *Since*, 142–44; of queer contagion, 70–75; in sinthomosexuality, 85, 252n62; of slapstick comedy, 67–68; of temporal regression, 253n71; Virilio's discarding of, 111; in Warhol's phallic murders in *Since*, 156–58. *See also* queer spaces
Shift (Gehr), 123–24
Shooting Kennedy (Lubin), 148
Siegel, Greg, 127
Siegel, Marc, 217
Signal 30, 113
Silverman, Kaja, 37
Simmel, Georg, 10, 14
Simon, Art, 147–48
Since (Warhol), 141–45, 148, 151–60; aesthetic of repetition in, 148–49; Bottomly's portrayal of Jacqueline Kennedy in, 157–60; camerawork in, 155–59; character uncertainty in, 154–55; homoerotic murder of Oswald in, 153–54, 156–57; location of, 141, 154; posthumous premiere of, 152–53, 259n10, 263n52; rupture and disrupted temporality in, 143–45, 152–54, 156, 157, 159, 259nn14–15; spectator mime and reenactment in, 151–54, 159–60, 263n54
sinthomosexuality, 85, 252n62
Sitts, George, 257n58
Situationist International (SI), 216
"Situationist Theses on Traffic" (Debord), 137
Sixth Section: A Documentary about Immigrants Organizing Across Borders, The (Rivera), 180
Slade, Mark, 242n24
slapstick comedies of the 1920s, 55, 60–104; anarchistic constructions of sexuality in, 84–91, 253nn70–71; autos' embodiment of narrative and gag in, 61–65, 179, 248–49nn23–27, 251n45; comedian-centered nature of, 66–67; gendered responses to, 65–68, 250nn31–38; industry regulation of, 60–61; Laurel and Hardy in *Two Tars*, 61, 69, 81, 90–104, 119; Lloyd in *Hot Water*, 68–81; role of social progress in, 63–65, 69, 84; speed and destruction in, 68–84
Sleep (Warhol), 144, 148, 168
Smith, Harry, 176, 269n57
Smith, Jack, 187
Smith, Marq, 266n34
Smith, Paul Julian, 186–87
Sobchack, Vivian, 6, 36–42, 242n24, 266n34
Sold at Auction (Parrott), 62
Sons of the Desert (Seiter), 65
Sontag, Susan, 148
space travel, 146, 261n26
spectators, 15; affective proximity to images of, 25–36; in afterlife of a film, 221–25; bodies on the couch of, 144–45, 151–54; embodied, 5–8,

spectators (*continued*)
36–42, 235nn8–9; encounters with looping images by, 229; mime and reenactment in *Since* by, 142, 151–60, 263n54; modern mobile, 8–11; topographical approach to, 48, 52, 123–24; trauma thrills of, 14–19; of Warhol's temporal drag, 143–45, 152–54

speed, 8; dangers to sexual norms of, 73; of early U.S. cars, 55; gendered metaphors of, 18–19; modern desires for, 11–14, 17, 111, 237n50; thrills and innervation of, 14–18, 20; of Virilio's speed machines, 106–9. See also the crash; technology of motion

Spencer, Steven M., 257n58

Springer, Claudia, 235n11

Stains (Ruscha), 176, 269n58

Stapp, J. P., 128–29

stasis and motion: in Ballard's *Crash*, 171–75, 178, 268n47, 269n49; gendered metaphors of, 18–19, 192–98; in Godard's cynical stasis, 208–9, 272nn5–6, 272–73nn10–11; in González Iñárritu's *Amores perros*, 183–85, 189, 192–98, 271n19; heterosexual stasis in *Hot Water*, 69–73; in *Two Tars*, 90–94. See also technology of motion

Sterritt, David, 207, 208, 211, 216, 268n47

Stewart, Garrett, 184, 270n12

still photography in cinema, 183, 185–98

Stills (Hannah), 271n19

Stop Driving Us Crazy, 12, 236n28

Stott, William, 113, 248n18, 255n34

Stow, Percy, 42

structuralism. See psychoanalytic film theory

subjectivity: in Deleuze's natural perception, 40–42; in Merleau-Ponty's universal masculine, 37; in Sobchack's phenomenological film theory, 39–41

Suleiman, Susan Rubin, 19, 165–66

Superstar, Ingrid, 155

Sussman, Eve, 271n19

Swift, Jonathan, 150

Tache Aveugle, La (Coleman), 185

"Task of the Translator, The" (Benjamin), 171–72

Tati, Jacques, 124, 245n65, 272n5

Tavernier, Bertrand, 268n47

Taylor, Elizabeth, 161, 167–68, 177

technology of motion, 8, 14–20, 61, 233–34; fixity of the camera in, 32; Godard's exploration of, 174, 218, 225–30, 268n47; illusions of movement in, 14; malfunctioning automobiles in, 28–29, 45, 56, 244n56; panning in, 240n12; social impacts of, 63–64; of vehicle-mounted cameras, 47–53, 246n70; women as the first vehicle, 13, 109. See also speed; stasis and motion

téléscopage, 107

television. See visual culture of the 1960s and 1970s

Television Assassination (Conner), 147, 148, 149–50, 151

temporality, 233–34; in Baker's understanding of photography, 183, 185–89; in Ballard's *Crash*, 167–68, 171–75, 178, 268n47, 269n49; in Davenport's *Weekend Campus*, 220–25, 229–34; gendering of, 18–19, 192–98; in Godard's *Weekend*, 208–13, 225–30, 272nn5–6, 272–73nn10–11; in González Iñárritu's *Amores perros*, 183–85, 271n19; in *Hot Water*, 69–73;

of narrative film, 145; in *Two Tars*,
90–94; in Warhol's *Since*, 143–45,
152–54, 159, 168, 171–73, 259nn14–15
Test Drive, The (Ronell), 131–34
"Test Track" ride, 131–33, 258n72
Texas Pieces, The (Chamberlain), 261n31
Thicker than Water (Horne), 76–77
Thin Man, the, 128–29
"Third Meaning, The" (Barthes), 141
Thompson, Kristin, 249n27
Thorne, Lydia, 255n34
Toledo, Goya, 197
topping the gag, 248n23
Traffic (Goldsmith), 220–21
traffic cops, 58, 248n21
Traffic in Souls (Tucker), 73–75
traffic jam sequences: in *Two Tars*, 90,
98–104, 225, 252n60; in *Weekend*,
209, 215, 218, 221–22, 226–29; in
Weekend Campus, 221–29
Traffic Problem, the, 55–61
transcendentalists, 36, 242n24
transportation systems, 9; bicycles,
29–30, 240n13; commodity-based
systems, 14–15; destruction of the
social in, 237n29; panning technologies of, 240n12; thrill-based systems,
14
trauma thrills, 14–19
travelers, 14–15
Tristana (Buñuel), 198, 270n8
Turvey, Malcolm, 37
21 Grams (González Iñárritu), 271n16
Twentyseven Gas Stations (Ruscha),
137–38
Two Tars (Parrott), 61, 69, 81, 90–104,
119, 239n9; female characters in,
94–98; movement and stasis in,
90–94; traffic jam sequence in, 90,
98–104, 225, 252n60
Tyler, Parker, 143–44, 242n24

university. See *Weekend Campus*
Unknown Quantity (Virilio), 11–14, 108
Unsafe at Any Speed (Nader), 125, 138
Untitled: Philippe VACHER (Coleman),
185
Urban Heat (Niemi), 264n13
Usai, Paolo Cherchi, 176, 186
Uthco, T. R., 138–41, 147–51

Vacche, Angela Dalle, 268n47
Vaughan (character), 161, 243n48,
259n9; death by car crash of, 167, 177,
269n57; as fictionalized Andy Warhol, 168–71, 266nn31–32; interest in
visual technology of, 172; scars of,
169–70, 177, 266n32, 269n62; sexual
organs and bodily fluids of, 163–64,
175–77, 264n10, 264–65nn13–14,
267n37; transgressive driving of,
174–75
vehicular suicide, 146
Velázquez, Diego, 271n19
vertical axis: of Bright's multilayered
roadways, 57, 247n8; cinema's neglect of, 47–49, 244n61; in fantasy sequences, 48, 245nn64–65;
of Hepworth's star-gazing camera,
244n59
viewing subjects. See spectators
violence, 13
Virilio, Paul, 236n23, 237n74; on desire
for speed, 11–14, 17, 23, 111, 237n50;
discarding of sexuality by, 111; misogynist vision of, 13, 109; on speed
machines, 106–9, 190; on transportation systems, 8, 237n29
virtual dimensions of film, 26, 39, 109
Virtual Life of Film, The (Rodowick), 28
visual culture of the 1960s and 1970s,
138–41; Ballard's probing in *Crash*
of, 166–71, 267nn42–43; celebrity

INDEX | 303

visual culture (*continued*)
car-crash deaths in, 259n9, 261n29; in Chamberlain's *The Texas Pieces* sculpture, 261n31; comedy and satire in, 149–51, 153; disaster images in, 146–51; in Kennedy assassination reenactments, 138–60; spectator bodies on the couch in, 144–45, 151–54; static images in, 147–48, 159; stretched temporality in *Since* of, 141–45, 152–54, 159, 259nn14–15; Zapruder film of, 38, 123–24, 140–42, 146–48, 150, 156–59. *See also* Kennedy, John F., assassination
Vostell, Wolf, 147

Waddington, Laura, 180
War at a Distance (Farocki), 180
Warhol, Andy, 7, 14, 105, 124, 262n37; Avedon's photo of, 169; body images of, 147; catalogue raisonné of, 148; *Death and Disaster* series, 147; disaster silk screens of, 147–49; Edie Sedgwick films of, 143; fictionalization as Vaughan of, 168–71, 266nn31–32; on inside-outside breakdowns in pop, 161–62; Kennedy assassination silk screens of, 147–50; media transpositions by, 166–67, 265–66nn20–21; painting with bodily fluids by, 176, 269n58; response to Kennedy assassination of, 151–52; temporal drag of, 141–45, 152–54, 159, 168, 171–73, 259nn14–15. *See also Since*
Waters, John, 147
Weekend (Godard), 61, 147, 197, 205–20, 239n9, 268n47; "Action Musicale" sequence in, 227–28; afterlife of, 216–17; critical response to, 213, 215–16, 273n19; cultural backdrop for, 208–9, 213–15; encounter of literature with cinema in, 206–7, 209, 210–11; endless tracking shots in, 218, 221–22, 225–30; responses in film to, 205–6, 217–32, 274nn31–32; sheep scene in, 213–15, 273n15; socioeconomic car crash in, 207, 230; soundtrack of, 226–27; terminal logic and afterwardsness of, 205, 209–13, 272nn5–6, 272–73nn10–11; titles of, 210–11, 272n8; traffic jam sequences in, 209, 215, 218, 221–22, 226–29, 274n31, 274n36
Weekend Campus (Davenport), 205–6, 220–34, 271n19; digital photographic montage and loop in, 220–21, 228–29, 274n37; media collisions in, 221; political passivity in, 230–32; setting of, 220–21, 230–32, 234, 274n38; temporal deferral in, 229–34, 274n38
"Weekend in Hell" (Kael), 215–16
Weltz, Alexandra, 135–36, 180
Wesselmann, Tom, 168
Wexler, Haskell, 147
What Made Pistachio Nuts? (Jenkins), 68
Wheels of Tragedy, 113
Whissel, Kristen, 73
White Noise (DeLillo), 233
Wiazemsky, Anna, 217
Williams, Lina, 264–65nn13–14
Wolff, Janet, 18–19
women: as static icons in *Amores perros*, 192–98; Virilio's designation as the first vehicle of, 13, 109. *See also* feminist perspectives; gendered approaches
Women Film Pioneers Project, 68
Wood, Michael, 270n8
Wood, Robin, 209
Woolf, Virginia, 26–27, 35, 44, 53
World-Information.Org, 180

world risk, 133
Woronov, Mary, 155, 263n56
writing/graphic interpretations, 243n50; in *Crash*, 243n48; in *How It Feels to Be Run Over*, 30–32, 42–43; in *Weekend*, 210–11, 272n8

Xala (Sembène), 205, 217–20, 273n25

Youngquist, Paul, 267n42

Zapruder (Abraham) film, 38, 123–24, 140–42, 148, 150; image of John F. Kennedy's wound in, 156; Jacqueline Kennedy in, 157–60; *Life* magazine stills of, 140, 146–47, 153; television appearance of, 147, 262n32

Karen Beckman is the Elliot and Roslyn Jaffe
Professor of Film Studies in the Department of the
History of Art at the University of Pennsylvania.
She is author of *Vanishing Women: Magic, Film, and
Feminism* (2003) and coeditor, with Jean Ma, of *Still
Moving: Between Cinema and Photography* (2008),
both published by Duke University Press.

Library of Congress Cataloging-in-Publication Data
Beckman, Karen Redrobe, 1971–
Crash : cinema and the politics of speed and stasis /
Karen Beckman.
p. cm.
Includes bibliographical references and index.
ISBN 978-0-8223-4708-8 (cloth : alk. paper)
ISBN 978-0-8223-4726-2 (pbk. : alk. paper)
1. Car-chase films—History and criticism. 2. Motion
pictures—Plots, themes, etc. 3. Motion pictures—
History. I. Title.
PN1997.8.B43 2010
791.43′6—dc22   2009053841